**Alan Hoe** joined the SAS in 1960 as a Trooper. He retired in 1980 in the rank of Major having voluntarily resigned his commission in order to 'check the true colour of the grass on the other side of the hill'.

His service (he has fought in the desert, amongst other places) has given him a deep understanding of the SAS. He can speak the language of soldiers, and has met all the surviving 'Originals' of 'L' Detachment (SAS). He was a trusted friend and confidant of David Stirling and wrote this book with the full cooperation of him and his family.

The author's previous books include *Terrorism: Threat and Response* (1987) with Eric Morris; the same pair are currently writing *Malaya: The Renaissance of Special Forces*. He also wrote a biographical work, *The Negotiator* (1988), under the pseudonym James March. He has written for a number of journals and magazines on military strategies and international terrorism, about which he also lectures from time to time.

# David Stirling

## The Authorised Biography of the Creator of the SAS

### ALAN HOE

WARNER BOOKS

A *Warner* Book

First published in Great Britain in 1992 by
Little, Brown and Company
Reprinted 1992 (twice)
This edition published in 1994 by Warner Books
Reprinted 1994 (twice), 1995, 1996, 1999

A CIP catalogue record for this book
is available from the British Library.

ISBN 0 7515 0245 6

Printed in England by Clays Ltd, St Ives plc

Warner Books
A Division of
Little, Brown and Company (UK)
Brettenham House
Lancaster Place
London WC2E 7EN

This book is dedicated to the Stirlings of Keir. Sir David Stirling founded and commanded 1st SAS; William Stirling commanded 2nd SAS; Peter Stirling provided a respite from battle; the whole family supported the cause.

# CONTENTS

**Book Three: Gang Forward**

# FOREWORD

General Sir Peter de la Billière KCB, KBE, DSO, MC

This book is a fascinating read about a great man who might well be described as the Robin Hood of the twentieth century. I can think of no better person to write it than Alan Hoe who, himself having served for many years in the SAS, got to know David Stirling extremely well. This book answers many questions; it cannot have been easy researching the actions and motives of a man with such diverse interests.

David Stirling was a legend in his time and eccentric in his day. Tough physically and mentally, he was essentially a visionary. Of course he was a man of action. He was a leader of the greatest distinction whose personality inspired others although he needed his lieutenant (for it was a rôle he never played and for which he was quite unsuited).

It has been my unforgettable privilege to serve for twenty years in a regiment with its founder, Colonel David, watching on the side lines. Throughout the post-war period David has made his mark on the SAS; kept it free of the harness of tradition yet fed it with a diet of inspiration and innovation.

The SAS is today the world leader in experience and the practice of matters Special Forces: David set it on that course and David has kept it on that course. With his death the responsibility lies with another generation and they above all others should read this work to understand the spirit that has made the Special Air Services what it is.

This is a book about the founder of one of Britain's best known regiments. It is a book of inspiration for the young and a book of contemporary interest for the old. It is a tribute to Colonel Sir David Stirling, appointed to Distinguished Service Order for Courage in Battle and many times Mentioned in Dispatches – a great British winner, a great British eccentric. Whatever your generation I feel sure you will find enjoyment in it.

# ACKNOWLEDGEMENTS

This is not an official history of the SAS; it is the story of the man who created that organisation. The SAS in its early stages obviously played a great part in Sir David Stirling's life and, having spawned the child, he maintained an avid lifelong interest in it. In his eyes it was the most significant objective he ever had. That is debatable for he set himself many objectives, most seemingly impossible; the reader will have to make up his own mind.

With regard to the part of the book which covers the SAS to the point of Sir David's capture I must stress one or two points. Some twenty-one books have been written which cover all or part of the SAS operations during the desert campaign. All of my material relative to this period has come directly from Sir David or those who soldiered with him; if there is some repetition of other writer's words this is accidental. I have tried to give a flavour of soldiering in the desert and to show the pressures on Sir David during the delicate stages of raising a regiment.

In putting together this book I am aware that some incidents and actions have been omitted. I do not apologise for this; those who know of those particular aspects of Sir David's life will be aware of the sensibilities. Sir David had a multitude of friends and close acquaintants and many will be asking why I have not referred to them in the text, nor interviewed them. It would not have been possible to do this; in writing the book I have tried to answer the questions I had about the man – there will be many other questions unanswered. There was always a private part of Sir David and I believe that should remain the case. If I have offended by neglecting to speak to various persons I apologise but it must be understood that there is a great sameness of opinion amongst all those I have interviewed.

I owe a debt of gratitude to many people who have been unstinting with their time and support; it is not possible to list them all. In particular I offer my deepest thanks to: the late Miss Irene Stirling, Lord Simon Dalhousie, KT, GCVO, GBE, MC, LLD, Lady Margaret Dalhousie; Mr & Mrs Peter Stirling, Major Jim Almonds MM, Peter Andrews, Admiral and Mrs Bartosik, Bob Bennett BEM, MM, General Sir Peter de la Billière KCB, CBE, DSO, MC, Field Marshal The Lord Bramall KG, GCB, OBE, MC, JP, Ernie Bond OBE, Jimmy Brough MM, M. Georges Caitucoli, Colin Campbell, Lord Frank Chapple, M. le Colonel Chateau-Jobert, Lieutenant-Colonel Peter Comyns, Donald Craven, Lieutenant-Colonel Ian Crooke DSO, 'Whacker' Evans, Terry Fincher, M. le Colonel Roger Flambaud, M. Raymond Forgeat, Paul Getty, General Sir John Hackett GCB, CBE, DSO, MC, Dep.Lt., Sir Stephen Hastings MC, Richard Hughes, the Rt Hon Earl Jellicoe KBE, DSO, MC, FRS, Lieutenant-Colonel Jim Johnson OBE, TD, M. Augustin Jordan, H.E. Kenneth Kaunda, Lady Sarah Keswick, Peter Kingswell Skinner, Major General David Lloyd Owen CB, DSO, OBE, MC, Kate Losinska OBE, Sir Fitzroy Maclean of Dunconnel, Bt, CBE, DSO, Paul McLoughlin, Bernard Mills, CBE, Peter O'Toole BEM, M. Jean Paulin, Major Jack Pringle MC, M. Philippe Reinhart, Major Pat Riley DCM, the Duke of Richmond and Gordon, Roger Rosewell, the Earl and Countess of Scarborough, Reg Seekings DCM, MM, Frank Sharrat, Colonel David Smiley MVO, OBE, MC, Arthur Stokes MC, MM, Mrs Margaret Thatcher OM, FRS, MP, The Viscount William Whitelaw MC, Lady Susan Wood

MBE, Lieutenant-Colonel John Woodhouse MBE, MC. To the host of others who have reminisced or passed on recollections (accurate or otherwise) in clubs, pubs and bars around the world, my thanks. In the true traditions of the British soldiery I will not appoint names, dates or faces lest I break alibis!

My thanks go also to the following authors and publishers for permission to quote from their works: Jonathan Cape, *Eastern Approaches* by Fitzroy Maclean; Harrap, *Providence Their Guide* by David Lloyd Owen; William Kimber, *Colditz Last Stop* by Jack Pringle; Michael Joseph for permission to use the photograph from *Soldiers and Sherpas* by 'Brummie' Stokes; the *Kenya Weekly News* for the leaflet entitled *The Way Ahead* (29 June 1956) by Rex Reynolds whom it has proved impossible to trace – this was so helpful in setting the scene for the Salima Convention.

My special thanks must go to Evelyn Le Chêne for her friendly, enthusiastic and professional assistance in 'opening doors' and translating so many documents from the French. To my friend and colleague, Donald Palmer, for carrying more than a fair burden in our working company for so long, and for his painstaking production of the maps in this book. To my wife, Janet, for being there, and displaying a forbearance well beyond the call of the marriage vows and my children, 'Heidi' and Andrew, for not taking me to task over my continual absences – thank you! Last but by no means least, to Alan Samson of Little, Brown for his endless patience and support, and to Sheila McIlwraith for an excellent editing job.

The responsibility for any errors of fact and expressions of opinion is mine unless so stated within the book. The author and publishers wish it to be known that 50 per cent of the royalties of this book go to the SAS Regimental Association.

# PREFACE

In 1959, I read a story which changed my life. Browsing through a bookshop in Newton Abbot, Devon, I spotted a newly published work entitled *The Phantom Major*, by Virginia Cowles. As far as I can remember the book cost me twelve shillings; almost two weeks' wages for me at the time.

I had joined the army in some desperation, to escape what was to my mind a singularly boring and very limited future as a farm labourer (and all under the eyes of a particularly obnoxious retired lieutenant colonel who decided that I should call him 'sir' at all times; on that point we disagreed – even then I thought such a title had to be earned). I had enlisted into the Royal Corps of Signals as a boy entrant some two years prior to reading *The Phantom Major* and although I was enjoying the military life, I could not happily envisage it as being my whole future.

*The Phantom Major* was a book of its time – a *Boy's Own* work which whisked me off to the deserts of North Africa and beyond whilst introducing me to the Special Air Service and a host of fascinating characters of the stuff from which legends are born. Great indeed was my disappointment when the book closed with the disbandment of the regiment.

Just weeks later I left the Junior Service and moved to a trade training camp in Lincolnshire, and on my very first day I spotted a tall, fit-looking corporal striding down the road. On the right shoulder of his battledress were the unmistakeable wings of the SAS! I approached him nervously, because a corporal was someone with only slightly less power than God in those days. Quite out of keeping with my expectations of a corporal's reactions, he smiled as I indicated the wings and said that he did not seem old enough to have earned them during the war; nor had he any wartime campaign ribbons on his breast.

Pat 'Doc' Travers explained that the SAS had been re-formed during the Malayan Emergency, where he had seen service with the regiment. The SAS was in the process of returning to the United Kingdom via Oman to set up base at Malvern in Worcestershire. Not only that, the regiment was seeking recruits through a difficult selection system held in the mountains of central Wales. For me the die was cast.

My enquiries to the fount of all knowledge, the Orderly Room Sergeant, met with total rebuffal and I determinedly set about making myself enough of a nuisance to have my application forwarded to the SAS. Blurred details in the date-of-birth box on the application form may have helped, but I think the SAS were not taking too seriously the edict that a soldier should be twenty-one years of age to attempt selection. My nuisance programme was an unwitting adaptation of one of the regimental founder's personal philosophies: 'If you need something – do not be put off by bureaucracy – find a way to take it.'

In early 1960, after a somewhat shaky start, I was into the regiment on a trial basis. Within weeks I knew that this was my way of life – they would have to drag me out in chains.

From my earliest days the subject of *The Phantom Major* fascinated me – Lieutenant-Colonel David Stirling OBE, DSO; founder of his own, highly successful regiment when he was not much older than twenty-one himself. Where was he and what was he doing?

Before long I had read and collected the entire plethora of books about or alluding to the wartime SAS along with the more modern works. It was, however, the man and the founding days which continued to interest me. None of these books gave me a satisfying insight into the fascinating aspects of creating a regiment against the active aggression and obstruction of very senior commanders and the often indifferent layers of bureaucracy between them and their fighting commands. From my own service experiences I knew that even though great successes by the SAS could be claimed in action, and cost-effectiveness proved, it still required an absolutely determined leader to fight the constant 'battle in the rear' to avoid disbandment.

If Stirling had been that figure in the rear, how had he managed to take part personally in so many operations? I talked to a number of his wartime comrades; none gave me reason to doubt his personal courage and great leadership abilities, but some were oblivious to the rear echelon manoeuvring. Although this did not detract from my interest in the beginnings of the SAS, it did cause me to focus more on the nature of the man. What perceptions (or instincts) guided his decision making? What part had pure luck played during the war? I wanted to know what forces had moulded his character, what his early ambitions had been and how much his wartime successes had shaped his subsequent endeavours.

Stirling, unlike so many war heroes, had certainly not faded into oblivion. From time to time I would read of his exploits in the national press; sometimes the articles were praising, more often, it seemed, they were disparaging – but they were always interesting and controversial, pointing to a man with original and imaginative thought processes who was unafraid to speak out, ask 'Why?' and act regardless of opposition. The press articles and subsequent discussions were tantalisingly scant on detail; they would only generalise on such organisations as Watchguard, the Better Britain Society, GB75 and the like. The man even had his own television company, so why were people so reticent?

He intrigued me. Every time I reckoned I had worked him out he confounded me by setting up a further venture along another tangent. I cannot now remember all the mental pictures I built up of Stirling but I can recall that they were constantly changing as new factors entered the equation, and my frustration became acute.

I decided that I wanted to write his story. Assuming that I was able to penetrate David Stirling's defences (I had been told that the press and writers were anathema to him unless he happened to be involved in a libel suit), would he co-operate? I did not represent the press in any way, but a book may capture the interest of many. He was an enigma to me and I determined to know him and one day understand him. I was to wait a long time.

Some twenty-two years after first reading *The Phantom Major*, after a mildly successful and hugely enjoyable career, I retired by my own choice from the SAS and the army. Even though my interest in Stirling never waned it was to be some years yet before I met him at a venue where we could talk freely. Meanwhile, I had been applying what I had learned in the army to the fickle demands of commerce and industry in such a fashion that I had some financial security.

At my first meeting with David Stirling I told him that I would like to write his story; I explained that the two books I already had under my belt were part of my plan to learn the craft of writing. He laughed. I did not know it, but writers with infinitely superior pedigrees had approached him. Why the reticence? In the first instance he truly did not believe that his life was in any way noteworthy; to write about it would be 'pomposo' in the extreme (he retained that stance for quite a long time) and, secondly, he did not believe that any writer he had met could understand and demonstrate the wide variety of situations in which his philosophies of warfare, life and business had been conceived and developed.

It was some months before David capitulated, and in true Stirling fashion he laid down conditions. Even though this book is not primarily about the SAS, when it came to the war years, I was to give full credit to his co-founders (L Detachment), tell a little about some of the key characters and demonstrate the truly international flavour of the wartime regiments. I was to be honest, and critical where I thought criticism fitting. These conditions gave me no cause for concern; I can only hope that I have succeeded.

This has not been an easy book to write; no one could accuse David Stirling of having been an industrious keeper of records, nor of blowing his own trumpet unless to reduce some other person's pomposity. At times I felt like a sneak thief as I pored over personal letters and memoirs. At times I was a bully as I pressed him for answers and opinions – sometimes when he was far from well. Lively argument often led to us both collapsing from side-splitting laughter; his humour was irrepressible. At times his perception amazed me. He avidly soaked up the international news and taught me the art of questioning everything.

This is not a book about the war; the reader of serious military history will have to look to the many authoritative sources. It is the story of a man, which covers part of a war from his perspective. Much of the book, of course, is taken up by the SAS; it is something by which the majority will remember him, and an organisation to which he devoted a great deal of time in his post-war life.

As I have worked almost entirely from the personal memoirs of David Stirling, the 'Originals' and other wartime witnesses, much of the SAS story will be familiar. Many stories of individual bravery are left untold though I have tried to give a little detail on some of those characters of the early days on whom Stirling placed so much dependence and trust; I have tried to concentrate on situations which forced David to make the major decisions which guided the future of his brainchild and to describe the forces which influenced his thought processes.

If there seems to be an overbalance regarding the SAS part of the story it is because he never lost the thrill of contriving situations and calculating how the SAS might play a leading rôle; he was never slow to pass his thoughts on to the modern day regiments. Many of his post-war enterprises were undertaken with the regiment in mind, and many of the early friendships were significant in later years. Indeed the SAS runs like the 'silver thread of karma' through his life, linking and cross-referencing much of his work.

Perhaps one of his greatest undertakings was the Capricorn Africa Society (CAS) to which sadly, I do not feel properly qualified to do justice. The CAS deserves a book to itself, written by someone with an intimate knowledge of the Africa of the middle forties, someone who can bear personal witness to the determination and dedication of David Stirling, Dr Oldham, Sir Laurens van der Post and that small band of brethren who tried to change the face of Africa. I hope I have succeeded in showing, in a small way, what they left behind for today's society.

As would be expected, some of David's work led him into close affiliations with government services, including those tasked with national security. Where such is the case there has been no attempt to embarrass government or individuals; this I feel as strongly about as David did.

To the end David was courteous, frank and humorous and for this I thank him. From my initial fascination grew a friendship in which I was the privileged partner. I hope I have been accurate in my interpretations, but above all I hope I have given the reader an insight into the mind and actions of a person whom I believe to have been one of the most forward-thinking patriots of our time.

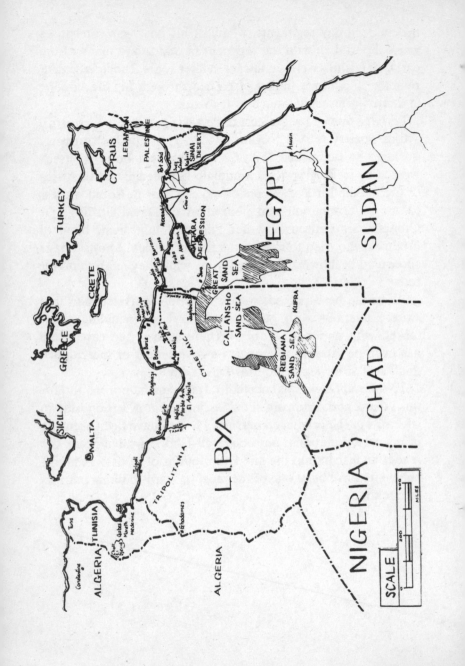

# BOOK ONE

---

# MAN AND BOY

# 1

---

# The Ideal – the Enemy of the Real?

> The Society's choice of a zebra on the map of Africa
> for its crest has a symbolic meaning. The zebra has
> black, brown and white stripes but is one living
> organism. If it is pierced to the heart it dies, and
> it does not matter through which stripe the wound
> has been made.
>
> The Capricorn Africa Society

The last of the chartered aircraft rumbled off into the rapidly dipping tropical sun, having disembarked its passengers alongside the orange-tinted waters of Lake Nyasa. Throughout the long, hot African afternoon aircraft, trains and cars carrying the delegates had arrived from all points of the compass; from Central Africa, Southern and Northern Rhodesia, Nyasaland, Tanganyika Territory, Kenya, Uganda, South Africa, the United States of America and Great Britain.

Eight years of dedicated work came to a culminating point on that evening of Friday, 15 June 1956, as farmers, businessmen, missionaries, journalists, tradesmen, housewives, and men and women from all professions assembled for the Salima Convention. The delegates gathered in hope, determination

3

and anticipation in the tented encampment at Salima on the shores of Lake Nyasa. Some were dressed in the natty tropical trappings of the time; some were in khaki drill and others were even more casual. The apparent common bond was a relaxation and trust tinged with excitement.

The general feeling can perhaps be summarised by an overheard snatch of conversation in the grass-roofed bar: 'How odd it will seem,' said one delegate, 'when we are back in civilisation and can't have a drink together.' 'Civilisation?' his companion of the evening responded, 'Ah well, in the meantime, it's my turn; let me get you another beer.'

An innocuous conversation? Yes, but this was Africa in 1956 and one delegate was white, the other black. And white and black mingled in all the groups of people who sat and chatted or strolled in the last warmth of the sun. It was an uncomplicated evening as the delegates unselfconsciously queued for their meal. Most retired early to recover from the rigours of African travel.

Next day, in the *bwalo*, an open-sided shelter of peeled log beams and grass thatch with trees growing through the roof, the convention proper would open. The Capricorn Africa Contract, drafted by the Capricorn Africa Society, was to be ratified.

As far as the western world is concerned Africa was 'discovered' because Prince Henry (the Navigator) of Portugal felt he must strike an alliance against the Moors with the fabled ruler of the African interior, Prester John. The Gulf of Guinea was reached in 1461, the year after Henry's death, and the Cape of Good Hope was first rounded by Bartholomew Diaz in 1487.

The mid-seventeenth century saw the beginnings of the Dutch migrations led by Jan van Riebeek via Table Bay into South Africa, and from that point onwards Africa became the set for one of the greatest and longest human dramas witnessed by mankind. Three centuries after van Riebeek's landing, native Africa could be said to be at the point of awakening; awakening as tribes, not as countries or nations. How could the sometimes accidental, often simply commercially convenient delineation of boundaries which cut through tribal domains encompass nationalist loyalties?

International newspaper and radio communications were now available to all and the Africans could see what was happening throughout the world. In size the continent of Africa is second only to Asia and throughout Asia there had been a very significant diminution of European influence during the late forties and early fifties. The important Chinese markets had been swallowed up in the move towards Communism; India's noisy demands had resulted in its political autonomy and France was about to lose Indochina. In every country or territory where the Western powers held influence a powerful upsurge of nationalism was being witnessed. On every 'colonial front' the European was giving ground. Was it not natural that the African should clamour for a voice in his own affairs?

In the eyes of the black African, the whites had failed to present him with any substitute for the disruption to his traditional values and way of life. Now, the commercial avarice of the European seemed set fair to disrupt security further with no lessening of degradation. Outside British East and Central Africa, segregation based on race, colour and ethnic origin was common though not invariable.

The year of the Salima Convention, 1956, saw the end of the Mau Mau movement. In the four preceding years a vicious campaign of sabotage and assassination had been waged by the Kikuyu people of Kenya. Predominantly this was a tribal uprising not a national one, associated with the ritual oaths employed by the leaders of the Kikuyu Central Association to promote unity in the independence movement.

By the end of 1956, more than 11,000 rebels had been killed in the fighting along with about 100 Europeans and 2,000 African loyalists. Around 20,000 other Kikuyu were put into detention camps, where intensive efforts were made

to convert them to the political views of the government,
i.e. to abandon their nationalistic aspirations. Despite these
government actions, Kikuyu resistance spearheaded the Kenya
independence movement and Jomo Kenyatta, who had been
jailed as a Mau Mau leader in 1953, became Prime Minister
of an independent Kenya about ten years later.

Industry, commerce and politics are dependent on the efforts
of man; man produces those efforts best under conditions of
harmony, stability, opportunity and prosperity and yet these
conditions were not apparently being sought. Great Britain,
with its Commonwealth experience, had realised long ago
that racial co-operation and understanding were prerequisites
to sound government – but Africa was different. In vast areas
of Southern, Central and East Africa many hundreds of white
men had made their homes – they were African and their
progeny would be African. They were not there as itinerant
administrators and transient governors. The same applied
to the thousands of Asians, the great coastal merchantmen
who had, through their international trading, breathed the
beginnings of economic life into the continent; they too were
there to stay; they too were African.

At first sight, this difference created by the longterm presence
of the 'white and brown Africans' should surely have alleviated
the situation. In practice it actually posed the problem. As the
blacks wanted their traditional values preserved in a working
atmosphere which gave them opportunity to progress within
their chosen spheres, so the Asians and Europeans wanted to
preserve what was dear to them and their families. Was there
a solution?

Prior to the meeting at Salima, a press statement was issued:

### The Capricorn Agreement

Next Friday evening . . . there will gather together . . . 140
men and women, Africans, Europeans, Goans, Asians and

Coloureds, from all the territories of British East and Central Africa. They are the delegates of the Capricorn Africa Society, meeting in convention, to endorse formally the draft contract between Africa's races – a contract designed to provide the foundation stone for a new citizenship in Africa . . .

Everywhere in British Africa north of the Limpopo, there is benevolent government conscientiously trying to meet the needs of the less advanced sections of the community but everywhere, if the facts are squarely faced, it must be admitted that there is a steady worsening of the relationship between Africa's different peoples. Opportunities for social and economic advancement and increased participation in the political management of the territories are too often given the African by governments – whose officials are predominantly European – in a spirit of concession, and are too often taken by the African as a reward for agitation and political pressure. The exclusive nationalism of race, white or black, the one stimulating the other, is strengthening year by year.

The Capricorn Society believes that this destructive spiral of racialism can only be broken by creating a central concept of citizenship and patriotism emotionally valid to each race. The definition of this concept has been the main object of the Capricorn Society since it was founded in 1948. For the last two years now over 25 Citizenship Committees, their membership drawn from each of the races, have been drawing up a contract between the races. From the start the Society was deeply aware that its contract would be worthless unless each race had been equally responsible for its preparation.

The Capricorn contract is an effective challenge both to militant black nationalism and to the Strydom creed of apartheid. The contract makes no pretence at compromise between the two, but sets up an idea valid in its own right. The Society's aim is to create a patriotism – by which it means love of country and all the people who live in it – and a political faith, by which it means a political order and a way of life capable of binding together Africa's peoples in a loyalty more compelling than that of race or tribe.

The Capricorn Society needs all possible support from public opinion in its fight to abolish racial discrimination in Africa and to establish in its place a new Citizenship common to all races.

Brave words? The Mau Mau uprising was still bubbling under the surface; growing African nationalism was now enhanced by highly articulate black speakers able to play on the powerful emotions of their listeners; there was an ever-increasing and jealously guarded Asian influence and personal experience of an increasingly luxurious Western civilisation which many black students were tasting in British, American and European universities and campuses for the first time. In short, the campaign was conducted amongst the most potent of human passions.

What was in the minds of the Salima delegates as they assembled in the *bwalo* in the cool of the morning? Excerpts from some reported keynote speeches point to a great optimism. Mrs Michael Wood, wife of the chairman of the Kenya branch of the Society, gave her qualifications only as being 'the third generation of my family to live and work in Africa' Nowadays, her warning note would seem to be pitched directly at South African nationalism:

> Fears are driving us to live outside our ethic. Our domination in the past was derived largely from circumstances. When the European came to Africa it was inevitable that he took the lead, as he had experience of the wide issues of life that was needed in a country as yet untouched by the growth of modern civilisation.
>
> We are inclined, now that the circumstances which require our domination are decreasing, to rely not on moral stature nor in winning the consent of the governed, but on a police force. We are a people nurtured in the democratic tradition: it is built into our history.
>
> If we were to forsake this tradition and say, 'Thus far and no further', what strength other than force would give us a place in Africa? What hope have we as a small minority dependent on force should we forsake the moral background from which men should derive leadership?

One of the speakers was Herbert Chitepo, the first black African to become a member of the Rhodesian bar. Chitepo was to be assassinated almost twenty years later; ironically the killer was almost certainly an ex-member of the post-war SAS. Chitepo referred to the new African organisations which were arising with specific aims to remove the Europeans. He stressed that time was short and 'this is not only a unique opportunity for Africa: it is also the last, for, if we cannot succeed together, Africans will be driven to adopt open racialist nationalism . . .' The European must '. . . accord Africans the dignity, freedom and security which is the right of every human being'

One of Africa's most famous figures and author of the book (amongst many others), *The Dark Eye in Africa*, Colonel Laurens van der Post, was a member of the Society from its early days. Unable to attend the convention, his speech was read:

Many prescriptions [for racial ills] have been offered to us from abroad by people who have not got to live the solutions themselves. But no worthwhile solution embracing the totality of the many-racial reality of Africa and coming out of the minds and experience of people who have to live the solutions has been put to Africa before. Now for the first time we have a movement dedicated to a concept which is concerned no longer with these crippling and paralytic preoccupations with race, but is concerned only with the maintenance and advancement of fundamental values. That is the essence for me of the Capricorn idea.

A number of speakers referred to Cecil Rhodes's precept of 'equal rights for all civilised men'. The speeches were not, however, without humour. A potent speaker, Mr K.J. Tsolo, a highly respected principal at the Waddilove Institute at Marandellas, Southern Rhodesia, deliberated the question of immigration.

To those who felt personally robbed through immigration, Tsolo suggested that they consider his own position. His grandfather had owned the site of City Deep, one of the richest goldfields in Witwatersrand. Tsolo's grandfather had not even known that gold was on his property; even if he had, he would not have known how to extract it or put it on the market – so there it was. Only a fool of an African would not grasp the opportunity to learn from the European. The same could be said for Asian immigrants – they were almost the same colour as himself and if they knew a thing or two then it gave him encouragement. Not that Mr Tsolo wanted poor whites or Indians competing with the more backward Africans. He wanted the good types – the sort he was surrounded by at the Capricorn Convention. If people were prepared to come to his country and teach him something, he would accept them as neighbours. 'Let 'em all come,' said Tsolo to exuberant laughter.

The Salima Convention lasted two-and-a-half days and at the close the contract was signed by 140 delegates and a number of supporters of the Society who had been present as observers. The final debate revolved around the question of a petition to the Crown. It was decided that a Loyal Address was the most proper next step. It was signed by the man who was the driving force behind the Society: 'To Her Majesty Queen Elizabeth II . . . We, the signatories of the Capricorn contract drawn from all the races living in the self-governing Colony of Southern Rhodesia, the Colony and Protectorate of Kenya, the Protectorates of Nyasaland and Northern Rhodesia, and the Territory of Tanganyika, being met together at Salima . . . as representatives of the Capricorn Africa Society and its members throughout these Territories, and having this day set our hands to a solemn Contract affirming our determination to establish in these Territories a society free from discrimination rooted in racial prejudice and acknowledging our human unity under God and our unity in one Loyalty to the Crown, trusting in Your Majesty's approval of this our purpose, hereby present for Your Majesty's consideration and with our humble duty a copy of the aforesaid Contract, and assure Your Majesty of our Loyalty and Devotion to your Crown and Person. Signed on behalf of the Signatories to the Contract, David Stirling, President.

What was the Capricorn Africa Society? What drove this man? What took the Phantom Major from the deserts of North Africa to Capricorn Africa?

---

# 2

# THE STIRLINGS OF KEIR

The imagination of a boy is healthy, and the mature imagination of a man is healthy; but there is a space of life between the character undecided, the way of life uncertain.

Preface to 'Endymion'
John Keats

There is a point at which industrial Scotland begins to fade into rich carse land as the country stretches north towards the Highlands. It is an area steeped in the history of clan warfare and struggles against the English. Off the main routes and within the tranquil triangle formed by Doune, Dunblane and Stirling stands Keir. Almost palatial in size, the white house with its large Italian-style terraces thrusts upwards through the formality of one of Scotland's finest gardens.

It is a peaceful house, but in 1924 there was the scurry of muted activity associated with one of the country's most well-connected, respected and hospitable families. The kitchens, dominated by Mrs Thompson, are a picture of quiet efficiency whilst outside the brown bowler-hatted figure of Mr Lunt, head gardener, keeps guard over the immaculate flower gardens and secluded kitchen produce areas. Peace does not always reign at

Keir – it is a house with children; children with the same spirit as their ancestors; children with a sense of fun. Keir is the seat of the Stirlings, an ancient, aristocratic Scottish family whose ancestors showed enthusiastic and distinguished service to their King and the Stuart cause.

His heels throwing up showers of gravel as his bicycle skidded around the corners of the ornate flower beds, the boy was oblivious to his surroundings. This was speed. He was Malcolm Campbell, even then preparing for his assault on the world land speed record. The thunderous applause of a thousand spectators did not detract from his concentration as he hit the straight at top speed. Suddenly, the worst happened. A track obstruction.

The brakes had little effect as the machine went into collision. The boy's eyes which a split second ago had been at a level with the midriff of the obstructing body were now tightly closed against the impact with the waistcoat buttons of General Archibald Stirling of Keir. David Stirling was having one of his rare daytime confrontations with his father.

Still holding the handlebars in the position at which he had stopped the machine, General Stirling, still erect and with no discernible expression, merely looked at the dishevelled crumple of a boy at his feet. No words were spoken as young David picked himself up, brushed nervously at his clothes and took the bicycle. He did not remount; looking apprehensively over his shoulder and with as much dignity as his nine-year-old body could muster, he pushed the cycle away.

Close to tears brought on by pain and shock, he remembered what his mother had said as, with his brother Hugh and sister Irene, they had made their way to the dentist a few days earlier. 'Now, David, don't cry, or Hugh and Irene will start bawling too.'

'Yes, Mummy,' with a confidence he did not feel. The local dentist's surgery operated by Messrs Platt and Common was not conducive to putting patients at their ease. Encompassed by the huge old leather 'operating' chair in the middle of the starkly furnished, draughty room the incumbent was treated to a view of the local railway station. If the approach of the primitive, treadle-operated drill coincided with the presence of a train then the gouts of steam and slowly revolving pistons produced images guaranteed to shatter the strongest nerve.

The tooth extraction had hurt abominably; he had desperately wanted to cry but such was his respect for his mother that he had somehow contained himself. He had not cried then and he would not cry now even though he suspected that the bicycle incident could lead to another visit to his father's study. On the whole, he reflected, he would rather take a stiff lecture or the loss of his bicycle for a few weeks. Perhaps he cheered himself up by recalling what happened next at the dentist's. David had been first into the surgery; after some minutes Mr Common entered the waiting room waving David's tooth triumphantly in his forceps. Hugh was next, but emerged some thirty seconds later to whisper to Irene, 'It's all right if you bite him!' Irene, who always did what Hugh told her, also came out in thirty seconds. (After that the dental care of the Stirling children passed into the hands of Mr Platt.)

David decided it would probably be a lecture; beatings were virtually unknown at Keir. The General hated physical punishment though there were certain things about which he felt very strongly; rudeness was one and his gardens were another – not only for their beauty, but also because they reflected the hard work and devotion of the gardeners, and the efforts of others must always be respected. In this instance the young David was quite wrong. There was neither beating nor verbal chastisement.

Archibald Stirling (to the Keir staff 'the General' or 'the Laird') had married rather late in life, aged forty-two; he was orphaned himself at the age of eight and arrived at fatherhood with little understanding of children's needs. A naturally shy man with adults, he was even less at ease with children and he tended to leave the rearing of the family mainly to his wife. The General had not had an easy war; he had suffered badly in a gas attack and he could be distinctly peppery. Not a regular soldier, he had answered the call to the colours at a time of need.

He was a scholar and poet by instinct and training, a true connoisseur of the arts with a great love for his wonderful collections at Keir. Spanish and Italian paintings; etchings; prints; china and furniture; much had been inherited, but he had added to it. He took his duties as a Member of Parliament seriously and prided himself on knowing his constituency. His courtesy and hospitality were renowned but his pepper could rise to the surface very quickly when four growing, energetic boys mishandled beautiful objects, fought, or were, in the way of youth, thoughtless. Severe though his lectures could be, the General had been a lonely boy and he loved his large family.

Another factor made him reluctant to chastise David too severely for his bicycle escapade, though punishment, he knew, was deserved. Of late there had been far too many incidents to ignore. The boy had discovered the delights of tearing around the grounds and the surrounding park at night and without lights apparently for the pleasure of terrifying staff and passers-by as he hurtled at them from the darkness. No matter, he would soon be back at school. And after all, here was a boy who, but for his mother's determination, would now have been on crutches following a leg amputation. A boy for whom a bicycle might have been an impossible dream.

Late the year before David had been on holiday on the Isle of Mull and during his wanderings in the heather had been bitten on the leg by an adder. He was a small child and not robust; that combined with the length of time it took to get treatment compounded the effect of the venom. The leg swelled horribly and seemed immune to all the doctor's concoctions. The doctor accordingly advised that amputation was the only certain way to save David's life. The answer from the boy's mother was an emphatic 'No!' David was shipped back to the mainland where the family doctor and his mother took over the nursing. The process was slow but he was now fully recovered.

David's mother, the Honourable Margaret Fraser, was born the fourth daughter of the 13th Baron Lovat. It was a large family and this was reflected in her attitude to her own children. Robust, with a sense of family history and tradition which augmented the sensibilities of her husband, she ran the great house with efficiency and a light hand. In her dealings with the children she insisted on politeness and respect for others at all times. Yet she understood children and their needs and this showed in a private gentleness and a sense of fun. In later life David confessed that whilst he loved his mother dearly, 'I had a great respect for her also. A respect which was tinged with awe. You see she always seemed to know what to do and what was in my mind and this could be quite, quite awesome. She never actually frightened me but I cannot remember ever disobeying her directly. I often did, of course, when we were separated by distance but never in her presence.'

A rather charming family story clearly illustrates the atmosphere; all (except father) were assembled at the breakfast table when David, late as usual, bounced in and brightly said to his mother: 'Good morning, Peggy.'

'What did you say, David?' responded his astounded mother.

Nonplussed, but only slightly, David looked around for support to find brothers and sisters giving him encouraging looks and nodding enthusiastically.

'Er, I said good morning, Peggy. Sorry, Mummy.'

His mother, torn between annoyance and laughter, took the matter no further.

There were six Stirling children: David, born on 15 November 1915; Hugh, who was killed in action in the spring of 1941; Peter, who was to feature in David's life in North Africa; Bill, who was to command one of the SAS regiments; Margaret, later to become Lady Dalhousie, and Irene. The children were as close as their different characteristics, interests and energies within a great house allowed. Closest to David was sister Margaret. Margaret was much more than David's willing companion in childhood adventures; she was, for a number of years, his interpreter to the rest of the family.

David was born with a speech deformity which remained unrecognised as such until he was about four years old. From the age of two-and-a-half, at which point he knew exactly what he wanted to say, he remained desperately thwarted by his inability to communicate clearly. Margaret translated his strange sounds to the others. Her sense of mischief was equal to David's and she would occasionally tease and anger him by misrepresenting his demands. This strange, frustrating world of second-hand communication continued until it was finally realised that David suffered from a tongue restriction which did not allow him full articulation. After a simple operation, David could speak normally.

The early disability almost certainly left its mark. Accurate, succinct communication became a hallmark of David's speech and writing and he was capable of displaying intense irritation with those who did not quickly grasp his point. In later years it was to assist him in understanding and getting the best from one of his most complex wartime colleagues. Most probably it also contributed to his many malapropisms – often these began as genuine mistakes, to be maintained thereafter for their comic effect.

This early inability to communicate effectively, coupled to the fact that he was obviously not growing at the same rate as his brothers, made David by far the most difficult child of the family. He was the notorious sulker, vanishing into his own silent world as a punishment to the others for injuries real or imagined. He was capable of maintaining silences for very long periods – until his brothers and sisters discovered that all they had to do was make him laugh and then he found it quite impossible to keep up the pretence. Invariably it was Hugh who broke down the barrier.

Laughter was never far from the surface in the Stirling

household and David caused a goodly share of it. The front entrance to Keir was of stone structure in the Victorian style and David decided this was a good medium for early artistic work. Taking a small, hard stone he tentatively scratched his name on the step. Pleased with the effect he continued to carve – the 'Davids' becoming more and more ornate with great flowing loops and curlicues. He became bored with the exercise and left to find other mischief. Perhaps it was a good time to persuade Margaret to collect peaches from the glasshouses.

He and Peter had discovered that the best means of extraction when they wanted a peach or bunch of grapes was to assist Margaret through a ventilation window whilst they took cover from Mr Lunt's patrolling activities. Margaret's initial protests had been easily overcome when they pointed out that the head gardener would certainly report Peter or David to the General had they been discovered.

Being a gentleman, however, Mr Lunt would not report a young lady for such a misdemeanour. Once more they were successful with the illicit snack, but on returning to the house David was summoned to his father's study.

The artwork had been discovered and David was subjected to one of the familiar lectures. On being interrogated by his sister afterwards he was full of chagrin. 'I wouldn't have minded being caught in the act – but how on earth did he know it was me!'

Religion was part of life at Keir; the house had its own chapel, designed by General Stirling, with a mosaic by Boris Anrep, where Mass was a regular feature and evening prayers the norm. The family numbered quite a few priests amongst their friends, who often stayed as passing guests and conducted religious devotions for the family. Children tend to take religion as it comes, often regarding it as an irksome necessity to be avoided if at all possible. The Stirling children were no exception, and, finding that the evening service could be missed if tennis was being played (on the pretext of not hearing the gong for prayers), made an undignified rush for the court at 6.25 p.m. every day. On Sundays, when there was Benediction, Peter and David would silently fight it out in the sacristy as to who was going to carry the thurible. The sedate to-and-fro swinging of the incense boat was boring – but it was fun to see how many times it could be swung in a complete circle without spillage or detection.

David was sent to Ampleforth at a younger age than his brothers, no doubt because he was reckoned to be incorrigible. He was handed into the tender care of the teaching order at the age of eight-and-a-half. The time at Ampleforth produced mixed feelings in the young David. Contrary to expectation a certain amount of nonconformism was allowed and opinions were expected to be freely admitted. The monks were dedicated teachers and exercised their vocation by reason and example rather than regimes of bread and water and the tawse. At that time the school housed about 350 boys from many walks of life. Neither wealth nor poverty was praised or despised and fees were a matter between the school administration and the parents.

A love of God and a responsibility to one's country and fellow man were the precepts of Ampleforth and a boy left to his own devices was expected to fill his hours with hard work. Although David was drawn towards the arts and languages he never quite accepted that at Ampleforth rules were not necessarily made to be broken. Self-discipline was not his strong point if it was a choice between unsupervised work and an expedition into the countryside.

'Brother Bill already had a reputation as an expert rabbit poacher; what's more he had secured an outlet through a local trader. What was good enough for Bill was certainly good enough for me.'

At Ampleforth David met the young Freddy de Guingand, at that time an under officer in the Officers' Training Corps, later to become Chief of Staff to General Montgomery with the 8th Army. As a friend with the ear of Montgomery he was of inestimable assistance to the early Special Air Service endeavours.

Organised sport, of which there was a multiplicity of choices at the school, was not Stirling's forte. He much preferred solitary ramblings in the North Yorkshire countryside which was so reminiscent of Keir country. Not physically strong at that time, he let his imagination run riot as he tracked wild beasts through the fields and hedgerows. The rules were inflexible for being caught out-of-bounds but David willingly accepted punishment as dues for his freedom. Six strokes of the cane were a small price to pay for an afternoon's adventure. Though his studies did not suffer too badly, he could have done better, and this he realised. His knowledge of the inevitable contents of his school reports made the slow rail journey from York to Causewayhead via Edinburgh pass all too quickly.

David's education suffered from constant and lengthy interruption. The adder bite took a large chunk out of one year, then, in his early teens, he was stricken with typhoid and during the long, painful recovery he was taught by a private tutor. The tutor must be given full marks for perseverance as he battled to capture the interest of a boy who was not above faking a relapse in order to avoid subjects he found boring or incomprehensible. During this enforced absence from Ampleforth, the young Stirling conducted his first successful raid.

The nursery and the kitchen were just about as far apart as was possible in Keir and the connection was via long straight corridors. It was about 7 p.m. and schoolroom supper had not satisfied David's appetite – he must do something about it even if it meant breaking the rules once again. Furtively he made his way along the top corridor, down one of the staircases and along further passageways to the unlocked kitchen. He was in luck; the room was deserted. With mouth watering, he helped himself to a whole ham and some tongue from the meat safe, stuffing his pockets with crisp bread and adding a jar of pickle. He was about to leave when he remembered dessert: he found apples, some pie and ice cream. The afterthought was his undoing.

He was spotted by the returning cook, who gave chase with a

loud yell. David made off at best possible speed, his precarious load balanced in front of him. He reached the first corner and almost collided with his mother's maid. She staggered, regained her balance and joined the cook in pursuit. They entered the occupied area of the house and muted their cries lest they disturb the Stirlings and their guests. The butler leaving the drawing room assessed the situation at a glance and joined the silent chase. Stirling scuttled up the third flight of stairs to nursery level and then decided on subterfuge.

Dashing along the upper level corridor he did a slalom turn at the end and went back down to the lower level via another staircase. The pursuit party made for the nursery door, then realising they had been foxed descended the same stairs as David. Stirling had meantime reached the first set of stairs again and with superhuman effort and a very creditable sense of balance ascended them at great speed, his supper still intact. Beating the posse to the nursery door by seconds he was inside and had the door locked as the butler reached for the handle and heard a distinctly pronounced 'Yum, yum' from the happy Stirling.

A perhaps satirical tale is told about the lengths to which he would go to provide for his ever-growing appetite. The family were at the shooting lodge which General Stirling had built at Ardchullary. The illustrious cook, Alice Thompson, was on one occasion set astride a pony by one of the keepers. It was her first ride, and she lost control of the animal, which tore across the lawn and flower beds wreaking havoc amongst the blooms. Alice was unseated. She picked herself up and walked back to the rest of the group just as the laughter turned to silence. General Stirling appeared on the scene, a grim expression on his face.

'Who is responsible for this?' he growled, swinging his arm around to encompass the damage. He looked from one pale face to another as he surveyed his brood. David, for reasons known only to himself, shouldered the blame. 'It was me, Daddy.'

After the inevitable ticking off David remained without consolation until dinner, whereupon his reward became obvious to brothers and sisters. David's portions were distinctly larger than theirs, and continued to be so during Alice's tenure at Keir. Subtle planning, or a sudden sense of protective honour?

Each summer in those early years the Stirling children were moved across Scotland to Morar on the west coast. Here Mrs Stirling's parents, the Lovats, had built a lodge on the edge of Loch Morar. The lodge itself was let and the children went to a house in Morar village. Many of the families in the area housed Glasgow 'boarded-out' children and at the house where David and Margaret were, there were four; the youngest, Sadie, was from the city. During a play session it happened that Sadie cut her hand and her status as a boarded-out child left David and Margaret culpable in the eyes of their nanny. In the dog-house, ostracised and given no lunch David decided that their only recourse lay in running away.

David calculated that to use the road to reach the railway station at Arisaig would be folly. Search parties would assume that they had taken the easy route. He decided upon the railway line. It was straight and it went to the station. Margaret was easily persuaded by his logic. She soon regretted her acquiescence however. Whilst David's legs were just long enough to step from sleeper to sleeper she, poor girl, had to totter along with very tiring foreshortened paces. The four miles or so to Arisaig were long miles indeed for Margaret. At the station they took stock – no sign of the searchers, but – no money for rail tickets! This and the ever-demanding stomach of young David decided him. 'We'd better go back for tea, Margaret, then we can think again.'

The final ignominy was not apparent until they returned. They had not even been missed. Setting out to punish they had succeeded only in punishing – themselves.

In many ways the attack of typhoid was a blessing in disguise for Stirling. Between the efforts of the school staff and private tutors he had progressed reasonably well, academically. Had he been at the school on a more permanent basis it is probable that his inability to accept a regulated life without resistance might have turned out badly for him.

David's voracious appetite was acquired during the recuperative period, and he began to put on weight and grow. With growth came confidence and he began to enjoy his brothers' highland pastimes: mountain walking, deer stalking, shooting and fishing became his great leisure pursuits.

Although he became an expert shot, David was a devotee of the hammer lock shotgun at that time, and was often in the habit of absentmindedly stroking the triggers whilst waiting for the duck to flight or the birds to rise. It was not uncommon for the early morning tranquillity to be broken by a blast from one or both of his barrels as a result of just a little too much pressure. Returning to Keir for lunch after a morning's shoot, David set his gun down on the floor only to have it unexpectedly fire and shatter the huge mirror at the end of the long corridor.

Amidst laughter and remonstration everyone helped to clear up the mess and disguise the pellet marks on the walls and ceiling before the arrival of the rest of the shooting party. David energetically claimed that he had followed the rule and unloaded before approaching the gun room, and that it had been a frame-up by one of his brothers. Too many similar stories make this unlikely.

The renewal of appetite and resumption of healthy outdoor pursuits had its effect on Stirling; at the time he entered Cambridge University he towered, at six feet five inches, over most of his contemporaries. Such academic interests as he had remained firmly with the arts but by now he also considered himself something of an expert on horse racing. Newmarket was close and he was a frequent visitor, often returning penniless but occasionally with 'sporran brimming'. When in the money the Stirling generosity was quick to show. David enjoyed the good life and had a wide circle of friends of similar ilk.

'Cambridge was fun in those days. If there was a serious side to life it totally escaped me. Although I knew I was doing scarce enough to get by academically I managed to persuade myself that there was time aplenty. I was encountering young Communists for the first time and took great pleasure in opposing their stuffy, secondhand arguments. I knew that eventually I would have to face the realities of my future but – not yet.'

Margaret, a fairly frequent visitor to Cambridge, arrived on one occasion to find that David had been 'gated'. This was not an unusual occurrence, but David had arranged to give a dinner party and was desperately keen not to cancel it. Stirling's tutor at the time was known affectionately as 'Granny G'. David liked and respected 'Granny' but knew that having decided to gate him he would not be open to pleas as insubstantial as a dinner party. As he was wont to do many times later in life, he turned to Margaret for assistance. By this time the Stirling charm was fully matured and already he had developed the knack of making people do things against their better judgement.

The ever-loyal Margaret was persuaded to visit the professor and use her charm to secure David's release for the evening. Before she could change her mind David deposited her outside the Professor's study, knocked and left. After some small talk with the puzzled 'Granny', Margaret had a brainwave.

'Look, Professor, David is supposed to be holding a dinner party this evening and it is very important to him. Could you please give permission for him to continue with it? It really is very important and also I know that David would be most pleased if you were to come yourself.'

It is a tribute to Margaret's abilities and obvious sincerity that the Professor agreed (though he turned down the personal invitation). David was delighted. 'Well done, Margaret. However did you do it?'

'It was quite simple. I asked the Professor to join you.' David's face turned white. 'What? That really is too much. We can't have him there. This is too awful for words.' He stopped as he saw the uncontrollable shake of Margaret's shoulders, and joined in the laughter at his own expense. The truth of the situation had not escaped 'Granny'. 'Never again should you send your sister to do your dirty work, Stirling,' he admonished.

Eventually the round of parties and jaunts to Newmarket took their toll and David was summoned to the senior tutor. Whether it was a tribute to his character, his family or whether the tutor was in a particularly benevolent mood on the day will never be known. David was read a list of some twenty-three offences which had accumulated against him and he was invited to select three on which to be sent down.

'I cannot remember now what the offences were – none seemed too serious to me, but I chose the three which I considered would be least offensive to my mother.'

On the tortuous journey back to Keir Stirling took his first long look at the life stretching before him and decided to follow his heart. He would become an artist.

3

---

# A Fully Grown Boy

Stirling adapted easily to Paris. The avant garde life-style of the Left Bank suited him well. The only pressures of work were self-imposed and social life was inexpensive and enjoyable. Generally speaking in those days an artist's life was one of penury with long evenings spent nursing sparse supplies of pastis and engaging in lengthy heartfelt dissertations about the capitalist society which paid no heed to the brilliant thoughts of the students. Apart from a somewhat mild exposure to the occasional youthful Communist at Cambridge, Stirling mixed for the first time with the 'angry young men' of the day.

He was stimulated by the experience and, as he was forthright in his conservative opinions, viewed with some suspicion by his companions. Not without money, he was careful to hide that fact and his background; not out of embarrassment but because he felt it might shut him off from other students and from stimulating debate. His experience of life had been, after all, that of the very capitalistic society of which his fellow artists complained so bitterly. The attitudes of the monks at Ampleforth, to which he had paid scant attention at the time, suddenly began to make sense. All men are born equal; all have their points of view, and these must be respected. However, respect is one thing, agreement quite another, and he cleverly argued the case for the 'real aristocracy'.

Although he enjoyed the night life and the discussions at

the pavement cafés of Montmartre, Stirling applied himself enthusiastically to his painting and felt he was making good progress. His work was a strange mixture of beauty and the macabre. Flowers were a favourite subject when he was in a light mood but if he was at a low ebb his paintings became strange creations of dark, interwoven shapes, sometimes with almost female curves and expression, sometimes with harsh, slicing lines of violently contrasting colours.

'I don't know what was in my mind, except that I sometimes suffered an immense frustration. I knew what I wanted to paint but it just would not come. It was the most awful feeling. I felt that I was going to burst with impatience. What was in my mind would not reflect on the canvas, I could see it so clearly but the translation was impossible. I went through quite a bad patch of what I suppose was depression. At that time painting was the most important thing in my life. What was a great help, of course, was that I was certainly not alone.

'Much of the time this was what caused the many frustrations of those young men and women in France. They had come to the great seat of learning in the art world and it wasn't working. Their escape became aggravation against the society to which they felt they were being forced back. They imagined that they had nothing to offer that society and there seemed no way of finding an outlet for their creativity. In some, you could detect a sort of hopelessness. What was most impressive, however, was that the ones for whom it was working never became "pomposo" about it; every way one turned there was willing help and advice. It was a warm-cold world, you have to live the life to understand it.'

Stirling, a generous man, occasionally managed to use some of his limited funds to entertain his colleagues. He would pretend to have had a winning streak at the gaming tables, or to have benefited from a repaid debt. He would then take a couple of tables for the evening at one of the regular haunts and buy in the pastis and food. In impish fashion he would make a provocative statement and eagerly anticipate the inevitable argument.

'I loved those evenings. They were full of fervent speeches, chest-beating and the pomposity of youngsters who thought they were being totally original. In fact their views were distinctly secondhand, bolstered by the booze and all the more plastic for that. I suppose I was a little false and plastic myself. I spent some of my brasso on buying clothes which I imagined allowed me to blend – corduroys which I deliberately made dirty and the regulation beret and scarf. No matter how cold it was I made my protest along with the others and never, never wore an overcoat.' (This was true to the end of Stirling's life.)

Stirling meandered through peaks of amiable contentment with his fellow men and troughs of depression as he struggled to produce the sort of work of which he knew he was capable. He was beginning to have doubts and thought that perhaps a change of environment would help him to break through.

'It remains the most bitter disappointment of my life. I looked to my tutor for advice, and he was obviously not surprised that I should have sought him out. He told me very bluntly, and for that I thank "le bon Dieu", that although undoubtedly had all the creative talent to make a passable artist, I lacked absolutely the necessary drawing expertise, and in his opinion I would never achieve it. He suggested that I forget any ambitions I may have had in that direction and look to another future – perhaps commercial art. I was quite shattered as I had honestly believed it was only a matter of time before I smashed the barrier.'

Somewhat disillusioned, Stirling returned to Keir to think again. In his opinion all he had gained from his year and a half in France was a vast improvement in his command of the language. This at least was to stand him in good stead. There was still enough of the artist within for him to desire to express his creativity in some form, and he settled on architecture. He was, he found, having embarked on a different discipline, still able to get a place again at Cambridge.

Although during this second session at university Stirling

applied himself somewhat more diligently to his studies, he was still far too close to Newmarket. Even worse he had now discovered the joys of White's and other convivial London haunts. Stirling drew a veil over this period of his life: 'It was entirely wasteful. I was unable fully to shake off the disappointment of what I regarded as a total failure in France. I managed to stay the pace for about a year in Cambridge before taking a position with a group of architects in Edinburgh – the senior partner was Reginald Fairlie, a friend of my parents. He was an extremely well-known Scottish architect and a frequent visitor to Keir. The simple fact is that though I still felt that I could create, there was little creativity called for in the projects set before me and I still couldn't draw. I was further disadvantaged by the fact that my mathematics was quite hopeless. I think Reginald and the other partners were probably quite relieved when I decided to quit.

'I was not allowed too much time to mope or idle when I returned to Keir. Within a few days my mother invited me to accompany her on a walk around the gardens. I had correctly anticipated her motives. I got the most shocking wigging. It was conducted in a quiet fashion (she rarely raised her voice) but it was crystal clear. My brothers and sisters were thinking positively about their futures. I, it seemed, was content to drift. I must learn to take defeat on the chin; if painting was out then I had to find something else which would allow me to leave my mark on life. The gambling had not escaped her attention either but I was not lectured on that, merely allowed to know that she disapproved of the habit in one with responsibilities.'

By this time Stirling was 'a fully grown boy', he had reached full height and was enormously strong. He enjoyed testing himself physically and mentally. The problem was to find a project or employment which kept both attributes at full stretch. It was also proper, to Stirling's mind, that there be strong fun and risk elements. Predictably, his plan was an ambitious one; he decided that he would be the first man to stand atop the lonely summit of Mount Everest.

Once the decision had been taken Stirling became thoroughly engrossed in making plans. His mother, if not entirely satisfied with his choice of target, tolerated it, albeit with some amusement. Stirling's climbing experience was limited to the Scottish peaks – thorough testing ground for short, savage winter climbs but not the best preparation for the High Himalayas. He decided to concentrate on two factors; skill in climbing and mountaineering at altitude and attaining peak physical fitness.

He planned to gain initial experience in the Swiss Alps under the tutelage of experts, then to set himself a goal which put more emphasis on endurance. He also had to conquer a personal problem; since childhood Stirling had suffered from acute vertigo. Certainly he had climbed in the Scottish Highlands and the Cuillins of Skye but always with others and as often as not he seconded rather than led. When he had led a pitch it had been on climbs with little exposure to sheer drops.

David's mother willingly financed the stay in Switzerland; 'The budget was not niggardly but it left me no change for excesses . . . I was certainly not going to be tempted to the casino.' A whole year was spent in the Swiss Alps with two German guides.

'They were brothers and possessed of less humour than a charging rhino. They were hard taskmasters and very, very good. The sheer scope of my task became more apparent. It frightened me but I felt challenged and I had to contain myself from getting too cocky and starting too soon. All this was long before I tackled the boring problems of logistics and sponsorship.'

Stirling returned to Keir in mid-1938 to plan the second part of his training schedule. He enlisted in the Scots Guards Supplementary Reserve to undertake part-time training at the depot in Pirbright. 'I thought this might help in some obscure way, and in any event my father had been in the Scots Guards so it seemed a right thing to do. There I would surely learn more about myself, brush up my navigation and harden myself off. It was of no help whatsoever; drill, drill and more drill with some basic and totally useless tactics thrown in. I decided to ignore the whole thing after a few sessions and get on with the next bit. I didn't even consider the penalties of my breaking a contract.'

The 'next bit' took him to Canada via New York City in late 1938. He was then twenty-three. His plan was to work his way across the continent, then climb all 'the worthwhile peaks in the Rockies' before finally hardening himself off with a horse ride along the length of the Continental Divide. But New York proved just a little too exciting to leave unexplored. Never one to do things by halves Stirling took a suite in the Hotel Pierre. This, quite apart from the gaming tables, took due toll on his resources and he often had to resort to subterfuge in order to get more of the 'indispensable stuff'.

'It was quite useful having the name Stirling. My account was in the Bank of Scotland, I was indisputably a "Jock" and my branch was actually in the town of Stirling. I never lied about my family owning the Stirling branch but I have to admit I was often guilty of not correcting those who thought we did. I rarely had trouble cashing a cheque – poor Mama often had to settle the overdraft.'

To cater for those occasions when the 'sporran' needed a 'substantial topping-up' Stirling developed the technique of calling the Stirling branch manager direct (reversed charges, of course). He would spend some time asking about the family, weather conditions in Scotland, cricket scores, the state of the shooting, or whatever. Just as it seemed he was about to hang up after his friendly call he would let it be known that 'I really could do with a few hundred pounds, you know'. It was usually successful!

There seems little doubt that Stirling's eligibility rating was high with the restless females of New York society and that he had 'more than a couple of close escapes'. He was not unattracted to the opposite sex (France had been quite instructive), nor was he unattractive, but courtship and marriage had rules and responsibilities; anathema to the young Stirling. He also required mental stimulus from his friends of either sex: 'I found coquetry and social foppishness very hard to tolerate . . . invariably I would quit the scene as soon as I reckoned that I may have become a target for some predatory female.'

Once he had had his fling in New York, Stirling set seriously about his preparations. In the beginning he worked for the Frontier Cattle Company Ltd, based in Vanderhoof, British Columbia, and with administrative offices on Wall Street, New York. Cattle driving was a new experience but he needed funds.

'I rode tolerably well but it took some time to adjust to the long stirrup, and adjusting was essential. If you had a few hundred pounds of longhorn lashed to the pommel of your saddle you needed to be able to brace the legs and lock the knees to avoid an undignified scramble in the dust. I had many of those in the early days. I soon found out that the well-trained mustang is a match for any polo pony. Those horses could stop on a sixpence and turn almost instantly in their own length. It was exhilarating at first and then it became a downright slog.'

Stirling enjoyed himself. It was a tough life and it seemed to him that his programme had been chosen well. He was hardening his body according to plan and he was in good company.

'The life of a cowboy was simple and hard. I was sleeping out in temperatures I had never before experienced without benefit of tent. A couple of blankets and the saddle as a pillow sufficed. I will never forget the cold. It was worse than anything I encountered in the Alps or the desert. We ate simple fare; salt beef, sourdough and piles and piles of beans. It was a boring menu but by the time one ate at night one just did not care. A full stomach, a few campfire yarns, maybe a song or two and sleep suddenly became the most desirable thing on earth.'

In between cattle drives Stirling found time to have a little fun which, inevitably, depleted his funds. His mother received few letters and these usually asked for money. A typical telegraphed plea was: 'Horse lost shoe – please send money. All well. David.' Usually the response was in the right vein. Stirling was not totally dependent on money from home; he earned reasonably well from the cattle drives, once took a very brief and disastrous job as a short-order cook and entered for rodeo events where he was moderately successful. It was just that the 'spare capital' seemed to dwindle.

'I religiously kept sufficient funds for my prime venture but the extra, for the little comforts of life, never seemed enough. During the season I tried the rodeos but I stuck to the horse riding [bronc-busting]; Brahmin bulls were a ride I never particularly wanted to try, they were quite fearsome beasts; noble too, and I always felt they were being made to look a little ridiculous.

'For much the same reasons I could never come to terms with elephants and lions performing in circuses. Zoos are one thing, after all they do a great deal towards the preservation of endangered species, but to have some of nature's greatest creations made to stand on little stools or be coerced into jumping through hoops is quite another.

'I'm afraid I often did cable to Keir for a little extra. I generally asked for twice as much as I wanted and usually got rather less than half of that. I seem to remember hearing, whilst I was in New York, that Margaret was coming to the States and would be visiting me. I fancied she might be carrying unwelcome instructions from my mother. I had said that my extended stay in the city was due to illness. I had been slightly ill but certainly it was not serious. That was just the prompt I needed to get me moving purposefully.'

Margaret was not coming solely to see David; there was no missive from mother except to wish him bon voyage. Margaret was due to visit family friends in New Mexico and Florida and was taking advantage of the air routing to spend a few days with her brother.

'I arrived at the Hotel Pierre and immediately enquired after David's whereabouts. The staff were vague but I was eventually told that "Master David" would visit me in my room at six that evening, and I was pleasantly surprised with the news. I was even more surprised when at six o'clock a complete stranger knocked at my door. It turned out that he was some kind of real estate representative!

'I returned later to reception and asked, "Are you sure you do not have any message from David Stirling?" After a little discussion with members of staff, the manager at last said, Yes, Mr Stirling had stayed in the hotel, there was no forwarding address but there was something else. I was presented with David's bowler hat, an umbrella and his hotel bill!'

During her visit to her friends, Margaret received the following letter:

My dear Margaret,

I hope you enjoyed your visit to Bill and Palm Beach, and that you understood why I left New York almost as you arrived. I hope that N.M. did not exaggerate things – you cannot believe what she says. She probably either told you that I was much iller than in fact or else that I spent the three months in New York merely gadding around.

The life out here is really tough – camping out without even a tent in temperatures below zero. One night there was even a snowstorm. Tomorrow myself and Dick Hobson start a cattle drive from here to a unit of the ranch about 70 miles away and after that I have to ride over to Bella Coola (on the coast) 215 miles and help to drive 50 head of horses to the home ranch. I shall start on my ride south about May 10th.

I'll write to you when I get to Banff on the way south – this is the most difficult and interesting part of the ride.

Your loving David

There is no evidence of Stirling having written from Banff but he duly arrived in the Banff National Park, via rodeos in Red Deer and Calgary, to begin his climbing and riding in earnest. He was by then very fit and ready for a change of scene and action. He had persuaded his companion to come along during long evening sojourns on the cattle drives; 'Panhandle' Pete, one-time prospector, cowboy, waggoner and rail-track layer. He was a fit, rugged Texan with a gift for tall stories and a humour as keen as Stirling's. From pioneering stock, it was quite natural for him to join David for a year of rambling, so long as it remained interesting and covered pastures new.

The journey down the length of the Rocky Mountains is not well-recorded but certainly the first climb was on Castle Mountain some fifty kilometres northwest of Banff. It was not a summit attempt, but a way of working out techniques and equipment needs. In 1938 the climber's requirements were not well served; unruly hempen ropes, inferior boots and clumsy crampons. Clothing was crude and the mountaineer relied upon layers of garments rather than the specialist down and synthetic fibre-filled items of later years.

It was now winter 1938 and in winter the northern Rockies, if not downright inhospitable, are certainly not pleasant; they rival (and can surpass) anything that the Swiss Alps can throw at the climber. It was not unusual to have windspeeds of 100 mph plus; the wind-chill factor at these speeds combined with temperatures which could be down into the minus thirties produced very severe conditions.

'I got it slightly wrong. I should have started my ride from the south and gradually worked my way up into more severe conditions. As it was I was tackling the worst situation first, but I couldn't switch direction and begin again. It was hard and dangerous, far more exacting climbing than I had experienced in Switzerland. I'd read somewhere that a man is quite incapacitated both mentally and physically at high altitudes in direct ratio to the degree of oxygen starvation at a particular level. This decided me to reduce my ambitions and take the technically difficult rather than the simply high masses. I could afford to leave altitude and acclimatization until I was in the Himalayas. It was a cumulative thing and whatever I achieved in the Rockies in that respect I would have to achieve again on Everest.

'I went for the difficult ice-faces, the lower glaciers and deep couloirs. I wanted to give myself maximum unprotected exposure to height – I still worried about vertigo; it never leaves one, you know. We did make some full summit climbs, by way of building up stamina, but they were the exception rather than the rule.'

There were frequent trips into the foothills to replenish supplies. Although there may have been some carousing in lonely bars, Stirling was taking life seriously now. The longest visits to the lower reaches were when the trips coincided with the locations of Indian Reservations. The first of these was just over the Canadian/USA border; the Blackfeet Reservation to which Stirling repaired after scaling Mount Stimson. Panhandle Pete was something of an authority on the Indian nations and it was he who first fired Stirling's imagination.

He was fascinated by the folklore of the Indian nations (distant ancestors of the Stirlings had been involved in the Indian Wars). In many ways the multitude of tribes reminded him of the clans of his native Scotland. Steeped in the history of inter-tribal warfare, they had unsuccessfully tried to rally against the westwards progress of the white man. Now they were almost forgotten, confined to areas of land which often bore little resemblance to their historic hunting grounds. Nomadic by nature and forced into stagnation, they were a strange mixture of resignation and bitterness.

'I would have liked to spend a lot of time with those people. They were dignified and proud. Their sense of history was still exemplified by handed-down tales around the campfires and in the communal wigwams which still appeared amongst the huts erected by the "Americans".'

As he progressed south, Stirling made a detour as he came off the Lewis and Clark Range southwest of Great Falls, a 350-mile round trip to visit the Fort Belknap Indian Reservation. After a few days there he decided to ride an easier route southwards to the start of the southern extremes of the Rockies. How long it took him to ride from Fort Belknap, Montana, to the Great Divide Basin in Wyoming is unrecorded but Stirling did not set a hard pace and indeed he covered some of the ground by rail. The months of climbing under severe weather conditions and on a restricted diet had left him tired and he looked on this part of the journey as a recuperation against his final work further south.

He made a point of stopping to visit yet another reservation as he passed through Shoshone country. By now the full scope of his venture was beginning to hit him. It was a mammoth undertaking and there was much that he had not considered. He was filling in the long hours of riding by mentally working out his expedition to Everest. Most of his waking minutes were concerned with logistics and administrative details.

'The one thing I cannot remember thinking about in any great detail was who was to come with me. Pete laughed outright when I invited him. I think I assumed that as it was such an exciting venture there would be no shortage of high-grade volunteers. I had a picture of turning them away by the dozen. Sponsorship would not be a problem – most worthy Britons would gladly contribute to such a splendid cause. How wrong I would have been.'

Mid-1939 arrived and Stirling was still some way from his target of Albuquerque and the Rio Grande, having moved roughly southwards through Colorado by following the Park, Gore and Sawatch Ranges. Rested and enjoying much more pleasant weather he was now thoroughly at home on the peaks. It is unclear from memories and diaries but at this point Stirling seems to have taken a train journey south into the area of the Sangre de Cristo Mountains before continuing on horseback. As he wound his way down into Los Alamos he decided to take a little relaxation time. Leaving his horses in the town he took a train to Las Vegas determined to turn his remaining money into a sufficient sum to have a 'really good time'.

He came out on top and was wise enough to keep the cash. He could now replace his very tired horses and spend a few nights in comparative luxury in Los Alamos. From there he made contact with Margaret, then with friends in El Paso. Stirling had one or two more climbs planned in the area of Arizona's Mogollon Rim before working his way down the Rio Grande to the Gulf of Mexico, whence he would return to Scotland via New York.

It was probably at Jarales, south along the Rio Grande from Albuquerque, that Stirling heard the news that Great Britain was at war. He immediately telegraphed to Keir asking for details of the situation in Europe and received a prompt and succinct reply from his mother: 'Return home by the cheapest possible means.'

Stirling, ever-obedient to such fiscally concise instructions, caught the first available first-class flight back. Thus the twenty-four-year-old absentee from the Scots Guards Supplementary Reserve returned to his country by the most expensive route to take up the colours.

BOOK TWO

———

# THE WAR YEARS

# 4

# 'AN UNREMARKABLE SOLDIER'

'Pirbright was hardly the best place to send a young man to train when he might be called forth at any moment. Being incarcerated in a barracks only an hour from London places a temptation before one which is simply irresistible. I suppose if the training had been a little more inspiring – less mechanical, and with the students being required to exercise the grey matter – it could have been tolerable, though I doubt it.

'If a chap is six feet six inches tall in his ammunition boots (why did they call them ammunition boots?) there is no place to hide. If that chap is also somewhat mystified by the intricacies of "saluting by numbers" and the "right about turn", then his presence positively demands recognition. Guards drill sergeants want for neither perspicacity nor expressive vocabulary. "Get those legs together, Stirling, the way you're prancing around you'll not damage anything that just might be dangling between them" was fairly typical of the sort of anguished bellow which resounded around the parade ground as a result of my more pathetic efforts.

'One developed a sort of immunity to it all. One did not get angry – those fellows were far too amusing for that and off-duty they were far more interesting to talk to about the real matters of warfare than the somewhat pompous officer lecturers. They had some real power too. I remember holding my rifle as near as I could get to the "port arms" position (this is to enable the instructor to look down the barrel without dirtying his fingers by having to touch the weapon). My sergeant duly peered and, obviously dissatisfied with what he saw, growled: "Ugh! Stirling, it's bloody filthy. There must be a bloody clown on the end of this rifle." "Yes, sergeant, but not at my end." My social life was severely curtailed for a couple of weeks.

'I think I just wanted to be off to join the war – I didn't mind where. It seemed to me, as it must have done to thousands of recruits, that a large percentage of what we were "learning" was quite irrelevant to tackling the Hun. I did develop various fairly successful techniques for avoiding attention, but really one just had to escape at every opportunity. This was not entirely frivolity; in men about to go to war there are tensions, there is fear (admitted or not) and the wild nights in London were a release of sorts.

'The officers really did lecture us in the truest sense of the word. "For this occasion the correct deployment and tactics are . . . That situation must be countered with a left flanking attack," and so on. Rarely were our opinions asked; when they were, they were usually not analysed and often treated with contempt.'

It might be construed that Stirling, then in the rank of Guardsman, was ne'er-do-well and pompous, holding senior ranks in utter contempt. This would be quite wrong. His father, after all, was a general, and Stirling had mixed with famous fighting men throughout his young life. High-ranking officers and clan chiefs (his uncle Lord Lovat was both) were constant visitors to Keir.

Not only did David Stirling have a very early perception of how the military mind worked, his deer-stalking days and sporting life in the Scottish highlands had given him a true countryman's sense of tactics and fieldcraft. The hard work in Switzerland, the USA and Canada had honed him to a sharp peak of physical fitness. Though he did not necessarily show it, he was supremely confident. He did not suffer the normal nervous reaction of most men when faced with authority; he was unafraid and saw no sense in not questioning those matters which were being put to him as inviolable tactical laws.

Once he realised that his refusal to accept things at face value resulted only in his being confined to barracks for ever-increasing periods, Stirling changed his methods. He would just go along with whatever was thrown at him. Training would not last forever and then the war would be upon him. Meantime he would hit the London circuit as often as opportunity and funds allowed. Trainees were not permitted to leave camp nightly, but the perimeters were easily breached and provided that he made it back before first light Stirling found no trouble in 'escaping' as often as he felt like it.

Long nights at the bar of White's Club or the gaming tables, coupled to the rigours of basic training, caused even Stirling's body to cry out sleep, so he took to dozing off during the more boring lectures. He would slump into a position between the two rear rows of students try to disappear between the legs of the men behind and the heads and shoulders of those in front and lapse into semi-consciousness. Often it worked.

TEWTS, in indulgence of the military's propensity for mnemonics, are Tactical Exercises Without Troops. An experienced instructor, with the aid of maps, pointers and military stick-on symbols, will design a battle situation, and students will dictate the moves of the pieces – a form of open chess designed to trap the unwary. One TEWT is worth recounting. An easily dislikable major whom we shall call Smith was, with a great deal of sarcasm, leading his class through such a battle. He spotted the somnambulant Stirling, twisted into an impossible position and apparently oblivious to everything.

'The enemy is here,' eyes obliquely cast in Stirling's direction, 'you have pushed them into positions along this crest.' More emphatically now, 'You are planning your advance along this ridge line,' a further glance at the offending trainee, when you come under fire. Your actions, please?' Stirling has not moved a muscle.

'Your actions, please?' Voice like thunder now. 'Stirling, your actions?'

Stirling opens one sleepy eye. 'Numbers 1 and 2 platoons will go to ground and return the fire. Numbers 3 and 4 platoons will move left. When I engage the target with mortars they will attack from that flank. When they are about to close I will cease the mortar fire. When they are through the position, 1 and 2 platoons will move ahead over the crest of the hill and take care of the survivors. We will then report ammunition and casualty states and regroup in all-round defence on the knoll while I make my report.' The eyelid drooped once more and there was the suspicion of a yawn followed by a gentle snore.

Major Smith's rage was easy to detect from the florid cheeks and rapid rise and fall of his chest as he fought for control. Stirling's answer had been almost textbook perfect – but it related to a question asked some time previously.

'In future you will kindly stay awake during my classes and make some effort to concentrate.'

'Yes, sir,' was clearly heard but there followed a mumble which witnesses testify to having been 'and bollocks to you too.' Whatever the truth, Stirling had made an enemy.

He made many such enemies with his refusal to conform. Viscount Whitelaw who was at Pirbright at the same time as him and somewhat younger, remembers Stirling's approach to military discipline: 'He was quite, quite irresponsible. I'd known the Stirling family most of my life and all the brothers were wild in their own way. Not eccentric but they could be relied upon to be different. As a junior officer I was, on one occasion, put under David for instruction. He was supposed to take me through the duties of Orderly Officer which included inspecting the guard and making night rounds.

'This was not for him. He would simply ignore the duties and go off to a party in London or wherever and he would invariably be found out. This didn't bother David at all but it was most unfair of the system to punish me for the misdemeanours also! He was quite incorrigible. He was great fun of course but he just couldn't tolerate the fact that, in the usual nature of the British Army at that time, we were being trained along the lines of the last major conflict with no apparent thought to the new tactics required for the present war. His reaction was just to ignore everything.'

Tactics being taught were indeed quite obviously based on the tactics of World War I; what is more, many instructors also knew this and admitted it. Stirling could not come to terms with what he saw as a situation that was simply not being thought out properly. Since his arguments fell on deaf ears (probably because of his then blunt, outspoken manner) he took the line of least resistance. He opted out; however, he carefully calculated the level to which he could frustrate the system before it took firm action. He enjoyed himself and waited his time.

Subsequently, when Stirling departed Pirbright as what the Guards Depot described as an 'irresponsible and unremarkable soldier', he had in fact scored something of a success by his own lights. He had refused to accept outdated teachings; he had had a 'damned good time and made lots of friends' and, above all, he had escaped any significant retribution. At least he was now off to war with a 'fairly unfettered mind'.

During late 1939 and January 1940 the soldiers of Finland had captured the imagination of Britain and France with their spirited resistance to the Russian advance. Using their innate skills in the winter snow they had neutralised the German Army's northern thrust towards the Gulf of Bothnia and the southern drive past Suomussalmi. If the Allies could secure the Finnish iron mines which were supplying Germany and also pose a menace to Germany's Baltic flank whilst assisting the Finns it could only be to the overall good.

With this in mind an expeditionary force was created. To Stirling's great delight he became part of the 'Snowballers' – the 5th Battalion, the Scots Guards. A proficient skier due to his days in the Swiss Alps, he was quickly promoted to sergeant and made an instructor.

'It was a privileged position and one I had scarce earned. I became part of the insulation between officer and other ranks. We went off to Chamonix and to my great delight I discovered other perquisites of the warrant officer and sergeant's mess. With the benefit of experience we were able to secure a far more comfortable billet than the officers, and thus attracted a much more meaningful element of the local French ladies. Despite the arduous and quite serious training, skiing is fun and the war seemed very far away.'

The British Expeditionary Force to Finland was not to be. Protests were raised by Norway and Sweden which delayed matters until Finland collapsed. The news of the Expeditionary Force's disbandment came to 5th Battalion as they were about to embark for the sea voyage to Finland. The Snowballers were no more. Back at Pirbright, and White's, Stirling again decided to enjoy himself until the moguls of the army made up their minds what was to happen to him. It is interesting that Stirling's brother Bill was en route for Finland at the same time, aboard a submarine. Torpedoed in the North Sea it had to make an undignified return to Scotland.

In White's, Stirling first heard of Robert Laycock's plans to raise the first unit of Army Commandos. There was instant appeal in the thought of highly trained men taking on specific and important strategic targets – what was more, he understood that it was to be raised exclusively from the Brigade of Guards.

Stirling volunteered, and joined Laycock's Commando as a newly commissioned subaltern. Once more back to refresher training, his approach was much more serious. He was no longer being instructed by depot sergeants, long in the tooth and out-dated in ideas. He was amongst first-line soldiers and he expressed his admiration frequently.

'These NCOs were different. I did not escape their attentions as I still had not mastered the arts of the drill square. They were kind to young, inexperienced officers but they were also very firm. It did not suit them to abuse even such a lowly form of life as a subaltern but they got round the situation very effectively. I was always put on parade next to a young Guardsman by the name of Starling. Whenever I made a mistake, which was frequently, the abuse from the sergeant, who had quite a turn of phrase even if his use of adjectives was somewhat limited, would apparently be directed at the young Starling: "Starling, you flicking, miserable, flicking idiot, how many left feet do you have? Get a grip on your flicking self or I'll stick this pacestick up your arse and run you round and round my drill square like a flicking lollipop!" Every time the sergeant spat out the name Starling he would look me directly in the eye. There was no doubt in anyone's mind whom he was referring to.'

Refresher training came to an end and the Commando was shipped to Scotland for the 'serious stuff'. Here endurance and fieldcraft were tested to the full and intermixed with unarmed combat and survival techniques. Stirling revelled in the work. Real soldiering was in sight at last. For the first time personal initiative was being challenged; plans for operations were tackled jointly and successes and failures in this new concept of army fighting were examined for lessons. But stimulating though the training and exercises were, Stirling was not totally fulfilled.

'There was a tremendous air of expectancy. We didn't know where we were to be deployed or when but we knew dammed well that we were going to be good. At the back of my mind though was always a nagging doubt. We plunged around the glens like one of the thundering herds of cattle I'd helped drive in America. It seemed wrong. There we were, being taught the art of silent killing and the like, signalling our presence to all and sundry as we ground forward in unwieldy groups of twenty or more.

'The consolation was that one was surrounded by as loyal and efficient a bunch of fighting men as the British Army then possessed. The constant exercises, broken by short periods of equally hard play, kept one pretty well occupied and I suppose that any ideas I had were pushed to the back of my mind. On the whole they were happy days – most of the officers were friends of mine from school days or gregarious evenings in London, and the conviviality left one with a great feeling of contentment, expectancy and also an impatience to be getting on with it.'

During this period, Stirling was developing as a man and an officer. He was a gentle person but his iron-hard physique was very noticeable and though he found it difficult to discipline his men for offences he found amusing (usually those ascribed to a surfeit of ale at local hostelries) he was uncompromising in the field. Self-effacing and still given to moods, at which times he preferred his own company, he often gave the appearance of being a little mystified by what was going on around him ('probably a hangover from my boyhood sulks'). He could be vague and seemingly uninterested in the business of soldiering when not actually engaged in training. Once in the field he changed character. He became decisive and alert but only when there was challenge. Without the stimulus of testing situations he would either lapse into his private world or play some sort of prank on a comrade regardless of his rank.

He took a great interest in his men – it was an instinct nurtured in him from childhood anyway, but he enjoyed encouraging others to talk to him just as he enjoyed gently challenging their ideas and concepts. Full of curiosity he never lost the need to ask, Why? Senior NCOs and soldiers alike responded to the young, gentle giant but it was often difficult for them to put a finger on the attributes which made him an undoubted leader even at that stage of the war.

Sergeant Ernie Bond, Stirling's Platoon Sergeant in the Brigade of Guards Commando, recalls: 'He could talk endlessly and convince you of anything. He was curious to the point of being nosey – he wanted to know everything. I had a good three years' soldiering under my belt and he would ask opinions on tactics then argue the changes. Exceptionally good on training and exercises; you had a great feeling of confidence in him. He never flapped and no matter how quickly things happened you always had the feeling that he'd already thought things out. A real gentleman in every sense, he was interested in his troops and never expected them to do more than he was prepared to do himself. In return they'd have followed him anywhere, I'm sure.'

In February 1941 the Guards Commando became part of Layforce and, as the newly designated 8 Commando, set sail along with 7 and 11 Commando for the Middle East with Stirling still a subaltern.

'Thank le bon Dieu that I was never a sailor. Life on board those craft was far from pleasant. Slow and vulnerable to air and submarine attack there seemed little we could do to defend ourselves. Our Commandos were exercised daily to keep fit and we all had duties to perform by way of the ship's defence. Our guns would be brought to bear in the event of an attack and of course we stood deck watch as observers. It was a monotonous existence and not my cup of tea.'

Sergeant Ernie Bond often found himself on duty at the same time as Stirling. 'He was quite amusing. He would chat for hours with the sentries and didn't seem to need much sleep. After each tour of duty there was the usual report to be filled in. Even if nothing happened the army insisted that you reported the fact in writing. This seemed to be quite beyond young Stirling and every time he would come to me and ask how the hell he was supposed to make the entries.'

One lightish moment came for Stirling with the realisation that Randolph Churchill (who had coincidentally volunteered through the White's Club network) was now also a young officer with 8 Commando and an inveterate gambler. In fact it was Churchill who sought Stirling out as a result of Evelyn Waugh's comments on Stirling's love of the cards and backgammon.

'He was a likeable chap,' Stirling told me, 'but dear me he could talk. Not a bad thing, as he could never concentrate

on his cards long enough to win; I really did stock up the
sporran at his expense. He ran up some pretty impressive
debts along the passage to Suez but it's not surprising; he
didn't really have the temperament for successful gambling.
He just couldn't resist holding forth about how the war should
be handled. Very good for us, I'd say, that father did not take
advice from the son. You know, of course, that he was prone
to unashamedly bursting into tears whenever he got frustrated
– not the most common attribute in a Commando officer, but
he was certainly brave enough. I suppose it was an indication
of passion rather than weakness but not one which endeared
him to the Jocks. If there was one thing which really got to
him it was the thought that he was disliked. His continuous
prattle did rather leave him companionless at times.

'We stopped off in Cape Town for refuelling and re-
victualling and Randolph was an enforced loner for most
of the time, people had had enough of his self-opinionated
diatribes. The stopover was a pleasant respite and a chance
to stretch the legs. I must say we were entertained royally
by the South Africans and I had good company for the few
walks I managed into the foothills of the mountains. I vowed
that I would go back some day to see more of the magnificent
scenery and wildlife.'

March 1941 and Layforce was in Suez set to begin their final
training for a combined attack on Rhodes. Winston Churchill's
concept of setting up a Balkan front had been given impetus
by General 'Dick' O'Connor's impressive successes with 7th
Armoured Division against the Italian 10th Army. All such
plans were thrown into disarray after the German Army's
brilliant seizure of Crete. All Commando units were despatched
to Geneifa near the Great Bitter Lakes where they were given
the title of Special Service Brigade.

Stirling, as part of 8 Commando, was repositioned in Mersa
Matruh whilst the other parts of the force were sent on
operations which included the holding of a small section
of the Tobruk perimeter; covering the evacuation of Crete;

opposed landings off the coast of Syria and raids along the coastline of Cyrenaica.

During this period 8 Commando took part in three such raids; two against coastal communications positions in the area of Gazala and one against an aerodrome near Bomba. All three were planned to the same pattern: an approach by either gunboat or destroyer, so timed that the landing took place as early as practicable in the night to allow the greatest possible period of darkness for carrying out the operation; a strong party left to hold the beachhead and a main attack party. After the operation the attack party would roll up through the beachhead and so out to the mother craft.

About two hundred officers and men took part in each operation. In the first two destroyer-mounted raids, failure was due to rough weather, and the gunboat operation failed because the craft was spotted by enemy reconnaissance aircraft on its approach. This was followed by intense bombing, loss of surprise, severe damage and a dispirited return to base.

At this point the history books are unclear but it is assumed that Middle East Headquarters' (MEHQ) reasoning behind the subsequent disbandment of Layforce would have been:

1. The Commandos had been brought out from the UK at a time when it appeared that the MEF had only the Italians, who appeared to be beaten, to contend with. It seemed then that a small, well-planned combined operation on Rhodes, carried out by well-equipped Commando units, would enable such a force to occupy the island. However, as already indicated, the situation had entirely altered with the appearance of the Germans in Greece, Crete and the Western Desert.

2. The Commando training, its establishment and its equipment were not adjusted to a defensive role; and the necessary facilities, such as naval units, could not be spared for offensive raids because the general situation was too grave.

3. The shortage of reinforcements due to battle losses in Greece, Crete and the Western Desert caused the AG Branch of MEHQ to look upon Layforce as a heaven-sent reservoir of

trained men which could be allocated to formations requiring
an influx of officers and soldiers.

The lack of success of the 8 Commando operations preyed
heavily on Stirling's mind, especially as he was now once more
forced into inactivity broken only by day and night exercises
which had no particular point except to 'keep the men busy'.
He was in Cairo and at the whim of MEHQ as they deliberated
what to do with the remnants of the force.

Stirling's brother Peter was then part of the British Embassy
staff in the city, and as such had the advantage of a rented flat in
the Garden City quarter. To this haven David made his way at
every opportunity to bathe in comfort before tasting the many
delights Cairo offered the bachelor officer. As often as not he
would sleep in the flat if his body was too weary to take him
back to base. There were the inevitable problems of missed
parades and the like but the Stirling charm worked wonders
and nothing more serious than a few nights' confinement
resulted.

Nonetheless he was not escaping the attention of some senior
officers who viewed the escapades with distaste. There was no
doubt a touch of envy present – the Stirling flat was a meeting
place for many entertaining members of Cairo society. It was
around this time that Stirling hit upon the 'oxygen trick'.

'I chanced, after a somewhat vigorous party, to be in the
company of a charming young nurse from the Scottish Hospital
and must have bemoaned the fact that the next day was going
to be quite intolerable because of the inevitable hangover. She
told me to pop around to the hospital the next morning and ask
for her. This I did and I was introduced to the magical effects
of taking a couple of deep snifters from the pure oxygen bottle.
Wonderful. The hangover vanished in seconds.

'This became a regular occurrence whenever I felt the need
to clear the head and eventually I saw the sense of finding a
quiet nook in the hospital in which to sleep. This saved me the
painful journey from the Mess to the hospital in the mornings.

There was always a little room to tuck oneself away in for a few quiet hours. It had to happen, of course, that I would at some point choose the wrong room. An irate matron rang my commanding officer to complain. I took considerably more care after that, presenting myself as quite sick with a debilitating and strangely recurring fever. The Middle East abounds with such agues and it was simply described as a "pyrexia of unknown origin". Most of the nurses were only too well aware of the origin but they were a loyal lot.'

Despite the roisterings, Stirling never missed any exercise with his unit. One occasion could have had very unfortunate ramifications, had his life not taken a different course.

An exercise, rumoured to be the prelude to an operation, required Stirling and his platoon to undertake a night march, during which he was unlucky enough to walk into a thorned branch. The result was a painful slash across the eyeball. He was hospitalised to have the wound stitched and while he was thus confined his superiors reviewed his service record. It did not make impressive reading when all the hospital visits were listed along with the reports of his adventures in the Cairo night spots. A Board of Officers was commissioned. Their instructions were unequivocal – to decide whether Lieutenant Stirling was a malingerer whilst on active service and, if he was, to determine the extent of the offence, and if necessary prepare papers for his court martial for cowardice.

Stirling was discharged from hospital some days later quite unaware of the existence of the Board. When he returned to the officers' Mess he met Captain 'Jock' Lewes who informed him of the acquisition of some fifty parachutes. No parachuting rôle was then envisaged for any troops in the Middle East and it is a matter of record that the 'chutes were destined for India. Lewes had obtained permission from Robert Laycock for himself and half-a-dozen others to conduct informal 'experiments'.

Stirling had met Lewes frequently and been much impressed by the taciturn Welshman. Superbly fit, the ex-Oxford rowing blue was itching to get on with the war. Inactivity was anathema to him and the parachutes were just a way of relieving the boredom of waits between operations. The idea appealed to Stirling for exactly the same reasons, and he talked Lewes into letting him become part of the experiment. Unknown to either man, this was probably to release Stirling from an ignominious (though innocent) departure from the Middle East due to the findings of the enquiry.

# 5

# THE FRUSTRATING WAR

The War Office

O.S./2698/S . . . (Casualties)
20 September 1941

Madam,

I am directed to inform you that it has been learned at the War Office, with regret, from a report received by mail from the Middle East, that your son, Lieutenant A.D. Stirling, Scots Guards, was admitted to hospital on the 15th June, 1941, suffering from contusion of the back as a result of enemy action.

It is possible that you are already aware of this information but you may, nevertheless, wish to have this official notification.

I am, Madam,
Your obedient Servant,
(R. Williams)

Hon. Mrs M.M. Stirling OBE, JP

Mrs Stirling did indeed know of the 'enemy action'.

Strange, there was no pain, but his legs simply would not move. Again he focused all his concentration on the big toe of his right foot. He lay absolutely still and forced the mental energy along the unfeeling leg, braced his shoulders and willed the toe to move. It did! Sudden elation as he relaxed. He was about to call for the nurse when he heard the voice of the dour, Scots matron.

'Aye, wheel he's nae going tae walk.' Stirling could picture the dumpy, ruddy face. 'He daesna' ken ye understand. It's the shock.'

David opened his eyes and let his face sag into abject misery attempting a smile. 'Hello, Evelyn. Very kind of you to come. Won't you sit down,' as he gestured weakly to the edge of the bed. 'It's OK. I can't feel a thing.' A further weak smile.

Waugh perched himself gingerly on the very rim of the mattress. It was a most uncomfortable position and soon he was sweating as he delivered a monologue of small talk. Every topic imaginable was covered – except Stirling's legs. Eventually Stirling could bear it no more. Each time Waugh peered surreptitiously at the end of the bed David, with superhuman effort, wiggled the now fairly co-operative big toe. It took four attempts before Waugh took in what was happening. He stared – the toe moved, rippling the sheet. He stood up with a huge grin, hauled the pillow from under Stirling's head and whacked it down on his chest. 'You bastard, Stirling, when did it happen?'

'Only minutes before you came,' said Stirling. 'It takes a bit of effort, but it's a start. Look, get Jock Lewes along tonight will you. I've been doing some thinking and I want his opinion.'

There was a commotion of nurses and doctors after Waugh left, pricking, prodding, pinching and squeezing, and it was some time before Stirling could relax and think over the events of the last few days which had resulted in his being in the Scottish Military Hospital in Cairo yet again.

A static line parachute depends for its function upon a line of webbing material attached to both the apex of the parachute and a cable in the aircraft passenger hold. There are requirements for the cable which at that stage of parachute development usually took the form of an overhead, sloping suspension attached to strong points forward and aft in the aircraft. The principle is that as the parachutist exits the aircraft his weight exerts pressure against the static line which unfurls through a series of loops and drags out the folded canopy until it is fully extended. At that point a thin connecting thread breaks and the canopy fills with air.

Aircraft prepared for parachutist use have special equipment; the ageing Valentia noisily rumbling through the turbulence of the hot air rising from the desert did not. The enthusiastic stalwarts preparing to jump had used the seemingly reasonable expedient of tying their static lines to the legs of the passenger seats. Certainly they were nervous, but what worthwhile new venture does not give a man that uplift as the adrenalin hits the bloodstream?

When a parachutist leaves an aircraft he is immediately thrown into the maelstrom of the slipstream of air created by the forward momentum of the machine. There is a proper technique for carrying out this drill, but when Stirling hurled himself into space in the spring of 1941, sandwiched between other initiates, he knew nothing of it. He was expecting to be buffeted in the slipstream for five seconds or so and then to experience a gentle falling sensation as the canopy deployed. Some ten seconds later he knew something was wrong. He wasn't falling, he was flying – or so it seemed. The force of the airflow kept his head jammed forward and he could not look over his shoulder. Suddenly he was indeed falling, and much faster than he had expected. He could now look up and saw to his horror that a large section of his canopy was flapping uselessly. He realised that his parachute had caught on the tailplane, held for a moment then ripped, and now the ground was rising towards him at an alarming rate.

The landing impact from World War II parachutes has been likened to jumping from a fifteen-foot wall. There is a technique to adopt as man closes with ground and goes into a natural roll. Stirling knew as much of this as he knew about the

exit procedure. He took the only apparently sensible course
– hunched up his body and closed his eyes. They were not
to open again until he found himself on the hospital bed. His
spine, which struck a boulder, absorbed the shock of the impact
and for the rest of his life he would have painful reminders of
the damage.

'Non-swanks [a favourite expression], once my toe began to
respond I knew it was up to me to get the rest of my body
functioning again. It took about a week for the toes and then
progress was quite rapid. It was bloody painful but a few days
later I was able to hobble around on crutches. I suppose the
hospital confinement was a good thing; I had little else to
do but think. Remember I'd thought from the early days in
Scotland that thundering around in droves, we lost something.
Even if the raids along the coast had come off I doubt if we
would have achieved anything of real value.'

The gunboat- and destroyer-launched operations along the
Cyrenaican coast had firstly depended upon getting undetected
to a point close enough offshore to beach the two hundred
officers and men sufficiently near to the selected target. A
beachhead had then to be set up and defended, which could
take as much as a third of the force depending upon the tactical
demands of the ground. The remainder of the force had then to
make their way to the target, again undetected, carry out their
task of attack or demolition, then return through the beachhead.

It is probable that any retreat to the beach would be a
fighting withdrawal causing casualties which would have to
be carried where possible. The beachhead then had to
be defended whilst embarkation on to the mother craft was
effected. By this time the craft would probably also be under
attack. All in all an expensive venture in terms of manpower
and support facilities against a pin-prick effect at best. Such
attacks were not only anticipated by the German forces, they
were expected as a classic Commando tactic and invariably the
element of surprise was lost at an early stage.

'There was the Hun sitting in secure defensive positions with all their attention focused on the sea and to the "left" and "right". All offensive probes came from those directions; they always had done, so why concentrate elsewhere? It seemed to me that the chance of taking them by surprise from those aspects was exceedingly slim. Even if surprise was achieved the way out again was slow and irksome; it was just not possible to get men from the beaches to the ships quickly; once on the water they were totally vulnerable. The Commando, used in that manner, were quite simply cumbersome almost to the point of immobility and far too numerous.

'Looking at the maps of the coastal defences a phrase struck me forcibly; the "Great Sand Sea". It was used to describe the vast sub-sealevel area of desert to the east of the Jalo, and south of the Siwa oases. This was one sea which the Hun was not watching. Why not? Because they felt secure – no one had ever approached from that flank because of the enormous difficulties. What were those difficulties and were they as enormous as all that? I realised that something along those lines had been disturbing me since the pre-Layforce training days. I had these thoughts loosely in mind when I met Jock Lewes and joined him in the parachute incident. That was the real trigger.'

Stirling still believed in the Commando rôle but would not accept that there were not better methods of using a highly trained, well-equipped fighting force. Surprise, potency and mobility must be the keywords. Surprise meant an undetected approach right on to the target and off it again if the same men were to be used time and time again. Potency required them to be able to spend as much destructive time on the target as possible, and mobility gave maximum chance of success.

Stirling instinctively thought that he was on to something and set about getting as much information as possible about German positions. Of desert conditions he was quite ignorant, but he swept that minor consideration to one side and concentrated on tactics and strategies. Some days later he had amassed a sheaf of jottings and was hard put to contain himself as he waited for Lewes to join him at the bedside. He had, he thought, convinced himself that something real could be done but he wanted to sound out Lewes whose calm demeanour, great professionalism and experience had impressed him so much.

'Jock, are you happy with the state of things?' asked Stirling.

'No. The Commando are being totally misused. No one's prepared to give us a firm direction. Our training's wasted at the moment.'

'I've had an idea. Let's see what you think. I believe it would be possible, not too difficult in fact, to infiltrate small numbers of men into selected German positions from the desert flank. I think we could then have a pretty dramatic effect on their efficiency and morale by sabotaging aircraft, runways and fuel dumps.' He was interrupted by Lewes.

'Hold on, Dave, small teams. It's not a new concept. Roger's Rangers operated like that as long ago as the American War of Independence. But this is Africa – the distances are huge and the desert's not an easy place to operate.'

'We go in by parachute. Dropped some distance from the objective. We watch the target by day, recce by night and the next night we carry in the explosives to sabotage whatever's there.'

'OK. How do you get out?'

'We walk out. At least for part of the distance. Then we get someone to pick us up. That can all be sorted out. What do you think of the idea?'

'Oh, the idea's got its merits, it's quite interesting. But I don't think you've thought out the real problems. Let's say that there's a way of getting parachuted into the right area, and I agree that is probably the best method – but you'd have to carry a hell of a lot of explosive to be effective. Have you thought about training for walking in the desert? Have you thought about who's going to authorise all this? Who's going to pick you up? I don't think you'll get very far.'

Stirling tried again. 'Jock, you've already said that the Commando training is being wasted. There is no sensible operation being planned for us. In fact it looks as though we're all going to be farmed out to other units as reinforcements to sit in trenches twiddling our thumbs while some bloody Hun pilot gets us in his sights. Come on. There are a lot of damned good soldiers getting cheesed off with inactivity out there. It's worth a try.'

'Tell you what. I'm under orders to go back to Tobruk in two days' time. If you manage to get anywhere with the idea, talk to me again. I don't hold out much hope.'

Stirling was only slightly deflated. Jock had talked sound sense. 'In retrospect, the chat with Jock was a key to success. I knew that I had to have all the answers to the questions he'd raised if I was to get anywhere.'

Over the next few days his energies were divided between enormous physical effort to get his legs and back working properly and hard mental application to the problems in hand. His approach was to take two or three typical targets and apply his theory to each. Eventually he was satisfied that he was on the right lines.

'One factor stood out by a mile. If such a force could be created then it had to come under the direct orders of the highest military authority. It had to be strategically tasked. Under the control of an area commander it would flounder – it would become involved in the tactical battle, and it would not be suited to that task. The theatre commander was the only one to direct the force and therefore he had to be able to understand it. Ipso facto it had to be the highest authority that I approached with the idea.'

The Deputy Chief of General Staff at that time was General Ritchie. Stirling was a lieutenant. He would need great luck to get himself before the DCGS, and if he succeeded he had to have something to leave behind in case he was forced to depart quickly. He had to condense his thoughts into a paper which could be read and understood within minutes. As far as it is possible to reconstruct the original appreciation it went along the following lines:

To: The Commander-in-Chief, Middle East Forces
From: Lieutenant D. Stirling, 8 Commando

Subject: *A Special Service Unit*

a. The enemy is exceedingly vulnerable to attack along the
line of his coastal communications and various transport parks,
aerodromes and other targets strung out along the coast. The
role of 8 Commando which has attempted raids on these targets
is most valuable.

b. The scale on which the Commando raids are planned, i.e.
the number of troops employed on the one hand and the scale
of equipment and facilities on the other, prejudices surprise
beyond all possible compensating advantages in respect of the
defensive and aggressive striking power afforded. Moreover,
the Navy has to provide to lift the force which results in the
risking of naval units valuable out of all proportion even to a
successful raid.

c. There is great advantage to be gained in establishing a
Special Service unit based on the principle of the fullest
exploitation of surprise and of making the minimum demands
on manpower and equipment. The application of this principle
will mean, in effect, the employment of a small sub-unit to cover
a target previously requiring 4 or 5 troops of a Commando,
i.e. about 200 men. If an aerodrome or transport park is the
objective of an operation, then the destruction of 50 aircraft
or units of transport will be more easily accomplished by just
one of my proposed sub-units than a force of 200 men. It
follows that 200 properly selected, trained and equipped men,
organised into these sub-units, will be able to attack up to 10
different objectives at the same time on the same night as
compared to only one objective using the current Commando
technique. So, only 25% success in the former is equivalent
to many times the maximum result in the latter.

d. The corollary of this is that a unit operating on these
principles will have to be so trained as to be capable of arriving
on the scene of operation by every practicable method, by land,
sea or air; and furthermore the facilities for the lift must not be
of a type valuable in tactical scale operations. If in any particular
operation a sub-unit is to be parachuted it will have to be from
an aircraft conveniently available without any modifications; if

by sea then the sub-unit will be transported either by submarine or caiques, and trained in the use of folboats; if by land, the unit will be trained either to infiltrate on foot or be carried within 10 or 15 miles of the target by another experienced unit.

e. The unit must be responsible for its own training and operational planning and therefore the Commander of the Unit must operate directly under the order of the Commander-in-Chief*. It would be fatal for the proposed unit to be put under any existing branch or formation for administration. The head of any such branch or formation would have less experience than me or my successor in the strategic medium in which it is proposed to operate.

f. It is no secret that an offensive is being planned for November 1941. Attached is my plan for the use of the unit in that offensive.

*Plan for the November Offensive*

1. *Target*: Enemy fighter and bomber landing grounds at TMIMI and GAZALA.

2. *Method*: In the night of D minus 2, 5 sections to be parachuted on to drop zones some 12 miles south of the objectives; this will preserve surprise. Each section is of 12 men (i.e. 3 sub-sections of 4). As cover a heavy raid is required on GAZALA and TMIMI using as many flares as possible to aid navigation to the drop zones.

3. After re-assembly on the drop zones each section will spend the balance of night D minus 2 in getting to pre-arranged lying-up points from which they will observe the targets the next day. The following night (D minus 1) each party will carry out its raid so as to arrive on the target at the same time.

4. Each party will carry a total of about 60 incendiary-cum-explosive bombs equipped with 2-hour, 1/2-hour, and 10-minute time pencils in addition to a 12-second fuse. The time pencils

---

* Stirling was aware even then of the octopus tendencies of G(R), the Middle East equivalent of the Special Operations Executive, and was determined that the Special Service Unit should not come under control of the Director of Combined Operations.

will be used on a time de-escalating basis to ensure almost
simultaneous detonation.

5. After the raid each party will retire independently into the
desert to a prearranged meeting place south of the TRIG EL ABD to
rendezvous with a patrol of the Long Range Desert Group*.


Stirling was satisfied with his memorandum. He also admitted that at that time he knew precious little about the Long
Range Desert Group (LRDG).

'We'd all heard that there was this unit operating deep in
the desert in an intelligence capacity. It was just an inspired
guess that made me mention that they could pick us up. Highly
pomposo.

'I suppose it was probably one of the worst pieces of military
writing ever submitted to a headquarters. I heavily overscored
sections where I wanted maximum impact; this I'm told is never
done. I went over it time and again until I reckoned it could
be read and understood in four minutes. Finally, I wrote it in
pencil – a cardinal sin when addressing a memo to a senior
staff officer. In part there was a sort of subliminal psychology
to the memo. I thought the scruffy appearance may have an
effect in itself – I may be letting time fool me into thinking
that, of course.

'Of course, the paper showed a bit of naïveté; my knowledge
of available explosives was limited to what I had gleaned from
Jock, who had a passion for such things, and my desert walking
experience was nil. These things I thought I could defend.
Well, I'd got it on to paper and after my chat with Jock I
knew I had some form of answer to any question that may
be thrown at me.

---

* This rendezvous was about 50 miles south of the coastline, and the desert
in that area was almost featureless, but there was a hill on which the Long
Range Desert Group (LRDG) were to be asked to leave a red hurricane
lamp at night and keep a watch by day for the returning units. Stirling
admits that the figure of 50 miles 'seemed a sensible distance'. He had paid
no real attention to the reality of having to cover 50 miles in one night.

'I was getting about quite well by then but if I tried to walk more than about fifty yards those damned legs would let me down. Every day brought a bit more progress but I had the bit between my teeth and I was impatient. I hadn't resolved the main problem though. I couldn't think of a certain route to the C-in-C. If I submitted the memo through the "normal channels" it would get no further than the first pomposo staff officer. I would either be summoned to re-write and thus lose effect or it would most probably be tossed into a wastepaper basket. I decided that the best thing would be to have a look at the MEHQ building.'

Stirling took a taxi to the main gates of Middle East Headquarters and spent a few minutes before getting out looking at the procedure for entry. It seemed fairly rigid with both sentries checking the passes of all visitors, except for one or two red-tabbed staff officers, obviously well-known to the guards. He decided to bluff his way through.

Adopting his most benign and innocent expression he moved as confidently as the clumsy crutches allowed, smiled vaguely at the guard nearest to him and carried on walking.

'Sir. Your pass, please.' The sentry's manner was abrupt. Lieutenants did not rate too highly in his books.

'Why, yes, sorry.' Stirling made to pat his pockets, looking perplexed and mildly embarrassed. 'Oh dear, I seem to have left it at the hospital. It will be all right, I have an urgent appointment with, you know, I'm sure it's OK. Can you possibly . . .?' The Stirling charm impressed the sentry even less than the lowly rank. He was firmly turned away. 'No pass, no entry, sir, you'll have to go back to the hospital for it.' No apology; he knew to a fine degree what he could get away with. Just the hint of an impertinent push between the shoulders as he turned Stirling round to face the direction whence he had come.

Stirling had already noticed the gap in the perimeter where the end post of the barbed-wire fence did not quite reach the corner of the guardhouse. He took up post behind the large tree some five yards from the gates and waited. Soon his chance came. A couple of staff cars stopped at the gate and both sentries were soon busily examining the passes of the visiting delegation. Dropping his crutches, Stirling slipped through the gap and eased his way behind the wooden hut. He was in!

Tucking himself behind the party of visitors he gritted his teeth against the pain and walked as normally as possible. Hands clasped behind his back, head down and occasionally looking towards the officer on his right he gave every appearance of being engaged in deep conversation with the puzzled recipient of his mumbled comments. All went well until the party reached the bottom of the steps leading up to the main building. They went straight past. They had travelled ten yards or so before Stirling realised that they were bound for some other part of the compound.

He turned abruptly and made to climb the steps. He was forced to move slowly and at a half crouch. The pain of lifting his feet the extra inches to ascend was agonising. He couldn't stop now. The sentry gazed out through the double gates and noticed one of the abandoned crutches on the roadside. He looked around in surprise and caught sight of Stirling's painful progress.

'Hey, you, stop. Stop that bloody man!' With a desperate effort Stirling made it to the top of the stairs and turned into the nearest corridor, aware of the shouts outside getting louder as the guard ran to the building. He stumbled around in the polished maze until a door marker caught his eye: 'Adjutant-General'. That sounded sufficiently senior. He raised his fist to knock, heard the sentry shout again, changed his mind and burst straight into the office. Panting heavily with the effort, he leaned back against the door and closed his eyes for a second. A voice brought him back to reality. 'Who in God's name are you? Where are your manners? Have you never heard of knocking? Well, what do you want?'

There was something vaguely familiar about the short,

plump, angry major. Sharply creased and brightly buttoned, he looked the picture of injured efficiency. God, was there really a war on, Stirling wondered, conscious of his own creased battledress. For a fleeting moment he wished that he had taken a little time to spruce up before he left the hospital. A salute was called for. The manoeuvre was difficult – it was not easy to stand erect.

'What's the matter with you, man?' Ignoring the question, Stirling said, 'Sir, I do apologise for bursting in. I have to speak with you urgently.' The apology had no visible effect on the purple-faced major. 'Explain' was the curt injunction.

'I'm Lieutenant David Stirling, Scots Guards and currently attached to 8 Commando. I came out with Layforce and you will know that the force is being disbanded. I have some ideas as to how I can harass the German coastal defences and supply depots which will require only a few specially selected officers and men. I need to prepare this unit for parachuting and explosives work before the next major offensive. I believe that we can severely disable the German air force on the ground. I have my notes and a plan here. Let me explain.' He began to take the memorandum from his pocket.

'Stirling? Ah, of course, Stirling! Don't you recognise me? No, because the last time we set eyes on each other, yours were closed for most of the time. (It was indeed his old instructor from the Pirbright days!) You were a fool then and you're a fool now. Left the Brigade for the Commando, eh? I suppose you think you've found a way out of going back to your regiment. Whatever lunatic idea you have, Stirling, forget it. I'll do everything in my considerable power to make sure that you do go back and as soon as possible. Furthermore, you'll go back with specific recommendations for your future and they will not include getting even the smallest command. Good day to you. Now, get out.'

The telephone began its throaty croak as Stirling saluted. He heard Smith's, 'Who crashed through the gate? Send the guard up here immediately.'

Stirling followed his hunch as he left the office. There was no point in retracing his steps. He was temporarily off the hook but it could not last for long. He turned away from the two men hurrying up the corridor and, walking in as dignified a fashion as his throbbing legs would allow, he scrutinised the signs on the doors as he progressed. DCGS – it would have to do; the sentry and Smith would be out of the other office in seconds. He knocked, but entered without waiting for the invitation. Facing him was the oft-photographed face of General Ritchie, Deputy Chief of General Staff. Without giving Ritchie time to register anger, Stirling opened: 'Sir, I am Lieutenant Stirling, Scots Guards. I apologise for bursting into your office without appointment but there was no time to arrange it. I have a matter to bring to your attention which I believe to be most urgent.'

Ritchie looked at the young man. Properly dressed, if a little unkempt, he was adopting a most unusual posture. His legs were locked tightly together, he stooped from the waist and his white, earnest face was a mask of pain. The voice had been normal, even gentle, with no hint of the apparent physical agony. Stirling's eyes held his own unflinchingly. Ritchie, as he confessed later, was intrigued. He took the proffered notes and motioned Stirling to a seat which Stirling took gratefully.

'My clearest memory is of thinking how the hell I was going to manage to stand again,' Stirling recalled. 'Ritchie read the notes twice, put them down and looked at me, then read them again. I was mentally going over the answers to the questions I knew must be forthcoming, but to my surprise he didn't ask a single one.

'"There may be some merit in this. We have been looking at ways of tying up German manpower. I will discuss this with General Auchinleck. You will hear from me soon. Just in case the Commander-in-Chief agrees to this, you ought to meet Major Smith, my AG branch officer."

'I can't imagine Ritchie having eavesdropped either deliberately or accidentally on my conversation with Smith but he expressed no surprise at Smith's obvious discomfiture when he came into the office and saw me in the armchair. Smith took it as a further sign of my bad manners when I didn't stand for the introductions but the truth is that I couldn't. I think I said something like, "Yes, we've met before; in fact just a short time ago we were talking about the good old days." The General told Smith that I had produced something of interest which might require his action at very short notice and that he should be prepared to assist in any way he could. Fortunately then, Ritchie left the office before I could stand. Smith's parting shot was a portent of things to come: "Stirling, I don't like you and I don't like this business. I will help because I have to help. You will get no favours from me or my branch." He left.'

Stirling was escorted back to the main gate by a sentry who was now in a much more pleasant frame of mind. 'Nice move, sir. Don't get that amount of exercise very often. Don't see the rules bent that often around here either.'

There is no doubt that both Ritchie and Auchinleck made enquiries about Stirling over the next few days. Whether Smith was ever asked for his opinion is not known but it seems probable that the possibility of court martial as a result of the inquiry in progress into Stirling's suspected self-inflicted eye injury would have transpired. It is, of course, quite possible that the episode with the parachute took away any suspicions about his moral fibre. More probably Auchinleck, as a Scot, would have knowledge of Stirling's pedigree and discounted any such nonsense.

Auchinleck had only recently taken over from Wavell as Commander-in-Chief and was already under pressure from Winston Churchill to make his presence felt by striking at Rommel. Husbanding and resting his resources, the Auk was immediately attracted to an idea which was economical in man-power and equipment, therefore of little risk to the material aspects of his command. Three days after his unconventional presentation at MEHQ, Stirling was summoned to return.

At a meeting with Generals Auchinleck, Ritchie and Smith

(Chief of General Staff) the whole concept was questioned. Stirling had prepared himself well, answered honestly and did not make light of the many difficulties which would be encountered in the formative days. Time was short; it was mid-July 1941 and the offensive was still planned for November despite Churchill's urgings for prior action. At the end of the meeting Stirling was promoted to captain and given authority to recruit up to six officers and sixty other ranks of which a high proportion could be senior non-commissioned officers. His prime recruiting pool was to be the remnants of Layforce and he was instructed that he could only approach other experienced, forward formations if he had a severe problem.

The naming of Stirling's 'unit' was almost haphazard. At that time Brigadier Dudley Clarke was responsible for deception operations throughout the Middle East. One of his creations, designed to unsettle the Afrika Korps, was the First Special Air Service Brigade, which did not exist. Dummy parachutists were dropped close to the prisoner-of-war compounds and mock gliders parked in the desert in order that the enemy's photographic reconnaissance aircraft and intelligence effort would become convinced of the build-up of a combined glider and airborne brigade.

Stirling accepted Clarke's exhortations to use the name SAS with good humour – he did not really care what it was called at that stage! Thus the unit became 'L' Detachment, SAS Brigade, Stirling wryly hinting that 'L' meant 'Learner'. It is of passing interest that Clarke helped the organisation a great deal in the early days, not least by using his communications system to get the word out that recruits were needed. In return, and some time later, the SAS was able to assist Clarke by leaving booby traps and deception 'packages' scattered around the desert where the Italians or Germans would be sure to find them.

Stirling's first action, after sending a message to remind Jock Lewes (then in Tobruk) of their earlier conversation was to list all the names he could remember from Layforce and the Scots

Guards who he felt might be interested. The SAS was now at least an embryo, and Stirling was dedicated to overseeing birth and weaning the infant – growth would come later. How true was his initial assessment of the early trouble spots?

'Most branches of Middle East HQ were helpful at the top level but astonishingly tiresome at the middle and lower levels. Amongst them all the AG Branch was, I knew, going to be unfailingly obstructive and unco-operative. Not helped, of course, by that little shit Smith. I used to refer to them as "that freemasonry of mediocrity" or, more rudely, but even more accurately, as "layer upon layer of fossilised shit". I had to get a small nucleus together fairly quickly. Until I got stronger I urgently needed one or two "leg-men".'

A letter to his mother shows that Stirling was far from certain of success. He had found enthusiastic support from Laycock, and had decided to make his brother's flat the focal point for his activities.

July 1941

My dear Mum,

Bob Laycock will post this when he arrives in England. He leaves tomorrow and will probably get to London in 3 to 4 days.

I wish I could crawl into the envelope myself – I would not mind the discomfort. Please address your future letters to Peter's flat as the Commandos are no more. I am not sure what I shall do now but I am attempting and may succeed in establishing a permanent parachute unit. It would be on a small scale but would be more amusing than any other form of soldiering.

I have got better quicker than expected from my back injury but it has left me with very severe headaches, and apparently very low blood pressure. The doctors seem to think that they are due to spinal shock and it need not mean that I will have them (the headaches) permanently.

I am very sorry for having had to wire for the £100. It has been made necessary by the absurd number of extra expenses I have had as a result of my various health setbacks:

a) 3 weeks in a nursing home with dysentry, with the doctor's bill thrown in followed by 3 weeks sick leave in Cairo.

b) The eye accident followed by 2 $1/2$ weeks leave in Alexandria. The buying of glasses, etc.

c) The back injury followed by 4 weeks leave in Cairo and Palestine with journey expenses, etc.

In addition to this I have had to buy a complete set of tropical clothes . . .

I wish I had known earlier that Bob Laycock was leaving tomorrow. I have got to give him this letter tonight and it is very late and I am feeling so dopey that I can't remember all the things that I want to say.

I have never in my life so appreciated letters as I do out here. I think that there must be a lot from you still in the post because the delivery of Commando letters has been fantastically bad.

Your loving,
David


Stirling later recalled: 'I'm afraid I really was the worst ever letter writer. I always had an excuse for a short letter rather than the long ones which my mother deserved. I blackmailed her in the most awful fashion to make sure that her letters kept coming – she wrote very regularly, you know. I don't know if she ever did her sums about the number of weeks I said I had been on sick leave but it simply isn't possible that I had as much as I said. I'm sure the money just went, as money did in those days.'

# 6

# THE BEGINNINGS

Never run; once you start running you stop thinking,
now remember that!

                    Jock Lewes, L Detachment

'Of all the names on my list I considered Jock Lewes to
be critical. He was sceptical enough to question everything
thoroughly and what's more put together a tough but pertinent
training programme. He was one of the best leaders I'd met
at that stage in the war, and he had established himself as a
brilliant exponent of the night-time raid behind enemy lines
in the Tobruk area. We got on well enough and if I could
capture his full interest I knew I'd have a real nugget serving
in L Detachment at first base. Jock had also seen some of
the potential recruits under fire and would be a great help in
picking the right men first time round.

'In retrospect it seems slightly pomposo that I should be
looking for people who had been under fire. My own experience was very slight; attacks on the boats and some artillery
fire and the like on our defences. At the back of my mind,
I was frightened but, non-swanks, I was sure that when the
time came I'd be able to control it. I suppose I just kept such
thoughts tucked away and concentrated on other matters. I

was put to the test quite some time before we saw action in our own right.'

Lewes did not respond to the messages and Stirling had to make three trips to Tobruk to persuade him to join L Detachment. Stirling always felt that it was he who was being tested for persistence and faith rather than the idea.

'I think Jock wanted to be sure that if we got the thing working, I was going to stay with it and also tackle the enormous problems at MEHQ which he possibly foresaw more clearly than me. It's true that he still wasn't in full agreement with the small unit concept but I reckon he thought that he would talk me out of the bits he didn't like. He just didn't want to get involved if it was going to be a short-term flight of fancy. Jock was a serious sort of chap, he could be very short on humour and I suppose I'd come across to him in the past as a bit of a good time Charlie. You wouldn't, for instance, find Jock catching a quick drink in Cairo or taking a flutter at the racecourse.'

Lewes eventually capitulated and brought pure gold dust with him in the form of the 'Tobruk Four'; Sergeants Pat Riley and Jim Almonds and Privates Lilley and Blakeney. Stirling's old platoon sergeant, Ernie Bond, was quick to follow. Whilst Lewes was given the immediate and urgent task of getting to grips with suitable training programmes and techniques, Stirling continued to recruit. He needed a core of officers quickly; not because he felt that they were particularly necessary from a leadership point of view, but he knew that he would have to satisfy MEHQ that his unit was to be 'properly commanded'.

At a meeting in a tent in Geneifa, Stirling supplemented the hard core of L Detachment, calling for volunteers to listen to him. He was vague about what L Detachment was going to do but his manner was infectious. There was a magnetism about this tall, slightly stooped officer still walking with a noticeable limp. His confidence showed despite his gentle delivery and occasionally misplaced word. Volunteers came forward for interview at a surprisingly rapid rate considering that he had told them very little except that they would have the chance to take a 'real crack at the Hun'.

Amongst those who came forward, later to become legends in the annals of the SAS, were Reg Seekings, 'Benny' Bennett, Johnny Cooper, Bob Tait, Dave Kershaw, Jimmy Brough, 'Whacker' Evans and 'Tubby' Trenfield. Many recruits were already comrades-in-arms. This nucleus was taken or made their own way to the allocated base camp at Kabrit. Here awaited their first surprise. The 'freemasonry of mediocrity' was excelling itself with the quality of support.

Kabrit, a village in the Canal Zone, lay about a hundred miles east of Cairo and about the same distance to the south of Port Said on the edge of the Great Bitter Lake. Flat, fly-ridden and exposed to the full power of the desert sun it was not an exciting place. The total accommodation and transport facilities took up very little space; one decrepit three-ton lorry and three dilapidated tents! Stirling's bivouac was recognisable as the command tent; it housed a battered card table and a teetering stool.

'It boded well for L Detachment that there was no moaning about the camp, or rather lack of camp. I told them that we should have to get used to this sort of co-operation from the Adjutant-General branch. I think I did mention my original escapade, to put it into perspective. I told them of the rather splendid New Zealand camp not too many miles away, which contained many things that would add to the comfort of Kabrit. Since the Kiwis had none of our supply problems, I felt no remorse at hinting that the men may care to make the construction of base camp their first operation. I left them to it.'

The dozen or so men who took part in the first raid in the Western Desert decided on a course of sheer bluff. Stirling had told them that the New Zealanders were out on exercise that night so they struck immediately. L Detachment's poverty-stricken status became quite clear when the large compound was reached; this housed British, Australian and Indian troops, as well as the Kiwis, in comparative luxury. Any finer feelings left the buccaneers very quickly as they stood off in their solitary, wheezing three-tonner.

Fortunately the sentries of that night were from the Indian contingent. The truck was driven straight through the main gate, the driver shouting, 'New Zealand Division, mate,'in what he hoped would pass as a Kiwi accent to the sepoy. The reply was a solemn salute. An uninterrupted drive through the British and Indian lines brought them into the New Zealanders' quarters. Lights were doused and the party disembarked and stood quietly to let their eyes adjust to the darkness. Quickly, and using torches only inside the tents, the small groups scurried around the lines and made a quick inventory. A fast meeting to decide the priorities and they were off to take their unsecured loans.

For five or six hours they laboured taking not only that which was considered necessary but also items which might be handy or downright pleasing. L Detachment's SNCOs were determined to have a Mess as a matter of rightful priority! It took four trips back to Kabrit before the raiding party was satisfied with its haul. Though there were plenty of curious onlookers at intermittent times during the long night there was only one moment of 'danger'. A military policeman approached. 'Has anybody got a light?' Friendly and mildly curious. 'What are you up to? It's a bit late to move house isn't it?'

'Too true and we don't get paid for the bloody overtime either.' The MP was kept talking with the expected complaints of a British soldier. At last, the truck full, the team said their goodnights to the unsuspecting policeman and left for Kabrit.

It appears that the New Zealanders never suspected that they had contributed so generously to one of the smartest camps in the area. No doubt the losses were put down to the local Arabs. In any event not only did L Detachment now have sixteen tents in excellent condition as sleeping quarters, they had a large, communal recreation tent equipped with bar, piano and an initial supply of drinks; they had lamps, tables, wicker chairs, cooking utensils along with all the necessary washbasins, mirrors and the like – a camp which was not only functional, but had that little touch of home.

Stirling was quietly pleased but he lost little time in ridding his small force of any feelings of euphoria, laying down the ground rules straight away: 'Well done. We now have a respectable camp. I don't ever want to see it at a lesser standard than it is now. Our standards of dress and discipline will be every bit as high as the Brigade of Guards. I want a high-grade performance in everything we do. We are under the eyes of MEHQ and they don't like us. We will give them no excuse to criticise us while we are in Kabrit. On operations we will be far less formal but that's another matter.

'There will be no bragging or swanking in the Cairo or Alexandria bars and that goes for scrapping too. Any energy you have for fighting will be directed at the enemy. Make no mistake, anyone who doesn't fit in will leave – there will be no second chances. Captain Lewes will be in sole charge of training and that includes my own. It's going to be tough because we have to be fit for the job we're going to do. If anyone has sensible and constructive comments to make on training, or any other operational subject, then make it. We are all here to learn.'

Soon after that short talk, Stirling left to go to Cairo. He had recruited more officers since Lewes had agreed to join; Bonnington, Thomas, Fraser and McGonigal. McGonigal had mentioned a fifth officer, Blair 'Paddy' Mayne, a close friend of his, who was languishing in prison awaiting his court martial for striking his commanding officer. Mayne was an Ulsterman, and an international rugby player of great repute. He had struck his CO under some provocation although, McGonigal explained, it was not an unusual thing for Paddy to hit out.

Provocation or not it seemed that Mayne's career as an

officer was over even though his courage was already proven (he was mentioned in despatches for his prowess during the Litani River action). It did not help that his commanding officer was Geoffrey Keyes, a lieutenant colonel at the age of twenty-four, holder of the Croix de Guerre and awarded the Military Cross for his valour at Litani River. Sometime prior to the incident which called for the court martial, Mayne had run Keyes out of their officers' mess at the point of his bayonet. Stirling was sufficiently impressed by what McGonigal had to say to want to meet the man.

'He was suspicious of me from the start. We were the same age except for a few months but here was a man who had already seen a fair share of battle and come out of it well. I probably appeared to him as a young whipper-snapper who could well have been out just to impress the MEHQ brass. We were the same height; he was somewhat broader but at least I could look him in the eye. He was very quiet and he spoke in that gentle Ulster brogue which could charm the faeries.

'After my introduction, at which point he told me quietly that his name was Blair and not Paddy, I explained what I had in mind for L Detachment and I saw the same doubts that I'd seen in Jock Lewes though Mayne didn't make any attempt to hide it. He questioned me rapid-fire style, but always in that gentle, slightly mocking voice. It wasn't in the least disconcerting for I had an immediate confidence in this giant of a man and by then I was well used to the sort of thing he was asking me.'

'I can't see any prospects of real fighting in this scheme of yours.' There was undisguised scepticism on his face.

'There isn't any. Except against the enemy.' It was the right reply because Mayne began to laugh.

'All right. If you can get me out of here I'll come along.' He extended his huge hand.

'There's one more thing,' Stirling said, ignoring the hand. 'This is one commanding officer you never hit and I want your promise on that.' He reached out for the hand.

'You have it.' A legendary partnership was sealed at that moment.

Ritchie took a great personal interest in the development of L Detachment, which probably accounts for Stirling being able to secure Mayne's release and the dropping of all charges. Keyes, despite being floored by Mayne, held him in high regard as a leader and no doubt would not have argued, since Mayne appeared to be going off where his talents would be put to the best use; in any event it was unlikely that the Scottish Commando would see him again. As Stirling put it, 'MEHQ's AG Branch did make the occasional wise decision even if they had to be pressed from both ends. There's no doubt, of course, that Ritchie's pressure was felt much more than mine.'

Stirling and Lewes were conscious that they had assembled a first-rate crew which would lose interest if training didn't get under way quickly. The training would have to be challenging, pertinent to the rôles and graduated in difficulty so that all of them could mark their progress. There was to be absolutely no distinction in rank – all would train equally hard to the same purpose and be subjected to the same exacting standards. The philosophies of the SAS were beginning to emerge. Night was to be their friend, therefore all skills with radios, weapons, explosives, first aid and navigation had to be practised in darkness.

They devised basic principles of training. The use of small patrols, as they were now calling their sub-units, automatically meant that they would have to react at greater individual speed than had been necessary in the Commando. There would be an even greater dependency on each other and so the system had to build up mutual trust. They would have to carry all their explosives on their backs and the weight could be significant. A training programme which concentrated on achieving maximum physical stamina, confidence and speed of reflex seemed to fit the bill. It had to be sufficiently demanding to give the recruits a real sense of achievement and any sub-standard material had to be ruthlessly weeded out. Only in that way would the true team spirit emerge.

It was not envisaged that any great distances would be covered on foot in the heat of the day, but it *might* happen, therefore physical toughness and endurance would be built up by day and night. Parachuting was high on the list of skills to be mastered and here L Detachment ran into a snag. The only parachute school then extant was Ringway in England. Stirling sent many signals to the school asking for guidance; he received only cursory answers and decided that they would have to devise their own methods of training.

Lewes was charged with setting the routines for parachute training and as usual made himself the guinea-pig. He decided that the best method of reproducing the lateral and vertical movement experienced by the landing parachutist would be to jump from the back of a moving vehicle. He tried it. It hurt. He experimented with various methods of throwing his body into a natural roll as his feet impacted with the ground. It worked if the timing was right and one went with the direction of the truck – that must be representative of wind movement. His trial was simple. Truck moves forward at 15 mph; jump off into a forward roll; land painfully badly; leave it out. Jump off into a backward roll; land unhurt and relatively smoothly; that's OK; let's all do it.

That's working all right. Let's increase the speed. Increase the speed they did – by degrees up to 30 mph. It was foolhardy, as Stirling and Lewes should have realised as more and more men succumbed to fractures and severe sprains. Ringway must take its share of the blame; jumping from trucks moving at 30 mph certainly never featured in their training syllabus. The chances are that if the 'Q' support from MEHQ had been better, Lewes's plan to use wooden rolling platforms to jump off would have saved many a casualty. Eventually the required materials were produced and parachute training became, if not correct, certainly more comfortable.

Lewes tackled the matter of parachutists having to locate

their supply containers and then regroup on the ground possibly during the blackest of nights in his own inimitable style. The answer surely was to devise a system whereby they all hit the ground together. Say the aircraft began to lose height fairly quickly, coincidental with the despatch of the first man; by the time the last man had dropped he would, if the calculations were correct, be at the same height as the first man. It was a once only experiment. Pat Riley, the last man to depart, reported that his parachute deployed only seconds before he hit the ground in a very positive manner. The chances of pilot miscalculation at night were high and out of all proportion to the possible benefits of the technique.

The training programme was critical. Stirling and Lewes were creating a corps d'élite; the principles of operation were known but the details were not. Many of the problems they must encounter could only be conjectured. There was little support from their main headquarters. It seemed that the one factor which was under their control was the quality of the volunteers. If they could get the training right then pride and competence would result in total dedication. The end product had to be men with great confidence in their own abilities, but not to the point of behaving recklessly; above all they must have a high degree of self-discipline. With the right team all the other problems would not matter.

Training, therefore, had to take the form of a course which was passed or failed. Those who failed must go immediately. The standards must never waver lest those who passed began to lose faith in the system. Stirling made one exception – it was possible that the unit might require technical skills not possessed by any of the men who passed the course; he was thinking initially of explosives experience and parachuting training. In this case they may have to accept having personnel 'attached' to L Detachment, whose function would be to pass on those skills to the operational teams – they themselves would never be allowed into the field.

Standards of navigation, weapon handling, enemy vehicle

and aircraft recognition, etc. are easily computed but how do you set the physical standards for a new course? The taciturn, self-contained Lewes was given this task and his approach was unorthodox but simple. He again set himself up as the guinea-pig. Often working long after the others had finished their day's training he would set out on desert marches by day and night. He would load himself with various weights and make rigid allowances of water; he would then simply walk until he arrived at a point where he calculated the return journey would be completed as he reached the limits of his endurance.

When he had achieved this he then repeated it with a smaller water allowance or a heavier burden. Through this process he arrived at a series of desert marches which he knew were possible within certain times and carrying particular loads. To these marches were added precise navigation tests and the first selection course was born. No wonder Stirling was to describe Lewes as one of his true co-founders of the SAS. It does not take great imagination to realise the risk Lewes was taking in experimenting with the unknown.

The effects of denying the body water are well known now but Lewes's experiments could have had very destructive effects on him. On top of this he never left details of his routes behind. Had he suffered collapse (and so often he nearly did) he could have died in the desert only miles from his base. His psychology was that if he knew that rescue was possible, he may have adopted the wrong mental approach and overdone himself! Witnesses who underwent the 'Lewes marches' testify that he did this anyway.

The stories of Lewes's marching discipline are legion. Well remembered by 'the originals' is the occasion when he called a parade under the midday sun and ordered the unit to assemble full operational kit for a training march to assess whether the water intake reducing exercises were progressing satisfactorily. He stressed that a good result was required – the underlying threat being that if the exercise did not achieve its aims it would be repeated.

Off on a compass bearing into the featureless desert they marched, and marched, making a great loop through the sand dunes before returning, on the point of exhaustion, to Kabrit Camp. The water bottles were checked and Lewes almost expressed satisfaction when it was discovered that none was empty. As they were dismissed he overheard a disgruntled comment that 'No one's checked his friggin' water bottle.' Lewes called the unfortunate forward:

'Are you thirsty, man? Here, you can finish what's left of this.' He passed over his own canteen. After about twenty miles of desert marching in the heat of the day, Lewes's water ration remained completely untouched!

During one of these marches, the secret of Lewes's navigational accuracy became known. It was noticed that he had the habit of shifting his hands between pockets at intervals during a march. When asked about it he explained, 'I carry a pocketful of stones in one pocket. I count my paces and after each hundred steps I transfer a stone to the other pocket. Assuming that an average pace is thirty inches, each stone represents approximately eighty-three yards. It's not absolutely accurate of course but it's a damned good guideline.'

There is no doubt that Lewes's dedication and professionalism set the psychology correctly not only for L Detachment selection and training but also for the SAS today, but it is interesting to note that he was still not in complete agreement with the small patrol concept; he still argued that the minimum number in any operational party should be ten and not the four which Stirling envisaged.

Despite this disagreement, Lewes readily set about formulating individual skills courses. Each patrol was to have a man trained in first aid; a driver/mechanic; a navigator, and a fourth who made explosives his speciality. Not only was this sound common sense in that no man could be expected to become an instant jack-of-all-trades, it created a dependency which would help prevent the emergence of a leader, along with possible acrimony. Indeed, the four-man patrol, which invites men to share in pairs, reduces this proclivity anyway.

It is worth considering the attitudes of L Detachment to their officers in those very early days at Kabrit. Many had come from the Commando and had an understandably jaundiced view of some of their officers. They had all volunteered to join Stirling, but it was the cause rather than the man at that stage. They had no reason to suspect that he was anything other than one of the many wealthy, smooth-talking, playboy-cum-gambling young blades who appeared to have jumped on the bandwagon when the Commando was formed. Of course there were exceptions, like Ernie Bond and Jimmy Brough, who knew him from the Scots Guards or Commandos.

This view of Commando officers was probably unfair; most acquitted themselves well when they finally got into action. Nonetheless, Stirling did little to change this pervasive opinion. Vague; often sitting for hours at the small table in his tent surrounded by maps and notes; often absent from training for days at MEHQ and uncommunicative with everyone, with the possible exception of Lewes. They all agreed on his capacity for work but felt that perhaps he was working on the wrong things.

Mayne, on the other hand, had truly entered into the spirit of the enterprise and was throwing himself wholeheartedly into training alongside the rest (and apparently suffering far less). Fraser, McGonigal, Thomas and Bonnington had all become part of the team. Lewes, though not as close as the others, was earning undoubted respect through his training demands, and in any event he had been 'to battle' with many of the recruits. Stirling, by virtue of the workload at MEHQ and his own somewhat distant demeanour, was growing apart from the men he commanded.

'I was aware that the November offensive would be upon us very soon. I was totally confident in Jock and Paddy and the others and it seemed to me that I just had to get the formalised establishment right at MEHQ. All those shits were against me; they sparked only when Ritchie took a personal hand and I couldn't keep bothering him. I also thought it would be unfair to burden the others with the problems. I didn't want to give anyone the slightest reason to doubt that what they were working for so hard was anything other than a reality.

'I did feel at one stage that Paddy was emerging as the natural leader and that I would have to find more time to spend in Kabrit. This is not a criticism of Paddy. He was naturally exuberant when he was being tested physically and it was not unexpected that his natural talents as a leader should emerge so early on.'

Any apprehension the Detachment may have felt about their leader was understandable in the light of comments such as, 'I remember Stirling all right, before the SAS that is; always at the racecourse in Cairo, liked a bet he did. Mind you, he was in good company, Lord Jellicoe, Randolph Churchill and the others. They were all part of the Silver Circle Club as we called it.' This comment was not made by a member of the original Detachment though the term Silver Circle stuck and was used to describe Stirling's occasional antics in a warm-hearted manner.

None of the men were disparaging about Stirling; merely ill-at-ease, if anything, and curious as to how he would turn out. Stirling's first opportunity to show what he was made of came before the first operation was mounted. It had taken some time to get MEHQ to make available a Bombay aircraft on a daily basis for parachute training. Ringway had still not produced any meaningful advice, so a certain amount of quite unnecessary guesswork was involved.

The Bombay had been used for parachuting, so at least it had the correct anchor line fitted to which the ends of the static lines could be fitted with a snap-link. On the first two jumps Stirling took his place in one of the sticks; both jumps were successful and, as is usual at that stage of parachute training, the jumpers were somewhat euphoric. Stirling decided to stay on the ground for the next jump to study movement in the air and landing patterns. He was mindful that at night a system of collecting on the ground would be required and this he wanted to consider in detail.

Disaster struck. The first two parachutists plunged straight to the ground with canopies still in their packs. The despatching sergeant managed to stop the third man exiting; the doors were closed and the aircraft landed. Stirling was shaken considerably; not showing his concern he greeted the subdued men with the instruction: 'The trials are cancelled for today. Once we have found out what went wrong we will pick up where we left off. Go away and relax and be ready to start again tomorrow morning.'

The fault was easily diagnosed. The snap-link which attached the static line to the cable had twisted under pressure as the parachutists had hit the slipstream. The pressure exerted against the twisted linkage allowed the static line ring to slip free. It was easy to find other clips which did not present this hazard but it was an exceedingly angry Stirling who found out, some time later, that the school at Ringway had experienced a similar tragedy some weeks previously. The loss of two lives could have been averted. The next morning parachuting was resumed and Stirling was the first to leave the aircraft. He later admitted that he hated parachuting anyway, but that that exit was the hardest he ever made.

Lewes, mastermind of desert marches, recognised better than anyone the appalling weight in explosives patrols would be asked to carry. The task was to destroy aircraft, trucks, ammunition and fuel dumps on the ground. The explosives were required not only to detonate and smash the targets, but to set them alight instantly. Technology had not then been tested with that particular problem and could offer only one option. An explosive device, fused in its own right, and an incendiary device which would have a separate fuse timed to ignite after the 'bomb'. The principle was that the incendiary would then light up the fuel released by the explosive. Such a device required about ten minutes to set up and would weigh not less than five pounds.

As a first measure Lewes and Stirling asked for the assistance of an expert. He was of little use. No doubt he had been briefed by MEHQ that he was wasting his time; he was totally unsympathetic and insisted that the problem had already defeated the scientists. A mixture of the usual constituents; gelignite, thermite, ammonal and anything else which could be thought of either exploded or ignited; never did both results take place.

Lewes rose to the unspoken challenge and obtained some of the new plastic explosive which was beginning to come into its own. The story of Lewes's persistence and almost accidental discovery of an effective device is well known. Within two or three weeks he had perfected a bomb, a mixture of plastic explosive, thermite and oil, which was not only malleable into various shapes to conform to the target but could be contained in 'blocks' weighing slightly less than a pound. Mischievous politeness demanded that Lewes and Stirling should invite the expert to return for a demonstration. Suitably embarrassed he observed in silence and raised no objection to the naming of the device. The Lewes Bomb was very soon to become famous.

In mid-October 1941, a fortunate encounter and Stirling's outspoken comments gave L Detachment the opportunity to put their training into effect – a full operational rehearsal before they went into action for the first time. A group captain of the RAF, whose name has been lost, was sent by Ritchie to view their training methods and give his opinion on their chances of success. He chose a date when the Detachment was parachuting. Stirling, forewarned of his presence, opted to remain on the dropping zone with him. The drop went without a hitch and Stirling asked the group captain's opinion.

'Parachuting isn't new. It's not even difficult, but I think your chances of success on the ground are practically non-existent I can't conceive how you managed to persuade MEHQ that you could infiltrate an enemy aerodrome and destroy their aircraft.

It's not on.' He appeared totally uninterested and Stirling's blood was up.

'You are quite wrong. Getting on to the aerodromes will be easy. The main problem as we see it will be to make sure your people drop us in the right place. After that we have to find our own way back. Destroying the planes will not be difficult. We will be approaching from an unexpected direction and it is a matter of common knowledge that aerodromes are always badly guarded including our own.' The last sentence was delivered in Stirling's usual mild manner as he made to turn away.

The group captain took the bait. 'A very innocent view you take, Captain Stirling; a presumption in fact. I can't speak for the enemy, though I'm sure that their defences will be every bit as good as our own, but I assure you that you wouldn't find ours an easy target.'

'Nonsense. It wouldn't be at all difficult to get on to one of your bases. If you'd care to take a bet of say, ten pounds, I'll wager we can get on to Heliopolis at any time we wish. By way of proof we'll leave labels on the aircraft in the exact position we'd place the bombs. By the way, I want to show you the bomb we've devised for the job.'

'The bet is taken. You've completely underestimated the job.'

'No I haven't. You can even warn the guard force at Heliopolis. We'll be there around the end of the month.'

The challenge came at exactly the right time for the men of L Detachment. The continual training effort was beginning to pall. A number of the early recruits had been sent back to their units. Many had failed to keep up to the high physical standards, some had failed in self-confidence, some jibbed at the parachuting and others just decided that L Detachment was not for them. The remainder were a close-knit team, confident in their own and their comrades' abilities, at ease with their officers and wanting simply to get on with the job. Here was the final test.

The timing was good; in October the desert sun is still very fierce and there is little wind. It would be physically hard. For a brief description of the exercise, I take Mayne's group. Even though it was to be an exercise without explosives, the weights carried were totalled up to an operational equivalent by stuffing stones into the packs, which were weighed by Mayne. The exercise was mounted directly from Kabrit; Heliopolis airfield was roughly ninety miles away. Four pints of water were allocated in addition to food.

Movement was by night only; during the day the group began to realise the true agonies of lying up in the flat, featureless desert covered only by pieces of hessian sackcloth. The scorching sun took its toll but no one disobeyed the water drinking instructions. Bob Bennett recalls one of the occasions when Mayne displayed his very individual form of discipline in the field.

'We had a lad called Chesworth with us and he did nothing but moan all the time. "There's not enough water"; "It's time for a break"; "What the bloody hell are we doing this for"; you know the sort, every troop gets one now and again. Paddy got pissed off with him and decided it was time to stop it. We were on the crest of an escarpment and Paddy suddenly beckoned Chesworth to him. He picked the bugger up and held him over the cliff – with one hand, mark you – and said, "Any more from you and that's your lot." I tell you we never heard another peep out of him.'

They did not reach Heliopolis until just before midnight on the fourth night; by this time the lack of water was causing some to hallucinate but all such distractions disappeared as they studied the target. 'By that time we were almost convinced that this was it. That Heliopolis really was a German airfield.'

A smooth operation then followed as they snipped through the outer perimeter fence and, unobserved, made their way on to the airfield and amongst the parked aircraft. Mayne's group placed between forty and fifty labels on the aircraft and before they retreated they moved around the target as much as possible just to prove to themselves that it could be done. They allowed themselves sufficient time to arrive at the army barracks of Abassea where they made contact with the guard force. Amusingly the guards assumed that they had been approached by Italian surrenderees. They were filthy, had five-day beard growths and were almost inarticulate through thirst (which they slaked before identifying themselves). The army provided them with trucks to return to Kabrit.

All of the groups had met with the same success. Although they had not seen each other on the airfield it turned out that some aircraft had a number of labels affixed as different groups had criss-crossed the target.

Although Stirling was told that the exercise had caused a great deal of consternation at MEHQ and that a number of quite senior ears had been 'blistered', he received his ten pounds along with a very complimentary letter from the group captain who admitted to admiration and expressly wished L Detachment good luck when it went fully operational.

The detachment learned a number of lessons on the exercise. The bold approach was sound. Although it would be foolhardy deliberately to understock with water it was possible, given tight discipline, to cover reasonable distances on limited supplies. Their technique of lying up was effective; they did not know until after the event but the group captain had sent out daily reconnaissance aircraft hoping to spot them. Last but not least, their confidence was now brimming. They were ready.

I have discussed those early days at Kabrit at some length for good reason. To arrive at an idea such as Stirling had is one thing. To have the tenacity to drive it through an unwilling and therefore unresponsive higher headquarters is quite another. To then maintain control and leadership of a group of energetic, well-trained, often experienced and sometimes outspoken men requires a particular strength of character; especially when it is appreciated that this was in competition (albeit not deliberate competition) with other officers of the calibre of Mayne and Lewes.

Beyond this is the ability, through discussion and close attention to detail, to create and implement with total confidence a training schedule which all accepted as being a supreme test. By the end of October 1941, though some individuals were still understandably curious about Stirling, he was accepted as commander and leader without reservation.

---

# 7

# CASE PROVEN

General Auchinleck's first major offensive was set for 18 November 1941; the aim was to relieve Tobruk and begin the push to remove Erwin Rommel's Afrika Korps from Cyrenaica. It is reported that 'the Auk' was not completely happy with the plan but the pressure from Churchill had become irresistible – there was to be no more waiting. L Detachment's rôle in the operation was exactly as Stirling had outlined it in his original memorandum to General Ritchie.

'I decided that we would use all the able-bodied men of L Detachment. A few were still unable to go because of training injuries and I think one was about to take compassionate leave. We would therefore have five operational sticks travelling in independent aircraft. The commanders were myself, Mayne, Lewes, Bonnington and McGonigal and each had twelve men as far as I can remember. This gave the ability to split into two or three patrols prior to attacking the targets but that was to be the decision of the commanders after the reconnaissance.

'It was known from intelligence reports that there were five forward airfields in the area of Gazala and Timini and we took one each. The drops were to take place on the night of 16th November giving each group the remainder of that night to reach a lying-up position from which to observe the targets. On the night of the 17th they would infiltrate the airfields and lay their bombs with fuses coordinated as far as possible to detonate in the early hours of the morning. All groups would then, by the most direct route, walk to the rendezvous with the LRDG, a distance of approximately forty miles. Exfiltration would be by LRDG truck to Siwa Oasis, thence by air to Kabrit.

'The whole unit knew, of course, that we would be taking part in the November offensive but the details were withheld until the 15th. This was not a security measure, I trusted all the men to keep their mouths shut, but the dates were not finalised until the last minute and the last thing I wanted to do was brief everyone and then call it off. I remember that there was great excitement as the plans were given out. The atmosphere was tremendous – after over three months of hard training we were being committed to action. There was no doubt in our minds that we were going to be successful and wipe the smirks off the faces of the obstructionists in MEHQ.'

The first operational parachute jump in the Middle East theatre was causing a great deal of interest; a pressure that Stirling could well have done without as events turned out.

The morning of 16 November brought the worst news a parachute troops commander can have. Parachuting is dictated by the weather – anything over a fifteen-knot wind and there is a good chance of the troops being well scattered; anything over twenty-plus knots and the business becomes downright hazardous with the prospect of parachutists landing very hard and being dragged over the ground. The forecast over the dropping zones area suggested that the wind speeds could be thirty knots or more.

The advice to Stirling from the Brigadier, General Staff who was co-ordinating the operation was succinct: 'It's no go. On a moonless night you would have problems enough in regrouping but with winds at thirty knots those of you who are not injured will be scattered all over the desert. My advice is to call it off. There will be plenty of other opportunities. However, the decision will rest with you.' The Brigadier's expression left no doubt as to the decision he expected.

'I was thoroughly depressed and told the Brigadier I would report back to him within the hour. I then sought out my officers and briefed them on the situation. I told them that it seemed to me that we had to take the risk but I didn't exert any other influence. Mayne and Lewes immediately went along with my suggestion and the others quickly followed. I said I would make my decision shortly and went away to think.'

By all the standards of current military thinking, Stirling's decision should have been to call off the operation. The chances of success must have been five per cent or less with the overall effect on the offensive being practically nil. In addition, valuable aircraft were being placed in jeopardy.

Consider first the weather effect on the parachutists; apart from the high risk of injury there was the problem of finding each other on a dark night when they could easily be separated by a mile or more. Supplies were being dropped in separate canisters and could be dragged off anywhere; in short, the survivors could reasonably expect to lose the whole of the cover of darkness provided by that first night in leaguering the injured and locating the supplies.

Navigation for the aircraft was going to be an immense problem; they would be lucky to see the flares on which they were so dependent for assessing the drop zone location (assuming that the weather allowed the other aircraft to drop them). The pilots, in addition to that hazard, were carrying parachute troops for the first time and the final decision to drop had to be theirs – was this a fair imposition of responsibility?

Why then was the operation not called off? The answer lies in the various pressures influencing Stirling. Although he must have realised that there was an odds-on chance of at least partial failure, he had utter faith in the concept that he had succeeded in pushing through MEHQ. He had made many enemies over the preceding three months – more than his happy band of warriors knew. Those enemies would be delighted to pervert the reasoning for calling off the job and use it as a lever either to have the force disbanded or make life even more difficult subsequently.

More important, to Stirling's thinking, was the morale of his men. He had been incredibly lucky to amass a body of men who had taken to the rôle like ducks to water. They were as ready as they ever would be; indeed any more training without action and they were likely to get stale. Furthermore, many had come from Layforce and had been on the same abortive missions as Stirling had suffered. To call off one more raid at the last moment was going to place a great strain on morale – it might even lead to key individuals returning to their units, which were now under great pressure. Finally, he knew that he had been accepted as a leader but he felt that only an operation would consolidate his standing.

Not for the last time in his life, Stirling made a decision based on human instinct rather than a clinical examination of the facts. It is true that the morale of L Detachment would have suffered a severe blow had the operation been postponed but men of that calibre would undoubtedly have put the upset behind them. Regardless of the rights and wrongs, L Detachment's leader made his decision and was supported by the whole of his command.

Stirling's letter home plays down the situation:

CTC Kabrit
15 November 1941

My dear Mum,

I am afraid it's a terribly long time since I last wrote. Thank you very much for your letters. I hate Egypt and I have never been so homesick since the Lower 2nd at Ampleforth. Letters certainly succeed in temporarily dispelling the gloom.

I have been very busy since July in forming a new unit out here and it has been extraordinarily interesting. The training is now over and we are going into our first operation tomorrow night. (I have just arranged for a Catholic padre to say mass, confession and communion to the Catholics of the unit at 4:30 a.m. tomorrow – we leave at 6:30 a.m.) It is the best possible type of operation and will be far more exciting than dangerous.

After it is over it is conceivable I may get home for a time.

It is very sad Bill has gone. Bill and Peter sharing a flat in Cairo made for a very amusing household. They fortunately had an Egyptian servant who was very good at anticipating orders never given and in compromising on conflicting ones. They employed a very good cook (sacked from the Embassy but not for bad cooking) which made the flat a very popular address around lunchtime.

I will write a much longer letter when I get back. Give my love to everybody,

Your loving David

Sergeant 'Gentleman' Jim Almonds, one of the 'Tobruk Four', was to the desert born in many ways. In this environment he was totally at home. He excelled in the velvet darkness and revelled in the vast emptiness of North Africa. His nickname was apt; six feet and two inches tall, his gentle, quiet and considerate manner hid enormous self-discipline and control which left him cool, efficient and deadly when the situation demanded it. Having done three years pre-war service with the Coldstream Guards, Jim Almonds was an experienced soldier when he joined L Detachment and held very high in Stirling's esteem.

A born innovator and skilled with his hands, Jim was responsible for most of the construction work at Kabrit to assist in parachuting training. A boat, a crossbow, tables, bars, exit training towers and mock fuselages all sprang from Jim's capable hands. A staunch ally of Jock Lewes, it was a bitter disappointment to Jim that he was not to go along on that first operation. Problems with the health of his wife and son made it seem that recall to England was imminent. Jim was left to await the recall and to continue with the building of Kabrit. Entries in his diaries reveal his mood:

*Sunday 16th November* The whole squadron left this morning to carry out a parachute raid on the enemy aerodromes in the western desert. Watched them embark and the planes take off.

They are a fine crowd of lads, how many will I see again. Left alone in camp I wandered around from tent to tent – all empty and yet so full of hope and faith. Photos of sweethearts, wives and mothers on the walls awaiting their return. May they none of them be disappointed. Did nothing all day just aimlessly wandered about.

*Monday 17th November* Tried to start work but gave it up as a bad job. The lads are now 280 miles inside enemy territory hiding in the sand and awaiting dark to start their reign of terror and destruction. After the massacre is over and the enemy planes blown up or burned there remains that terrible march back through the desert. No one who is sick or wounded can possibly make it and none can afford to help. The weight already carried by each man is as much as he can bear, great supplies of water and food are so essential to such a trek.

I am not there. I sit back here in the safety of camp and wish I were, one more would have made the load lighter and a few words of encouragement when hard pressed go a long way. When in action before and hard pressed I have managed to get a smile or two out of them which has helped a lot along the way. Anyway had I been with them at least I could have tried. Reality beats fiction for sheer, cold, calculating courage. Some of these lads cannot be beaten. Films and books of daring and adventure fall far short of the real thing. More will be heard of the SAS should this raid go through as planned. The war in Northern Africa should soon be brought to a successful conclusion.

*Tuesday 18th November* Wandered around the camp again today, think I must have been overdoing the work. Reaction is no interest in anything, not even things I used to like doing. Had a letter from home, Dad wrote about a page, extracts from the bible, enjoyed reading it so much. Wish I had a bible.

*Wednesday 19th November* [Personal comment on no news regarding his wife and baby] . . . also my mates somewhere in enemy territory. Heard today that the plane my section went off in is missing. Poor devils, they need all the luck possible. In this tent there will be Mrs Bond and two children waiting for Ernest, Mrs Stone and son waiting for Barney, Mrs Quinton waiting for Spike. May it please God that they don't wait in vain. Had it not been for Sonny's illness, Mrs Almonds and son would be waiting for Jim. I should have been with that plane, the terms of fate are past all understanding.

Records show that it was at 19.30 hours on 16 November 1941 that five Bristol Bombay aircraft of 216 Squadron took off from the forward base for the final run to the operational area. Weather in the local area was fine; the night was clear and there was no discernible wind at cruising altitude. As the target area was neared the weather deteriorated alarmingly. Cloud appeared and thickened and soon the aircraft were flying through a storm of impressive proportions.

From memory, and later talks with the pilot of his aircraft, Sergeant Ernie Bond has rendered a graphic account of the experience of Lieutenant Bonnington's group.

'We were bound for the area of Tmimi and were pleased with the state of the weather when we took off. It seemed that the forecasters had got it wrong. There wasn't much room in the aircraft as most of the interior was taken up by a huge, long-range fuel tank fitted along the length of the plane. We were expecting some sort of flak as we got near to the target and it wasn't the most comfortable feeling in the world having a few hundred gallons of fuel right before your eyes.

'The storm hit us fairly suddenly and then we were bucketing about all over the place. We could hear the thunder above the noise of the engines and the lightning was plain to see.'

In the pilot's cabin there was chaos; Warrant Officer 'Charlie' West was in deep trouble with his navigation. There was no way of even crudely estimating the direction and force of the wind. He had taken a course over the sea and had expected to be able to use well-defined coastal configurations as navigational aids before making his run inland. It was impossible even to see the ocean. He dropped a sea marker flare and managed to make a guess at the speed and direction of the wind. His check showed him that he was well off course and could not hope to make the zone area in time for the planned drop. He decided to descend and get a visible fix and plan his route from there.

Ernie Bond picks up the story. 'We knew we were losing altitude but we didn't realise how much until suddenly tracers from the anti-aircraft guns began flicking past the windows. There was a great shudder and then we were groaning upwards again.'

The port engine had taken a hit and was losing power; worse perhaps, the entire instrument panel had shattered. Charlie West's Bombay was now blind and crippled and to make matters worse he was conscious of petrol draining from a holed wing tank. The only undamaged instrument in front of the pilot was the magnetic compass. He set this due east and, assuming this to be the course for base, turned for home. Within an hour of this decision, fuel draining rapidly away, West was forced to conclude that he should land whilst he still had power.

The wind was so strong that the huge Bombay was being pushed backwards despite locked brakes. It took some minutes before ice-frozen weapon containers could be freed to use as chocks.

'The weather improved as the night wore on and just before dawn we took a patrol out to try to get our bearings. We were pretty sure that we were in friendly territory but surprise, surprise, we came across an Italian position. There was a short, sharp skirmish and we took one very frightened Eytie back to the aircraft. By the time we returned, Charlie West'd discovered that his compass was jammed by a piece of shrapnel. So we must have been trundling round in a bloody great circle the night before.'

West and Bonnington made a hasty decision. The amount of flying time was unknown as the fuel gauges were out of action but there certainly wasn't much. If they stayed where they were either the Germans or the Italians would be upon them within minutes. If they took off there was the unknown factor of fuel. The decision was to take off and gain as much altitude as possible whilst heading for Allied territory; Tobruk and the British lines seemed the best bet – if they ran out of fuel at least there was some comfort to be gained from an incalculable glide factor.

'We got back into the plane in a hell of a rush. The poor, bloody Eytie was jammed on top of the fuel tank and told to sit still. Poor sod, he was even more terrified than we were. Charlie managed the take-off OK, but the engines sounded pretty ropy.' No sooner were they airborne than the Germans opened up with small-arms fire. West flew as low as possible in the hope of avoiding anti-aircraft fire but their luck was out. The fuselage received a direct hit.

'I felt something hit me hard and almost at the same time the Eytie took off and it seemed that he flew right through the opposite side of the aircraft. The plane was wobbling about all over the place and it was obvious that we were going down. All we could do was brace ourselves. The next thing I knew I was lying in the sand some yards from the plane. Charlie West was pretty badly injured but the only one killed was the co-pilot.

'We were pretty quickly in German hands and taken off to their nearest field hospital. We were treated well which was a surprise. I was bedded down next to Charlie. He was unconscious for some days and didn't know what had happened when he woke up. Some days later we decided to escape. We were a pretty sorry sight with our bandages and bits and pieces but we just walked out of the hospital and down the street. We had a bit of bad luck as we turned one corner. Two Panzer officers, pissed as newts, were heading towards us. If we'd been fit we might have got away with it.'

Ernie Bond was to spend the remainder of the war in PoW camps until he was repatriated in 1945. On the way to Germany via camps in Italy he tried to escape once more but his luck was out; even so, he was luckier than many that fateful night.

Stirling's experience was no less disastrous. Pleasantly surprised by the weather on take-off, he became concerned as it deteriorated, but hoped for a reprieve at the last moment. The pilot was having the same navigational problems as had hit West; the flares which Bomber Command had agreed to drop were obscured by cloud. He lost altitude and got a semblance of a fix on the coast just as the anti-aircraft guns began to engage, and banked into his inland turn. Stirling's men were given a six-minute warning and were soon in the air.

'I was surprised. The plane had been thrown every which way but now I was under the canopy everything seemed so smooth. I knew something was wrong when I realised how long it was taking to hit the ground – I was being blown along like a kite but without any real sensation of speed. I tensed up and waited for the impact – it was wrong to be so tense but impossible to avoid. When I did hit the deck it was so forceful that I was knocked out.' David calculates that he must have been unconscious for about two minutes though it is not possible to know.

When he came to he was being dragged at speed by the still inflated parachute over gravel and small rocks. It took a moment or two to release the harness and it was with great relief that he found that despite the blood there appeared to be nothing broken. He was in a raging sandstorm in a wind so powerful it was difficult to stay upright. The worst fears had been realised.

It took almost two hours to regroup by means of shouts and wildly waved torches. A further two hours were spent looking for the one missing man and the scattered supplies. Two men were virtually out of action with a suspected broken wrist and a broken arm; two more were able only to limp painfully with either broken or badly sprained ankles. The remainder all had cuts of varying severity. It was a miserable picture as Stirling took stock.

Their search had failed to locate the weapons container so they were armed only with the revolvers they carried. Half-a-dozen blankets and one day's food plus a dozen Lewes Bombs (with no fuses) was their total haul. Of the missing man there was no sign.

'I was so damned angry. We were in a sorry state but with weapons and explosives we could still have achieved something.

As it was we were impotent. There was no action we could take; I could only hope that the others had been more successful. At least I could have a look at the enemy – I might learn something useful. I decided that I would take one man with me, Sergeant Tait. He was in reasonable condition, like myself only a few cuts and bruises. The others were out of action so I detailed Sergeant Yates to lead them at best possible speed to the LRDG rendezvous.

'Tait and I calculated that the coast should be about ten miles away but at first light, when the weather turned, there was no sign of it despite very good visibility. We must have been blown well away from the drop zone. We kept going in daylight until about mid-morning when it seemed that there was a haze on the horizon which could be the sea. I decided to stop until dark to conserve our water supply which was pretty low; one bottle each I think.

The weather changed in the late afternoon and as we reckoned there would be no enemy flying, we pressed on. We managed to reach the long escarpment before full darkness and from there we could see the coast road and the sea. We could see movement along the road but none of the airfields. It whetted my appetite I suppose for it proved that given the right conditions what I had thought of was possible. We couldn't do anything so we made for the RV.'

'We made for the RV.' A simple statement, but in fact it was Stirling's first test as a desert navigator. They had to cover in the region of fifty miles – on the remains of the one water bottle each. They were fortunate in that the weather turned again and it poured with rain for the next few hours. It was cold and there was water. The two men also learned of that desert phenomenon, the flash flood. Water coming down in torrents hits the baked sand and gravel and because of the sheer volume, it takes the line of least resistance at such speed that a wadi bed, dry one minute, can become a raging torrent the next.

To find the RV would have been relatively simple had they

been starting from a known reference point. The Trig El Abd was a track line in the desert, laid many years ago by camel trains and later by the vehicles of war. The principle of navigation was to use a deliberate intersection error: a line formed by the track would be intersected at a point which was deliberately off the line of the intended RV. When that track line was reached the navigator knew which way to turn along it. Fortunately Stirling and Tait had discovered that they had been dropped or blown off target and when they hit the Trig El Abd they knew they had to turn to the right. Sergeant Yates had not been so lucky – he had allowed himself to be persuaded to turn left and subsequently was picked up by an enemy patrol.

All that day and the following night they walked, spotting the LRDG lamp in the early hours of the morning. Looping around, Stirling's route first took him into another LRDG position, manned at that time by Captain David Lloyd Owen (later to command the LRDG), though this had not been planned. Stirling and Tait were treated to tea with a strong whisky base and after introductions asked whether any of their men had come through the position on their way to link up with Jake Easonsmith who was manning the RV proper.

Mayne and his party had passed by and were at that time with Easonsmith. During that pleasant lull Lloyd Owen suggested it would be more practical if the LRDG were to deliver L Detachment to their target areas and collect them again after the attacks had gone home. Probably because the bitter taste of failure was still with him, Stirling was not particularly enthusiastic. 'Too slow,' he mumbled. He and Tait moved the short distance to the RV and linked up with Mayne, Lewes and Fraser to review the situation.

Mayne's experience had been similar to Stirling's. He had lost two men with injuries so severe that they had to be left behind; he, too, had marched to the coast to get accurate bearings. He had arrived in the area before Stirling but had laid off for a while to make sure that the figures he had seen were not German. Lewes and Fraser had managed to get eight of their men back to the RV; one had to be left behind with a broken leg and one was missing. Of Bonnington's group there was no news. McGonigal's party was never heard of again – tragically it has to be conjectured that they were all killed. Out of the original sixty-two-man force only twenty-two had made it back.

Rest was the first priority. Depressed to a man they covered themselves as best they could and tried to sleep. Pat Riley shared a tarpaulin with Stirling and Lewes, dozing fitfully between them. Sergeant Pat Riley, six feet two inches tall, was a great bull of a man. Born in Wisconsin, USA, he had not found it easy to join the army without changing his citizenship. A few masterly strokes with the pen and some obscure details on the recruiting forms had got around the problem, however. He had been in the Coldstream Guards before the war and had rejoined them as hostilities broke out. As one of the Tobruk Four, and with the highest possible recommendations from Lewes, he had been one of the first to join L Detachment.

Riley had been with Lewes's group along with a close friend, Jock Cheyne. Jock dwarfed even Pat, and when it came to fitting their parachutes Pat's was too big and Jock's too small. It seemed a matter of common sense to exchange. As it happened it was Jock who went missing after the drop and it gave Pat Riley an 'uncomfortable feeling' for some months. A cool and very courageous soldier, Pat Riley was one of the most significant figures in the early SAS. Promoted RSM in the field by Stirling and later commissioned, his broad-based knowledge and total faith in the unit were tremendous assets.

'I remember at some point during the night, David leaned across me and said to Jock, "I think that's the end of parachuting for us, Jock." Jock's reply was affirmative. We were all pretty shocked by the failure and the loss of all those guys. I don't think any of us thought it was all over, though. David and Lewes discussed using the LRDG for a bit – a "taxi service" I think – but pretty soon we all fell asleep for a couple of hours.'

It is typical of Stirling's faith and thinking that he turned his mind completely away from the failure and looked to how, with the remnants of his force, he could gain a success. He knew the concept was right. Both he and Mayne had gone right up to the enemy's unprotected flank without incident, despite the fact that the Germans had known the aircraft were in the area the night before. He had learned that though parachuting could not be totally written off as a means of delivery, it could not be relied upon for operations where timing was critical. The LRDG seemed to be the answer.

He also recognised that the failure would be manna from heaven for the Doubting Thomases at MEHQ and that if he returned there the chances of anyone listening to his arguments would be slim. Auchinleck and Ritchie would be too tied up with greater matters to be relied upon for direct support. During the two-hundred-mile drive back to Siwa Oasis, Stirling had plenty of time to talk to the LRDG about their techniques and he became convinced that this talented band could provide the perfect combination of skills. Their navigation was impeccable; their camouflage and movement drills were excellent as were their almost uncanny abilities as desert drivers and masters of mechanical improvisation. What was more, and perhaps most importantly, they were kindred spirits, totally committed to their rôle.

Nevertheless, his chances of driving that idea through MEHQ were remote. He had to find a means of proving L Detachment's worth before he set foot in Cairo again. He was a solitary figure once he had decided on the requirement, keeping his own company some distance from the others during the many halts and apparently deep in thought when they were travelling. He had the ability to switch off completely from outside influences. A number of decisions had been made by the time the group arrived at Siwa.

Firstly, he would not return to base; he would not even contact base nor would he be available if anyone tried to contact him. Secondly, he would plan a raid based on the abilities of his remaining twenty-two men. Thirdly, that raid would be against an airfield – airfields had been the focus of his initial incentive and enemy air power would be giving Auchinleck his biggest headaches at this point of the offensive. Two problems stood out: where were his supplies going to come from? Would the LRDG agree to support them?

On the second score he had no need to worry, Colonel Guy Prendergast's agreement was quick in coming. Provided that his own rôle was not interrupted he was happy for his patrols to oblige. It was the beginning of a unique relationship which was to set the SAS on its feet. The supply problem was not so easily settled. 8th Army Headquarters was not too far from Siwa – maybe they would help. Stirling sent everyone back to Kabrit under Lewes with instructions to collect every item of useful equipment and weaponry and return to Siwa as quickly as possible. They were to scrounge their air passages discreetly and on no account to go near MEHQ.

What news had in fact filtered back to MEHQ? Jim Almonds's diary shows:

*Thursday 20th November* . . . our troops have advanced 50 miles from Sollum on their advance to Tripoli; according to this progress Tobruk should be relieved in another 2 days. God, will this happen. Will they find our boys safely hiding up there somewhere. Each night I say my prayers . . .

*Friday 21st November* . . . advance in the desert continues this morning only 10 miles out of Tobruk. No news of the boys as yet . . .

*Sunday 23rd November* Heard news today that some of the boys have been picked up, out in the desert, feel very pleased and relieved about it . . .

*Wednesday 26th November* Today the remnants of the SAS returned, 21 as rumoured. Pat Riley one of them, Blakeney missing. In my tent the beds remain empty and their personal effects lie strewn about where they left them. I have not got the heart to alter things; you see I still cannot give them up as lost although the government has. What happened to that plane no one knows. Was it shot down? Anyway I will keep the hope for another month, may their wives never really know of this.

The LRDG report arrived at 8th Army HQ before Stirling and he was summoned to meet the Commander, General Cunningham. Aware that Stirling had been in a position to overlook the coastal road between Gazala and Tobruk he asked for news of enemy movements. All that could be passed on was the sighting of supply columns – no news of German armour. The offensive was falling short of expectations and within a few days of the meeting with Cunningham, Stirling learned that Auchinleck had ordered Ritchie to take over the 8th Army. Ritchie he did not want to meet, and he arranged his return to Siwa. Too late. Ritchie sent for him. The meeting was brief; Ritchie questioned him about traffic movements on the coast road, commiserated with him about the abortive operation and a relieved Stirling made his exit.

Stirling then met with some luck in the form of Brigadier Marriott, ex-22 Guards Brigade, whom he had met in Peter's Cairo flat. He was a sympathetic man, liked the fervour in what he heard and provided an introduction to Brigadier Denys Reid, currently occupying Jalo Oasis which he had recently captured.

'If you're looking for a supply base to leech on to, Denys is your man. You'll like him and he's well placed to help.'

Jalo was about 180 miles inland from L Detachment's area of operational interest; well away from 8th Army (Stirling was worried in case Ritchie suddenly took the wrong kind of interest in his force) and out of the immediate fighting area. At Jalo, Reid lived up to Marriott's promises. Whilst they waited for Stirling's men to return from Kabrit, maps were studied and the likely dispositions of German aircraft discussed in detail. From Almonds's diary.

*Wednesday 2nd December* Asked by CO to go on new operation,

saw news film of SAS at aerodrome cinema. Quite a good
show. Leaving by plane first thing in the morning to start
a new 'adventure', shall be away 1 week, 2 weeks, I don't
know . . .

*Thursday 3rd December* Left by Douglas airliner from Kabrit
aerodrome and flew to Pergush . . . Spent a night in a tent
beside the airfield. Leaving in the morning for Jalo Oasis.

*Friday 4th December* The plane did not leave this morning.
Sandstorm raging all day. Spent a miserable day in the tent.

*Saturday 5th December* Left by Bombay this morning for Jalo
at 07.45 . . . and arrived at Jalo the same night.

*Sunday 6th December* The Oasis is about 7 miles in length and
2 miles wide and is abundant with water and palm trees . . .

By the time L Detachment was together once more, Stirling
had met Major Don Steele of the LRDG and agreement had
been reached in principle for transport to and from the first
operation wherever that was to take place. The right occasion
did not present itself until early December. Stirling wanted
a significant operation, and one which would be of positive
assistance to the immediate battle, in order to put paid to the
Doubting Thomases. Reid's Flying Squadron was under orders
to link up with Marriott's force in the area of Agedabia and
to be in position by 22 December. The move was severely
threatened, almost to the point of being suicidal, by the German
aircraft at Agedabia, Sirte and Agheila. A classic challenge to
Stirling.

As usual the outline plan was simple and stark. Stirling
and Mayne would move out on 8 December with ten men.
They would be lifted by LRDG vehicles to within striking
distance of the airfield reckoned to be the most important, at
Sirte. Lewes would embark on 9 December – target Agheila;
action required by both groups on the night 14/15 December. Fraser to move on 18 December and attack Agedabia
in support of Reid's move. Jim Almond went with Lewes:

*Wednesday 9th December* Started away early this morning travelling east by north. The country has changed, deep wadis and escarpments have taken the place of the level sand and in the wadi bottoms there is a sparse growth of shrub. Progress is much slower, negotiating the steep hills and rocky ridges very dangerous. Sharp lookout kept all day for enemy aircraft. Covered 60 miles and camped for the night.

*Saturday 12th December* Captured a native near the camp and held him prisoner by fastening his legs together with the tow chain of the lorry. Looked after him well but could take no chances of allowing him to escape, a slip now would prove fatal to us . . . Enemy aircraft overhead several times during the day.

*Sunday 13th December* Mr Lewes and party returned with a prisoner, a corporal from an Italian native regiment. We called him Sambo, he was as black as ink, a good sort of chap and very friendly . . . The aerodrome at Agheila was deserted but they found some lorries of ammo which they blew up and blew down a mile of telegraph lines along the main Tripoli road. Except for Corporal Sambo and his platoon they encountered no one. Cpl Sambo's platoon laid down their arms and wanted to be taken prisoner and were very disappointed when only Sambo was taken.

During his slow move towards the target, Stirling was struck again by the likeness of desert to ocean. He felt infinitesimally small against the vastness of the sandy, gravelly, sometimes rocky wastes. It was a learning period for all as they observed the LRDG in action. Navigation drills, camouflage techniques and daily routines – all were soaked up by Stirling's men as they were inexorably carried forward. Unfortunately they attracted the attention of a Gibli scout aircraft, and for a few days they were harassed and bombed. As they reached the coast road it became obvious from the activity that the hunt was on. A decision was called for.

Stirling decided that the operation could not be jeopardised. He would drop off at that point with one man and take his chances of moving through the enemy patrols. He did not want to risk more than the two of them. Mayne was given command of the remainder and asked to make as much noise as possible when he moved off, so the Germans would think the whole party had left. They took to the vehicles' running boards and jumped off on a gravel patch to avoid leaving tell-tale tracks. Stirling's companion was Sergeant Jimmy Brough, who had served in the Scots Guards and Layforce and had been personally sought out by Stirling on his first recruiting drive. They had met during Commando training in Scotland and Stirling had a high regard for this canny Scot, who was reputed to have an extensive repertoire of artful dodges. Jimmy takes up the story:

'We felt a bit exposed after the truck disappeared but we had to be moving. We both had big rucksacks – I'd enough food in mine to feed an army – and between us on the ground was the bag of Lewes bombs and fuses. Captain Stirling didn't actually tell me to carry it but he made some comment as to how it might be best if I did because I'd been trained for it and he was going to navigate. We played quite a game of hide-and-seek with a group of Eyeties before we suddenly found ourselves right on Sirte airfield. God, we were tempted to lay our bombs there and then, there were planes all over the place, but Captain Stirling said we must stick to the plan and hit them at the same time as Paddy Mayne.

'We tripped over a couple of sleeping men, off-duty guards I think. They started firing – then other guns started and then anti-aircraft guns opened up. None of the bullets were coming our way though. Captain Stirling reckoned they must have thought they were being attacked from the sea and said it was a good thing that they seemed more scared than we were. We made a place to lay up back on the ridge and when daylight came we found we were in the middle of a bunch of Arab women grubbing around with mattocks.

'We were very still for about three hours and they went away. That afternoon we noticed that the aircraft (we'd counted about thirty Eyetie Capronis) kept taking off in pairs and nothing seemed to be landing. By late afternoon the airfield was empty.

It looked as though they'd been flown away for safety after we'd disturbed the sentries.'*

David, despondent, cursed himself for having gone too close the night before. He was hoping against hope that one of the other groups would pull something off. Shortly the pair had the great satisfaction of seeing flashes in the sky some five miles to the west; seconds later the thunder of Mayne's bombs reached their ears. Tamet was burning!

'We didn't grab each other and dance for joy but damned nearly,' said Stirling. 'In a fit of devilment we put a mine on the road and had the inestimable pleasure of watching an Italian truck disintegrate some minutes later, made even more pleasurable by Gus Holliman turning up smack on time at the RV.' Parachuting was most definitely out, thought Stirling as they trundled back to Jalo.

Mayne's group did not arrive back until the next day. The occupants of Jalo spotted the returning green and pink vehicles some distance away and decided to give them a traditional salute by firing into the air.

'We had no brakes, and we thought we'd been mistaken for the enemy. We were shaken but it turned out to be a welcome,' said one of the triumphant party.

Bob Bennett, archetypal Cockney, full of humour and quick to play shop steward if conditions suited, was an ex-Grenadier Guardsman (by accident, he says, but that's another story) and a quick learner in the desert. Devoted to Paddy Mayne, he makes a good witness to the raid on Tamet:

'It went without a hitch. We didn't meet anything on the way in and before we knew it we were groping around the airfields. Black as pitch it was, couldn't see a thing. Then Paddy spotted this Nissen hut affair and sneaked up to it. He obviously heard something inside because the next thing we knew he'd dragged the bloody door open and was letting rip with his tommy-gun.

* It was of little moment; the aircraft simply flew to the airfield which Mayne had as a target.

Screams from inside and the lights went out.

'The buggers inside soon started firing. Paddy put a couple of guys on the ground to keep the Krauts' heads down and the rest off us went after the planes. We got through all our bombs pretty quick – brilliant those Lewes Bombs. Quick and easy. Afterwards Reg [Seekings] said there wasn't a bomb left for the last plane and Paddy got so pissed off that he climbed up to the cockpit and demolished it with his bare hands. What a feller.

'We got moving fast, but even so the first bomb went off before we were clear of the airfield. We had to stop and look, didn't we. What a sight, flames and muck all over the place. We headed straight out to the LRDG lads. There was a bit of a kerfuffle when the Krauts caught on to us using flashing lights to find the RV – they started flashing their own but we used our whistles as a back-up and we got back OK.'

Mayne's party had destroyed twenty-four aircraft on the ground without a single casualty. The result of Paddy's somewhat undisciplined foray into the hangar was unknown, but he was a first-class shot so there would have been some dead Germans. (Mayne was later to admit that it had been a mistake to alert the enemy before laying the bombs.) Three days later Lewes returned from Agedabia; he had been unlucky, in that he arrived at an empty airfield, but instead he had targetted a building nearby, at Mersa Brega, which intelligence reports had identified as a regular meeting place for German brass. The plan misfired, and Lewes's only alternative was to place about thirty-eight bombs on vehicles parked in the vicinity.

Last to return to Jalo was Fraser's group. Theirs was the icing on the cake. In a totally unhindered operation, once they had bypassed the sentry posts, that four-man patrol had infiltrated Agedabia airfield and destroyed thirty-seven aircraft. L Detachment was overjoyed: sixty-one aircraft, at least twenty-five trucks and an unknown number of soldiers destroyed without a single Detachment casualty.

Vindicated, Stirling might well have chosen to return to Cairo and MEHQ. Instead he decided to have another crack at the airfields straight away. He had not destroyed any aircraft himself, but this was not the only reason for staying on.

'We had tasted success, we had all the support we needed on site and the targets were easily accessible. It seemed folly to pull out then. I decided that we'd go the next morning. Bill Fraser had only got back that morning. I just suggested that if he was not too tired he might like to go along, and take on the Marble Arch airfield which was quite close to our areas.' This was typical of Stirling's method of giving orders. He rarely did so directly; if he were to suggest that something might be 'worth doing' or 'fun', it was difficult to refuse. This was quite a calculated business of course – but it did hold the 'volunteer spirit' together.

The targets selected were Tamet and Sirte again, with Nofilia and Marble Arch added on for Lewes and Fraser. Stirling again found an empty airfield. Mayne struck gold. Jock Lewes's party found only two aircraft on their target and on the return journey were attacked from the air; Jim Almonds relates:

*Thursday 31st December* On the move this morning travelling northwest to pick up Mr Fraser and party. 10.00 a.m. sighted lone Messerschmitt 110 fighter heading our way. Kept still in hope he would not see us. He passed right overhead and was going away, everyone breathing a sigh of relief, when one wing dropped and round he came. Circled us very low and then attacked, armed with four machine guns forward and two cannons. He gave us a hell of a time not to mention the gun in his tail. A sharp fight followed and we gave as good as we got. His second burst got our truck but did not hurt anyone or set us on fire. It soon became obvious that it was only a matter of time before we should all be killed if we stayed with the trucks so we left and got behind a rock. Mr Lewes had been wounded in the leg . . . for a time we played ring of roses with it round the rock, three members of the LRDG, Bob Lilley and myself. We had that plane beat, it took him some minutes to get round the rock but we could do it in a few strides and his rear gunner must have been killed earlier in the engagement, the cannons were out of action.

The patrol was split and all that day was harried by Stukas, but somehow they survived. Of Fraser's party they could find no sign; they were presumed dead or taken prisoner since it appeared to Lewes's patrol that the enemy had been waiting for them. On the way back to Jalo Almonds's party made contact with other survivors and found out that Jock Lewes had died of his wounds. The closing paragraph of that last day in 1941 in Jim Almonds's diary reflects the whole of L Detachment's thoughts on Lewes:

> I thought of Jock, one of the bravest men I have ever met, an officer and a gentleman, lying out there in the desert barely covered with sand. No one will stop by his grave or pay homage to a brave heart that has ceased to beat – not even a stone marks the spot.

Fraser's party, having missed the rendezvous, survived an epic march of two hundred miles in eight days, having to steal what water they could. Jim Almonds, then in Cairo on leave, recorded:

> *Saturday 16th January* Met a party of ghosts in town today. The New Zealanders we left for dead in the desert [part of Fraser's group], they walked the 210 miles back to Jalo, but Cpl White did not come with them. His feet were bad from the effects of his previous march, so he left them at the Marauder Road to wait and hold up a German truck.

Stirling was hit hard by the death of Lewes – he had returned to Cairo before learning of Fraser's survival. Bearing the news that his survivors from the disastrous parachute insertion had stayed in the desert and destroyed no less than ninety aircraft in two weeks, he reckoned it was reasonable to beard Auchinleck in his den and insist on more officers and men. It was more than desirable – it was vital.

# 8

# INDEPENDENCE AND THE REBUILD

To me David Stirling was an inspiration and a hope. Of the SAS which owed its being to him, it is difficult to speak too highly – its services were, without exaggeration, invaluable. The courage, spirit and endurance of its leader and of the wonderful team he collected can seldom, if ever, have been equalled.

General Auchinleck

L Detachment had travelled back to Kabrit together with the exception of Fraser's section which had still not reappeared. Stirling took only the time needed to have a bath and change into a respectable uniform before heading for MEHQ; he did not bother to shave.

'I'd taken stock of my position over the last few days. Jock Lewes's death was tragic. Apart from losing a trusted friend I knew I was going to miss his very fine brain. Jock had become fully sold on the idea of small patrols after the last operations and I had intended to ask him to take over all recruiting, rear administration and training. I think he would have objected strongly because he was such a fine front-line soldier and leader; but in the end he'd have done it to perfection.

'We'd not had as much success as I'd have liked but certainly there was sufficient to show that the concept was sound and despite the dismal failure with the parachuting I now had a very workable and even more effective alternative with the LRDG, fully supported in principle by them; they obviously had to be able to continue with their own invaluable work. It looked as though Auchinleck's offensive was going to be successful and that Benghazi would be in British hands within a few days. If this came to pass then Rommel would surely be forced to use Bouerat to harbour his fuel supplies.

'I reckoned we could get into the port and blow up both tankers and dumps. I didn't want L Detachment to be linked in bureaucratic eyes only to airfields. They had to grasp the true strategic concept which meant that I had to grip the nettle with Auchinleck. I'd taken a chance that he would agree with me and already set the wheels in motion with the LRDG at Jalo. My problem now was men.

'There were a few rude comments from the Director of Military Operations' (DMO) staff. I'd asked to see General Auchinleck but apparently protocol dictated that I follow an ascending route to the top. I ignored the comments on my beard, which was really rather a fine one, and asked why I was being kept waiting. Hadn't they seen my signal stating that I had business with the C-in-C?'

In fact Stirling did not have to wait long. Auchinleck was expecting him, and congratulated him both on the successful raids and the magnificence of his beard and asked what his plans were.

'I was a little taken aback – I'd feared that I was going to be given instructions rather than an invitation to expound on my theories. I explained that, in my opinion, the enemy's storage depots were even more important now that the offensive seemed to be growing in momentum and that I intended to raid the harbour of Bouerat. I told him of the proposed affiliation with the LRDG and how precisely they could deliver L Detachment to any given point with good security.

'Security was paramount to our continued success – if we could get to the target areas undetected then all was possible; the limitations, given manpower and good support, were boundless. He blinked but didn't comment when I repeated my initial stipulation that I must work only to him directly and that there must be no radio or written traffic regarding our movements and targets. He asked very few questions.'

'How many men do you think you will need?'

'About fifteen.'

'Where do you propose that the Bouerat operation should be launched from?'

'Without a doubt, Jalo Oasis.'

'Why Jalo?'

'There are good facilities there. It is one of the LRDG bases. It is within an acceptable distance of the target and anyway planning and preparation is in progress.'

'Really! And when do you think you might be ready?'

'If I get back to Jalo by about 10th January I will be ready towards the end of the month. We have to strike when there is no moon if we are to go in with the minimum risk of detection; the best time seems to be about the 24th.'

Auchinleck closed his eyes for a few moments before concluding the meeting. 'Fifteen is not enough men for you. You have the authority, as of now, to recruit up to six more officers and, let's say, a further forty men. Well done, Stirling, and from now you have the rank of major which may help a little.'

Stirling had about a week before he would have to return to Jalo for final preparation. He would have a variety of problems, not least the recruiting of extra men. He was not too concerned about that because he knew the Bouerat operation was feasible from his existing resources. His main concern was that his enemies in MEHQ should not know of any problem unless he chose to share it.

'I reckoned I had three enemies at that time. Firstly, the fossilised layers of shit which I've already described;

I considered them unwitting but nonetheless close allies of
the second enemy, the Germans, and lastly SOE who were
taking a great interest in us since the concept had proved
itself. They were functioning in the Middle East, I believe
under the label of GR. They claimed that as the planning of
strategic operations behind enemy lines was their remit and no
one else's, L Detachment, which was after all a tiny unit which
could only "tease" the enemy, should logically be under their
aegis. I saw this as a classic case of escaping the frying pan only
to land in the fire and refused to submit to their blandishments,
arguing that I was under the direct command of the C-in-C and
that our prospects would be damaged if the planning of our
operations was carried out by staff officers unfamiliar with our
methods.

'The office I was expected to work from in MEHQ gave
me no privacy; I wouldn't be able to make a single move
without being overheard and I'd have to carry every scrap
of paper away with me each evening. I decided to move into
my brother's flat.'

To use the lack of privacy offered by MEHQ as an excuse
to use Peter's flat was perhaps less than honest. The flat, in
what was then known as the Garden City quarter of Cairo,
was opposite the British Embassy where Peter worked as a
diplomat. Peter was to *savoir-faire* what Shakespeare was to
English drama. Witty, sophisticated and dedicated to living
life to the full, he was a magnet to many like-minded transient
officers in Cairo.

The very spacious three-bedroomed, two-bathroomed apart-
ment with its sitting room and long hall was a cross between
banqueting venue, temporary barracks, spare equipment storage centre and dead-letter box. It was also said to boast the
finest telephone directory for the best-looking 'party girls' in
Cairo. The atmosphere was at once relaxed and chaotic. The
degree of occupancy was always uncertain but the occupants
were invariably 'of the right sort'.

To Peter Stirling, of course, this was home. In the past it

had been to brothers David and Bill a refuge from which to launch expeditions to the Gezira Club, Shepheard's Hotel or the racecourse. The major-domo responsible for cleaning, messing and general party arranging was Mohammed Aboudi, 'Mo', a Luxor-born Egyptian of remarkable presence and talent.

Before Mo would render service to any of Peter's friends, it was necessary for him to like them. He liked David, and David's servant, Guardsman MacDonald. Within a few days, Mo became Stirling's somewhat unconventional PA.

'He was far more efficient than anyone the army could have given me. He was very discreet and I had no hesitation in leaving maps, photographs and notes around the flat. I only had to tell Mo I wasn't home and no one would get past the front door. Possibly because his English was limited, he would not take no for an answer on the telephone. If someone hung up on him he would simply re-dial until he got an answer. He was quite happy to liaise directly with anyone in MEHQ; I used him to chase up ammunition, rations, vehicle spares, anything. He was like a terrier – I just used to tell him to use his own imagination to get things done and he did! MEHQ never complained to me. I don't know what they thought and I didn't care. The system worked and I never bothered to explain it to them.'

The flat was the scene for many a wild party and it was not unusual for the evening to culminate in a revolver shooting match between the Stirling brothers. Peter was generally reckoned the superior shot though David disputed this. Much of Mo's time was spent patching up bullet holes or re-hanging the only two pictures in the flat (framed cut-outs of King George VI and Queen Elizabeth) as a temporary concealment measure. He did not seem to mind; he loved the Stirling brothers. Not only were they great landowners in 'Scotchland', but David was also in the 'Scotchguards'.

Stirling was pleased with his successes to date, but thought them infinitesimal, considering the detachment's potential.

The war in North Africa was not going to last forever, but would go on through the islands, up the length of Italy and through France and Germany and he did not want his small force to vanish into obscurity with the closure of the desert campaign.

The opportunities exploited thus far in Africa could just as surely be turned to advantage against unprotected lines of communication, headquarter fortresses, and fuel and ammunition dumps in Italy and France. Stirling wanted to be ready for this, with targets already isolated. He realised that it was premature to make overtures to Auchinleck (who in any event, by Stirling's calculation, would probably not feature in the European war) but nonetheless, and it is a measure of his foresight, his notes of the time reflect that thinking. And when an offbeat opportunity arose Stirling had the mental flexibility to recognise it and seize the advantage.

Literally lounging in Alexandria was a group, almost squadron strength, of Free French parachutists, recently sent down from Syria where they had hung around for some time without either equipment or rôle. They were immensely frustrated – they had trained long and hard and wanted a crack at the German Army; indeed it was almost a passion. Here, then, were well-trained troops motivated and with nowhere to go! Would they join up with Stirling?

Very aware of the shortage of time before the Bouerat operation, Stirling went to Alexandria to meet the Frenchmen. His discussions were held with Captains Bergé and Jordan. Two more different personalities it is difficult to imagine. Bergé, the commander, was a Gascon, quick-witted, humorous and possessed of an unpredictable temper. Jordan was quiet, well-mannered and very precise. The one often spoke before he thought whilst the other never gave an opinion without careful consideration. Their dedication to the destruction of the Germans, however, was mutual and Stirling realised immediately that here he had potential recruits of excellent quality.

Stirling's French was more than adequate and Jordan's English was impeccable so there was no difficulty in understanding; both Bergé and Jordan were quick to indicate their acute interest in L Detachment's work and their willingness to soldier under Stirling's command. Language would not present an insurmountable problem if the mixing of patrols was kept to the minimum, operational tasks were carefully worked out and procedures well rehearsed. Stirling was elated – the next hurdle was to get official permission for the alliance.

Stirling realised that the greatest objection would come from the Commander of the Free French Forces rather than MEHQ. He was convinced that Auchinleck would put up no resistance provided that he had the necessary authority from the French. If, however, the middle levels of command and administration became involved the plan would be thwarted immediately; the answer was not to tell them at that stage. General de Gaulle was then in direct command of the Free French Forces. Stirling was quite prepared to meet with de Gaulle, but where was he? Time was of the essence. Local power resided with General Catroux, and an initially uncomfortable meeting took place in Cairo.

'Non. These soldiers are waiting to go back to France, they are not to fight here and certainly not under the command of the English.' Catroux was adamant.

'With my organisation they will operate in France and to good effect. We also intend to fight in your country. Here in Africa they can perfect their skills, gain experience against the German Army using tactics which will be very effective in France and furthermore they will not be sitting on their backsides which I can tell you they do not like.' Hard words from one strong man to another.

'They are already experienced. They are already trained and they *will* be going back to France very soon.' Immovable.

'You know they will not be going back to France for some time. I know they are highly trained. I know they are experienced. That's why I want them. They want to fight *now*. I can take them to the front. I need them. They *want* to come with me.' Equal immobility.

'Enough. They will not fight here or elsewhere under English command.' The final dismissal. Stirling, apparently calm, turned away muttering under his breath but just loud enough for Catroux to hear, 'Les sales Anglais. What about the auld alliance?'

Catroux reacted sharply 'What did you say?'

'I am not English. I am a Scot. What about our old alliance?'

Catroux laughed. Thus the ice was broken in a carefully calculated manner by Stirling. The day was won and consent was given for the French squadron to join forces with L Detachment.*

Within hours the Free French were at Kabrit, fully kitted out and undergoing L Detachment training. As trained parachutists the exercise hinged mainly around the use of the Lewes Bomb and the vulnerable points of aircraft, fuel dumps and the like. They were a hard bunch, many having undergone their own form of savage selection course in escaping from France and making their way through the Pyrenees or via Britain to Africa. Some of those individual journeys are epics of survival. It is not surprising that they fitted in so well with Stirling's men.

Stirling by now had taken steps to create a more solid identity for L Detachment.

As trained parachutists, they should have wings, but not the normal Airborne Forces wings. L Detachment was different

---

* In post-war years Stirling remembered the meeting as having been with General de Gaulle in Beirut. This is highly improbable. Records show that de Gaulle visited the Lebanon only twice during this period – between 25 July and 18 August 1941, which is too early, and between 12 August and 8 September 1942, by which time the French contingent was already working with the SAS. General Catroux, de Gaulle's second-in-command as far as the Free French were concerned, was moving frequently between Cairo and Beirut. When pressed, Stirling appreciated that his memory could be at fault; he had seen de Gaulle as the 'top of the tree', and it was always his policy to approach a problem at the pinnacle of power.

and should be seen to be so. They were from mixed regiments but as they were serving in their own unit they should have their own cap badge. Application to MEHQ for permission to design insignia met with a sharp written rebuff. L Detachment was simply that – a detachment, not a regiment – therefore the men would continue to wear the insignia of their own regiments. In typical Stirling fashion the offending letter was torn up and cast to the desert winds.

To Sergeant Bob Tait goes the credit for the design of badge and wings. The badge, now well-known, consists of a flaming sword (not a winged dagger) crossed at the base with the scrolled motto 'Who Dares Wins'; the wings owe their inspiration to a pharaonic device of similar shape and are depicted in Oxford and Cambridge blues. Stirling said:

'They were good designs with which I was entirely satisfied, and to hell with MEHQ, we were damned well going to wear them. The white berets were not a good idea – they provoked too much devilment and often resulted in scraps breaking out, and we could ill afford trouble at that stage. On the whole medals are good things but I wanted a mark of recognition within the unit as well as outside and, in consultation with Paddy Mayne and others, I decided that on completion of parachute training our recruits could wear the wings in the conventional manner on the shoulder. Those officers and soldiers who had completed two or three successful operations, I can't remember which, could wear the wings on their breasts. It added to the sense of pride and belonging which I thought so important to a special unit. It was a highly prized medal in its own right.

'MEHQ didn't like it one little bit but I ignored them. In fact General Auchinleck admired them the first time he saw them (at Shepheard's I think). Anyway, I wore them to his office thereafter, he never objected and that was enough for me. I took that as the official blessing, the stuffy beggars in the Adjutant-General's office could live up to their reputation and really get stuffed. I think that was the day the SAS was truly born. Success and an accepted identity of which we could all be proud. What more could a unit want – traditions? The only relevant thing about traditions is that they take an age to test and season. I am probably guilty of the fact that so many of those L Detachment men were under-decorated, but I can tell you that they took as much pride in having those wings on their chests as they would have in any medal. It was mark of respect and recognition of one of our own.'*

Planning was well advanced and it had been arranged that the RAF would hold off a planned bombing raid on Bouerat until the night of 24/25 January. It was therefore critical that the SAS strike by the night before at the latest. It was imperative that Stirling return to Jalo Oasis as soon as possible to fine tune the planning and preparation.

At this point Stirling had to make another difficult decision. He had always had it in mind that Jock Lewes would take over the recruiting and training based on Kabrit. Jock was dead – who could fill the gap? Here Stirling made one of his rare wartime mistakes. He appointed Paddy Mayne.

'It was a bloody stupid thing to do but you must remember that we were just getting to know each other. What I had seen and heard of Paddy demonstrated a most remarkable officer and leader, courageous to an incredible degree and with the most remarkable battlefield intuition; those who had operated with him were devoted to him. He had taken to SAS soldiering like a duck to water. Surely this was a man who would inspire recruits and exact the highest training standards.

'I should have known from his reaction when I faced him with the task. I was as diplomatic as possible, pointing out that there was nothing personal and that I felt I was acting in the best overall interests of the SAS, appointing the best officer in the unit to secure its longevity through the officers and men he would be recruiting and training. Paddy didn't

---

* Like Stirling I shall use the term SAS rather than L Detachment from this point. Though it is not strictly accurate, Stirling and his men had adopted the title anyway and used it in normal conversation.

lose his temper – he went icy cold and practically accused me of leaving him behind so that I could overtake his "bag" of aircraft. He reminded me of our first meeting when I'd told him that he would be joining me to fight the enemy. I told him that it would be a temporary measure only – until Bouerat was finished – then we'd have more men and we could get properly organised.

'In the end he accepted the decision but not with good grace; he informed me in a somewhat ominous voice that he'd do his best. I left him with some misgivings. Fortunately, by that time we had secured the services of a most marvellous Sapper, Bill Cumper, a very likeable and professional chap. He took on all the explosives training and improved our techniques tremendously. He also had the happy knack of getting on amazingly well with our new French contingent.'

By this time Stirling was beginning to get reasonable support from the Air Reconnaissance Unit (ARU) at MEHQ; a support engendered by his charm and enthusiasm rather than by the edict of staff officers. Critical to the Bouerat raid was the positioning of the enemy fuel storage tanks and bowsers. It may seem strange to those who have never worked in the desert but on a jet-black night when no shadows were cast, it was quite feasible to pass within yards of buildings, trucks and the like without having the least inkling of their presence.

Peter Oldfield, then in charge of the ARU, and a willing convert to Stirlingism (he later joined the SAS) undertook to transmit the latest results of air photography to Stirling by radio before 21 January, the critical date if the raid was to take place before the bombing run. With this firmly agreed, Stirling returned to Jalo.

Stirling knew that the presence of tankers would be largely a matter of luck as they stayed in port for the shortest possible time and their movements were, according to intelligence, unpredictable. Even so, Bouerat was a viable target as fuel had to be stored there in some manner. He still needed to attack a target which was not solely linked to airfields in order to implant and maintain the idea that the SAS was capable of attacking a wide range of facilities.

Within the SAS there was little expertise with regard to waterborne operations and sub-surface mining of vessels, and tankers could well be moored offshore at Bouerat. Stirling turned to the Special Boat Section for assistance. Captain Duncan and Corporal Barr arrived at Jalo about 13 January with their folboats. Compared to today's canoes the folboat was a beast. A complicated device consisting of rubberised canvas and an assortment of wooden struts, it was the very devil to carry and had a mind of its own when the time came to assemble it quietly in the dead of night. Once in the water it was clumsy and unpredictable if not in the hands of experts; Duncan and Barr were well used to the folboat and Stirling had utter confidence in them.

Bouerat lay to the west of Sirte and Tamet, so the ground between the target area and Jalo was familiar to the raiding party which set forth on 17 January. The LRDG escort, commanded by Captain Hunter, was guided by the eminently capable Mike Sadler, veteran, almost legendary desert navigator. As the routes had been used before, the group decided to lay off to the south as far as possible in case the area was part of an air surveillance pattern due to the attacks on Sirte and Tamit. They would then enter the Wadi Tamit at a suitable point and use it for much of the covered approach to the target area.

In North Africa a journey across the desert poses many problems. There are occasions when it is almost like travelling along a tarmacadam road and good speed is possible. Without warning the terrain can change to a boulder-strewn moonscape which tears at the vitals of vehicles, threatening half-shafts and sumps. From this it is not inconceivable to slip into soft sand covered by a deceptively solid-looking hard crust which suddenly leaves a truck belly-down and immovable without strenuous physical labour.

Punctures are common and with the lengthy repair times of these and other mechanical ailments, it would be hard to guarantee more than eighty to a hundred miles in a long day. Always there is the sand. Sand thrown up by the vehicles in front choking throats, weapons and air intakes. Sand which without warning is whipped up by a sudden storm and hurled abrasively against any surface be it human skin or metallic. Add to this the constant threat of air reconnaissance and attack and it will be seen that there was little romance in wartime desert travel in daylight.

By contrast the desert nights can be a wonder. For the amateur astronomer there is the fantastic panorama of stars presented by crystal clear nights. From the staggeringly debilitating heat of the day the body can be subjected to often sub-zero temperatures. There is, however, a strange peace about a desert night. Not the total silence that would be expected in the sandy wastes, for the desert is alive. The ever-present flies of the day slumber in crevices whilst the night creatures take over. Gentle warblings and strange clickings can be heard leaving the shape and form of the perpetrators to the imagination. Shifting sand makes hypnotic creakings as the temperature changes and body and vehicle weights settle. Above all is the feeling of man's sheer insignificance in the order of things, a mere pinhead in the vastness. But the night does bring peace to the raider and the quiet blankets each man's thoughts and fears of tomorrow from the other.

The Wadi Tamit was reached at nightfall on 22 January and Stirling had received no confirmation of air photograph interpretation from Oldfield. He was anxious, not because he was unsure of finding some kind of worthwhile target, but because he wanted to make sure that the SAS success was total. With Hunter he decided, against all normal rules, that they would break radio silence. The area, having been attacked before and having great strategic significance to Rommel, was known to have excellent radio direction-finding facilities. Contact was made and the raiders were told to expect details the next day. It was cutting things fine.

Dawn broke to reveal the paucity of cover on the brink of

Wadi Tamit and the route to the wadi bottom was precipitous.
If the radio interchange had been detected there was a very
real threat that the enemy would put up air reconnaissance
flights. Undesirable as it was Stirling and Hunter decided to
risk dropping into the wadi at that point and take cover rather
than move along the escarpment looking for an easier route
and risk being caught in the open by strafing fighter aircraft.
It was not unusual for the LRDG and SAS to face difficult
descents and ascents but the drop into Wadi Tamit caused
particular problems.

Extremely fit and physically very powerful, Reg Seekings,
ex-Brigade of Guards and one of Stirling's first recruits, was
a key part of the Bouerat operation. In a chronicle made
available by Stirling, he takes up the tale:

> It was a precarious point to get down into the wadi. All
> the trucks were lined up along the edge with bonnets facing
> downwards. [It was obviously decided that it made sense to get
> all vehicles down at the same time in the interests of speed. It
> also indicates that the cliff really was difficult otherwise surely
> they would have gone in line down the easiest route.]
> Tow ropes were fastened to the back of each truck. The
> driver stayed in the vehicle, two men were in position to check
> the front wheels and the rest hung on to the tow ropes for dear
> life to try to slow it down. My vehicle hadn't gone far when
> the back end started to swing. The driver didn't bail out –
> he put his foot down hard. The vehicle straightened and he
> went down at a hell of a speed. He must have had real nerve
> because he kept control and got it safely to the bottom.
> We got to the bottom none too soon. An Italian plane
> skimmed the wadi edge and it had us spotted. I was behind
> some large rocks which suddenly became the size of peas. Our
> driver got into the truck to move it but a pair of pants had
> been hung over the radiator and got caught in the fan so he
> gave it up as a bad job and took shelter with the rest of us.

As the plane left the trucks dispersed along the wadi and
took shelter as they could. They were lucky. The wadi at
that point had many little overhangs and caves but they were

fortunate to survive the five or six hours of blind bombing and strafing which followed. It was just before last light that they regrouped to bad news. The radio truck and operators were missing and were never heard of again.

Stirling, though upset by the loss of men and communications was philosophical. 'Losing men is always hard, one never got used to it, but we had to press on. I accepted that there would be no intelligence confirmation of the fuel dumps and that we should just have to search and hope to strike lucky. We stopped at the point which Hunter (good chap) decided would make the best rendezvous and we checked weapons. I decided, having seen how bloody the folboat could be to assemble, to have it put together there and then. Not a good idea as it turned out.'

The convoy travelled at first with low lights and then in total darkness as the target got nearer. As they had been spotted it was more than probable that Bouerat would be alert and there may be outlying mobile and static patrols. A few miles before they were due to take leave of the vehicles the one carrying the assembled folboat struck a boulder or a pothole and the shock smashed the boat beyond repair.

'I was not a happy man. No communications and now no boat. I thought about it briefly. There would still be worthwhile targets and, of course, one couldn't possibly write off a situation without first looking at it. I certainly couldn't predict what I'd find. There may have been a rowing boat or something we could use just waiting for us. This made it easy for me to take Duncan and Barr along – I'd have found it hard to deny them anyway. I asked Duncan to take a few chaps and go for the wireless station which we knew from air photographs was only a few miles up the coast. I think he was quite pleased even though he had the furthest to go and would have to wait until the following night to be picked up.'

Precise navigation in the desert on foot is extremely difficult especially on a moonless night and when speed is of the essence. Though the early SAS men developed a very accurate 'ground feel' and good memories for areas they had already travelled through it was necessary to cater for mishap. Usually RVs were selected along a track line and the point at which to turn off would be indicated by a branch, twigs or a heap of rocks. These were unlikely to be noticed by the enemy and the system invariably worked.

It was late when Stirling's group arrived at the target and he split his force into two groups; one under Sergeant Pat Riley, one with himself. Stirling's instructions were to work inwards from opposite sides of the harbour, place bombs with lessening time fuses on whatever targets were available then make for the RV. Bombs should be calculated to detonate as close as possible to 0200 hours. On no account were weapons to be used except in emergency. Stirling's party reached the pier by taking a route along the edge of the beach; they neither saw nor heard any sign of sentries or patrols. Great was his disappointment when he realised that there were no tankers in the harbour. Perhaps this was why there was no one around; it was probably hard work offloading the tankers and no doubt whatever force was committed to Bouerat felt inclined to get their heads down.

'It was a strange, eerie situation. Total silence which in itself was uncanny. Great storehouses on each side of us as we left the pier end. We entered them all without any problems, conscious of the noise we were making as we pushed doors open. I remember one storehouse with a large piece of important-looking machinery in it, it could have been pumping gear I suppose. We placed bombs everywhere; on the pumping machine, crates of rations and what looked like boxes of aircraft or tank parts. In the last of the big buildings I told my chaps to stay where they were and went out to see what else was around. As soon as I got out I heard someone coming.'

Pat Riley's party had a similar experience. 'We found an assortment of buildings stocked with rations and crates of spare parts. We placed our Lewes Bombs as instructed and moved out of the buildings to quarter the area we had been given but came hard up against barbed wire. It could have been the perimeter and the last thing we wanted to do was bump a guard post or a prowling sentry. I reversed the direction and we moved over to another set of warehouse-type buildings. Just as we were making our way to what seemed to be the door I heard someone coming out. Before I could move I bumped into him. It was Major Stirling. Good thing neither of us was trigger-happy!'

'What the bloody hell are you doing here? This is my end of the business,' Stirling snapped, obviously relieved it was not the enemy. He still wanted an entirely uncompromised operation. On hearing Riley's explanation the groups reorganised and set off in opposite directions. Stirling took a course close to the road in the hope of stumbling over an underground petrol store. They had covered sufficient ground for him to begin to think that they were out of luck when Seekings, who had a phenomenal ability to smell petrol (an odour he detested), pointed out some vague shapes dimly silhouetted against the darkness.

The delighted team soon found themselves in the midst of what appeared to be dozens of huge fuel tankers. What a godsend. Within seconds they were placing their bombs, time fuses now set for under an hour. Whilst bending down to lay one of his bombs, Stirling again became conscious of movement. Slowly straightening up he again bumped into the second presence. Riley again! This time both men were hard pressed not to let out loud guffaws of laughter. Placing bombs is a tense business at the best of times. Fuses can be unpredictable and there is, inevitably, a moment when 'the rectum gives a distinct twitch'. There is always the knowledge that whilst concentrating on this deadly business a man cannot look around or listen properly for the approach of a stealthy sentry. Stirling and Riley, on recognising each other, must have felt immense relief. It speaks highly of SAS self-discipline that neither man fired his weapon.

Stirling decided to have the last word: 'I'm glad you've learned the art of moving quietly, Sergeant Riley.' The tone was acid but Stirling's tongue was pressed firmly into his cheek. 'We'll stay together from now on, we don't want to shoot each other.' The RV was reached with no problems and it was with great satisfaction that the party later felt the tremors of the explosions and watched the desert sky turn red with the flames of burning petrol turning to dense, black smoke as dawn broke. Duncan, Barr and Rose were collected from the RV the next night. They had successfully blown up the radio station, though not without difficulties. Unlike Stirling's group they had had to contend with sentries which slowed them down considerably.

Pat Riley takes up the tale. 'After we had picked up [Duncan's] party, Major Stirling decided that as he had never actually seen one of the bombs detonate, since we were always some miles away at those moments, it might be fun to watch one. He decided we could follow the road for a while and we might find 'something worthwhile'. It was crazy really, we should have been long gone into the desert, but no one cared to argue – he was that sort of man.

'I reckon we drove for twenty miles or so before we spotted a big vehicle slotted into a sort of cut-away alongside the road. We coasted to a halt and Major Stirling took someone with him to have a closer look. It was a fuel tanker and it looked as though it had been abandoned. Major David thought it was just right for the job in hand and said he would lay on a demonstration for the LRDG; I knew it was for himself! Major Stirling went forward with Reg to lay the bomb. The crazy beggar put it on with a ten-second fuse. We all took cover but nothing happened.

'Then Major S. and Reg went back and picked the damned bomb up just as the time pencil decided to go into action. The bomb was dropped and they took great dives across the road and down the bank as the bomb went off with a ruddy great bang. It then got hilarious – out of the cab jumped this Eyetie driver. No boots and no trousers either. Somebody fired his gun, into the air I think, and the poor bugger saw us and ran forward to surrender to Reg. I'm surprised he didn't die of fright. There wasn't a man amongst us under six foot two, all with dirty, matted beards and bulging with warm clothes.

'Unknown to us the CO had gone back to the truck with another bomb on a ten-second fuse and when he shouted "Take cover" it took less than a second. Major Stirling got his wish though, that truck burned beautifully. I think the Eytie legged it into the night. He was of no worry to us as we were pulling out anyway, or so I thought. It seemed we were to go a little further to see what was about.'

It was almost Stirling's undoing. The party ran into an ambush a little further on which they were very lucky to survive. 'Flash' Gibson, driving Stirling's vehicle, chose either not to hear or to ignore the order to turn off the road. He accelerated through the ambush and turned off some distance later. Reg Seekings and Johnny Cooper put down a withering hail of small-arms fire as they roared through the ambush and all parties agree that they should have been killed by the laws of firepower against them. Gibson's action undoubtedly saved the day. (He was later awarded the Military Medal.) The RV with the remainder of the group was reached without further incident.

Although Bouerat was a relatively small operation compared with what was to come, it had enhanced the reputation of the SAS significantly and proved a number of things. The men taking part had been 'turned around' and put back into action in a remarkably short time. They were not now purely associated with aircraft and airfields. The co-operation of the LRDG had proven the vehicle-borne approach concept. Working without communications, Stirling had demonstrated total flexibility. Not an iota of explosive or ammunition had been wasted, neither had one operation compromised another closely adjacent one, i.e. Bouerat and the nearby wireless station. The group had survived an air search and bombing operation by an enemy who knew for certain that they were in the area. Against the devastation they had wreaked on the enemy's desperately needed fuel reserves there had been only three casualties – the three radio operators – and even they might still be alive.

When Stirling was finally back in communication with MEHQ
he found that the war in North Africa had taken a turn for the
worse. Rommel, far from being backed against a wall and on
the verge of defeat, had counter-attacked with skill and vigour.
Not only had he retaken Benghazi but he had won ground along
the whole length of Cyrenaica and now threatened the 8th Army
which was in defence around the Gazala area. Stirling had never
intended the SAS to rest on its laurels but the situation decided
him to act on an idea which had been turning in his mind since
he had walked so easily along the harbour frontage of Bouerat.
The SAS would attack Benghazi and all airfields in that area.
He returned to Kabrit with a light heart.

# 9

# THE FRUITS OF ENDEAVOUR

Stirling did not, however, underestimate the difficulties of his position. He had proved to himself that harbour attacks were feasible – but, through no fault of his own, he had not destroyed any shipping at Bouerat. He had to persuade MEHQ that an attack on Benghazi was feasible and that it would not mean a suicide mission for the SAS. So far he had not had access to air photographs or intelligence reports of the town; he knew of no one with first-hand knowledge. He had to arm himself with basic geographic facts before approaching General Auchinleck. He decided to discuss the idea with Paddy Mayne at Kabrit.

Stirling was appalled to find Mayne morose and resentful. He knew little of what was going on regarding the training of the French and other recruits and seemed to care even less.

'I realised at once what a dreadful mistake I had made in committing this superb soldier to a training and administrative rôle. He had withdrawn into himself and left his tent only when necessary. His conversation was desultory – he spoke in monosyllables and didn't even look me in the eye. He was not the Mayne of a few weeks earlier. He had become thoroughly bored with administrative minutiae and infuriated with the red tape and stubbornness of MEHQ. In retrospect I'm amazed that he didn't let fly at a staff officer – a measure of

a self-discipline witnessed by few people. He wanted the SAS
to succeed but he wanted also to do his bit at the front end.
I suppose that was when I first began to get an understanding
of Paddy.

'I don't think I had realised until then just how close Paddy
had been to Eoin McGonigal or what the relationship had been.
McGonigal, of course, had been lost on the first operation and
we could only presume the worst had happened. McGonigal
had been a friend of Paddy's before the war [as had the
whole McGonigal family] and knew something of his inner
frustrations and, because of this, Paddy was able to relax
totally with him. Perhaps due to the family friendship, Paddy
also felt in some way responsible for Eoin, yes, I'm sure there
was a little of that.

'Later I came to realise just what strange forces were working
away in Paddy's mind. I can remember talking him to him in
the mess about the pre-war days and our families; Paddy had
reluctantly forgiven me for being a Roman Catholic and the
progeny of a landowning family (being Scottish helped a little).
I told him about my bitter disappointment when my art teacher
had told me I was wasting my time, and related how the intense
frustration had led me into taking up the challenge of climbing
Everest.

'Paddy was by then quite drunk and pretty maudlin, but
he suddenly came to life, and I realised that here was a
man suffering from an equal, if not greater frustration, as
his subconscious need to create searched for an outlet. I
suddenly had the explanation to his deep depressions which
led to the drinking sessions and also, I think, to the violence
of which Paddy was capable in action. I am sure this is correct
because it also explained the reverse side of him.

'He was an instinctive leader in battle; his intuition regarding
ground, tactics and situations was infallible. He had the knack
of touching exactly the right chord in each of his men; these
were things he never had to think about – they were there, just
waiting to come out. And, of course, he was as brave as a lion.

If he had fears, and he confessed that he had, they were well hidden. It was as though he had some sort of blockage when faced with having to sit and deliberately plan something; as though he had no confidence in his abilities and his mind would become blank if called upon to untangle administrative needs. The more he tried to cope with them the greater the blockage would become and then the frustrations would take over. I believe that Eoin McGonigal had known all this and was able to communicate with Paddy on a different level. Paddy had to be kept away from those irksome responsibilities of command which would have infuriated him, lessened his effectiveness in the field and led to impossible situations. He had to be committed to the front line, where he was the finest soldier I ever met.

'He gave me something too, you know, I was afraid – on many occasions. I've little doubt that we all were from time to time, but the secret and perhaps the hardest thing of all is to control that fear. With someone like Paddy in competition, and we were competitive, there was little danger of fear taking over. It was also a great help to know that Paddy understood my many absences from the mess after operations. The unit would be carousing together whilst I was back in Cairo doing my damnedest to make sure that we survived, getting supplies sorted out and obtaining clearance for the next set of ops. He saw the necessity for this and was intensely relieved that I never again used him in that area. It is interesting that after I was captured and the SAS was fighting in Europe there came a period when disbandment looked likely and Paddy did take up the cudgels with the bureaucrats in a very resourceful way.'

Stirling was quick to undo his mistake in leaving Mayne at Kabrit. Mayne remains something of an enigma. Setting aside his black depressions he could be a most convivial drinking companion, with a great sense of humour. Stories of his evenings in the Kabrit mess are legion and well recorded elsewhere, but Pat Riley passed on two tales which show yet other facets of this remarkable man:

'I came across him once when he had been drinking and he was taking to task a person who had upset him, setting about him in such a way that I thought he was going to do him serious damage. Without thinking too much I laid one on him and knocked him down. It was when I saw him on the floor that I thought I was in for a rough time. Not a bit of it. He stood up, looked at me for a while and then quietly went off.

'He was always concerned about his men. Dave Kershaw was a good example. Dave and Paddy were playing cards one night, Dave had some back pay and he loved his cards. He was losing heavily and pretty soon he was down about sixty quid – a lot of money then. Paddy asked Dave how much he was going to send home to his wife and Dave said, "Not very much at this rate". Paddy stopped the game, handed him a fiver and told him that when he proved that his wife had received it he would give him the rest to send home. He did as well!'

It was Pat Riley, then Sergeant-Major, to whom Stirling then gave the job of training supervisor and recruiter.

'Pat Riley was far from happy with the decision but I could not have selected a better man. He had been into the thick of it with the Commandos, had been on all our operations and loved the SAS. He did a superb job for which I will always be grateful. The French were about half way through their training and would not be ready for the next operation but there was a number of other recruits, so things were looking quite hopeful – no shortage of volunteers but the pass rate wasn't high. Certainly Riley didn't drop any standards though.

'It was a bit of shock to find that we'd lost Bill Cumper. Apparently, with the eternal wisdom of that mediocre MEHQ freemasonry they'd sent him to supervise the engineering works at a bloody hospital. Imagine that, the best and most ingenious explosives man we had was now fitting toilet seats in Alexandria. I soon got that sorted out. I had him located and asked him to join the SAS formally – forget the course, we needed him; he did so and then he was safe with us. He did all the training as far as I can remember in between running sabotage courses, and soon he took part in operations.'

Stirling, having sorted out his immediate Kabrit problems and found Mayne as enthusiastic as himself about the Benghazi raid, set out to educate himself about the target area. He had time on his side; it was going to be about ten days into March before the next moonless phase. Auchinleck was resisting pressure from Winston Churchill to make an advance against the German Army. Churchill was determined to force him into early action, but he was equally determined not to move until his reserves of equipment and manpower had been built up to what he considered a sufficiency to ensure success.

On learning this Stirling decided that he should not limit himself to the town and harbour of Benghazi. There was a significant number of airfields in the area and it seemed sensible to hit as many as possible. Close to Benghazi were Berka and Benina, with Slonta and Barce lying due northeast. They would send a patrol to each target with his (Stirling's) also taking a look at Benghazi. Whatever the outcome, and there would surely be some success, a strike in that area could only assist Auchinleck in a material way and demonstrate to Churchill that the war was not stagnating.

Stirling discovered the existence in MEHQ of detailed ground models of the town of Benghazi and also managed to recruit Gordon Alston from the Middle East Commando – Alston had actually been in the town as an intelligence officer. His knowledge of the target built up and he secured the volunteer services of Captain Ken Allot and Lieutenant David Sutherland of the Special Boat Section. The team was completed by Bob Melot, an Arabic linguist, and two Senussi soldiers who 'may be useful for recce purposes'. After being obliged to leave Jalo, the LRDG had set up a rear base at Siwa Oasis, a much more attractive proposition than Jalo. On the edge of the Qattara Depression, Siwa was almost luxurious by comparison. It was possible to enjoy a relaxing swim, pick dates from the many palms and generally enjoy some greenery after the yellow-brown wastes of the desert.

Stirling was now the proud possessor of his own 'Blitz Buggy' which he had 'liberated' in a somewhat devious fashion in Cairo where it 'seemed to have no real purpose in life'. It was a Ford V8 utility car which had undergone radical engine tuning and could be adapted to resemble a German staff car. Large and powerful, with the roof and sides removed it could hold a crew of six along with basic equipment and explosives. The boot space was modified so as to take the mounting for twin Vickers K machine guns and extra petrol, and a single Vickers K at the front completed the armament. Both guns could be removed quickly and hidden on the floor of the car.

The whole thing was finished off in a dark, matt grey highlighted with German recognition symbols (these signs, designed to aid identification from the air, were changed every calendar month by the Luftwaffe). Stirling hoped there would be occasions when such 'Q' cars could be used on enemy-held roads behind the lines. A genuine captured German car completed the SAS fleet of vehicles. As they set out on 15 March 1942, the rest of the SAS contingent was ensconced in LRDG vehicles under Lieutenant John Olivey.

The target area was approximately 380 miles away and the going was good until the Trig El Abd was reached. The Trig El Abd is a centuries-old track originally laid by camel caravans; it is rutted and covers a wide area and the going is good. The Germans and Italians, realising its value as a means of navigation and speedy movement, had seeded great patches with Thermos mines. LRDG and SAS alike distrusted the 'Trig' and rarely travelled along it; they used it as a navigational marker when adopting the 'off line' or 'deliberate error' techniques mentioned earlier. Nonetheless it had to be crossed on the move to Benghazi. For once their luck was out and the German staff car commanded by Sutherland hit a mine which resulted in an injury to Sutherland's arm; he was dispatched back to Siwa courtesy of the LRDG.

The ground out from Benghazi and the coast in the sector Stirling had chosen was tactically excellent for approach and observation purposes. The foothills undulating downwards and coastwards from the Jebel were sufficiently high to benefit from light rain and heavy early morning dews, making them more fertile. Water means shrubs and shrubs mean cover. Unfortunately vegetation also attracts humans and their flocks of sheep and goats. This was (and is) a Bedouin and Senussi area. The Bedouin tended to let well alone and held allegiance to no other nationality although they could be bribeable; the Senussi on the other hand were passionately anti-Italian and had no love for the Germans. On the whole they were guardedly trusted by the LRDG and SAS as a source of information and sometimes food. A freshly slaughtered sheep can be a great morale booster to a patrol which has lived on army rations for a few weeks.

From a rendezvous point within this 'friendly' environment Mayne departed with his small patrol to raid Berka airfield. The two Senussi soldiers brought along by Melot were sent to carry out a reconnaissance of the main road between Benghazi and Regima. On their return the next day they reported the road to be clear of blocks and check points and, embarking in the Blitz Buggy, Stirling's patrol was under way at last and headed for Benghazi. As they left the words of the MEHQ pundits were ringing in Stirling's ears; 'suicidal', 'brainless', 'sheer fantasy'. They would soon see.

Stirling knew from air photographs that the harbour area was wired off and there was every reason to suspect that it was patrolled. He had originally decided to get as close to the harbour as he could by simply driving through the perimeter gate. On the fast journey down the Regima road he changed his mind. They would find a place short of the wire where they could hide the car, launch the folboat from a point outside the perimeter and navigate round the end of it to attack the tankers. This would prevent the enemy from sealing the road and halting the car on its exfiltration journey if anything went wrong. A suitable hiding place was found within three quarters of a mile of the quay. Leaving a couple of men to camouflage the car and guard it until his return, Stirling took Allot and the SBS party to the quay.

What happened from then on was an acute disappointment. The party reached the waterfront without problem. They simply walked quite openly through the darkened side streets. They encountered nothing by way of enemy except a drunken Italian who ignored them. When they reached the water it was obvious that a launch was going to be difficult but Stirling decided to try for it. This time the folboat had been kept in its webbing pack until the last minute, and had been treated with more care than a case of eggs.

'The bloody thing was useless. Allot was desperately trying to fix the damned thing together and I was urging him to get a bloody move on but the two ends of the frame just would not marry up. I swore then that we'd find something to replace that idiotic device.'

It is probable that even if the folboat had performed correctly they would have been unable to launch as the wind was whipping up creating very large waves against the quayside and the folboat is difficult to handle under the best of conditions. They packed up the canoe and returned to Cooper and Seekings at the car, who had also had an uneventful time. Stirling decided that it would not be wise to show that they had been into Benghazi by leaving explosives on targets which would give the enemy no real problem. He intended to come back.

To fill in the few days before Mayne and the others were due back at the RV, Stirling's party carried out reconnaissance patrols, principally on the Benina airfield, which were to stand them in good stead. On one occasion they were able to blow up a small munitions dump, but more importantly, he ascertained that Benina was a main repair facility, and though it was heavily guarded they knew the way in.

The others arrived back at the RV on time. Apart from Mayne, they had had no more success than Stirling. Slonta airfield had been too heavily guarded for access; Fraser, raiding

Barce, had managed to destroy only one aircraft and some vehicles; Alston had been unable to locate his target at Berka main airfield. Mayne, however, reported with a huge grin that he had taken care of fifteen aircraft on the satellite strip just outside Berka.

Stirling returned to Kabrit to take stock. The French were approaching the end of their training and could probably be committed to operations in early April. His SAS reinforcements were growing with the completion of each course. Riley had done a superb job of recruiting and training and Stirling congratulated him – Riley wanted to get back to operations, but was prevailed upon to wait a while. The SAS still had to prove themselves against waterborne targets in harbours and this Stirling took to be his priority task. On both occasions he had been let down by unsuitable equipment; he did not have the time to get personally involved in the search for suitable boats and he thought of Fitzroy Maclean, who had completed his SAS training.

This most remarkable soldier had been seduced into joining the SAS because Stirling had said that 'it was a good thing to be in'. Not that he needed second urgings; he was interested in the concept, had known Stirling before the war and was excited by the opportunities. Maclean was briefed on the problem, told that he would be taking part in the next operation and invited to find the right equipment and become familiar with it. The parameters for the boat were simple. It had to be as light as possible, stow into the smallest possible space, be robust and easily assembled and 'IT HAD TO BLOODY WELL WORK!' Without a significant success this could be the last chance for the SAS to take a crack at a harbour.

Fitzroy Maclean's arrival at the Kabrit camp was typically unceremonious. Arriving after dark he was handed into the care of Guardsman Duncan, a dour Scot from Aberdeen. He found an empty tent for Maclean expressing dismal regret that the previous occupant would appear to have no further use for it. Early the next morning Maclean was disturbed by a dirty, dishevelled, bearded figure who announced sardonically that it was his tent. This turned out to be Bill Fraser who had just returned from his two-hundred-mile walk across the desert after the Marble Arch raid.

Maclean eventually solved the boat problem by obtaining two reconnaissance craft which were on the equipment scale for the Royal Engineers. Small, dark-coloured and reasonably lightweight these boats were inflated by hand bellows in a fairly short if noisy space of time. They had just sufficient capacity to hold two men, their personal weapons and some limpet mines. This was as good as they were going to get, the next thing was practice. The make up of patrols for the next Benghazi operation was to be Stirling, Alston, Maclean, Seekings, Cooper and Rose. The boat crews were to be Stirling and Cooper and Maclean and Seekings.

Stirling, Seekings and Cooper were almost inseparable in the operational sense. It is probable that both men accompanied Stirling on all his operations and both were immensely fond of him. Cooper was the youngest of the originals and was still a teenager when he went on his first operation. It is doubtful if anyone younger has ever joined the SAS. He and Seekings formed an impressive team; good friends, they spent much of their leisure time together. Stirling's opinion of them was extremely high:

'They were utterly dependable and there was an almost intuitive rapport between them. A marvellous team, they could laugh easily regardless of the circumstances. I interrupted their rest on a number of occasions in Cairo. When I happened to be using Peter's flat and needed things doing I'm afraid it was often Seekings and Cooper who were telephoned. Paddy Mayne and I would study the intelligence reports and photographs and decide our next jolly and then we'd hand over all the details to the pair of them.

'They would be left to calculate things like petrol, ammunition and ration requirements and then liaise with Riley to decide if any sort of 'top-up' training was necessary. As far as I know they never got it wrong – they took a lot of the boring administrative stuff off my shoulders.'

The Great Salt Bitter Lake became the SAS training ground and night after night shadowy figures could be seen sneaking the boats down to the water's edge. Various methods of muffling the sound of inflation were tried but nothing could hide the distinctive wheezing of the hand bellows. There was every chance, based on experience, that the normal harbour noises of lapping water and floating tin cans and other garbage would hide the sound, so no one worried too much. Their boatmanship improved dramatically and soon they were able to paddle the small craft in relatively straight lines with the minimum of paddle noise on the blackest of nights. It would be nice to have a real try out against alert sentries.

Using the Blitz Buggy, still covered in its German look-alike paint and recognition insignia, the group set out one dark night for Suez where they were admitted into the dock by a guard who, if not alerted by the strange vehicle, should have been alarmed by the men's strange clothing. 'God, if the Germans had had a unit the same as ours they'd have had even less trouble than we did in getting on to enemy installations.' Later in the war, of course, Otto Skorzeny was to copy Stirling and do just that.

At the waterside the boats were unpacked and inflation began.

'What are you blokes on then?' asked a friendly passing gunner.

'Never you fucking mind. Fuck off.'

'All right.' Miffed. 'Didn't mean anything.' Hadn't they had similar experiences with Italian personnel in situations where an enemy presence was not suspected?

In exact rehearsal for the forthcoming operation Stirling and Cooper took one boat, Maclean and Seekings the other. Leaving the remainder on guard by the Blitz Buggy they homed in across the far from still waters on their target – Royal Navy vessels!

'We learned a lot on that trip. It took us longer than we thought and it was difficult to maintain bearings when the little boat kept dipping low into the troughs and we lost sight of the lights. It would be even more difficult if the enemy tankers weren't showing harbour lights. It was also quite hard to hang on to the ships' lines and keep the craft steady whilst one laid the limpets. The noise over the water when the magnet connected sounded loud enough to wake the dead but the crews didn't seem to notice anything.' Stirling's experience gave him confidence in the boat and he felt easier about the coming raid.

Both parties were successful and after clearing away, still acting cautiously and tactically, they made good their exit before contacting the expectedly angry Port Authority. Now both the RAF and the Royal Navy had been offended by 'unfair actions'. The SAS was not gaining popularity. The chosen group was under strict orders not to confide in anyone the details of the forthcoming raid, not even their closest SAS comrades. If it were successful, Stirling wanted the most dramatic effect when it was reported.

At this point Stirling broke one of his own strict rules. Randolph Churchill, who had reacquainted himself with Stirling during 8 Commando's journey out from England, desperately wanted to be a member of the SAS and approached Stirling, who was not happy with him.

'He wasn't a popular man with soldiers, or most officers for that matter. He really could talk the most awful nonsense about the war and tactics. He was also a rather chubby fellow. He was so persistent that I eventually allowed him to do a parachute jump. I reckoned that would put him off and not leave him feeling too aggrieved. Remember that his father was by then Prime Minister and it was well known that Randolph wrote to him daily and made no secret about the contents of his father's return letters which were hardly couched in terms of good security. It would be as well to keep him on side for the time being. In fact I accompanied him on his first jump which was quite out of character for me. I found the whole business of leaping out of aeroplanes most unpleasant. There was also a little of the devil in me at the time – it would be good to get a few pounds off his portly midriff.

'I remember the jump well. It has been said that he bribed the despatcher to kick him out if he got cold feet but I didn't hear that until some time later so I don't know if it is true, it would be in character – he didn't lack the courage to let people know he was scared. At least he didn't cry, that would have been the last straw. He jumped right after me and as he passed me he shouted that he was glad the bloody thing had opened. I took a perverse pleasure in pointing out that he would be on the ground long before me.

'He had quite a hard landing and claimed that his parachute was faulty. Of course it wasn't, he was just too bloody fat. If I'd hoped that would be the end of it I was wrong. The trouble was, Randolph wasn't really interested in joining the SAS to fight the Germans, though as I said he didn't lack courage; he wanted the insignia. He would wear whatever badge and rank seemed the most appropriate at the time for getting the best out of a situation and no doubt a SAS badge and wings would have suited him admirably from time to time.'

Stirling could not remember what exactly persuaded him to break his rule about taking men on operations before they had been fully trained. There seems little doubt that Churchill would have failed; even if he had survived the physical aspects of the course it is unlikely that his loose security and generally disruptive behaviour would have passed the scrutiny of Sergeant-Major Riley.

In a letter to his mother Stirling makes no mention of motive:

May 14 1942

My dear Mum,

I am terribly sorry for having been so long in writing. The

longer I leave it, the more impossible in length I felt the letter would have to be and therefore the more difficult; now it is really impossible to write a short letter because I have accumulated so much to tell you. This can only be a note.

I am writing from Mersah Matruh while waiting for an aeroplane to take me further forward. I am leaving on a small and short expedition which will be the last I will go on for some time – which is a pity because they are tremendous fun.

From your letters it is clear that you have heard and probably believed an amazingly exaggerated account of L Det. activities. I wish they were all true.

My newest recruit (he is only attached at the moment) is Randolph Churchill. He did his first jump yesterday – which was tremendously entertaining. Preceding this he had had 3 weeks building up or rather in his case breaking down exercises, which had removed $1^1/_2$ stones. He is still damn fat.

I shall have to stop in order to catch the a/c.

Your loving David.

It is my opinion that Stirling's motives were of the finest for an officer in his position. Randolph Churchill's presence on a successful raid would mean that the Prime Minister would get a first-hand account of the SAS in action even though it would probably be embellished in favour of his son. This alone could be important to the long-term survival of the unit. Stirling also made it known to Randolph that he was not happy with the way the French were being treated – there was still resistance at MEHQ to those soldiers coming under his command. He had made the approaches to Catroux and MEHQ had taken them under their wing even though they clearly did not know what to do with them. At the time of the Benghazi planning Lieutenant Jordan and a detachment had been sent to Libya for unspecified operations without reference to Stirling. There was little time for him to do anything but complain.

It is a tribute to Stirling's powers of leadership that no SAS members objected to the inclusion of Churchill on an operation upon which so much depended. It is immaterial that Churchill was simply to wait at the LRDG rendezvous with the transport;

that job was as important as any other. The lack of complaint cannot be explained away as normal military discipline. Every member of the unit was a strong individual. Confident and superbly trained, they were all determined to see the SAS succeed. Under normal circumstances curiosity alone would have prompted a question to Stirling, but Churchill's presence was ruefully accepted even by Seekings and Cooper, who not only would have to rely on Churchill's steadfastness but who were closer than anyone to Stirling and could have raised doubts without any fear of recrimination.

The raid was again launched from Siwa Oasis. The LRDG guiding patrol was under the command of Robin Gurdon and using a similar route to the last venture they made their way across the Trig El Abd minefields to the escarpment of the Jebel Akhdar (Green Mountain) and the known good cover. Here, on 21 May, Seekings had an unlucky accident. Whilst he was checking the battle stores and fitting fuses and detonators to the Lewes Bombs a faulty detonator exploded in his hand. It was not a serious wound but he was disabled by a temporary paralysis and, to his disgust, instructed to remain behind. Stirling decided to take Churchill along.

The Blitz Buggy, considered so necessary to the deception, slowed down the fifteen-mile journey to the main road. Not equipped for rough cross-country work it had to be nursed over boulder-strewn areas down the line of a minor wadi. The LRDG escorts left Stirling at the main road and almost immediately, as the Buggy picked up speed on the smooth surface, the comedy began.

'The car made a noise like a hundred rampant East End tomcats out for a good time,' Stirling reminisced. 'We had obviously taken some damage on the wadi bed. We got the beast off the road and tweaked and hit various parts of it but it seemed the wheel was off-line and it was a major repair job. I was annoyed. We were hardly going to make a stealthy approach with that racket but we were going on, of that I was certain.'

Speed was unaffected and good progress was made towards Benghazi. The team's main memory now is of exhilaration, but one can imagine the picture; a car, only reasonably German in appearance, speeding along behind enemy lines with a noise which shattered the desert peace and signalled its coming over a considerable distance in the still air, on board six desperadoes not remotely resembling Germans or Italians and an array of guns of a distinctive silhouette.

On that drive, Stirling had occasion to reprimand Churchill. 'We had stopped for something, perhaps a mileage check, when I smelled rum. I looked into the back and there was Randolph with his water canteen in his hand. I threw it away and cursed him roundly.'

Stirling took the precaution of asking Cooper to shin up a telegraph pole and cut the wires. There were very few blind corners on the Benghazi–Regima road and visibility was good. Regima airfield was fading into the distance when the first corner was negotiated and straight in front was a roadblock.

Stirling braked violently and crashed down through the gearbox halting just in time. He hunched over the wheel and appeared to take no further interest in the proceedings as he waited for Maclean, the Italian speaker, to get on with it. Maclean sharply told the sentry that they were staff officers and in a hurry. He noted two or three men behind the sentry and what may have been a machine-gun post, and heard the unmistakeable click of a safety catch being eased off. It appeared that a fire fight was unavoidable when the sentry suddenly relaxed, made a comment about the brightness of the headlights and motioned them through.

Within minutes they were on the outskirts of Benghazi. They began to slow down when a vehicle which had passed them from the opposite direction suddenly turned and began to follow. Stirling slowed but the vehicle chose not to pass. They had clearly aroused the suspicion of the occupants and could only either shoot it out (far from desirable as it would call for their instant departure), or take flight and lose it in the back streets. Stirling opted for the second and floored the accelerator; the stealthy infiltration into enemy-held Benghazi took place at seventy miles per hour.

Stirling evaded the pursuer simply by driving into a side street and switching off his lights. Shortly after this the air was rent by the scream of air raid sirens. An air raid was unlikely; Stirling and Maclean had confirmed that the RAF would leave Benghazi alone for two nights to give the SAS a fighting chance of avoiding detection. Had they been given away somehow? It preyed on Stirling's mind. The Blitz Buggy, with its distinctive noise, would have to be dumped. An explosive charge was set by Cooper to detonate thirty minutes later and placed in the boot beside the petrol tank. The patrol set off into the Arab quarter.

Maclean's linguistic abilities were useful again immediately, when they bumped into a uniformed, armed member of the Carabinieri. When he and Maclean had finished what appeared to be a light-hearted conversation, the impatient Stirling asked for a translation.

'I asked what all the racket was about and he told me it was another English air raid. He thought it was really funny when I said it might be English ground forces. He said there was no danger of that, they were all back in Egypt.'

It was hardly necessary for Stirling to tell the patrol to race back to the Blitz Buggy and retrieve the bomb. They had obviously not been compromised and the wagon was still their best means of escape. They made it with only minutes to spare. Churchill was left with one man to find a place to hide the car and the others set off in search of a worthwhile target.

They made their way to the harbour with the boats, Maclean taking care of the occasional Italian. One soldier was asked whether he knew of a hotel where they could sleep. They were very tired having carried all their luggage (indicating the boats) from the scene of their motor accident. At the harbour edge Maclean and Cooper were instructed to inflate the boats while

Stirling set off to look around the harbour. Maclean takes up
the story:

> Crouching under a low sea wall, we unpacked the kitbag and
> set to work with the bellows. There was no moon, but brilliant
> starlight. The smooth, shining surface of the harbour was like a
> sheet of quicksilver, and the black hulls of the ships seemed no
> more than a stone's throw away. They would make good targets
> if only we could reach them unobserved. At any rate, we should
> not have far to paddle, though I could have wished for a better
> background than this smooth expanse of water. Diligently we
> plugged away at the bellows, which squeaked louder than I
> liked, and seemed to be making little or no impression on the
> boat. Several minutes passed. The boat was still as flat as a
> pancake. We verified the connection and went on pumping.
>
> Then suddenly we were hailed from one of the ships. It was
> a sentry. 'Chi va la?' he challenged. 'Militari!' I shouted back.
> There was a pause and we resumed pumping. But still the sentry
> was suspicious. 'What are you up to over there?' he inquired.
> 'Nothing to do with you,' I answered, with a show of assurance
> which I was far from feeling. After that there was silence.
>
> Meanwhile the boat remained flat. There could only be one
> explanation. Somehow, since we had inspected it in the wadi
> that morning it had got punctured. There was nothing for it
> but to go and get another. It was fortunate we had two.
> Hiding the first boat as best we could under the shadow of
> the wall, we crossed the docks, slipping unseen through the
> hole in the wire, and walked back through the silent streets to
> where we had left the car. There we found Randolph and Rose
> in fine fettle, trying with the utmost unconcern to manoeuvre
> the car through a hole in the wall of a bombed-out house.
> Occasionally passers-by, Arabs for the most part, gaped at
> them with undisguised interest and admiration.
>
> Wishing them luck, we pulled the second boat out of the
> car and started back to the harbour. Once again we got safely
> through the wire and down to the water's edge, but only to
> find that the second boat, like the first, was uninflatable. It
> was heart-rending. Meanwhile there was no sign of David. We
> decided to go and look for him.*

* From *Eastern Approaches* by Fitzroy Maclean.

David was located and it was decided that, as dawn would soon be breaking, they would have to retrieve all signs of their presence from the dockside and hide up. The next twelve hours were tense but not without hilarious (retrospectively) moments. En route back to the hiding place Maclean was prodded vigorously with a bayonet wielded by a Somali Askari (with the Italians) before his impersonation of an angry Italian officer turned the unfortunate away. When two sentries tacked themselves on to the end of the file of British soldiers, Maclean marched pompously to the main guardhouse and delivered a potent rollicking to the guard commander on the sloppiness of his command.

As they passed through the gate: 'The bloody sentry actually presented arms. Fitzroy was quite magnificent that night. I'm sure he enjoyed the whole thing enormously,' Stirling summed up.

It was almost light when they reached the camouflaged car and they decided to make their temporary home on the top floor of what Randolph Churchill had christened 'Number 10 Downing Street'. That the house was opposite a German Area Headquarters was of no concern to the party of course! What would the Germans have given to know that they had the son of the British Prime Minister so easily within their grasp. The day passed undisturbed except for a visit by what was presumed to be an Italian deserter or looter, who fled in fear when he saw the fiendish-looking occupants.

During the day Stirling did a foolhardy but brave thing. Dressed in his uniform of corduroy slacks and polo-necked sweater, and with a towel round his neck, he strolled out for an hour's reconnaissance of the harbour. He decided that two patrol boats moored to the quay would be worth taking out. Meanwhile the team worked on the vehicle and succeeded in improving but not curing the misaligned wheel and track rod.

It was not possible to blow up the patrol boats as the arrival of the raiders coincided with the changing of the guard – they

were forced to move on. The departure from Benghazi was
unhurried, the patrol took time out to stroll around the town
and a petrol dump alongside the main road was bombed on
the way out. The patrol left by the same route and enjoyed
themselves by joining an enemy convoy as far as the road
block. Once more the 'staff officers' passed through without
remark and drove their still protesting Blitz Buggy back to
the Jebel Akhdar and an overdue RV with the LRDG and
an anxious Seekings.

In strategic terms the patrol had achieved little, but in
knowledge, which was to stand them in good stead, the
returns were very significant. For over thirty-six hours, six
men had moved around the harbour area of Benghazi virtually
at will. They had quite openly attempted to inflate boats in full
view of the targets with no more than passing interest shown
by the sentries. Those damned boats – it seemed that Stirling
and shipping were never to come together.

Stirling had to hasten back to Cairo to sort out the French
situation; on the drive between Alexandria and Cairo he had
one of his many motor crashes. On overtaking a convoy of
lorries he misjudged the distance and caught a wheel. Churchill
crushed a vertebra (he was later sent back to England where
he did indeed regale his father with stirring tales of Stirling's
prowess); Fitzroy was put out of action for some weeks with
a fractured skull and concussion; Rose suffered very bad
fractures of radius and ulna; Stirling used one more of his
nine lives and got only a cracked wrist bone.

The state of the war had changed during Stirling's absence.
The Afrika Korps and the 8th Army faced each other across
a fifty-mile frontage of infantry, armour and artillery. Neither
side seemed to want to take the next step. Auchinleck was
under severe pressure from Winston Churchill to attack
Rommel; the Auk was adamant after his earlier setback not
to advance until he was sure he had numerical superiority.
Rommel beat him to the punch and in late May (the 26th) he
attacked. He was initially held and suffered heavy losses but

his long supply lines were well established and efficient and it was only days before he advanced again.

Churchill was under desperate pressure from Malta to get ammunition and food on to the island. The German-held airfields of Cyrenaica gave them total dominance over any naval convoys moving into the Mediterranean; if Malta were starved into submission and taken by the Germans then their stranglehold would be complete. Their supply lines would be impregnable and Egypt would quickly fall. In Churchill's eyes, therefore, the safety of Malta was paramount; Auchinleck was equally convinced that the time was not right for him to counter-attack. It was into this battle of the Titans that Stirling stepped. Wrist in plaster he was summoned to the Director of Military Operations at MEHQ.

He was informed that in response to the dire needs of Malta, a convoy of Allied ships was going to run the gauntlet of the Mediterranean. What, if anything, could the SAS do to assist in relieving air attacks on the convoy? It was timed for the middle of June.

Before leaving for his last operation Stirling had applied pressure on MEHQ to get formal authority for the French, under Georges Bergé, to act under his command. What progress had there been? Stirling was shown a signal sent by Bergé shortly after his departure. This signal showed that his exhortations for the use of the French had, after all, been heard and it confirmed Bergé's personal dedication to the SAS cause. In it, Bergé actually outlined future targets – aerodromes in Libya, Crete, Rhodes, Greece, even Sicily; depots between Tripoli and Benghazi, which may have been jumping the gun, but it showed his initiative: Stirling was assured that the French were now well and truly under his command. He left with the assurance that he would be back within twenty-four hours with his outline plan.

# 10

# THE GOSPEL
# SPREADS

Stirling could not shake off the feeling that the visit to Benghazi had somehow been compromised and that they were expected. There was no proof of this – he just felt ill at ease. On the journey in to the target area they had encountered two strange characters who had passed themselves off as being members of the South African Survey Unit. Their accents were foreign and they were driving a British truck of which there were many in enemy hands. An investigation into the Survey Unit in Cairo proved fruitless.* This was not conclusive, of course, and Stirling looked to other quarters. Halfway between Cairo and Kabrit there was an Arab restaurant used a lot by the SAS men. Just in case there was anything untoward within the staff of the establishment the unit was given instructions never to discuss operational matters in the building. (Stirling's instinct here proved sound as it was later discovered that the Germans had installed a particularly competent intelligence agent in the restaurant though it is not known whether he was ever responsible for betraying a SAS operation.)

---

* It is just possible that the two men were part of the Africa Kompanie, a specialist German unit drawn from the Brandenburgers with the intention of setting up a LRDG 'equivalent'.

Stirling himself was certainly not beyond reproach when it came to security. His brother's flat was often left strewn with maps and plans whilst Stirling went off to MEHQ to discuss his affairs. Peter Stirling remembers: 'He used to leave everything there, you know. It is almost certain that nothing was ever taken or copied because we knew all our visitors, but Fitzroy and I decided to throw a scare into David on one occasion to teach him a lesson. We invited a particularly handsome girl to lunch one day; she was the absolute epitome of Mata Hari in appearance and manner. After she left we cleared away all David's papers and told him she seemed to have stolen them. He was most distraught, but of course it wasn't possible to keep a straight face for long and he soon realised the joke.

'David used always to lunch with me before setting off on an operation and his jeeps would usually end up waiting outside for him. I mentioned this to those concerned and they decided that this was a possible security breach so they ordered that a jeep should be permanently stationed outside my flat. This didn't last long, as the Egyptian traffic police were soon complaining about the obstruction. I don't think that there ever was a breach of security from the flat, however.

'It was most amusing when, later on, I had to hand the flat over to the original occupant, an Admiral. The bullet holes had been disguised as best we could, thanks to Mo, but a few surprises remained in the attic roof space. I think the Admiral uncovered bullets, grenades and a variety of explosive bits and pieces – of course, I denied all knowledge! I'm sure that David wasn't to blame for all of them, people just had a habit of hiding "unwanted" things there. I've no idea how the Admiral explained them away.'

Maybe because of the early open hostility of the Adjutant-General branch of MEHQ, Stirling always believed that security leaks had emanated from those offices. This is perhaps unfair but certainly his unusual style of operating was the subject of loose conversation in many clubs, bars and messes. In the last analysis it is not important as the suspicions served to create a greater awareness of security within the SAS generally, though Stirling did not change his own habits noticeably then or thereafter.

Stirling was now beginning to take risks with his own health. A day off was a rarity; he would return from operations in the desert and throw himself mercilessly into negotiating better support with MEHQ, planning the next operation and continuing to try to establish the SAS as a permanent force in the British Army. True, he would still carouse with convivial company in the evenings, but generally speaking he was totally committed both physically and mentally. Like the rest of his unit he had become the victim of desert sores; unlike the rest he did not seek treatment for them. A quick wash and a piece of sticking plaster was his ineffective remedy.

There is no doubt that Stirling recognised the value and effectiveness of his unassuming, modest, almost shy style of leadership. That he managed to maintain that façade of utter unconcern is remarkable. He achieved it by total concentration on the job in hand and not allowing himself to think about the dangers to which he was exposed. From periods of total operational concentration he would move straight into a different sort of battle in Cairo which nevertheless demanded the same sort of mental effort. This supreme exertion was taking its toll; he was getting very tired and run down. It is difficult to criticise his lack of care of his own body for that is the man he was and he would probably not have functioned so well had he adopted a different style. I asked if he had been aware of his tiredness.

'Of course I was aware that I was doing myself down a little. You have to see it as I saw it. It was not a matter of trust that stopped me appointing a second-in-command to take some of the administrative load. I had no one at the time. It would have been a great folly to put Paddy back into that sort of harness, he was performing marvellously where he was. I had no other officer with the right bent for the job at the time.

'Those who were looking hopeful had not been with me long enough to have the necessary operational experience. Fitzroy was too badly laid up to help; he'd suffered a broken arm and collar bone in addition to the severe concussion. I had my eye on Robin Gurdon, one of the LRDG officers. I had pretty well talked him into transferring but he didn't want to leave the LRDG until his slot could be filled. He was a very, very fine man. Anyway, I only really felt tired when I stopped to think about it and there didn't seem to be too much of a hurry to appoint an assistant.

'You must also remember that at that stage a quite momentous thing had happened. Instead of my having to go to MEHQ and explain the next operation I'd planned, I'd been confronted with one of their problems and asked what I could do about it! That was certainly not the time to start reorganising the SAS command structure. There was the chance for real impact, and what is more the French were up and running. Pat Riley had got quite a few recruits through the course so we could bolster our patrols. I had a numerically realistic force to deploy.'

On the face of it, Stirling's plan was a masterpiece of simplicity. He and Mayne, however, knew of the problems behind the apparently blasé briefing to MEHQ. The next dark period, though not moonless, would be 13/14th June; eight patrols would be committed to eight different targets, all airfields. They would take the areas of Benghazi, Derna and Barce; in addition they would send a force to the Heraklion base on the island of Crete. They would be ready to move within the next nine or ten days. If 'that was OK. We'd like to get cracking'. It was indeed OK. At the Stirling flat in Cairo and the mess in Kabrit there was a frenzied buzz of activity as supplies were calculated and issued; the latest intelligence reports and photographs were scrutinised and routes were fixed.

Stirling had decided to deploy a mixed force in the following manner:

1. Benghazi area: Stirling, Mayne, Jaquier
2. Derna: Jordan (3 patrols)
3. Berka (main site): Zirnheld
4. Heraklion: Bergé

Out of eight patrols of a maximum of five men each, six would be French. Stirling not only wanted to rest and retrain some of his own men, he felt that the French had been kept in a state of uncertainty and anticipation for far too long and that to make this a mainly French operation could only be good for the long-term integration of the two nationalities. The decision to put Bergé in command of the Crete operation seems a little incongruous considering that Libya was to be the main operational scene for the foreseeable future. Stirling, however, had his reasons.

'I had, a few weeks previously, got hold of George Jellicoe who'd spent quite a lot of time with the SBS. The operation had to be mounted from a boat of some sort and his experience would be most useful. He spoke French fluently and had some knowledge of the island. More than anything he got on extremely well with Georges Bergé and there was obvious trust between them. At first sight that seemed the most difficult of the targets and I was tempted to take it on myself. That would have been foolish for two reasons; I knew the Benghazi area quite well, and secondly it was likely to take longer to get back from Crete and I wanted to be back at HQ soon after the operation. Georges was certainly very keen on the job. He and George Jellicoe planned their own way from then on.'

Difficult though Crete appeared to be it did not present any problems greater that those faced by Jordan. Derna was situated one hundred miles or so westwards along the coast from Tobruk. The site made a natural reinforcement-holding area for the German Army, so it was a hive of industry with active patrols and some training taking place. The surrounding ground was rough and broken which, although it gave good concealment, presented a tough challenge to vehicular movement – speed was not possible. The available maps were not good and air photography was limited to the close target area. Stirling and Jordan scratched their heads for hours trying to determine the best way into Derna.

'For once MEHQ gave me something both gratuitous and useful. I was told about Captain Herbert Buck and his little band of German Jews.'

This was the unit which went under the misnomer of the Special Interrogation Group. It was a volunteer organisation consisting of Jews mainly from Palestine who had offered their services against the Germans in any capacity. A role was seen for them in behind-the-lines intelligence gathering and sabotage where they could masquerade as soldiers of the Afrika Korps. These brave men knew that capture would result in speedy execution. Herbert Buck MC was one of those strange adventurers so often found in the ranks of the British Army during times of war. He had been captured at Gazala and escaped; a fluent German linguist, he had acquired some items of German uniform and had simply walked out through the German lines with the greatest of ease. This had planted the germ of an idea in his mind and this became the SIG.

Buck's training regimen hinged on linguistic perfection and a deep knowledge of German Army routines and customs. To this end he had recruited two German prisoners of war. Both ex-French Foreign Legionnaires they had been questioned thoroughly and screened to the best of MEHQ's ability. They seemed secure and got on well with the Jews. Stirling's proposition to Buck was that the SIG might care to provide Jordan's patrols with Afrika Korps vehicles and drivers. The Frenchmen could hide in the trucks whilst Buck's men took them through the German perimeters. Buck accepted with alacrity – it was a classic task, apparently well within the capabilities of his small unit. The SIG would link up with

Jordan and the SAS at Siwa Oasis. Jordan was pleased with the concept and his team left Kabrit on the first stage of their journey shortly afterwards.

Stirling, Mayne and Jaquier moved along now familiar ground to the Jebel Akhdar where they fixed their rendezvous point. They spent one night together before moving on. There was complete integration between the British and French now and they entertained each other with songs and stories round what would be the last relatively safe campfire before the return journey.

'Those periods were very pleasant, almost relaxing. We were as safe as you ever could be behind the lines and we always got as much sleep as possible. It was also the point at which one had time to get to know people a little better. Once a raid was under way, concentration was total. On the target it was a matter of getting the job done quickly and pulling out. There was then a short period of joy as we watched the bombs go off, hopefully from a safe distance. After that we knew that unless we were very lucky, we were going to be harassed by aircraft and the first twenty miles or so could be hair-raising.'

Stirling was to take Benina, Mayne would go to Berka and Jaquier would attack Barce to the east. Stirling took only two men, the redoubtable Seekings and Cooper. Benina had already been identified as a prime target; it was the main repair base for fighters and bombers, and supported all the coastal airfields. Supplies of spares were as important to the enemy as airframes. A placid panorama lay before them as they established an observation point on the escarpment just over a mile from the target; the air was so clear it seemed they only had to reach out to touch the aircraft waiting for a test pilot.

Benghazi, for all the world like a picture postcard, shimmered in the hot June sun. Low, white, innocent buildings with silhouettes which formed a patchwork of peace against the blue backdrop of the Mediterranean. The scene of tranquillity was completed by the brightly dressed women toiling in the field oblivious to the scorching heat and the shepherd boys indolently urging their flocks not to stray. The mind plays tricks at times like that – would it not be easy to remain in the observation post for a few days, luxuriate in the peaceful atmosphere and watch the war go by? A feeling quickly banished by the perpetual flies drinking from the ever-present rivulets of sweat trickling down grimy faces.

With darkness came the need for action. Stirling had been informed that in support of his sortie the RAF would bomb Benghazi just before the moon subsided and he intended to be on Benina before the aerial attack took place. The enemy response to the attack would probably be to stand-to all sentries and if the patrol was already inside the perimeter they would have more than a sporting chance of locating all the guard positions before moving about with the bombs. The bombing took place on time and coincided with the patrol's arrival at the very centre of the airfield.

The patrol was some distance from their targets; having located them by sight against the illumination of the bombs, they were able to take compass bearings for use later. Now came one of the most difficult aspects of any operation behind enemy lines – the waiting. Stirling's party had at least an hour to while away in order to make their play at about two in the morning, in co-ordination with other patrols: action on one target might inspire enemy reaction on another. And at this time of the morning human reflex is at its lowest ebb; this lack of efficiency on the part of sentries became an SAS weapon in itself.

Waiting in the dark in exposed positions is nerve-racking. Shadows begin to move. The bush which a minute ago was in line with the corner of a building has suddenly jumped a few feet to the left. The noise which you identified as a piece of loose corrugated iron tapping something in the night breeze is now definitely a signal between two sentries closing in on you. The night air cools your sweat-soaked clothing and the shivers begin; your teeth chatter and you know that the noise can be heard hundreds of yards away. The temptation to move prematurely becomes almost irresistible.

Stirling, well aware of the tricks of the night, used his own ploys to cure the effect. On that night he regaled Seekings and Cooper with a lecture on the art of deerstalking in his native Highlands. In detail he described the patient stalk, often flat to the ground in the cold, dew-covered heather; the long, circling crawls to stay downwind of the quarry; the camouflage methods and the critical eyes of the expert ghillies; the need, for the sake of humanity not pride, for the one-shot, clean kill; stories of inexperienced stalkers and self-important 'trophy-hunters' who filled him with disgust. He had an avid audience and in a trice the time was right for movement.

A number of Stirling's original L Detachment soldiers made an interesting observation about him – that while he could be quite awkward, almost clumsy, in his movements by day, at night he had the most incredible ability to walk around in total silence without a stumble or hesitation. He also had an unerring knack of retracing his footsteps almost exactly under the darkest conditions.

The first opportunity target of the night was a real bonus; they had not known of its presence. It was a vast fuel dump; the ground had been excavated so that the containers were below ground level, out of sight of observers (no doubt this construction was also a safety feature, as it would contain oil and petrol spillages). This was given two or three bombs. The hangars were the real attraction, and they were delighted with their content. The first hangar was chock-a-block full of ME110s and Stukas, so full that the total complement of sixty bombs was soon used up.

There was more than a little tension in placing a Lewes Bomb under those circumstances. The actuating device, the time pencil, relied for its operation on the action of acid eating away at lead elements of varying thicknesses. The lead element was the one device which held back the firing pin or striker which was under spring tension. The thicker the lead, the longer it took the acid to eat through it and so release the striker. The acid was contained in a breakable vial within the body of the time pencil; this was squeezed by finger pressure at the appropriate time releasing the acid to work against the lead.

There were a number of variables in those devices. Both acid and lead elements could degrade in storage. Once the acid had been released the degradation time of the lead could be affected to a degree by any movement which caused the acid to swirl around the element. Temperature could shorten or lengthen the action time of the acid. The vial was sufficiently fragile for it to be inadvertently broken and a dent in the pencil body was not easily detected on a cold night when the fingers could be numbed. The in built safety system was a safety pin which obstructed the passage of the striker pin. This was always the final arming action. Thus a Lewes Bomb would be placed on the target and the safety pin withdrawn. If there had been a serious malfunction then it was technically possible for the bomb to detonate instantly. This had not yet happened but there was always a prickling of adrenalin when the pin was pulled.

In order for spasmodic sabotage of the SAS type to be really effective it was necessary to think further than just the destruction of airframes and parts. Aircraft and vehicles can be 'cannibalised'; part of one vehicle or aircraft can be removed and fitted to another, making one functional vehicle out of two immobilised ones. The SAS developed a fine technique of limiting possible cannibalisation. If the best method to destroy an aircraft explosively on the ground was to place the bomb on the wing, how much more of a nuisance it would be if all bombs were placed on the port wings. No way then that the enemy can retrofit the 'spare' wings to other aircraft. If the attack was to be on the undercarriage (on bigger aircraft), better to attack the same side of all the undercarriages and then destroy the appropriate spares in the depots if they could be identified.

The operation had gone very smoothly and there was time to spare. Stirling decided to do something which he later said was out of character. The patrol had spotted the guardhouse a short distance from the hangar. Stirling told Seekings and Cooper that they would give the Germans something to remember them by. Removing the pin from a hand grenade he opened the guardhouse door and tossed the grenade into the crowded room with the words, 'Here you are, share this amongst you.' He closed the door and the patrol beat a hasty retreat. Later he was to recall: 'It was a silly show of bravado, I suppose. In a fight I would shoot to kill with the same enthusiasm as the next man but I was not at ease with that action. It seemed close to murder. The other thing which made it silly was that if the grenade had not gone off I would have alerted the whole damned camp to the fact that we had been there and they may well have got organised sufficiently quickly to search the hangars and save a few planes.'

There are two things to remark upon regarding Stirling's mention of the incident. Firstly it showed the gentler side of his nature, which was never very far from the surface. There are many witnesses to his calmness and efficiency during small-arms actions with the enemy and I have met no one who would consider the action at the guardhouse as anything other than a professional act of war. Secondly there was almost a code of honour during the North African campaign which was held by both sides. Prisoners of war did not expect to be put to the sword or treated much worse than the soldiers of the capturing side. It was, as many have said, a clean war; nothing like what was to come in Europe where the influence of the Nazis was extensive. No doubt Stirling, quite unnecessarily, felt slightly dishonourable. He was certainly to take Mayne severely to task for what he considered a particularly brutal action later in the campaign.

The patrol were able to enjoy watching the results of their endeavours from a relatively safe distance; in fact the explosions started before they had passed back through the perimeter. Stirling, moving uncharacteristically slowly, was forced to admit that he was feeling unwell. Weak and unsteady, he was suffering a massive attack of migraine. He could not have been in better hands. Seekings and Cooper helped him over the rough ground and into a covered position where they could sit back and watch the fires raging. The journey back up to the top of the escarpment was difficult with Stirling half blinded by migraine, but to stop on the low ground would be to invite discovery.

The patrol was lucky, they lay up close to their observation point of the day before and Seekings went in search of water. He found a well, and the cold water had a slight recuperative effect on Stirling. Rather than move slowly the pair decided it would be best for one of them to locate the LRDG RV then return to assist the other to take their Commanding Officer back. Cooper found the RV quickly and they were soon together again sipping the brew which had become habitual on the safe return of a patrol – tea heavily laced with rum.

Mayne, with Lilley, Storey and Warburton, had a tough time. The satellite airfield at Berka was strongly defended by alert troops. The patrol managed to get on to the target but their arrival coincided with a RAF bombing run which should not have strayed further than Benghazi. Within minutes the airfield was awash with troops. They could only lay bombs on a fuel dump before they fought their way out. The Germans, knowing what had happened and having experienced previous raids, quickly despatched vehicle-borne troops to cut off the raiders.

All night they moved this way and that in a desperate game of hide-and-seek. As dawn broke Mayne decided that they should split and double their chances of survival in what seemed a very bleak situation. During the day Warburton made a break from cover when he thought discovery was imminent; from the sounds of shooting heard by Lilley it was fairly certain that he was killed. Oddly Lilley (after strangling an Italian who foolishly thought to take him prisoner) ran into Mayne and Storey on the way back to the RV, and one day late they were back with Stirling and the LRDG. Undoubtedly the explosions created by Stirling's patrol and those of Jaquier who had successfully infiltrated the airfield at Barce (and blown up petrol dumps), had heightened the Germans' awareness that they were being attacked by a large number of patrols. In addition the members of Zirnheld's patrol were fighting for their lives at Berka having experienced similar problems to Mayne.

'We had a bit of fun after the raid,' related Stirling. 'I had told Paddy, with some glee, that it was rather nice to see the results of my own bombs for once. I was well behind him on results. I half jokingly said that it might be fun to go and see if the bits and pieces were still burning; we'd never seen the after-effects of a raid. Paddy, naturally, immediately said yes. It was foolish of course, but that's how we were. We had no transport of our own and I did a bit of pleading with Robin Gurdon to let us have a wagon. He moaned good-naturedly a bit about us inviting trouble, because the Germans were all over the place, but he agreed in the end. He wasn't too enthusiastic about rules. We were under pain of death though to return the truck intact.'

The events of that night have their place in the annals of SAS history as feats of sheer audacity and remarkable navigation.

'I was being a little pomposo,' said Stirling. 'There were seven of us in the truck. Reg Seekings and young Johnny Cooper were not going to let me out of their sight and Storey and Lilley must have felt the same about Paddy. I invited Karl Kahane to come along too [Kahane was a member of the SIG]. Paddy was driving as I still had my wrist in plaster; we got to the main road and turned west, I told Paddy not to be so cautious as there were no roadblocks until we passed Benina. I was the expert and I knew there was only the lone Italian. How wrong I was. The Germans had got their act together at last. We hit a proper German block fairly quickly.'

In the halted truck there was all the tension which could be expected. Men, apparently relaxed, had their fingers curled around their triggers, trying to breathe slowly and naturally whilst remaining sufficiently tight to spring into action. Kahane came into his own by snarling at the sentry who had asked for the password, snapping that the party had been at the front line for six weeks and couldn't possibly be expected to know the password. When would the silly man open the gate and let them all get through for a decent bath. The guards had all had a life of ease whilst they'd been fighting for theirs. There was a click as Mayne pulled back the hammer of his revolver, followed by the sounds of safety catches being eased off in the back of the truck. The German sentry heard all this, and, assessing his own position as being far from comfortable if guns went off, he let the vehicle through. He almost certainly telephoned through to the guard posts further along the road and Stirling suspected this.

'It would have been stupid to drive right on into Benghazi though I have to admit the temptation was there. I was determined that having come so far we shouldn't leave without dropping a calling card somewhere. We passed a petrol store, quite a small one, but we reversed and planted a couple of bombs for good measure. A bit further on we found some trucks and did the same. I seem to remember there was a fire fight there. I decided with Paddy that the best thing to do was strike out across the desert to Wadi Qattara. There was a bit of a race to beat the Germans to it.'

'A bit of a race' was a typical Stirling understatement. The Wadi Qattara was rough and strewn with huge boulders. Once inside, a driver had to pick his route slowly and carefully, and would often have to retrace his tracks as an impassable obstacle was reached. Stirling's patrol knew that there was only one point within reasonable distance where they could the wadi with relative ease; they had to cross to take advantage of an easy route up the escarpment and into the desert beyond.

Stirling calculated a compass bearing to the crossing point and Mayne drove as fast as he could. This sounds simple but with no lights and the vehicle heaving up and down and from side to side like an unbroken stallion it was no picnic. Even in broad daylight it can be difficult maintaining a bearing as obstacles are circumnavigated and lines of movement have to be corrected to compensate. The five men in the back must have been going through their own form of hell as they were thrown around the interior, crashing against the bombs and fighting to keep a grip on their weapons and to stay inside the vehicle.

Mayne noticed the headlights of what could only be a German vehicle some two or three miles away headed on a converging course. The local commander had done his homework. He too knew where the crossing point was and now there was a desperate race to be first there. The Germans with full lights on were making much better time and they would surely win. They probably had not seen the SAS vehicle but if they got to the crossing point ahead of them an ambush would be simple. There was nothing for it – Mayne flicked on his lights and increased speed.

It soon became apparent that Mayne had picked up a short lead. The crew in the back tried to bring their guns to bear on the German's headlights but it was impossible to steady a weapon as they lurched from boulder to boulder. They would be there first but that was to no avail if Stirling had got his bearings wrong. Continuously shouting to Mayne above the din of the vehicle, his, 'Left, left, left', 'right a bit' had seemed very confused, but he had remained calm. They arrived suddenly at the edge of the cliff. 'Turn right,' instructed Stirling and within a few yards there was the break which signified the crossing point.

'Paddy went down it like a bat out of hell and I don't know how he kept the truck on its four wheels. The Germans, of course, didn't follow. It would have been too easy to ambush them and they knew that. If they'd known the trouble we would have in getting the big truck up the other side they might have been tempted. We practically had to manhandle it up and over the lip.'

The going was better now and the patrol relaxed. After the last few miles everything seemed an anticlimax and some began to doze off as Mayne, now driving at a reasonably comfortable speed, headed for the RV with the LRDG. This was better than most post-operational journeys. It was still dark, there was no danger of aircraft and the going was good – life was good.

Lilley shook the patrol alert with a shout: 'Get out. Move, quick. There's a fuse burning.'

It speaks highly of their reactions that everyone was out within seconds – Mayne did not try to stop the truck, which was either quick thinking or human reaction. It was just as well because it travelled a few yards before exploding in a great ball of flame. During the desperate race to the wadi edge a time pencil must have been activated and the safety pin must have been faulty or slipped out as the bombs were thrown about the floor. Stirling and Mayne, who had given their earnest oath to Gurdon to return the truck in mint condition, laughed as loudly as the others when they surveyed the pathetic remains. The journey was continued on foot, the RV eventually reached and the bad news delivered to Gurdon.

'He was very good,' remarked Stirling, 'he just looked at us and said, "I suppose you've had a good time then." Remarkable chap and I couldn't wait for him to take up my offer of becoming my second-in-command.'

It took about five days for all the patrols to reach Siwa Oasis. Zirnheld's patrol had successfully infiltrated the airfield at Berka and placed bombs on eleven aircraft before being spotted by sentries. They were quickly immersed in a raging and highly mobile battle during which they accounted for a large number of guards and amazingly suffered no severe casualties. He had managed to get the whole patrol back safely and had returned with Stirling to Siwa.

André Zirnheld was not cut from the same cloth as the other Frenchmen; in many ways he was quite like Stirling in character. He was an intellectual but his sense of duty to his country was very strong. A 'militant' before the war he taught philosophy in Tunis. He joined the army as a sergeant in Lebanon but, frustrated with the inactivity, joined the Free French and was soon commissioned to be sent to Cairo where he worked in public relations trying to bring the Free French cause into recognition. All he really wanted to do was fight and he was one of the first to answer Bergé's call for volunteers for the SAS.

Something of a mystic he had an aura which inspired confidence despite his very quiet, unassuming manner. Devoted to his men he quickly acquired a high reputation. He is remembered for the prayer he wrote in the Western Desert which demonstrates the complexity of his character:

> I bring this prayer to you, Lord,
> For you alone can give
> What one cannot demand but from oneself.

> Give me, Lord, what you have left over,
> Give me what no one ever asks you for.

> I don't ask you for rest,
> Or quiet,
> Whether of soul or body;

> I don't ask for wealth,
> Nor for success, not even for health perhaps,

> That sort of thing you get asked for so much
> That you can't have any of it left.

> Give me, Lord, what you have left over,
> Give me what no one wants from you.

> I want insecurity, anxiety,
> I want storm and strife,
> And I want you to give me these
> Once and for all,

> So that I can be sure of having them always
> Since I shan't have the courage
> To ask you for them.

> Give me, Lord, what you have left over,
> Give me what the others want nothing to do with.

The Stirlings of Keir. Left to right: Hugh, Margaret, General Stirling, Mrs Margaret Stirling, Irene (on lap), Peter, David (on floor). (*Family collection*)

Keir. (*Family collection*)

Stirling in the Swiss Alps during his training for Mount Everest (1937). (*Family collection*)

David Stirling and Jock Lewes hatch a plot (1941). (*Family collection*)

Stirling with an 'L' Detachment Patrol in the Western Desert (*c*. October 1942). (*Family collection*)

Kabrit Camp: Parachute training aids – construction by Jim Almonds. (*Courtesy of Jim Almonds*)

'Paddy' Mayne (on right) lends a hand with a bogged-down jeep. (*Family collection*)

The first SAS Reunion Dinner, 1946. (*Author's collection*)

Stirling at Salima. Susan Wood is on the extreme left. (June 1956).
(*Courtesy of Jeanine Bartosik*)

David Stirling and Leopold Takawera at Salima (1956). (*Courtesy of Jeanine Bartosik*)

The Salima Convention of June 1956. (*Family collection*)

*Left* : Stirling in the Capricorn Africa Society office in Salisbury. (*Family collection*)

*Right* : The first Zebra House in Marloes Place. (*Author's collection*)

Television International's office in Sloane Street: 'Bally Shoe & Bally Hoo'. (*Family collection*)

'The Global Perspective'; in the TIE office at 21 Sloane Street. (*Family collection*)

But give me courage too,
And strength and faith;

For you alone can give
What one cannot demand but from oneself.


Stirling was very disturbed to hear Jordan's tale. His patrol had surrendered themselves completely into the care of Herbert Buck and his men. They had travelled concealed in the back of three trucks manned by the SIG. They had two Afrika Korps vehicles and one British truck disguised as a captured vehicle and decorated with German Army insignia. All Buck's men were dressed in authentic German uniforms and carried German weapons. They had been obliged to depart Siwa on 6 June without the German passwords for that month. They travelled without any incident of note, bluffing their way through an Italian checkpoint without the password, until they were halted by a German just before last light. To their relief he was not checking identities but he advised them of the presence of British saboteurs and told them that they should spend the night at the camp along the road. It was then 12 June and they had only one night left in which to carry out their raid.

In a whispered conversation with Jordan, lying under the tarpaulins with the rest of his men, Buck decided that it would be provident to stay at least for a while at the camp. It was reasonably safe; the SIG men even lined up with the enemy to share their evening meal. After a couple of hours they decided that it would not attract attention if they were to move and so they covered another ten miles or so and camped just off the road so that the Frenchmen could stretch their legs and prepare a meal. Without the password they would not get much further along the road.

Buck's soldiers carried out a most impressive bluff. Carrying a message typed by Buck which instructed the recipient to give his men the password, two SIG men dressed as Nazis returned to visit the German NCO who had advised them to stay at

the camp. After much goodnatured joshing and cajoling they
were given the password. The next day Buck was able to
drive Jordan's patrol commanders around the area for their
reconnaissance. They were delighted to see a great number
of aircraft on each site they visited.

During the late evening the patrols were assigned their
tasks: Tourneret would take Martuba, Jordan and Bourmont
the two Derna airfields. Their driver would be Brückner (one
of the ex-French Legionnaires recruited by Buck to assist with
authentic training). The move to the airfield was fraught with
problems. The truck misbehaved continually and Brückner
spent a lot of time under the bonnet. The journey, planned for
twenty minutes, took well over an hour. Brückner eventually
halted close to the airfield and said he was going into the
adjacent German guardroom to get assistance with tools.

Moments later the truck was surrounded by Germans and a
loud voice ordered, 'All Frenchmen get out.' The French patrol
retaliated with the desperation of cornered men. Grenades were
thrown and they laid down as much fire as they could. Jordan
managed to escape in the confusion but saw the truck explode
seconds after he got out. (It subsequently appeared that one
of the SIG Jews had blown the truck up with himself on board
rather than face capture and interrogation.) Jordan made a
superhuman effort and ran for the RV with Buck. No one
else appeared. Buck was staggered to learn of Brückner's
treachery; the problems with the truck had obviously been
of Brückner's own making. This was not the end of it.

Bourmont and one other who had escaped at the same
time as Jordan had chosen to make for the RV set for the
patrol attacking Martuba. They found that this point had also
been betrayed to the Germans! Seven Frenchmen with limited
supplies gave battle against hugely superior numbers until their
ammunition ran out. All were captured and several had severe
wounds. Jordan, the sole survivor of his part of the operation,
was more determined than ever that the SAS concept should
continue.

Stirling was shocked to hear of the treachery, but had to admire the unbroken spirit of the French second-in-command. He had to wait until he got back to Cairo before he heard about Bergé's adventures.

After departing on HM Submarine *Triton* it took Bergé's patrol until 8 June to reach a position offshore from Heraklion airfield. The party consisted of Bergé, Jellicoe, three French soldiers (Sibert, Mahout and Leostic) and a Greek guide called Costi. They got ashore without hindrance and the inflatable boats were sunk as planned. It took most of two nights hard climbing through the steep, unfriendly mountains before they reached the edge of Heraklion airfield. They had encountered only some Cretan peasants whom they had no reason to distrust. Bergé had decided to attack that night since they were undetected but on the way in a sentry challenged them and opened fire. It was pointless to go on to an alerted airfield. They would hide up that day, hope the incident was passed off, and go in the next night.

They were on to the airfield quickly and taking cover in a small shed when a patrol passed and the hole they had cut in the perimeter fence was spotted. As the guard patrol was about to pass through the hole and discover them, they had a stroke of luck as a RAF bomber made a lone run over the airfield, providing sufficient distraction for them to escape from the shed. They didn't make the obvious move and leave the airfield, however; they went deeper and whilst crossing the field managed to lay Lewes bombs on twenty-one aircraft, some trucks and a petrol store. Hiding up the next day they were confident of a smooth pick-up; that night they reached a point some three miles from the beach. They had only to survive one more day and they would be on the way home.

That morning their hiding place was stumbled on by a Cretan well known to the guide Costi who said he was a friend who would not give the patrol away. Knowing the strong Cretan sense of honour, Bergé allowed the man to go to collect the food and water he had volunteered to obtain. Jellicoe and Costi were sent off to make arrangements to signal the submarine and as dusk arrived Bergé prepared to move to the beach.

They had been betrayed. As they broke cover they saw two columns of Germans approaching from opposite flanks. There was about an hour of usable half light before escape would be possible and Bergé opted for resistance. Outgunned and outnumbered the patrol put up a spirited fight during which the fourteen-year-old Leostic was killed. As they tried to break away, Sibert, Bergé and Mahout were wounded and taken prisoner. The other two were picked up without further incident and a much saddened Jellicoe made his report to Stirling in Cairo.

Stirling judged that the raids had been relatively successful despite the French losses. It was tragic to lose Georges Bergé on his first operation, but looking coldly at the situation, Augustin Jordan was well suited to take command.

Augustin Jordan was no stranger to the desert. Before the war he served in the Governor General's office in Morocco until he was mobilised in 1939 into 2nd Spahi at which point he was equipped 'with sword, burnous and horse' and sent to the Ardennes. He went to officer school in Saumur which was soon to be overtaken by the German offensive. Jordan vanished from sight, got a visa for Spanish Morocco and went from there to Tangier, Gibraltar and Great Britain where, in September 1940, he signed up with the Free French Forces. His organisational talents were used to bring order into chaos, but he was willing to carry out administrative duties for a limited period only. He wanted to fight.

At the end of 1940 he met General Legentillomme and joined his headquarters, the hub of the French Expeditionary Force for Ethiopia. The force was too late to join in the battle and a frustrated Jordan moved across to take part in the liberation of Syria. He met Georges Bergé in Damascus and the two became friends. From there it was but a short exciting step to Kabrit and the SAS; Jordan had got his desire – to fight the Germans.

Stirling calculated that the total destruction figures were thirty-seven aircraft accounted for, plus some thirty or so aircraft engines (Benina) and an unknown quantity of ammunition and fuel. How much this contributed to Malta's survival cannot be calculated, of course, but two ships had made it through the blockade and the island lived to fight on. At MEHQ, Stirling was to receive his most dismal briefing to date on the state of the war.

---

# 11

# STATIC YES –
# STAGNANT NO

Everybody in uniform must fight exactly as they
would if Kent or Sussex were invaded . . . Egypt
must be held at all costs.
> Winston S. Churchill, *The Second World War*

As Stirling left Siwa Oasis the LRDG were making their
plans to evacuate and move some 350 miles south to Kufra
Oasis. Tobruk, the 'impregnable fortress' town, had fallen to
Rommel's Afrika Korps and his advance troops were well into
Egypt. Auchinleck had ordered the British Army to effect a
fighting withdrawal back to a line between El Alamein and
the northern edge of the Munkhafad Al Qattara (Qattara
Depression). In Cairo and Alexandria the normal precautions
were being taken. Aircraft and shipping were being moved out
of harm's way in case Rommel broke the forty-mile front line.
Auchinleck remained quietly confident that the line would hold
and that the over-extended Rommel would grind to a halt.

Conditions were perfect for Stirling – Rommel's long supply
lines screamed out for attack and it was easy to persuade
MEHQ to let him avail himself of ammunition and equipment.

They had more to worry about than the antics of the SAS. He had not forgotten the anxious moments in the vehicle under the guns of the German sentry and when his eye was caught by a consignment of new jeeps, his imagination was fired. It appeared to be the ideal vehicle for the desert; true the payload was limited but it was light and highly manoeuvrable; light enough to be manhandled out of trouble by the crew. If effective firepower could be fitted to the jeeps, it opened up a whole new concept. If he could get his hands on the jeeps, and there were fifteen of them, plus some heavier vehicles as support trucks, the SAS could stay in the desert for months rather than weeks. Within two days Stirling had possession of all the jeeps with the promise of more to follow, and eighteen three-ton lorries. He was self-contained at last.

'I was perfectly happy with the LRDG but we were a burden to them and I was conscious that their support could be withdrawn at any moment; indeed, Colonel Guy Prendergast (commanding LRDG) had expressed concern at the extent of their support to us – not because he disapproved, far from it, but their own vital effort was reduced whilst they escorted us. Under the war conditions of the time, they could be needed more and more by Auchinleck in their reconnaissance and observation rôle. We had learned so much from them; it is debatable whether we could have got off the ground so swiftly without them. We had some pretty good navigators, drivers and mechanics by then so I thought we could reasonably go it alone should we have to.

'I was lucky in finding about a dozen Vickers K machine guns and I got the local Sappers to fit out the Blitz Buggy and most of the jeeps with fore and aft guns. The Vickers was a superb gun, and designed to destroy aircraft.'

There were then at least a hundred trained members of the SAS, the majority already battle-hardened. It was a force to be reckoned with in anyone's language and with Stirling and Mayne at the helm success was pretty well assured. The whole of the SAS was set to scrounging and 'requisitioning' anything which would be useful for a protracted stay in the desert. That week probably took more out of Stirling than any other similar period. He flogged himself mercilessly, ignoring the migraines and the worsening desert sores in the haste to get ready. Capable though he recognised Auchinleck to be, Rommel was a determined foe and if Cairo and Alexandria fell, Stirling wanted to be independent and out in the desert where he could inflict most damage on the German rear echelons.

On 1 July the SAS was ready to move off, planning to raid six or seven airfields and the coastal road on the night of 7 July. This was to be co-ordinated with Auchinleck's planned offensive which was aimed at regaining the coastal ground as far as Mersah Matruh. Any attacks on airfields, supplies or lines of communication would be of great assistance to the 8th Army. The main SAS force was despatched under the wing of the LRDG to meet with Stirling north of the Qattara Depression.

The Qattara Depression formed the southern 'anchor' to the Allied line which stretched northwards to the coast at El Alamein. The Depression covers about 7,000 square miles; shaped like a huge pork chop, it contains salt lakes and marshes. It descends to 435 feet below sea level and with steep, encircling escarpments up to 1000 feet high it was an imposing obstacle, thought by the Germans to be impassable to military traffic, hence its use as the anchor. There were two crossing points which had been set up by Arab traders and their camel trains. The thick salt crust was an unknown variant. In some places it would take considerable weight, in others it would crack and the offending vehicle would slowly disappear into the quicksand. Stirling had decided to infiltrate the enemy rear through the Allied line along the escarpment of the Depression. The move was successfully carried out and the whole force was soon assembled in the launch area.

Two new factors now influenced SAS tactics. Firstly, they had more vehicles on the ground than ever before, which created concealment problems with regard to tracks and leaguer positions. Secondly, the front-line British troops were not aware of the SAS plans for sensible security reasons – this meant that they would be targets for both German and British aircraft. Stirling did not even brief his own men on the operation until they were well into the desert. One large group was to split and, under command of Stirling and Mayne, hit all airfields along the line of Fuka and Bagush. A second party, commanded by Schott and Warr, would raid Sidi Barrani, and the last group, led by Jellicoe and Zirnheld, would attack the airfields in the area of El Dhaba. All attacks would be co-ordinated for one in the morning of 8 July.

'I got as angry as I have ever been with MEHQ during the early part of that operation. There was a British column swanning about which I had been told nothing about. It did not present a danger to us but their presence had alerted the sentries along the length of our attack line and kept all traffic off the main road thus depriving us of ambush potential. Paddy Mayne had a disappointment which actually turned to our advantage. He had taken a long time to get on to Bagush because the sentries were on the ball. He laid quite a lot of bombs but only a few went off. We found out later that the primers were damp. Someone had primed the charges too early and the lubricant in the charge had seeped into the primer. It was against instructions – the priming was supposed to be done at the last minute. I don't know what Paddy did about it.

'The incident did, however, crystallise my thinking about the jeeps. There we were with guns aboard which were designed for the RAF to shoot down aircraft in the air – why couldn't we do just that from the ground and keep the bombs in reserve? Paddy was all for it and we decided simply to drive on to the field and shoot the beggars up. It was amazingly easy – it was a total surprise to the Jerries. We used only the Blitz Buggy and one jeep. We did a circuit of the perimeter and runway and poured down as much lead as we could. We left the whole place littered with burning planes. A very satisfactory night's work, but we had been entirely frustrated by MEHQ with regard to George Jellicoe's raid on El Dhaba.

'I received a message from our "experts" instructing me not to raid El Dhaba as it was not being used by Rommel. I accepted this, of course, and George was sent to do some mischief along the main road. He was unlucky as it was very quiet, but the point is that André Zirnheld took some German prisoners who later told us that El Dhaba was indeed in use and always had been – it was Rommel's most important forward air base. I sent a message back to base that could have had me court martialled under different circumstances. We had missed a glorious opportunity through their bloody negligence.'

By this time the Afrika Korps had felt the effect of the SAS and a legend was beginning. The title Phantom Major was being freely used by the Germans and had been picked up by the British press. Back in Scotland, Stirling's mother was fighting her own battle with the media who had made her a target for their enquiries. Surely she knew what her son was doing? Surely he wrote to her and told her of his adventures? What could she tell them? Far more security conscious than her son, 'Mum kept mum'. Stirling was now even beginning to feature in Rommel's diaries.

'I have to say that I derived a certain pleasure from all that nonsense as it had to be an indication that we were hurting the enemy. It didn't make the battles with MEHQ any easier however. The Phantom Major tag merely served to reinforce the Private Army image, which had the psychological effect of portraying the SAS as a product of North Africa to be shoved under the carpet when that campaign was over. I still had not succeeded in getting those morons to understand that this was a new form of warfare we were developing, not a young man's whim. The SAS was a new weapon; this was an absolutely fundamental principle and, if it was allowed to develop and mature, it would be accepted as a permanent feature in the British Army Orbat [Order of Battle]. It was all very tiring. I was constantly having to make trips to Cairo to try to make them understand when I should have been in the field.*

'MEHQ, and SOE for that matter, still insisted on labelling us as saboteurs. Damn it we were not saboteurs, we were a strategically effective force which could use sabotage as a tactic if the task called for it. The SAS was a military unit, properly structured, properly commanded and subject to military discipline in the same form as any other unit – much harsher discipline in fact; any officer who came to me had to prove himself to the men he commanded before he could consider himself part of the SAS. I trusted my sergeants completely. No matter how well a patrol had seemed to operate, I would always have a few words with the sergeant afterwards; if he had anything untoward to say about the officer's performance on an operation then that officer left us immediately. There could be no room for any mistrust or lack of confidence within a small patrol behind enemy lines.

'The SAS was based on maximum achievement for minimum cost; who could possibly argue with that? I don't believe that even Auchinleck who had helped me so much had wholly grasped the awesome potential of the SAS as a permanent unit. I have to say that though he was pleased with the effectiveness of the unit, his thinking, by virtue of the command position he held, was limited to the task in hand and dealing with Rommel.'

Over the next week a series of raids were carried out during which Robin Gurdon, whom Stirling had hoped to make his second-in-command, was killed. Stirling accepted this blow

---

* Stirling hugely understates himself. There were very few operations in which he did not play his part on the ground.

with his usual philosophical outlook but it meant that there
was to be no reprieve for him; he must remain in the forefront of
both 'forward and rear' battles with precious little time for rest.
It is a quite remarkable feat of mental and physical endurance
that he maintained his equilibrium and still presented to his
men that calm, unflustered, almost benign attitude which they
found so endearing.

'He had a power over men which I had not seen before.
I believe that if David had asked his men to jump into the
midst of an enemy armoured division in broad daylight
they would have gone with him without question and in
the knowledge that he would find a way to subdue the
tanks and bring his men out unscathed and the overwhelming
victors.'*

Stores were now very short and there would have to be
an expedition to Cairo. Stirling, as always accompanied by
Cooper and Seekings, moved on ahead. Mayne was to follow
with heavier vehicles and a party was left behind to secure the
rendezvous. Stirling, in his light vehicle, crossed the Qattara
Depression without too much trouble using the Kaneitra
Crossing. Mayne decided to cross further to the south along
a route reconnoitred by the LRDG. He knew it would not
be easy and he was right, and it was two more days before
he joined Stirling in Cairo.

When the combined party returned to the desert RV it was
a close-run thing. The holding group were down to their last
rations and water. The 'goodies' from Cairo were a great
morale booster but not as satisfying as the twenty new jeeps
all fitted with Vickers K machine guns. Stirling went straight
into his briefing; his earlier success with Mayne using the armed
vehicles on Bagush airfield had prompted him into an ambitious
concept. The SAS now had more than thirty jeeps and it was
time to change tactics.

'It was not change for change's sake,' said Stirling. 'I was

* *The Desert My Dwelling Place*, David Lloyd Owen.

concerned that once the Germans fully caught on to our tactics it would be quite simple for them to make life very difficult for us. Certainly it would tie down manpower, but all they had to do was double up on their airfield sentries, keep them alert and we would have problems getting in. Taking it one step further, they knew we had to escape over the desert and that in some key areas the routes were limited; a well mounted and armed cut-off force would have severely limited us. If we could keep them guessing and use a variety of tactics in such a manner that they never knew what was coming where, and how it was being delivered – we could sow real confusion in the rear.'

The target was the major airfield at Sidi Haneish in the area of Fuka. It was reported in a signal from MEHQ intelligence to be a major staging post with an abundance of aircraft at all times, but more to the point it held a significant quantity of JU52s. These heavy transport aircraft were the mainstay of Rommel's supply system and he was known to have less of them than he required. Stirling's plan was to use the unexpected tactic of attacking while the moon was full. They would have good driving light and conditions in which the SAS had never raided before, which could mean that the sentries would be more relaxed. He wanted 100 per cent success.

The plan was daring and dangerous. Stirling proposed to use eighteen jeeps, approaching the airfield in single file to minimise track signature and vehicle damage from potholes. On reaching the target area the jeeps would fan out into line abreast and breach the perimeter using maximum fire power to kill and confuse the enemy guard force. As the runways were approached Stirling would signal with a green Very light for the jeeps to move into file formation with seven jeeps to each flank line. Spearheading the formation would be Stirling's vehicle with two others flanking it and slightly to the rear; completing this inner diamond would be Sadler's vehicle assigned to maintaining accurate navigation. All gunners would

observe the strictest arcs of fire outwards from the 'box', with
the command diamond covering the forward 180 degrees. All
in all there would be a point at which sixty-eight machine guns
could be firing, all capable of putting down up to one thousand
rounds per minute.

The efforts of the legendary Mike Sadler were never in
greater demand than on the night of the move to Sidi Haneish.
The convoy was far too large to risk hiding on the way in,
therefore the intervening ground had to be covered quickly
and accurately if the attack was to go home at the planned
hour of 1.30 a.m. Loss of direction would result in lost time
and Stirling required at least three-and-a-half hours of darkness
after the attack in which to get away, split up and hide from
the inevitable air search.

Sadler had to resort to accurate dead reckoning which
meant that a compass course had to be followed with as little
deviation as possible. This brought the inevitable surprises as
boulder-strewn areas and minor cliffs presented themselves
as obstacles. The men worked with a quiet efficiency to
reduce time-wasting. Sadler was pinpoint accurate and the
jeeps fanned out into line abreast as the ground flattened
signifying the closeness of the airfield. Everyone was aware
that the full moon exposed them very clearly and the noise of
eighteen jeeps, albeit moving quite slowly, seemed thunderous
to their ears. Tension was high.

'It was becoming difficult to suppress the order to pick up
speed and begin the attack,' remembers Stirling, 'but if we
were premature we would just waste valuable ammunition.
I was on the point of giving the order when I got the shock
of my life. The whole damned airfield suddenly lit up. For
an instant I thought we'd been spotted or betrayed again
but it was an aircraft coming into land. It was perfect for
us. We were still further away than I'd have liked but I
hit the accelerator and charged straight for the aircraft and
about two hundred yards away from it I ordered my gunners
to open up.'

The force was on to the airfield proper before the landing lights were out and almost immediately Stirling used his Very pistol and the jeeps screeched into file with guns swung outwards. Thanks to his gratuitous view of the airfield Stirling had no hesitation as he sped along between the parked aircraft. Not all burned, but many did; it was afterwards proved that those that did not were put out of the war for some time. The enemy were quick to react with mortar fire. This could not be accurate against the fast-moving vehicles but Stirling's jeep was put out of action and his crew clambered aboard others.

At the end of the airfield, cool as ever, Stirling stopped the column and had the engines switched off for a few moments while he took stock with Mayne. Mayne had already got off his vehicle once to lay a bomb on the wing of an aircraft which had been missed by the gunfire and upon which he didn't think it safe to engage with his Vickers. He had spotted a further group of aircraft off on a flank but before heading for them he wanted to make an ammunition and casualty check. They made another run and took out the remaining JU52s and Stirling gave the signal to head for the desert. On the run out Stephen Hasting's vehicle went out of action. They placed explosives on board and hitched a ride with the others.

Sandy Scratchley's gunner had been killed but his body was still aboard the jeep. The gunner was the only human casualty which seemed remarkable; three jeeps had been lost and many had taken hits but were still functioning. The force headed back to the RV in small groups of two and three. Time was short and in the haste Stirling had gone off course. In no time they were in the early morning ground mist, blinded to anything more than twenty yards away. The mist would clear almost instantly, leaving the patrol at the mercy of the aircraft, which would be airborne and searching at the first opportunity. The fog began to lift; Stephen Hastings takes up the story in a post-war note:

Then the desert became our friend. The fog cleared away and we found ourselves on the edge of a small escarpment dropping about fifteen feet. Before us lay what appeared to be a large bowl-shaped depression about a quarter of a mile broad, the walls of which were cut by fairly deep wadis with thick greenish brown shrub up to three or four feet high. A few minutes before, our position had seemed very grave; now suddenly we had been shown exactly the place we were looking for.

The vehicles were hidden and the group brewed up the essential tea. Stirling quietly asked two men to bury the dead soldier; he said that they would stand round the grave for a minute or so. Hastings again:

The officers moved away into the scrub and stood gathered round the pathetic little heap of sand and stones. There was no cross, some of the men were trying to make one from the scrub and a piece of old ration box . . . We stood bareheaded, looking at the grave, each with our own thoughts. Most of us had not even known this man, who was one of the more recent arrivals; he was just a name to us or perhaps a cheery red face and a shock of black hair. It was indeed a curious burial, just a two minutes' silence with a handful of tired, dirty comrades. Yet for this short fraction of time, lost in the middle of nowhere, there was dignity.

It took a further three days for Stirling's party to reach the RV and this they did with fuel tanks on the verge of drying out. Despite fire fights and air attacks all the other patrols made it back. There was one further casualty; André Zirnheld had been killed during a particularly long series of attacks by Stukas. It seemed reasonable to calculate that the raiders had accounted for some forty to fifty aircraft but Stirling appeared not to be pleased. He berated his small force for extravagant expenditure of ammunition, claiming that better discipline would have led to better results.

'Privately, I was very pleased but I didn't want the men to become too blasé about the business. What we had proved to my satisfaction, and it was something I could use to positive effect at MEHQ, was that we could operate under a variety of tactics to the same end, and what was more, we were no longer dependent on moonless nights. This was always providing that MEHQ would keep me supplied with men, jeeps and Vickers guns. We had one small problem in that a couple of the guns seized up. I know that it wasn't bad maintenance because the men looked after the weapons superbly well. We decided that the Vickers, which was air-cooled, wasn't getting anywhere near the same volume of air rushing past it as it would when mounted on a Gloucester. We could minimise the problem by using shorter bursts of fire.

'There was an amusing incident during that action; one of the patrols, LRDG I think, had taken prisoners. A light aircraft had landed near them – the pilot had naturally thought them to be Germans. The two officers who got out were arrested and brought back to the RV. One of them was a doctor and a Baron [von Luteroti] to boot. It turned out that George Jellicoe knew his wife before the war. The men thought this was very funny and I think George was credited with all sorts of sexual exploits with the Baroness which I'm sure were not true.'

The prisoners were later to escape; it seems that their passage was unobstructed. They were within forty miles of their own lines and safety, and it is rumoured that they were given guidance on basic navigation along with water and rations. Stirling planned to press home his advantage by remaining in the RV area for three to four weeks getting resupplied by parachute or light aircraft, and conducting nightly attacks over a wide area using their new-found mobility. He had taken the precaution of organising this before he left Cairo. He and Mayne began to plan the next series of operations when they were interrupted.

'I got a personal message from MEHQ ordering me back to Cairo to take part in an operation which they had planned. They still hadn't got the message. The only persons who would plan SAS operations were SAS officers. I retaliated with a signal to this effect and stated that if I were to be "supported and not thwarted" my force could have a devastating effect on Rommel's communications. I seem to remember saying that if the SAS were to come under anyone else's authority I would refuse that instruction under "pain of court martial". It didn't change anything. I was ordered back and told that the operation was vitally important and that I would have "a free hand". Free hand my backside, if I'd been given a free hand I'd have had patrols moving out within a few hours. There was no real alternative, I had to go.'

Stirling had planned to spend up to twelve days harrying soft-skinned enemy targets in the immediate vicinity of the El Alamein line. This at first sight seemed ridiculously dangerous but, 'It was a further change of tactics. We would certainly not be expected so close to the front. All sorts of soft convoys were moving around just behind the German front line carrying rations, ammunition and personnel. If we could get amongst them I was sure we could create some havoc and have the enemy feeling that they weren't safe anywhere. They would have had to pull soldiers and armoured vehicles back from the front line to take on escort and guard duties. The signal to return thwarted this. I decided to change the time schedule. They'd instructed the whole force to return but I wasn't having that. I left about half the force there and told them to spend four or five days shooting up soft targets and then to make their way back to Cairo. There wasn't time for them to be more than moderately effective but they did upset the applecart for the Germans in a small way.'

Stirling was already in Cairo when the remainder of his force came in, so he did not hear the story of their harrowing experience until later. They had chosen to drive through the Qattara Depression and, after three days driving through rugged country, the dirty, tired group reached the bottom of the Depression. Here is the description of the rest of the journey written by Captain Carol Mather, one of the patrol commanders, and published in the *Royal Geographic Journal* in April 1944.

By the starlight we only got a vague impression of the surrounding land; our route descended gradually amongst broken country, and as I was navigating I had to concentrate wholly on the wheel marks I was following. It was very tiring and exacting work. After about fifty miles we swung south-east passing over a flat gravel surface scattered with stunted acacias, giving, in the gentle light, a rather park-like appearance. This scanty vegetation showed us that we were at the bottom of the Depression.

At about three o'clock the crescent moon began to rise, and we hit the track at exactly the correct mileage. We would have to hurry if we were going to get out of the flat bog by daylight, but we stopped to check our bearings, then drove on for four miles until we lost the track and on turning round we found, to our horror, that we were missing ten vehicles. The drivers were so dead tired they had all gone to sleep at the last halt, and even the cries of 'start up' and the noise of the engines had not awakened them. After an hour's search we found all ten of them standing motionless in the desert, with drivers slumped over their wheels.

The situation was getting critical now. There was an hour until daylight, and here we were in the middle of the Depression with no cover within miles. We drove on fast for a few more miles, but after two bad collisions we gave up the attempt and raced back to the escarpment where we would find shelter for the day. We turned and saw in the dim light of dawn the great cliff towering behind us, but it was more than two hours before we plunged into its deep shade.

Here, lying beneath the 400 ft cliff, we spent our second day. We must have been about twenty miles from the Qattara Spring. It was intensely hot but we felt secure from any enemy planes . . . It was pleasing having cheated them so far, for there was no doubt that they had been after our blood for the past three weeks. From where we lay under boulders and wedged between rock clefts, we could see as far as the eye stretched – to the east a firm but broken coast, to the south-east a flat gravel plain, we were unable to see any sign of bog or marsh. However, we thought it would be wiser to retrace our old tracks of the night before until we should come to the main Qattara Crossing track. From here we could follow it slowly and carefully until we had passed over the bog.

That night we made our second attempt to cross the Depression. We followed the beaten track carefully until it became only a few wheel marks. Then we found ourselves following a single wheel track only, very difficult to see by starlight, and so cast left and right to locate the main routes once again. A few miles more and it petered out altogether. Then we found ourselves travelling over a rough rocky surface which continued for about 200 yards. At the end of this distance lay a hard salt crust with a quaking bog beneath. We sent out four jeeps to the four compass points. Three returned and reported bog on all sides, the fourth with all its kit sank beyond recovery, bonnet deep into the bog itself. Again only one hour till daylight. The unfortunate thing was that as the surrounding surface was hard rock we were unable to trace the route we had entered by, and so we seemed to be stranded.

Then we found an outlet. It was undoubtedly bog beneath, but there seemed to be a fairly stout crust. It might lead us into a further bog – we had no idea what lay beyond, but it was our only chance. For three hundred yards the surface held even our heavy trucks. Then we came to a dyke of soft mud . . . only about ten feet across.

We put tarpaulins, steel sand channels, sand mats and more tarpaulins over this, and each vehicle charged it at top speed. It had to be done very quickly because the stationary vehicles on the near side soon began sinking slowly through the crust, in fact we were too late with our last three-tonner for when its time came to take the jump it had sunk up to the axles and soon the tailboard began to disappear. We abandoned it and hurried on to the next dyke. This we bridged in a similar manner, and a third, and just when we were beginning to think that to continue was foolhardy and to return was impossible, the ground began to steady. The upper surface became spongy but there seemed to be a firm foundation beneath, and before we knew where we were we had entered a wide flat gravel plain.

We halted for a few moments to get our direction. Took a bearing on a low constellation of stars, switched on all our headlights and raced at 50 mph towards the north-east. The dawn was just beginning to break, the billiard table surface lasted, and we covered thirty miles in less than an hour. We raced on until we reached a large grove of acacias under whose friendly shade we finally came to rest.

This almost matter-of-fact narrative belies the extreme limits of endurance reached by all the patrols. Stirling's group had also crossed the Depression, and he was to have no significant rest before he reported to MEHQ.

The 'grand plan' outlined to Stirling by MEHQ was to force him to make perhaps the most difficult decision of his war. In a strange way it was also the key to the future of the SAS though he did not know it at the time.

Some time before Stirling had, in a fit of enthusiasm, explained his ideas for the SAS to a man who had successfully operated as a British agent for almost a year along the Cyrenaica coastline. This was Colonel John Haselden, a pre-war Arabian traveller and expert on Arab languages and affairs. It was Haselden who had built on Stirling's original concept of a massive raid on Benghazi town and harbour with full air and naval support.

Auchinleck would not be persuaded into an offensive until around October; MEHQ intelligence believed that Rommel was going to make his drive for Alexandria and Cairo before then. Any operation which stood a fighting chance of disrupting his supply lines would make his plans more difficult. Haselden's proposal, with some fine tuning, was therefore attractive to MEHQ.

The basic plan outlined to Stirling was thus: the SAS, heavily reinforced by troops allocated to him by MEHQ, would attack Benghazi. The force would number in the region of 250 men and 80 to 100 vehicles split between heavy support duties and armed jeeps. He would destroy everything and hold a number of positions. The LRDG would attack and destroy Barce airfield. A force (probably the Sudan Defence Force) would take Jalo Oasis, and in a major operation Colonel Haselden, with naval artillery and Commando support, would take and hold Tobruk. On paper, simple; in reality, to Stirling's mind, ridiculous. There were too many major flaws.

The MEHQ planners had got the measure of Stirling's ambitions now even if they still didn't understand the philosophy behind them. They requested him to lead the Benghazi attack and promised that, in the event of a successful operation, he would be given area command with the responsibility of destroying all enemy installations in Cyrenaica according to his own plans. MEHQ would further ensure that the SAS would be expanded under his direction. This seductive measure alone did not convince Stirling.

'It was patently obvious that I couldn't accept their word with any real confidence. The operation was against every single principle of the SAS. It had been planned by persons with no training or experience in our operations. It was, in part at least, a tactical use of the SAS. I was expected to take completely untrained men with me. Lastly, there was just no way that surprise could be achieved with those sorts of numbers – I was back to the "thundering herd". On top of that, look at Haselden, an intelligence officer! He was to command a taskforce which not only meant leading infantry-men but required close co-operation with naval artillery and Commandos; units and tactics quite unknown to him. At that point I made my feelings known in a very sharp fashion but I had to agree at least to attend the planning meeting at HQ.'

At the meeting were the Director of Military Operations (DMO); representatives from both A and Q Branches; RAF and Royal Naval intelligence units; an air vice-marshal (AVM) and an air commodore (AC) whose names have been lost and, of course, Stirling. The atmosphere was tense. Stirling's objections were by then well known and he was not exactly popular with MEHQ.

The AVM lost no time in making his personal views known:

'This is a job for regular troops and not the colourful individualists which seem to have been attracted to the SAS.'

'The SAS is as well disciplined and led as any regular unit but I agree, it is not a job for us,' retorted the nettled Stirling.

'I don't mean to say that the unit is not courageous but I dare say that the word enthusiastic better describes them than disciplined. I believe that on the evidence I have seen in this headquarters some of the claims made by the SAS have been exaggerated.'

'If anything we have always under-claimed on our results. If I, or one of my men, see an aircraft in flames we feel reasonably confident that it is on fire. If we see one explode we feel equally confident that it cannot fly for at least some days. If we plant a bomb on an aircraft and see neither of those things taking place then we make no assumption whatsoever and this is reflected in all our reports.' Stirling could keep neither the sarcasm nor the distaste out of his voice.

The AVM stuck to his guns: 'This is nonsense. It has to be tried and tested regular troops for Benghazi.'

Stirling, having spotted a heavy glass inkwell on the DMO's desk, was stretching his hand towards it, possessed of an uncharacteristic rage. The DMO noticed the movement as did the A Branch staff officer to Stirling's side. The one locked eyes with him and the other reached out a restraining hand but not before the AVM had also seen the movement. The situation could have become even more explosive had not the AC interjected.

'I believe Major Stirling is right. His unit has been phenomenally successful, post-operation air photography has confirmed everything he has ever claimed. Even though he does not consider this to be an SAS task, and I think I appreciate his reasoning, I am in favour of his taking the initiative in Benghazi if simply because he is the only commander we have available who has actually been there – and on more than one occasion I believe?' He turned to Stirling inquisitively.

'The game was lost in that moment. I could still have

refused and I believe that I should have done so, but I feel that I would have been replaced on the spot. I also felt that I had lost ground and would appear merely to be bleating unnecessarily. I found out later that the AVM was aggrieved because someone, Marriott I think, had suggested that as the SAS had knocked out more aircraft than any RAF squadron I should be awarded the DFC.'

There is little doubt that Stirling's acquiescence was due to the gambler in him, but the gambler might have been controlled had he not been so utterly weary. Even then he was to have no rest. Looking forward to twenty-four hours' sleep in Peter's flat, Stirling was summoned to a dinner which was to change the course of history for the SAS.

'At first I thought we had been invited because Peter was, of course, very close to the British Ambassador, Sir Miles Lampton. This was not the case; Randolph had been talking to his father in much the manner in which I'd hoped but not really expected. The Prime Minister was in Cairo and, with Generals Smuts and Alexander, he was being wined and dined at the British Embassy that night. Fitzroy and I were invited.'

Stirling's tiredness was shed like an unwanted cloak. If he could get into conversation with Winston Churchill there was hope yet for the SAS.

'Fitzroy and I were warned not to discuss the Benghazi raid with Churchill and were amazed that the reason given for this was his apparent inability to maintain security. We decided to ignore the advice anyway if we got the opportunity. It was a superb dinner; it is difficult to conceive now of a table set with the best of silver and served with the best food Cairo could offer, with the British Prime Minister at the head of the feast, just forty or so miles from the Allied front line. It was a little unreal even for Cairo. It was amusing to see that Winston wore one of the famous siren suits that I'd only read about until then – I do believe he had a bow tie though.

'I was called across to meet him after dinner and I was not surprised to hear that some of our exploits had been a little titivated by Randolph – not that it did any harm. He invited Fitzroy and me to join him in a stroll round the garden, during which I told him everything about the Benghazi raid from the SAS point of view and even said I did not consider this one of our classic rôles. I mentioned that I saw us being used in Europe at a later stage. I was told afterwards that he had used the "Don Juan" quotation to describe me to Smuts. I'm not certain of this; I always understood it had been used to portray "Shimi" Lovat.'*

Churchill's interest was sufficiently aroused for him to ask to see Stirling again the following evening. Stirling literally bumped into Churchill on the Embassy stairs. As Stirling reeled back from the solid body, Winston said, 'Hmmph. The irresistible force meets the immovable object, eh?'

During this second meeting, Stirling was able to make some significant observations to Churchill upon which the latter was to act. He conveyed his absolute conviction that the SAS had a positive rôle long after the desert war was over. He, Stirling, was looking to Sicily, Italy and then the 'the soft underbelly of Europe'. His immediate problems were that the concept of usage of the SAS was not fully appreciated by the local commanders and in any event it was still only a detachment which could be disbanded at any time. If it were to become a properly constituted regiment, no one could deny it the continuing task in Europe and beyond.

'Winston did not comment very much, apart from asking me if he could use the phrase "soft underbelly of Europe". He thought it was a good hunter's expression and properly described the Mediterranean flank to which I'd applied it. I

---

* Churchill is reputed to have said: 'He was the mildest mannered man that ever scuttled ship or cut a throat.'

was a touch disappointed but there was little more I could say about the SAS.'*

A veil is drawn over the Benghazi operation; not because it was a disaster, though it certainly was, but it has little bearing on Stirling himself except to show that he was wrong to accede to MEHQ's blandishments and misuse the SAS. Not only was the force expected by the Germans but many of the liaison duties went tragically wrong. The operation encompassed many individual acts of immense bravery, and the SAS fought with the courage and tenacity of lions. Though it was a task they should never have been committed to, no other unit could have bettered their performance. Nevertheless, Stirling lost 25 per cent of his force killed, wounded, captured or missing, and 75 per cent of his transport was disabled or destroyed. Tobruk was even more of a disaster. Only the LRDG attack on Barce was successful and they destroyed thirty-two aircraft by operating in the classic SAS fashion.

As ever with the SAS there was humour in adversity. In a

---

* In a personal letter to Mrs Stirling written in 1943, the writer refers to Winston Churchill's enthusiasm: 'I saw Randolph Churchill on Friday and . . . he talked about David for 1½ hrs! . . . He told me that Winston had been bowled over by David and saw him three times in Egypt. He personally introduced D. to Gen Alex. and Gen Montgomery and told him they were to give him a free hand in everything – later Gen Alex. asked David how many men he had and when he heard 400, told him he should make it 4000. He then offered him a Brigade which D. courteously but firmly refused. Later David saw Mr C. and Gen Smuts together and Randolph said Gen Smuts considers David the most brilliant soldier in the M.E. Apparently Mr Churchill came home talking not of Stalin but of David whom he calls the Scarlet Pimpernel – Randolph gave a life-like imitation of his father, which would earn him a fortune on the stage . . . Randolph then described the only raid he'd been on with David where they spent 4 days in an enemy-held town. As a raid it wasn't a success but as a story of courage it's unparalleled. It was on their return that they had the car smash. David was driving but the accident was not his fault as it was caused by the last truck of a big convoy pulling out in front of them and meeting them practically head-on. Randolph's back was quite badly injured but he hopes to be all right in 2 or 3 months and then his one wish is to rejoin David. His unbounded affection for D. is touching – all the more so as D. treats him as a dogsbody, if that! This he in no way resents or conceals. He was struck by D's intense faith . . .

post-war interview, Sir Stephen Hastings recalled, 'After David had flown out to Cairo we went back by different routes. My party arrived at the River Nile and took a steamer back up to Alexandria. We were a sorry-looking lot and we'd had a pretty hard time one way and another. We were literally in rags and tatters; the French looked even worse as they still had their beards. We tied up one night and I remember we had a visitor in the shape of a Medical Corps corporal.

'"Sir, you are invited to a party on board the hospital ship."'

'We were in no shape to go to a party dressed as we were and I told the fellow that.

'"Sir, the matron 'as asked me to invite you and that's what I'm doing." A smart salute and off he went. We looked across at the hospital ship and sure enough the deck rails were lined with nurses in their sparkling white uniforms, waving and calling to us. So, off we went. The expressions on their faces as we climbed the ladders was a sight to behold especially as the French hove into view. That was one party which was definitely not a success.

'We eventually ended up in a barracks just outside Alexandria and we reported in to the quartermaster's stores to get kitted out with new clothing. As we lined up we realised that we still had an Italian with us. We'd got so used to him that we'd forgotten that he was a prisoner. He was really quite a useful chap. His name was Antonio – we called him Tony. He used to make us pots of tea, cook and generally carry out the more boring camp duties; he was perfectly happy – he certainly preferred our company to the alternatives.

'"Boots, pairs one; shorts, khaki drill, pairs one; socks, knee, pairs one; shirts, khaki drill, one," intoned the Quartermaster Sergeant as each man was issued with some basic replacement clothing. "Name? OK, sign 'ere," he went on.

'It came to Tony's turn; he was quite impressed with the fact that he was apparently to get the same uniform as his captors.

'"Name?" demanded the Sergeant. "Er, Tony, signor," respectfully answered our man.

'"Tony? Tony what?" At that moment the penny dropped and the Sergeant almost dropped his millboard in his haste to get Tony rushed into the guardroom as a prisoner of war. He completed the kit issue with muttered imprecations about a variety of "hirregularities" and "wot's the bloody war comin' to".

'We did manage to put in a good word for Tony eventually and make sure that he was properly looked after but we missed having him around.'

Stirling took some heart from the fact that the Benghazi raid was the first real débâcle he had experienced. He rightly didn't include the parachute operation – tragic though it had been, it was part of the learning process and had put the SAS on the right track. Furthermore, the only successful attack, on the Barce airfield by Jake Easonsmith and his LRDG patrols, had been conducted according to standard SAS tactics and was further proof that these were correct.

Even so Stirling was expecting derision from the MEHQ officers. He could not have been more wrong! During his absence, and it explained Churchill's presence, General Alexander had taken over command from Auchinleck and General Montgomery had relieved Ritchie. Stirling was sorry about the Auk, they had become very close and he held the General in high esteem.

He was greeted with the news that he was now Lieutenant Colonel and invited to meet General Alexander, who bore more good news. He was to be allowed to recruit up to full regimental strength because the Special Air Service Regiment was now an accepted part of the British Army Order of Battle! From Stirling's perspective the operation had been a failure, and indeed it had been in terms of true effect. But it had borne home to MEHQ the force's speed of planning and deployment; its versatility in action; the outstanding competence and courage of the troops and the powerful leadership abilities of David Stirling. Ironically, therefore, it was the Benghazi débâcle and not the SAS's previous successes which finally convinced MEHQ staff what a potent force they had at their disposal if Stirling's rules were obeyed, and led to the SAS's formal recognition as a unit with a full rôle to play in the remainder of the war.

Not since the Boer War, when David Stirling's uncle Lord Lovat had raised the Lovat Scouts, had a new regiment been added to the Order of Battle. In little more than a year Lieutenant David Stirling had risen from that rank with detachment command to Lieutenant-Colonel in command of his own regiment – this at the age of twenty-six years. The tide was surely turning – or was it? Stirling had yet to meet General Montgomery.

---

# 12

# THE FLEDGLING SOARS

The Boy Stirling is mad. Quite, quite mad. However,
in war there is often a place for mad people . . . Who
but the Boy Stirling could think up such a plan?
General Sir Bernard Montgomery

Pause now to look at Stirling's achievements for it is a good
point at which to examine the still-developing character of the
young man. Promotion from Lieutenant to Lieutenant-Colonel
in just over a year was exceptional, but in time of war it was
rare rather than unique. But in the same short year the man
had forced the acceptance of a new concept of warfare, and
had personally led L Detachment.

Stirling's critics have said that the SAS was simply an idea
waiting to happen and that, had it not been Stirling, some
other outstanding officer would have taken the lead. The fact
remains that it was Stirling – anything else is conjecture. The
comparisons with Orde Wingate and Vladimir Peniakoff do not
hold water. Wingate and Stirling were both original thinkers in
terms of their concepts, and their exploits had similar effects on
different campaigns; not only material effects but also dramatic
improvements in morale throughout the 8th and 14th Armies.
Wingate, with his Chindits, struck deep and daringly into the

jungles of Burma and proved that the Japanese were not invincible – but he stayed with the 'thundering herd' and suffered heavy casualties.

'Popski', a somewhat piratical raider-cum-intelligence gatherer, though undeniably brave, probably earned his reputation more through his flamboyant character and rumour than measured damage to the German war effort. This said, he was certainly wise enough prior to the fateful Benghazi raid to stipulate that he would operate only in conjunction with the LRDG against Barce. Not in cause, method or effect does he stand comparison with Stirling.

Stirling has said that he had three 'enemies' to contend with in the Middle East, 'the Hun, MEHQ and SOE.' His reasoning was straightforward. 'The Hun was the enemy to us all and on that we agreed. The divergence came when it came to deciding how to use the SAS to help achieve his destruction. My secondary enemies made life very difficult at times. MEHQ was a strange mixture of talents and jealousies. At the lower end of the scale were the young, thrusting officers full of adventurous and often romantic ideas but basically wanting nothing more than to join the fight. At the top were some marvellously competent, very experienced senior officers getting on with the job to the best of their abilities and resources whilst shouldering immense political pressures from London. In the middle – and not always bridging the gap – could be found my "layer of fossilised shit". There was the stratum of jealousy, frustration and, often, incompetence: middle-ranking officers shifted into a major headquarters because of staff qualifications earned during peacetime or because they fitted nowhere else.

'Those who wanted to join the fight (and some undoubtedly did not want to) were frustrated; they saw no reason to give support so that some other officer could go off and "have a jolly good time at the front". Some, brought up to the strict traditions of textbook soldiering, were obstructive purely because "it wasn't done", despite the fact that many of them had no battle experience whatsoever. Some just didn't seem to give a damn anyway and the fact that I was outranked did not help.

'I believe that SOE saw the SAS as a ready trained pool of manpower heaven sent for their purposes. They never got it into their heads that we were strategic troops. Troops. Uniformed, disciplined, military troops with a proper military part to play. Not spies in civilian clothes; not individuals to be sent off here and there to blow up the odd bridge or factory. Through MEHQ they brought a lot of pressure to bear to have us brought under their control – and they got a lot of support from some quarters. You ask what the keys to success were. Non-swanks, I think it was because I thought things out in great detail and I truly believed in what we were trying to do; on top of this we had more than a little help from le bon Dieu at times; I certainly placed great demands on Him. I suppose the MEHQ attitudes actually helped me in a perverse way – they put me on my toes certainly.'

Many people bear witness to the fact that there was much more to it than Stirling's 'non-swanks' statement. An analysis of his character and actions of the time displays a remarkable perspicacity.

He had recognised his 'enemies' early and his first shrewd observation had been that he must never lose personal command of the SAS and he must be under the direct command of the highest military authority. Thus he maximised his chances of gaining authority for the operations he considered most suitable, and minimised the ability of others to interfere. His utter belief in the rightness of his concept is undeniable; in a very determined man who was not above taking comfort from the Almighty when he needed it, this produced a formidable figure. Alone, it was not enough.

If his SAS was going to achieve what Stirling knew to be possible it had to *want* to partake. He realised that a special force not only had to attain the highest order of training and discipline it had also to *feel* that it was special. The mechanical procedure of physically producing the right nucleus was not particularly difficult – first-class fighting soldiers were there in quantity. Stirling recognised one fundamental during the early stages; the SAS had to be led and not just commanded; led in such a way that if the leaders fell motivation would not fail, nor the force be stopped. He therefore chose his first officers with specific qualities in mind: different though they may have seemed they were all able and willing to do everything they asked of their men, and demonstrated a deep respect for those soldiers.

'There was no point in one's having high ideals and good, meaty targets unless the force was fully behind one. I never lied to the SAS and I never demanded anything which I did not fully believe to be possible.'

Stirling's quiet honesty and courtesy is well remembered although he is often fondly accused of some understatement in assessing the odds! His style of leadership inspired admiration, loyalty, and indeed friendship amongst the whole of his command. His success against the MEHQ 'enemy' was certainly partially ascribable to 'thinking things out'. He would spend a lot of time imagining as many of the questions as he could and formulating passable (but not always honest) answers. Not that he was unable to think on his feet; he had a most alert brain and could instantly recognise a threat or an opportunity and act accordingly. 'It was a case of "prenez maximum garde" from the moment one stepped into MEHQ.'

He exercised firm self-discipline in his dealings with the staff. Though naturally courteous, Stirling was prone to bouts of immense frustration when the perceived need for speed of decision and action was thwarted. This could lead to flashes of fierce temper brought on by the migraine from which he suffered during times of stress. He knew he must control this and the only time he almost succumbed was during the inkwell incident mentioned earlier. He won most of his battles by sheer power of argument. He had the enviable knack of explaining something so apparently clearly that the listener felt foolish if he should question it. This was a deliberately calculated and well-rehearsed tactic and Stirling continued to use it throughout his life.

'To fight within MEHQ would have got me nowhere. Occasionally I would pretend to get angry, but I preferred the quiet approach and sometimes lead a discussion so that my opponent appeared to have the idea himself; thereafter it was a simple matter of flattery to get what I wanted. One had to recognise the jealousies within the HQ; the staff were mainly concerned with the major battlegrounds – they were unable to correlate our successes with our ever-increasing demands for ammunition and equipment and vehicles; the fact that bullet for bullet it was well-spent seemed to escape their calculations. There were frustrated officers in there and the least sign of self-aggrandisement or boasting on the part of the SAS would have fuelled the jealousies and could have been catastrophic.'

At times, Stirling employed more direct tactics with MEHQ to get what he wanted, as is demonstrated by his recruitment of Wilfred Thesiger. Thesiger was with SOE; he was frustrated by inactivity and heard by chance of Stirling and the SAS. He was advised that Stirling was about to set off on a raid and was directed to the Cairo flat. The twenty-five-year-old Thesiger was already a desert veteran, having spent several pre-war years in exploration and served with Orde Wingate in Abyssinia; he was also fluent in Arabic. He explained his position to Stirling (whose main concern was how Thesiger had known about the raid) and found himself instantly acceptable. Stirling's resolution of the problem of gaining MEHQ's authority was quite simple: he telephoned the Military Secretary, a brigadier.

'This is Colonel Stirling. With me in my office I have Major Thesiger. I am going to take him with me on an operation. Would you please release him at once.'

Thesiger was then directed to make his own way to Kabrit, acquaint himself with the men and await Stirling's arrival the next day. These two had much in common and after the war they became firm friends. (Thesiger, perhaps the last of the great explorers in the nineteenth-century mould, still lives in the Africa he loves so much.)

On 4 August 1942, Winston Churchill had arrived in Cairo to make a personal assessment of the situation. His mind was already made up that Auchinleck must be replaced. Despite a huge influx of men and materials the Auk was still strongly resisting Churchill's exhortations for an offensive before September. Although the British now had a healthy superiority over Rommel's forces a large percentage of the men were new to action and to the desert. Auchinleck was not going to make his move until the training phase was completed. Smuts, a powerful influence, agreed with Churchill.

Churchill decided that Alexander would become the new Commander-in-Chief and that 'Strafer' Gott would take over as Commander of the 8th Army. Gott died in an aircraft crash the day after the decision was made and command passed to General Bernard Montgomery. The hierarchical change was completed with the arrival from the United Kingdom of Lieutenant-Generals Oliver Leese and Brian Horrocks as commanders of 30th and 13th Corps respectively.

Rommel's eastward thrust at the end of August was repulsed and he was forced to yield ground. Alexander decided to hold rather than follow up the success. The British offensive (unknown to Stirling) was scheduled to resume in late October. Morale in the 8th Army was beginning to rise as a result of this first significant 'victory'. Rommel's supply lines were sorely stretched over the thousand-mile line between Bouerat and Alamein.

One further change within MEHQ was to affect the SAS. Stirling was briefed by the Director of Military Operations on the new branch which had been established to coordinate all 'special activities' to ensure that they conformed with the tactical aims of the 8th Army. Stirling was filled with

foreboding, but it disappeared when he met the General Staff
Officer 1 (GSO 1) of 'G Raiding Force'. He had imagined
having to face more proposals along the lines of the Benghazi
débâcle. Not so. Colonel Shan Hackett and Colonel David
Stirling liked each other the moment they met at Peter Stirling's
flat. Hackett and Peter Stirling already knew each other well
and Hackett was familiar with the exploits of the SAS.

General Sir John Hackett commented on his rôle as GSO1,
GRF in a post-war interview. 'After the Benghazi raid, which
was a cock-up, there was a growing awareness in MEHQ that
the Mediterranean and the Middle East generally was a small
raiding paradise most apt to exploitation by the British whose
maritime background had made them very sensitive to, very
much aware of the opportunities for exploitation that lie in the
open flank. There was the Mediterranean full of open flanks; if
there wasn't sea there were islands, there was desert, there were
mountains; the thing was a divine complex of open flanks and,
of course, raiding-minded Brits dropped into this and began to
find ways of sporting around in it.

'The thing had got wholly out of hand. The place was full
of private armies. So GHQ reckoned they ought to sort this
out and they set up a new staff cell at GHQ Middle East
which they called G Raiding Forces with a GSO 1 in charge
of it. Freddy de Guingand had just gone up to 8th Army as
Chief of Staff to the newly arrived Monty. I knew him well,
we were old friends. They wanted a chap to take charge of
this G Raiding Forces and I drew the short straw. I was then
Second-in-Command of a splendid armoured lot, much looking
forward to the next encounter and getting ready for it – the
last thing I wanted to do was to go and sit in a bloody office
in Cairo. I protested loudly with a very rude note to Freddy
but they were merciless and I had to take the post.

'This was really where my association with David began
because he was one of the prima donnas I was there to try
to control. My business was therefore first of all to try to
sort out this extraordinary array of private armies; after that

to try to make special operations comprehensible to senior commanders and thereafter to try to make them palatable so that it was possible to get them what they wanted to carry out the operations. David and I became very close allies naturally enough – if he couldn't get what he wanted he'd go and purloin it. There was this extraordinary array as I've said – there they were, the LRDG, absolute maestros at what they were doing with their deep reconnaissance with the occasional beat-up just to keep their hands in and cheer them up a bit; there was L Detachment, wonderful beaters-up occasionally doing a bit of reconnaissance just for fun. But a little later on as I was trying to handle this circus, I came across this difficulty, that the LRDG would perform a circuitous route of say a couple of thousand miles with dumps up and down the desert to put two men in the Tripoli road watch which was brilliant, absolutely brilliant. Fine, and there they'd be two hundred yards from the main artery logging all the men that came down and signalling GHQ in Cairo. It was remarkable – invaluable – one of the most important reconnaissance operations of the whole war.

'Then the SAS would come out to blow up some aeroplanes on a handy airfield and they were the most untidy operators, they'd leave everything around the place. Then the Axis Force would mobilise a security operation to cleanse this lot out of the place, search around and find the LRDG you see. Well, I couldn't have this so I adopted the device of an ancient pope who, discovering that the Portuguese and the Spanish tended to get in each other's way in the Atlantic and the New World drew a line down the middle and said, "West of that only Spaniards; east of this only Portuguese."

'I did the same in the desert, drew a line down the middle and said, "West of that – LRDG, SAS keep out. East of this – only SAS. LRDG enter at your peril." This was later on of course, but I was much concerned with that cock-up of earlier on and I wanted to inject as much order as I could into these things and it began to develop into a going concern. Very heterogeneous, not at all orderly, but like-minded people working very hard to do their best. There was the LRDG, the SAS, Special Boat Squadron, the Libyan Arab Force, the Greek Sacred Squadron, a bunch of Turkish assassins called the Kalpaks and then Popski's private army.

'During all this time I saw quite a bit of David and we saw absolutely eye to eye. My business was to find work for him, to get people accustomed to having him working in their patches and to see that he was adequately provided with everything he wanted, to do what he felt inclined to do, which was the main thing. He was by far the best chap to choose the targets he would operate most effectively against. We had a very close alliance and before Alamein we needed recruits. Monty was then in charge.'

Hackett's reputation as a fighting man was already remarkable and he totally understood Stirling's ambition. It was likely that the next British offensive would be a key to the campaign and Stirling could see the immense potential for the SAS harrying, on a nightly basis, Rommel's over-extended supply lines and rear echelon airfields. If aircraft and fuel dumps were to be destroyed it might be that Rommel could find it impossible to withdraw from some of his locations. Stirling's quiet excitement was intense and infectious. All he needed was more men – and quickly. He already had an appointment to meet Montgomery, and Hackett would be with him.

Although Stirling grasped the 'big picture' of the campaign with crystal clarity, his views on 'the Generals' (shared by Hackett) were somewhat jaundiced. He had liked and respected Auchinleck, Alexander and Ritchie but he saw them more as targets to be manipulated to reap maximum support for the SAS than as keys to success in North Africa; they came and they went. Montgomery was just one more in the chain of commanders who would be sent on his way if Churchill became dissatisfied with progress.

'I was surprised when I met him. Quite a short man, not at all fully grown, but he had a way of fixing his eyes on you without flinching. The eyes were a very bright blue; he reminded me of an underweight fighting bantam cock. He never interrupted as far as I can remember and even if he was economical with words, he made himself quite clear.

'Montgomery maintained his forward headquarters quite close to the front. He had a few tents and his personal caravan some ten or twelve miles along from the Alamein Line and that was where Shan and I met him. He asked me quite abruptly what I wanted. I told him how I believed the SAS should be used to best effect during the coming offensive. I explained that I could arrange for nightly raids along a two-hundred-mile line of communication peppered with fuel dumps and aerodromes. Intelligently carried out these operations could cripple Rommel. To do this all I needed was his immediate authority to recruit about 150 men. I urgently needed a lot of senior non-commissioned officers, along with other experienced officers and men. I had to move fast therefore I had to go to the desert-seasoned regiments of all arms. My direct approach to him was not the correct one!'

Montgomery spent long seconds looking first at Hackett and then Stirling before responding. The conversation which followed is recorded in a number of works; from the memories of Stirling and the now General Sir John Hackett it was along these lines:

'If my understanding of your brief is correct, you wish to take some of my men. You want only my best men; my most experienced and dependable men.' Stirling seemed to be about to interject but Montgomery went on. 'I am very proud indeed of my men and I expect them to do great things in the very near future. What, Colonel Stirling, makes you assume that you can handle these men to greater advantage than myself?'

Stirling was amazed. He did not think he had cast any aspersions on the General's abilities to lead – he saw only that in order to get the SAS back into action he needed men quickly. He felt the beginnings of anger and he was very tired.

'Sir, I don't know what you are talking about. I have to bring the SAS up to strength and to do this I need experienced men. I can't carry out the plan I have put to you without them. It will take me far too long to train raw recruits.'

'I also need experienced men,' sarcastically. 'How long does it take you to train your recruits?'

'Raw recruits a couple of months,' replied Stirling, 'experienced men I can train in three or four weeks.'

'My offensive will begin in a fortnight. If I keep my seasoned men they will be used very quickly. If I give them to you they will miss the offensive.'

'Perhaps they won't be ready for the next offensive – but they'll be ready for the one after,' Hackett entered the conversation showing his acute irritation. Who did this man think he was? Didn't he have the wit to see the urgency?

'I don't intend another offensive. The next one will be the last one. What's the matter? Why are you smiling, Stirling?'

'Nothing really, sir, but we heard that from the last general, and the one before him.'

Montgomery treated Stirling to a look of utter contempt. He was obviously nettled. 'My answer is no. No. I find your request arrogant in the extreme. It seems that you think you know the commander's duties better than I do. You failed in Benghazi and come here asking, no, demanding, the best of my men. In all honesty, Colonel Stirling, I'm not of a mind to associate myself with failure.' He held up his hand at Stirling's protestation. 'I am leaving now to lunch at the Guards Brigade Headquarters. I cannot join you but I would be pleased for you and Colonel Hackett to lunch in the officers' mess as my guests. I'm sorry if I disappoint you, Colonel Stirling, but I prefer to keep my best men for myself.' Montgomery brooked no further conversation by turning and leaving.

'God, I was angry,' Stirling remembered it well. 'Shan cooled me down considerably but not sufficiently to let Monty off the hook when it came to his lunch bill. We ate in royal fashion and put a considerable amount of boozo on to his mess chit, the rub being, of course, that Monty was teetotal. If nothing else it cheered us up – Shan was as disappointed as me. After lunch, in fine fettle we returned to Monty's caravan to collect Shan's document case and we ran into Freddy de Guingand who it seemed was then Monty's Chief of Staff. I knew him from my schooldays and had shared the occasional hot meal with him in town before the war. Shan also knew him well.

'We set about the poor beggar mercilessly. I berated him about his new boss's arrogance and told him that without the SAS being injected fairly quickly, the next offensive was doomed. I suppose our mood was more than a little heightened by the wine and Kümmel but we both enjoyed it. I began to pull his leg by saying that the only hope for the offensive was if Churchill persuaded the Yanks to land in North Africa and open up a second front. It was a total throwaway line but we both spotted Freddy's look. It was unmistakeable. A second front *was* planned! Poor old Freddy told us to keep our mouths shut so I tried a bit of not too discreet blackmail by telling him that if he didn't persuade his boss to give me the men I wanted then we would be forced to let it be known that he (Freddy) had leaked the information on the Yank landings to us.

'It didn't help. Freddy told us what a determined beggar Monty was once he'd made up his mind. We had to settle for Freddy's promise to mention the SAS in favourable fashion at every opportunity. I had to reconcile myself to having to recruit soldiers fresh from home and train them as quickly as possible.'

It didn't take Stirling long to find out that Operation Lightfoot, the offensive, was to take place on 23 October and that Operation Torch, the Allied landings, which were to take place at Algiers, Oran and Casablanca, would follow some two weeks later if all went to plan. He had to make the SAS presence felt before then otherwise he could see that given Montgomery's apparent lack of support the regiment could founder into obscurity. After much soul-searching he made his decision.

He looked at the structure of the SAS; it now had regimental status and so he formed his remaining troops into a formal squadron under Major Paddy Mayne. He extracted just sufficient men to form a recruiting and training team and despatched Paddy and his squadron first to Kufra with instructions to cross the Sand Sea with the aid of the LRDG and establish a forward base from which to attack targets along the Matruh railway line and the coastal road as effectively and frequently as possible. Stirling would remain behind to recruit and train the next squadron at Kabrit.

'I was bitterly disappointed to remain behind. I felt I was betraying one of the principles; I had removed myself from front-line command. I had no choice. There was no way I could repeat the business with Paddy Mayne and leave him in base and there was no one else with the experience. There was another aspect, of course; I would be close to Shan Hackett and his GRF headquarters and between us we could keep plugging away at Montgomery and Alexander to make sure that whatever successes Paddy had were quickly made known to them. It became apparent very shortly that Monty's offensive was successful. The line held and from that moment I think we could all see the end of the war in North Africa; albeit many months away, there was a certain inevitability about it.'

Stirling's feelings were understandable, but his decision gained him much. He may have got off to a bad start with Montgomery but Alexander was still staunchly 'on side' and Hackett spared no effort in furthering the SAS cause. Stirling refused to give in to his fatigue but his desert sores eventually forced him into hospital; not that this was a rest period – he simply transferred his office to the ward much to the annoyance of the medical staff.

A letter to his mother in Keir written from hospital shows some interesting approaches to paperwork, military authority and a humbleness regarding his own efforts:

My Dear Mum,

Here with George Jellicoe. He joined the unit about 6 months ago and has been absolutely indispensable. He is much brighter than he appears at 1st sight and I have the greatest confidence in him. I have sent him home for a spell because he has been unwell but also to acquire equipment and bodies.

. . . I thought for a time that my present job would force me into the habit of writing at least official letters, but unluckily this is not the case. I seem to be able to get by without writing anything at all! This is probably my 1st letter of any sort . . . since I last wrote to you – excluding the many abortive letters I began to you or failed to post.

At the moment I am in bed with severe desert sores. As they are probably indistinguishable from bed sores it becomes rather a problem to know when I should get up. I maintain that they are already turning into bed sores but there is general disagreement on this view – especially by the doctor. It is a long time since I have been on an operation. The last one I went on was a long and completely unsuccessful one. Andrew Maxwell asked if he could come and as he assured me there would be no repercussions I said OK. I heard afterwards that Andrew was fully extended in negotiating the permission from his battalion in order to join me for 'a week to 10 days maximum'. But you can imagine how much more fully extended poor Andrew was on returning from the operation which altogether lasted nearly 10 weeks. In fact the repercussions were terrific but fortunately did not break my way. However I hear he is now reinstated and likely to be given command of Right Flank. He was very good value on the operation. But he was far more windy of what the Colonel was going to say on his return than any immediate threat from the enemy – I think he was hoping for a slight wound.

I have just heard that George Jellicoe instead of leaving the day after tomorrow is now leaving this afternoon. This spoils the opportunity of writing a long letter. But I shall be home myself in about a fortnight's time. I am tremendously looking forward to it.

Your loving David


'During that short spell in hospital I got the news that brother

Bill had been given permission to recruit and train a further unit of SAS in Britain. We had never thought it possible that this would come to fruition. The plan was for Bill to recruit and give the boys basic training then they would pass through Kabrit to be desert-hardened and then become 2nd SAS Regiment. We were getting a steady flow into the French squadron which was performing exceedingly well. Further to this I was told that I would shortly have the Special Boat Section under command. From a recruiting point of view I managed to take maximum advantage from what was left of those very fine soldiers from the old Middle East Commando. The better ones who needed the least training we managed to filter through to Paddy to join A Squadron.

'It would have been towards the middle of November 1942 that I made a full assessment of the SAS potential. With the end of the war in North Africa in sight, though distant, I had to follow up on what I had said to Winston. I had to be ready with a plan to move out of the desert and into other pastures. To gain credence for the plan, which would first have to be presented to Montgomery, I must ensure that we had maximum impact in Africa before the end of the war. We had to be remembered.

'I drafted a plan which reasoned that A Squadron should shortly be sent to the Lebanon to take a familiarisation course in mountain work and skiing so that it could fit smoothly into any operations in Persia or Turkey if the Caucasian passes came under threat. Prior to that I would extract from the group under training the most advanced personnel to form B Squadron, appoint the best commander and send them to link up with Paddy and exert pressure on the German Army along the whole four-hundred-mile length of the road and rail between Agheila and Tripoli. We would mount between four and six operations each night regardless of the moon phase. This would mean dividing into sixteen to eighteen troops depending on how many men I could muster from Kabrit.

'If we got a move on we ought to be able to coincide with

Monty's next offensive which was planned for December. If we could tie down Rommel by night the RAF should be able to contain his supply lines by day. I sent my plan to Shan Hackett for his approval and submission to Monty. I did not want to chance meeting him personally in case he disagreed and the rift created at the first meeting should broaden.'

In fact Stirling had had a number of meetings with Montgomery since that early incident, and had come to regard the 8th Army Commander in a different light. He was positive and he was determined. He appeared to accept Stirling but remained, though polite, distant and aloof.

Hackett approved the plan but not without reservations; B Squadron could not be considered fully trained by any means but he acquiesced under the weight of Stirling's enthusiasm and secured Montgomery's unreserved agreement. At this point Stirling slipped in his *coup de grâce*. He acknowledged Hackett's point that the men were not fully trained; however, they were very enthusiastic and he, Stirling, would continue their training en route to the RV with Mayne. On the way to the RV in a wadi at Bir Zalten (160 miles south of Agheila) there would be time to hone the troops; it would, with an allowance for being slowed down for tactical training, take about ten days.

Overriding Hackett's objections by pointing out that he must command unseasoned troops himself, he appointed George Jellicoe his second-in-command, tasked with completing the training of the remaining men. Hackett did not protest through lack of confidence in Jellicoe; he was thoroughly taken with the long-term plans for the SAS and wanted Stirling to be at Kabrit at a time when he knew that key organisational and planning decisions were to be taken. Hackett agreed only on the promise that Stirling would return as soon as was humanly possible.

B Squadron left Kabrit on the morning of 20 November and as soon as the convoy of forty-five vehicles was under way Stirling forgot about taking time out to train. He wanted to get his ninety-six men into action as soon as possible. They covered the ground in nine long, arduous days to find that Mayne had prepared the reception well. He had constructed hides for the vehicles in the soft sandstone overhangs and was carrying out a full maintenance schedule on A Squadron's vehicles and weapons.

Planning got under way with great intensity; Stirling still felt that time was short for him to consolidate the position of the SAS with Montgomery. The outcome was an apportionment of responsibility between the two squadrons: Mayne to take the area east of Bouerat and to begin his attacks immediately; B Squadron to operate to the west under command of Vivian Street. Stirling with his mobile headquarters would initially move with Street and 'blister' himself on to whichever troop he wanted. His reasoning in this sub-division was that Mayne's experienced squadron was well able to go into action at short notice whilst it would take B Squadron some days to reach their operational area thus giving them more time to gel together. By his reckoning it would take the 8th Army until late January to reach and occupy Tripoli and the SAS would keep just far enough ahead of the advance to inflict the maximum hindrance on the retreating Rommel.

Unknown to Stirling, he had made a deep impression on General Montgomery. Shan Hackett was present at a dinner at which Montgomery said, 'The Boy Stirling is mad. Quite, quite mad. However in war there is often a place for mad people. Now take this scheme of his. Penetrating miles behind the enemy lines. Attacking the coastal road on a four-hundred-mile front. Who but the Boy Stirling could think up such a plan? Yet if it comes off I don't mind saying it could have a really decisive effect on my forthcoming offensive.'

Stirling was not to hear this until some time later, but he got an intimation of Montgomery's change of heart in a signal from the delighted Hackett shortly after the dinner: 'Army

Commander feels your activities could have decisive effect on course of battle.'

Stirling's pithy reply was 'Congratulate Army Commander on perspicacity.'

Mayne's A Squadron were in action within two days, and they soon hit problems. The going was the toughest they had ever encountered and four jeeps and their crews had to be discarded along the way with instructions to operate locally and make as much of a nuisance of themselves as they could. Stirling pressed on but it took until 13 December for them to take up their attack positions based on Bir Fascia – the date coincided with D – 1 of the 8th Army's major offensive.

Stirling, conscious of his promise to Colonel Hackett, duly made his way back to MEHQ but not before enjoying a 'little fling'. Montgomery's push was successful and the efforts of the SAS were certainly significant. Successes in material terms were mixed but the SAS tied down an immense amount of German manpower by day and night and Stirling was keen to lay plans to assist in the next offensive.

Lieutenant Fraser was to recall, during a visit to Stirling's mother, that over Christmas 1942 when the SAS were enjoying a brief respite in a wadi south of Misaurata, Montgomery sent a bottle of whisky and five hundred cigarettes for each of Stirling's men. He also sent a personal message to say that the force had, since Alamein, done more than any division for the war effort.

'I had lost a lot of men but the accomplishments were undeniable. In terms of manpower it was, in percentage terms, as great a loss as the very first parachute operation. The men were in tremendously good form, however, and in the first week in January 1943 we managed to get them a short rest period but we kept them up-country in the area of Bir Guediffia.

'I told no one, not even I believe Shan Hackett, but I felt

that this was the time to try to achieve brigade status. I think I may have mentioned the possibility in one of my rare short letters to my mother. Brother Bill was now on the 1st Army front with 2nd SAS Regiment. The French were at sufficient strength to become a regiment in their own right and I had enough men in 1st SAS to carve a line down the middle and produce two regiments. On top of this I had been given command of a very energetic bunch of chaps from Greece.* They were a proud bunch and based their battle traditions on the wives' farewells to the ancient Thebans: 'Return – with your shield or upon it'.

'If I could achieve brigade status I would be well placed to push through the argument which I had only touched upon with Churchill – a regiment each to the Eastern and Central Mediterranean, the Italian theatre and the fourth to be held against the inevitable second front in Europe.'

Bold thoughts, but why not? Stirling had, or shortly would have, the requisite manpower. His successes were undeniable and well-supported now by Montgomery. There was not a single man in MEHQ who was against him and Churchill would almost certainly be in favour. He decided, however, that he needed an 'edge'. There was a lot of ground still between the advancing 8th and 1st Armies. What if it were to be a SAS fighting unit which made the first contact between those armies? The opportunity it offered Stirling was irresistible. The 8th Army Commander was on his side; he needed the backing also of the 1st Army Commander (Lieutenant-General Kenneth Anderson), and the opportunity to discuss the plan with Bill Stirling.

To manipulate events to suit his purpose required more than the usual daring. Stirling worked around two precepts; Montgomery had requested assistance west of Tripoli and this he would organise. He was also aware that mapping

* This was the Greek Sacred Squadron under command of Colonel Tzigantes.

and intelligence in the area of the Mareth Line was poor – he could provide input. He decided upon a four-way split of the SAS: the French Squadron (still commanded by Augustin Jordan) would raid between Gabes and Sfax; Harry Poat would take a group to raid Tripoli and satisfy Montgomery's request; the third group, under Paddy Mayne, would operate in the area of the Mareth Line. Stirling intended to move into northern Tunisia, conduct a detailed reconnaissance and link up with the 1st Army. A true journey through the unknown.

Stirling's route took him through the difficult terrain on the eastern stretches of the Grand Sea Erg and on northwards to the Gabes 'Gap'. The 'Gap' was created by the Mediterranean coast to the east and the salt marshes of Lake Djerid to the west. The German Army was thick on the ground and caution was the keyword of the journey. First through the Gap was Jordan's group, aiming for the Sfax–Gabes railway line. They were given strict instructions to avoid the enemy at all costs regardless of the ease or quality of target which may present itself – there was time enough for action later. Stirling was to follow the day after.*

Jordan's group, despite the utmost caution, made contact with the enemy twice before they got to their operational area. The going was so difficult and the enemy so heavily deployed throughout the area that it was 25 January before they could blow up the railway line at two different points. On the way back to their 'hide' in the El Hama hills close to the Gabes–Gafsa road they were confronted by German armoured cars and were forced to split. The Germans were now well and truly alerted by this and other SAS activity and Jordan's luck ran out two days later when he drove into a re-entrant only to have his exit sealed

---

* Shan Hackett had been well aware of Stirling's intentions to operate into and beyond the Gabes Gap and had issued a direct order that he was to go around the Gap and *not* through it. Intelligence knew full well just how many German and Italian troops were amassed in the small bottleneck.

by an Italian Army company. He had no option but to surrender.

Stirling knew nothing of the Frenchmen's contacts with the enemy but as they neared the area they were spotted by a German reconnaissance aircraft. They had been without sleep for two days and were on the point of exhaustion. A valiant effort over atrocious terrain took them through the Gap and into a small, deep wadi in the foothills of Jebel Tebaga (it turned out to be quite close to Jordan's intended base). As dawn came the patrol became aware of enemy movement within a mile of their position but they were confident in their concealment – in any event they could not have moved. Sleep was essential.

Stirling and McDermott rested beneath a shallow overhang while Cooper and Sadler moved to a position from which to cover the mouth of the wadi. The Frenchman Taxis took up station across from them in a small depression. Within moments all five were in a deep sleep. The SAS soldier of today may consider it strange to allow all the patrol to sleep without posting a sentry. It should be accepted that they were certain that their presence was unknown and there were no discernible tracks to lead the Germans to that small, well-concealed wadi. Furthermore, even if they had been awake and aware of an approach they could have done little. First Cooper then Sadler awoke to the sound of infantry boots scrunching up the wadi. Taxis came to within seconds and all sat up to be confronted by two German soldiers whose only action was to indicate, as they continued up the wadi, that the trio should remain quiet.

Remain quiet the three certainly did not – with a speed which surprised themselves they shot to the top of the wadi side, hurled themselves into the nearest cover and began to inch away from the scene. Stirling and McDermott had no such chance. They were awakened by shouted orders, and confronted by a short, dumpy, nervous German clutching a Luger pistol. Alert to any chance to escape the pair initially had no option but to follow their trembling captor. As they cleared the mouth of the wadi they were staggered to see Germans amassed in at least company strength. That evening the two men decided they could only get away by simply running for it after dark and hoping to evade pursuit by a combination of speed and stealth.

The chosen moment came: 'I let out the most horrendous rebel yell. It had all my frustration and all my anger in it. I think I almost frightened myself. McDermott and I were away. I covered at least ten miles that night, trying to attract McDermott along the way. We had arranged a series of whistle signals but we did not find each other. Despite the distance I covered I was still on the fringes of a built-up area when I was forced to stop just before dawn. I took a big chance and stayed the day with an Arab. He fed me as well as he was able on dates and tea but I moved off as soon as it was dark.

'I was a bloody fool. I noticed an aerodrome which I did not recognise and like an idiot I went to recce it. I should have moved at all possible speed towards the RV at Bir Soltane but I couldn't resist a check to see whether it was a worthwhile job for the boys. I was convinced I was going to make it back, you see. There were lots of planes, Junkers, it would be an easy target from my assessment of the defences. The trouble was it took me about three hours to sneak around the place. I wasn't too worried – I'd planned on making about twenty miles that night and I still had a good five and a half hours' darkness left.'

The unpredictability of the desert let Stirling down. The terrain became painfully tough and his progress was slow. Just before first light he took cover in an inadequate depression and hauled bits of scrub and grass over himself in a pathetic attempt at camouflage. He slept all that day, he was so acutely tired. In the late afternoon he awoke to hunger pains and decided to get moving. As he stood he was confronted by a young Arab who offered to take him to food and water. He was led straight into the arms of the Italians. These were professionals and they were in strength. The Arab pressed a revolver into Stirling's ribs and motioned him forward to meet his enemy.

As he handed him over to the Italians the Arab made what could have been his last mistake. He came within Stirling's reach. Stirling did not hesitate. He stooped and grabbed the Arab's ankles and with the superhuman strength which rage can give, he straightened up and whirled the hapless man around his head to the amazement of the Italians. With every intention of dashing his brains out he whiplashed the traitor against the rocky ground. The Italians dashed forward and pinioned his arms before he could complete his intention and Stirling was once more a prisoner. He was bound and taken heavily guarded to the nearest headquarters at Menzel.

Three points of irony: had Stirling stayed at MEHQ he would have met with Antony Head, deputising for Mountbatten (Combined Operations), who was looking at the prospects of using special raiding forces in other theatres. Head had been tasked with conducting detailed discussions with Hackett and Stirling in order that Eisenhower could be advised of the potential. It seems very likely that at this venue Stirling's desire for brigade status and prolonged involvement for the SAS would have been granted with alacrity. Stirling, in fact, had no need to seek extra prestige by trying to link the 1st and 8th Armies. (Sadler, Cooper and Taxis did escape, linked up with the Americans and put their knowledge to good purpose by acting as guides to General Freyburg's New Zealand Division as he moved it around the flank of the Mareth Line. McDermott was recaptured and remained a prisoner until the end of the war.)

Secondly, Stirling's capture was in no small way due to profound fatigue, not just brought on by that particular patrol, but by months of self-denial throughout the interminable 'negotiations' with MEHQ between operations.

Finally it seemed that the patron saint of dentists, whoever he may be, remembered how the young Stirlings had behaved so cruelly to Mr Platt so many years ago. No doubt it was he who manipulated fate so that David Stirling's first captor in the small wadi in the Gabes Gap should turn out to be the dentist of the unit specially formed to seek out the SAS and LRDG patrols! Pure luck had taken them to the wadi – they were on a shake-down training exercise.

---

# 13

# A MODEL PRISONER!

Sadler, Cooper and Taxis, who made it to the 1st Army, were not the only ones to fulfil Stirling's designs. The day after they had made contact, Lieutenant Martin with his patrol arrived at the Allied line. Not quite as planned, but those seven men, British and French, of 1st SAS Regiment were the first fighting soldiers to link the 1st and 8th Armies in February 1943.

Stirling's capture inevitably resulted in initial confusion. Only he had known the locations and tasks of all the units. Patrols appeared unexpectedly to report on missions which MEHQ knew nothing about – others were summoned by radio to return and report their activities. During Stirling's reign the SAS had been successful out of all proportion to the expenditure of men and material and this was now acknowledged by all.

The destruction of four hundred aircraft was logged along with a large number of fuel dumps and ground transport – this apart from the severe disruption which the German and Italian Armies had suffered at the hands of the regiment. Just in the area between Tobruk and Darba the coastal railway had been cut twelve times and was out of action for thirteen of the twenty pre-Battle of Alamein days. The aircraft numbers were probably even higher, since the SAS reported only certainties.

To some it was amazing that Stirling's only British decoration

should be the DSO. When Major-General Laycock took over from Lord Louis Mountbatten as Head of Combined Operations (1954) he offered the following description of David Stirling: '. . . a leader of quite exceptional resource and one of the most under-decorated soldiers of the war. More than once he would have won the highest military honour that a Sovereign can bestow, were it not for the rule that a senior officer must be present to vouch for the circumstances of the citation – and senior officers were never well placed to witness Stirling's raids behind the lines.'

In a personal letter to the Hon. Mrs Stirling written shortly after her son's capture, Robert Laycock had expressed similar feelings:

> Combined Operations HQ
> War Cabinet Office Annexe
> 1A Richmond Terrace
> Whitehall SW1
>
> 8 March 1943
>
> Dear Mrs Stirling,
>
> Thank you so much for your letter . . .
> When I sent my last letter, I did not know the details of David's capture, which I was not, therefore, prepared to accept. Now, however, it seems irrefutable, which in a way one should be grateful for since at least we know that he is safe and well. If he had still been missing, one could not but have been tormented by uncertainty.
> I hope, as you say, that David will remain in Italy, but even if he stays in a prison camp until the end of the War, he has done more for his country than any single individual of his rank in the army.
> If anyone ever deserves the VC, it is David. I am sure too that others feel this. I wish that he was still under my command, so that I could take a more legitimate part in recommending him . . .
>
> Yours ever,
> Bob

The capture of the commanding officer placed severe strains on the whole SAS organisation. Paddy Mayne, probably the most charismatic figure of all, took over command. Brilliant soldier though he most certainly was, he lacked Stirling's deft touch when it came to long-term planning and manipulating the hierarchy. As new causes will, the SAS began to founder, but any organisation of such quality will continue to attract the cream of the military and soon the sense of purpose was regained and some of Stirling's far-reaching ideas reached fruition. More of that later.

On the home front, Mrs Stirling was officially notified by the Casualty Branch of the War Office, on 11 February, that Lieutenant-Colonel Stirling, DSO, was reported missing in action on 8 February 1943. The exact date of his capture is uncertain but it must have been during the last week of January. On 5 February two letters were despatched from Africa in the same envelope:

Algiers
5 Feb. 1943

Dear Mrs Stirling,

I saw George Jellicoe in Tripoli yesterday, and he asked me to send you the enclosed letter.

I will not add to what he writes as I know nothing except what he has told me. Personally I am hopeful that David may yet turn up. At the worst he is a prisoner.

You know how we all loved David and I hate having to send you this news, incomplete and unreliable as it is.

But George and I both thought you would like to hear at once. I have arranged that any further news will reach you promptly.

Yours very sincerely,
Randolph S. Churchill

The enclosure:

Tripolitania
4 February 1943

Dear Mrs Stirling,

I am writing this with only a moment to spare if it is to return swiftly so I will be very brief.

I heard yesterday that David had been captured. As I am almost certain you will hear rumours of this before it is confirmed I am writing to tell you what I know.

The message, from the neighbouring area in which he was, said that his patrol had been captured. It was not absolutely clear as the process of deciphering had rendered it slightly corrupt. But it mentioned that 2 members had escaped and these did not include David. I will see the survivors directly they get here and will then get as accurate a knowledge of what occurred as is at present possible. I am *certain* that if David had been killed the message would have specifically stated so.

Please forgive me if I am breaking this news to you but I thought the risk – if it meant a slight lift of uncertainty – was worth taking.

Bob Laycock will be informed, as will the PM when definite news of David is received.

I don't think it is necessary for me to tell you what even a temporary loss of David's company – and his genius for command – means to me. I am, I think, a fairly discriminating person – and a harsh judge – but I am quite unashamed in avowing my devotion to him.

I am so sorry for you as I know how you will hate the idea of David in prison.

Yours ever,
George Jellicoe

Jellicoe wrote to his own mother: '[Stirling's capture] is a very great personal blow to me and a great loss to the unit, the army and England. David would undoubtedly and may still (because he's almost certain to escape) have been of great use to us in helping to shorten this accursed war.' And Peter Stirling wrote home: 'David's capture is regarded as a great blow here as there is literally no one of the same stature and prestige to replace him. It was particularly bad luck as the operation he was engaged on was of no particular importance in itself. I am afraid he will be a rotten prisoner and hate it.'


Lady Luck and 'le bon Dieu' were to smile on Stirling in the days immediately after his capture. He skilfully maintained a façade of gentle, bumbling blimpishness and the violent incident with the Arab seemed to be quickly forgotten. The Italians knew they had captured one of the SAS (he still had his cap with its badge) but it is equally certain that they did not initially realise that in their hands they had the Phantom Major. They probably imagined the latter to be eight feet tall with huge shoulders, bristling with machine guns and aggression. This quiet, stooping fellow could be of little consequence, but he may have information and must be sent off without delay.

Ironically Stirling was despatched under heavy guard from the very airfield he had reconnoitred thoroughly the night before. He slept deeply on the flight and arrived in Italy refreshed and alert but very, very angry. He had to escape; he had to get back to the SAS.

A soldier who suffers capture is subjected to acute shock, though it may not manifest itself immediately. Freedom is a thing of the past. Life is now controlled – he eats whatever is put in front of him and the nights, heretofore spent under the quiet blanket of stars, find him confined to a gloomy cell. The noise of the shifting sand or the throb of the jeep engine is replaced by the murmurings of disconsolate prisoners. It did not hit Stirling hard until he reached the first transit camp. A free spirit since youth, his every waking action was now controlled or supervised.

'At first there was a sort of numbness and a complete refusal to accept the situation. I felt almost insulted. Then I began to feel rather sorry for myself but that didn't last long. I think the main feelings were anger and the most acute frustration imaginable. Anger at myself for being so stupid as to hang around that bloody aerodrome and anger because I'd trusted the Arab. I do believe that if I had not been so tired I may have acted more sensibly. I was full of desperation – I had to get back. I was due to return to England to discuss the formation of the SAS Brigade and to talk to Winston about the part we were to play on the second front. I knew the SAS was in good hands with Paddy and brother Bill but I had not had the chance to talk over long-term plans with them. Shan Hackett had an idea but we hadn't argued detail. It really was immensely frustrating.

'I was surprised to hear from the other prisoners just how widely news of SAS activities had spread. A lot of it was grossly exaggerated, of course, but it gave one quite a morale boost. I remember giving a brief on the state of the war in North Africa to a group of officers. I used a white towel and bits of pencil or whatever to mark the Allied and Axis battle lines on it and show some of our operations and the battle dispositions. An Eyetie officer came in part way through my talk and got very excited and ordered me to shut up. I just ignored him and he soon settled down to listen. Do you know, he thanked me afterwards.

'There was a sort of apathy in the camp which I think had a good effect on me – I was determined that I should not get into that state. Looking back I suppose I was a little unkind in those thoughts as most of the men were fairly recent prisoners, still in a state of post-capture shock or whatever it's called, and many were also very, very tired. It's quite a thing to be roaming the desert one minute and locked in a prison compound the next. I had thought about it in the past – we all had – but somehow I had always imagined that the end of my war would be death. Not that I wanted to die, of course, but it always seemed that the danger point was during the active part of an operation not the period when we were getting our heads down. I also realised that very few prisoners, whatever their rank, seemed to know much about what we fondly called the 'big picture'. It's not surprising in retrospect; the SAS knew more about what was

going on than many local commanders because we had to fit
our operations into a wider perspective.'

On 5 February 1943 Stirling wrote four letters to his
mother. The two which reached her show something of his
feelings, though as usual they are somewhat understated.
Here is one:

Campo Concentramento P. G. p.66
P.M. 34000

My dear Mum,

I have written all the letters to you they will allow here. I
hope some of them get to you. There is plenty to eat here
but no books and no space for taking exercise – so it is very
boring. What is so especially exasperating is the thought that
my address at the moment would have been Keir had I not
been captured. However I am not staying here very long – it
is only a transit camp.

If you send anything, books and clothes are the most
required. Letters make an immense difference.

I have not met anybody I know yet, but probably will fairly
soon. It is a disadvantage being a colonel because one is liable
to be made to associate with other colonels. I am allowed to
write one of these letter forms and one postcard a week.

Love, David.

Uncharacteristically Stirling did not try to escape from the
transit camp. This was probably a good thing as he slept a
lot and within a few days was as fit and alert as ever, just in
time to find that he was being moved to another, temporary
resting place before being moved to Gavi in early March. He
fell amongst friends, as he wrote to his mother: 'There are 8
or 9 chaps here whom I knew before, including Jack Pringle.
Simon Ramsay [Stirling's brother-in-law, later the 16th Earl
Dalhousie] was captured about the same time and is I think
in Germany.'

I had met Jack Pringle before the war and liked him
enormously. I didn't realise, when we met again in Gavi,

that we were going to have so many high jinks together. Jack is the most amazing man; a real scholar with a quite remarkable memory; he speaks Italian, German and French but what I remember so well about him was that everything seemed to him to be fun. He was absolutely fearless and the most steadfast partner one could have had in those days. We have chatted quite a lot from time to time about the prisoner of war days.'

Gavi looked exactly what it was – a fortress, sitting atop a rocky outcrop with a design akin to the sixteenth-century strongholds still to be found in France and Spain. It was of three-tier construction with the central and highest enclosure being the final redoubt of the early defendants. Many of the lower level passages and cells were excavated out of solid rock. Dank, gloomy and depressing it was to Italy what Colditz was to Germany – a place so forbidding that escape seemed impossible.

'I was subjected to the most undignified search when I got to Gavi. Every cavity in my body was examined – quite unnecessary and very unpleasant; I didn't have a damn thing anyway. They even ripped the seams of my desert boots which was a pain as I had no spare clothing. I met Jack almost as soon as I arrived and he introduced me to Alistair Cram. Cram was a climber as well and we had quite a lot in common. I remember talking of my ideas on Everest – I'm not sure that he took me all that seriously at the time. I didn't know then that Jack and he were such kindred spirits. In truth, my main memory of those early days is of an overpowering hunger. I just never seemed to get enough to eat. The Germans were much better organised when it came to the Red Cross goodies.'

Stirling soon broached the subject of escape with Pringle and Cram, who were already in the advanced stages of a plan. Since early January they and eight others had been cutting a tunnel through an outer wall on to the top of the guards' quarters. This simple statement belies the dangers of the ingenious plan. Access to the outer wall was through a cavity wall which actually housed a reservoir of water. Once through the outer wall the team would have to traverse a steeply pitched roof, circumnavigate part of the lower compound along the top of a wall, descend into the compound then climb the perimeter wall and fix a rope to lower themselves to freedom. Most of this route was covered by sentries in high turrets manning machine guns.

Stirling was not told of this plan at first. Even though Pringle knew him and Cram had immediately taken to him, they stuck to a very sensible 'escape etiquette'. Prisoners had to earn their places on an escape attempt. Those who qualified were: the man who had the feasible idea; the men who worked on the project; men who had demonstrated their resource through past escapes; men whose continued contribution to the war effort was considered highly important, or perhaps men who had skills such as languages to heighten the chances of success and a 'home run'. Stirling convinced Pringle and Cram that he had a real need to get back to his beloved SAS to mastermind the link-up between the 1st and 2nd SAS Regiments and, through his planned discussions with Churchill, set to work in the Aegean, Italy and Europe.

The final arbiter in granting both permission to escape from a prisoner-of-war camp and the constitution of the escape team is the Senior British Officer (SBO), assisted by the Escapes Officer. Jack Pringle took Stirling's case to the SBO, who was sufficiently convinced to interview Stirling. Not for the last time Stirling's persuasive personality won the day for him as a prisoner. He became the eleventh man in the team.

On a cold, wet April night the plan went ahead. Stirling was sixth in line with Pringle following. All went well until Stirling was spotted crossing the open compound by a group of guards leaving their hut. Shots were fired and the compound was flooded with light. Stirling fought free of the first guards to seize him but was overpowered as he reached the perimeter wall.

Pringle managed to stay undetected as Stirling was being hounded by the guards, but as he went over the wall the rope broke giving him a fall he was lucky to survive unscathed. Even if Stirling had evaded the guards, therefore, he could have been severely injured. Pringle turned out to be the only one to stay out of prison for a significant time. All the others were either caught in the local area or seized before they made it to the wall.

Now began a strange period of uncertainty. The daily news broadcasts announced that the Axis Forces had been forced to withdraw from the Western Desert, and it seemed likely that Italy would be made to surrender. If so, surely the Germans would not bother about PoWs in Italy – they must certainly be ignored in the panic, repatriated, or overtaken by the Allied advance, in which case it made no sense to escape. Gavi, however, was a special case, as a letter from Peter Stirling shows:

> British Legation
> Athens
> 1 April '43

My dearest Mother,

   . . . I got news of David today from one of the naval prisoners of war who were exchanged a few days ago, a lieut. called Brown who is flying home immediately. He was at the same camp as David – *Camp 5, Post 3100*, at a place called Gavi near Genoa. You probably already know the address from the Vatican who have just sent it to me. David arrived at the camp about the end of February and was well and in good spirits. Brown told me he won £100 at roulette the first evening so there can't have been much the matter with him!

   Camp 5 is the special camp for escapees or the 'molto pericoloso', David having qualified for the honours either by his reputation or because of an escape he made while still in Africa and which resulted in his recapture two days later. His present camp, though regarded as a hopeless proposition to escapees, is supposed to be one of the most agreeable and Brown told me all the best people graduated there in the end!

Your loving Peter.

So, they were considered to be 'very dangerous' and the Germans had no intention of leaving them behind. After the Italian capitulation the Germans surrounded Gavi prison and a minimal show of force was sufficient to convince the prison commandant to surrender. Some prisoners attempted to evade the Germans by secreting themselves in pre-constructed 'hides' but the determined Feldpolizei went through the fortress with a fine-toothed comb. Everyone was rounded up (Stirling and Pringle were in the last batch after hiding for two days in a cavity beneath a lavatory seat), loaded into cattle trucks and despatched by train; destination, apparently, Austria.

Any notions of running which Stirling and Pringle may yet have entertained were ended when the Feldpolizei coldly gunned down two Italian prisoners who were mistakenly walking in the wrong area. These were the Field Police, ruthless and apolitical, normally used for controlling the Jews on their way to Poland for extermination. They would just as soon shoot a prisoner as take the trouble to recapture him.

The train eventually stopped at Innsbrück for the night and the Wehrmacht took over guard duties. These were professional soldiers with all their inherent ethics and the intrepid pair were prepared to take a chance with them. The rainy night and a light mist gave them their chance. Slipping out of the unlocked cattle truck Stirling and Pringle sneaked out of the railyard and through the backstreets of Innsbrück travelling west towards the Swiss border, which they reckoned to be about 100 miles distant. On the second night, after a scare when they bumped into a member of the Landwacht, they took refuge close to the road. Jack Pringle takes up the story:

> Half an hour later we stopped running and crawled into a huge haystack just off the road.
> Then took place an incident that was so extraordinary that David and I have never been able, properly, to explain it . . . Dead tired, we were soon asleep in our haystack. We awakened with a start when we heard English voices close by. We peered out through the hay.

There, standing in a group and clearly visible by the light of early dawn, were the three officers who had left the cattle truck just after us. They stood there talking in loud voices. We got out to confront them. They were Ian Howie, Waddy Wadeson and Peter Griffiths.

'For God's sake, what are you doing?' David whispered. 'Someone will hear you. Clear off or they'll be after us. And shut up!'

'We'll join up with you,' one of them offered. 'We can all rest up in the haystack and move on together.'

We were furious.

'You bloody well won't! Get out – get moving!' David was using his most intimidating manner. The little group drifted off in the half light and disappeared.

The strange thing was, they had never been there at all.

Months later in a prison where we all found ourselves after recapture, we asked them why they had done such a rash thing, risking capture for all of us.

They didn't understand. They had never met up with us after the cattle truck, they said, nor could they have, as they had gone towards Switzerland on the opposite – the north side – of the River Inn. They looked at us as if we were mad. David and I said no more. We were quite shaken . . .

If only one of us had had the experience it could be put down to a dream. But not only had we both had the same vision, but we had heard each other talk to the intruders, and heard their replies. In every respect it was real for both of us, and we agreed in every detail.

We have often talked about this strange event, but have never been able to explain it. Perhaps lack of sleep and hunger had brought on a joint hallucination with a telepathic element due to the nearness of the others on the far side of the river. Whatever the explanation, it was an uncanny experience.*

In an interview Jack Pringle recalled having recently read a study by army psychiatrists on the effects of lack of sleep on soldiers. They assessed that for every day a soldier went without sleep there would be a 25 per cent reduction in judgement and that after four days hallucinations would probably begin.

* From *Colditz Last Stop* by Major Jack Pringle.

With soldiers in a fox-hole, for example, it would be quite feasible for two of them, if they had suffered the same sleep deprivation, to be subjected to identical hallucinations. As a professional opinion this has to be accepted as the probable explanation of the haystack incident though, as Jack said, in the course of his escapes he was frequently without sleep for four days and longer but this was the only occasion upon which he hallucinated.

Two days later the pair were captured by the Landwacht. Within twenty-four hours they found themselves in a camp for Russian prisoners-of-war, Markt Pongau, in Austria. A few days after that they were free again, having taken advantage of a misty morning to throw a blanket over the barbed-wire perimeter fence, scale it and dive into the swirling currents of the River Pongau amidst a hail of bullets from the machine guns in the watchtowers. There followed a hair-raising chase as they were pursued by guards and tracker dogs through the forested hills. Their efforts took them into the lower reaches of the Alps.

'We were quite sure we were not going to make it. There was a lot of tough country ahead with not much prospect for filling the nosebag with the sort of fodder we would need. It was the most marvellous feeling though, just to be out in the countryside again and though we quickly tired no one could take away the pleasure of freedom, no matter how temporary. Our plan, I suppose, would have been to head for Jugoslavia – at any rate we travelled eastwards.'

They were betrayed to the Landwacht by an Austrian farm worker who had offered them sustenance and handed into the custody of the local police, to hear, with some trepidation, that they were to be sent to Berlin for interrogation.

'This was not good at all. Berlin was over 700 kilometres away – why should we be taken there unless to be handed over to the SS and eventually shot. I can't remember the area of Berlin we were taken to [it was Lückenwalde] but we were put in a prison which was indeed run by the SS and very efficiently too. There was no interrogation as such except that a pretty pathetic Irishman posing as a British sergeant was thrust upon us in our cell to ask questions – it was obvious that he was some sort of stool pigeon and probably an IRA man to boot.

'We were soon sent to a camp near Nürnberg I think, a most unruly place and really quite jolly in many ways – the Germans were totally incapable of maintaining discipline. In fact those escapes had taken rather a lot out of us. Jack had to go to hospital on one occasion. What was pleasant was that the Red Cross and postal services were very well organised and we seemed to get sufficient to eat. I know we spent Christmas there so it must have been in early 1944 that we went on our travels again.'*

Jack Pringle describes their arrival at Märisch Trübau:

Cold moonlight lit the streets of this old Sudeten-Czech town as we were marched through the snowy streets to our new camp, not far from Austerlitz, scene of Napoleon's great victory over the Russians in 1805. It was stimulating to think that we were out of Germany itself, in Czechoslovakia, scene of one of Germany's first aggressions in Central Europe.

This new camp was on a slope, with the town below and a thick pinewood above. At one time the Czech military academy, its layout made it better adapted to housing prisoners than most of the places I had been in. An enormous wooden building which we called the biscuit factory was the central complex, and it was surrounded by thirteen satellite wooden barracks and several large games fields. It was nearly a mile around, enclosed by two rings of barbed wire about ten feet apart, and guarded by sentry towers at regular and rather close intervals.†

In Märisch Trübau prison camp Stirling achieved what was probably one of the greatest feats of persuasion and leadership

---

* Stirling's 1943 Christmas postcard to his mother was indeed sent from Oflag VII-B (Eichstätt).
† From *Colditz Last Stop* by Major Jack Pringle.

of his life. 'It was Jack who sparked the idea when he mentioned that we would not be in the camp for long – we had, for once, friendly countries on two flanks and when we got out it should be fairly simple to find assistance. It came to me in a flash and I spoke out without really thinking. I asked Jack why we didn't simply turn the whole camp into one organisation all working towards a mass escape of about two hundred officers.

'The place was in absolute chaos. It was a new camp and both the guards and the three thousand prisoners were still settling down. Of course it would take some organisation, but it was a thrilling idea. Jack pointed out just what type of man I was dealing with and he was quite right. There is very little personal time available to a prisoner and he becomes very much the individual in his efforts to protect what little "freedom" he has. No one was going to take kindly to any form of regimentation or structured effort. But no one could be allowed to go off at a tangent and start organising his own escape attempts lest the major effort be compromised. Besides it is an officer's duty to escape, and what I had in mind would mean many officers being told that they would not make any escape plans.

'I knew the first step would have to be convincing the SBO. He was a delightful cove called Waddilove, a full colonel, but he was already having difficulties trying to enforce basic discipline. What I wanted would give him even greater problems. I talked it through with Jack; it seemed to me that the greatest benefit would be the effect on camp morale. If every man in the camp was motivated by a single aim, knowing that every face they looked at was part of the same commitment – a mass break-out – it had to be a binding factor even if a large majority of them would be staying behind. The effect on the Germans would be of major proportions and such a break-out would tie down a hell of a lot of troops.

'I went to see Colonel Waddilove, determined that he was not going to thwart the plan. In fact he was immediately intrigued by the idea but could not see how it was going to work. I had to give him some "carrots" (not that he was a donkey – far from it); I said that I would take on the onus of selling the idea to the camp as a whole, that I would act as Escapes Officer and that everyone would have to bring their ideas to me, and that I was prepared to hold the powers of veto. I would set up a team to exercise full security measures over all plans. I also knew by then a little about prisoner psychology; enough to know that accurate news from the outside is the one thing for which everyone desperately yearns.

'Without knowing at all how I was going to achieve it, I promised Waddilove that I would organise an intelligence cell to procure local information as to political and military situations – more, I would get the camp a wireless. It was an offer no SBO could really turn down. The thing now was to find a way to make it all happen. I knew one thing for certain – I wanted Jack Pringle to take a leading part. His experience as an escaper was beyond compare; he knew prisoners of war and what made them tick; he was clever and resourceful and he believed in the project. The fact that he had a marvellous sense of humour was also a great asset!'

David appointed Pringle as his second-in-command and the two set to work. The first and most difficult task was to persuade all the other officers that the plan was feasible and worthwhile. This was approached on a hut-by-hut basis and never was Stirling's power of persuasion more severely tested. He used calm, logical argument backed by the intensity of his demeanour. Still deeply tanned and with his disreputable pipe clamped firmly in his teeth he stared down from his six-feet-six-inch vantage point and fixed every questioner with those piercing eyes. The Phantom Major's reputation helped; and his charismatic presence softened even the hardest antagonist. Within a few days the camp was alive with a new raison d'être.

Organisation was kept simple though the tasks were far from easy. Four cells were nominated: Pringle, as well as being Stirling's immediate deputy to take over in the event of his demise, was placed in command of the intelligence cell. Access to accurate information for each escapee was paramount to success. Stirling's initial plan had been modified only slightly. Instead of 200 men he had reduced the figure to 150. Pringle was given a four-fold task. Firstly he would, with Stirling, assist in the overall analysis of the work of all cells. Secondly, he would build up an accurate knowledge of topographical, geographical and communications factors from the area immediately outside the prison to as far afield as possible. Thirdly, he was to find a way of contacting local resistance groups; initially, the Czech Underground Movement. Lastly, he would determine the feasibility of making contact with friendly locals – if this looked possible he was to use his own judgement and act.

In charge of the second cell, tasked to cover all aspects of security, was Anthony Simkins. Simkins was a superb analyst with pre-war experience as a barrister and his was, in extremis, the most important job of all. One whisper of an impending escape would have brought the German search parties in with a vengeance. It required immense attention to detail and great powers of leadership to keep his deputies motivated and efficient. Many years later, Simkins was to become Deputy Director General of MI5.

Simkins's greatest headache by far was Stirling himself. Whilst he could be most uncompromising in dealing with people who breached security no matter how innocently, Stirling was quite capable of making awful gaffes himself. The cell soon learned that any report or other piece of paper, any sample of forgery, dress or equipment had to be taken away from Stirling as soon as he had examined it. Once he had scrutinised a paper and the contents had transferred to his brain, Stirling seemed to lose interest in the medium and would very likely leave it lying around the hut. Such was the esteem in which he was held that those responsible officers were content to look after him in this respect, consoling themselves with the occasional amused comment.

The third cell was initially created as a result of Stirling's promise to Waddilove. A 'news office' was established and run by Ben Aharon, a Palestinian Jew. Once the requisite radio had been obtained (through the courage of a local labourer employed on maintenance duties around the camp) Aharon's cell worked with a will. Accurate news is meat and wine to the prisoner and under cover of translating and distributing official German newspapers, the broadcasts from the BBC Foreign Service were passed to all.

Lastly came the support cell with the dual functions of logging and reporting all movements of German guards, visitors and administrative staff, and supplying British 'sentries' to protect those working on the preparations necessary for a mass escape.

'We were extraordinarily lucky in Märisch Trübau in that the prison was full of experienced escapers or would-be escapers. Most had been involved in at least making escape preparations in the past and we had a wonderful complement of forgers, tailors, carpenters, architects, engineers, 'confidence tricksters' and innovators. It would perhaps surprise you to see just how much equipment has to be manufactured and then securely stored against an escape attempt by five percent of a prison's populace.

'Apart from such items as compasses, clothing, maps, money and rations, we had an immense amount of bumph building up. Every cell was swiftly producing the most remarkable amount of detail and it all had to be lodged away from the prying eyes of the Germans who were prone to making unexpected searches. We organised a methodical interrogation of all officers in the prison. Everyone, myself included, who had ever escaped or spent either war or peace time in any of the countries of interest was patiently questioned by our intelligence staff and asked to note anything of possible importance to an escaper. Trains, bus routes, locations of churches, stations, main roads, everything was carefully recorded.

'There were many sub-cells working in addition to the main ones. Everyone was committed to something – it wouldn't have worked otherwise. We met daily, myself and the main heads of cells to discuss progress. The ingenuity was amazing. Not a day went past without new input, really quite, quite satisfying.'

Stirling fails to comment on the variety of ranks from brigadier downwards who happily took their orders from him and his designated cell commanders. At no time was there overt disgruntlement or any attempt to take over what was obviously a superbly well-organised affair. At no time was there disagreement as to who would form the escape contingent even though some could not fully believe in the project. Stirling's word was accepted without rancour even by the non-believers.

'We had a number of projects running simultaneously; two of them were large chambers, one underground under the floor of Colonel Waddilove's hut and the other in a roof space. These were designed primarily to hold the vast amount of stores and equipment which was being consolidated but the underground one was well within tunnelling distance of the outer wire. We didn't have much luck with the tunnelling. The water table under the camp was quite high and the four tunnels we did get cracking on all flooded. We tried to get some measure of security out of this by deliberately letting the Germans know about them. I reckoned that if they thought they had an informer they may be less inclined to carry out snap searches.

'Our prime escape route was to be over the wire and we had an amusing plan which involved men hiding in platforms and officers practising highland dancing on the top. We had hoses ready to play on the sentries, and it was arranged that all the lights would be fused at the critical moment. All highly improbable in retrospect but there had to be a focal point until a better idea was formulated.'

Stirling does not say just how dangerous the prime plan was. At the point when the escapers were to burst from under the platforms and breach the wire, a party would turn the hosepipes on to the sentries. When someone doubted the efficiency of water as an armour screen, Stirling merely bent slightly towards him and repeated the plan slowly, so that the questioner felt ashamed of having asked.

The overall plan included the temporary 'escape' of a number of officers who were to make local reconnaissance before being 'recaptured' or staying free in the immediate area to organise local assistance. This ambitious plan soon looked feasible. The contact with the Czech who had purchased the radio extended to other workers who agreed to accept escaped 'lodgers' into their homes whilst they carried out their tasks. Five German speakers were selected for intensive training, to learn the basic elements of the Czech language and get physically fit.

During this phase, Pringle conducted a masterly suborning of one of the camp doctors, an alleged South African called Van Zouco. As he spoke perfect German and English with an accent, he was suspected of being a 'stooge'. Stirling and Pringle put him through a series of tests which half convinced them that he could be trusted. Then suddenly coincidence produced an opportunity. Pringle had been having trouble with heart murmurs and was to go before a medical board to decide whether he should be repatriated to England. Van Zouco would be in charge of escorting him to the hospital where the board would sit.

During his short stay in hospital Pringle, at great personal risk, persuaded Van Zouco to get him out to the nearby town and put him in contact with a member of the local resistance group. A tense but fruitful meeting in a Roman Catholic church followed where Pringle was able to extract much useful information including addresses of Czech resistance men who would help escaped British officers. He got back to Märisch Trübau shortly afterwards to discover that the camp had suffered its first casualty. Peter Griffiths, one of those who were to make local reconnaissance, had been placed under orders to transfer to another camp. He decided to escape from the train and carry out his task anyway; this he attempted and tragically died in the process.

'Because of the amount of critical information Jack had collected we were in a position to put down the slight drop in confidence caused by Griffith's death. We couldn't determine whether Griffith's orders to move were the start of other such instructions and I decided to accelerate the whole business and get out as soon as we humanly could. A plan was devised to get men out to establish where we could expect immediate help and to prepare the Czechs to expect significant numbers. We got four out in disguise – they simply walked out as two Russian prisoners under escort by two Germans. The lock posed no problem as one of them, a very skilled locksmith, had been practising for weeks. Two of them were caught quite quickly but the others made it.

'Events took a turn for the worse shortly after. The Germans apparently discovered that the Czechs were planning to liberate the camp (we knew of this of course) and they made a huge number of arrests. The immediate repercussion was that they doubled the guard force and fortified the camp – making it as hard to get out as in. We also found out that they had located many of the 'friendlies' on whom we had planned to rely. It was really looking quite bleak again.

'The news Jack brought back from the Czech he met in the church gave me food for thought. Their antagonism against the Germans was growing even greater if that were possible and pro-British feeling was high. I decided that to have maximum effect during what seemed probably to be the closing year of the war we should think again about our actions after the escape. I was not at all happy with Churchill's treating with the Russians – it seemed logical to me that they would move to establish a Communist regime in Poland and Czechoslovakia after the war and where would the British be? Surely if our escapers were to stay with the Czechs it would establish a memorable degree of British solidarity with their cause. I was not advocating taking up arms with the resistance group against the rules of the Geneva Convention but I dare say it would have happened to some degree; I doubt if any soldier would have been able to deny himself another crack at the Germans.

'To me it seemed that 150 British officers making friends with the Czechs could do an enormous power of good. Given the knowledge we had, it is quite possible that we could have saved Czechoslovakia from going over to the East. Britain paid scant attention to them before the war and they were ripe for an appeal by the Communists. I still believe we could have struck a real blow for Czechoslovakia'.*

The escape attempt was set for June 1944, but fate again prevailed against the escapers when, in May, the Germans suddenly moved a large force into the camp and informed the prisoners that they were to be moved to Brunswick.

'It was a bitter disappointment but there was no option but to call off the escape and rescue as much as we could from the months of hard work. All escape materials were packed into secret compartments in packing cases and all the loot survived the searches. I decided that I was going to remain behind in the space under the SBO's quarters and I was pleased when Jack Pringle agreed to see it through with me. Everything was ready, we had all the necessary documents and food and water for about three weeks. The intention was to secrete ourselves away and wait it out until the Germans had moved out, then strike for Prague.

'Jack found out from his doctor contact that the German Commandant suspected that he and I had been running something of major importance. He didn't know what it was but it seemed that we ought to make ourselves scarce. Not easy at my height so I merely kept out of the way. Jack masqueraded as half a dozen other people, but just as it looked as though we would get away with it the Germans found the bunker. We made an attempt to get into the roof space which was

---

* Had Patton not been stopped from taking Prague, and given the presence of escaped British officers living locally, a better understanding of the Czech situation may well have resulted, and the post-war-map might have been a very different colour.

still pretty well stocked, but I was grabbed by the guards as I left my hiding place. That was the end of the plan as far as I was concerned and I didn't see Jack again until I arrived at Brunswick.'

By some miracle Cram eventually rejoined the pair. A miracle because the news filtered through that the remaining escapees from Märisch Trübau (Wadeson and Mackenzie) had been recaptured and 'shot while trying to escape'; a German euphemism for cold-blooded murder. Shortly after this Stirling and Pringle were informed (by Van Zouco) that they had been tried in absentia by a military court and sentenced to death as 'enemies of the Reich'. Van Zouco told them he had heard this personally from the German Commandant whilst delivering his daily medical report.

'This news really scared the hell out of me and I worked le bon Dieu very hard that night. It's a very nasty feeling to know that one's future is quite outside one's control. I could cope with being shot in action or even while trying to escape; after all at those times there was adrenalin and fluid motion, extreme mental and physical effort which took one's mind away from the bullet. This was different and quite unpalatable. I think that I was more frightened then than I have ever been before or since.'

It is a matter of conjecture as to whether sentence was actually passed on Stirling and Pringle. The latter came to believe that it was a ploy by the Camp Commandant to try to make himself and Stirling behave. The SBO was never informed of the sentence, which would have been a logical first step by the Germans, and the Commandant knew that they were in close collusion with Van Zouco. Nonetheless this did not enter their calculations at the time and they had a few very uncomfortable days.

Stirling may have confessed to having been very frightened but it did not affect the façade he continued to present to his cell-mates in Brunswick. He was then sharing a tiny cell with Jack Pringle and Arthur Gilbey. They had taken delivery of their Red Cross parcels; these were usually eaten with great care as delicacies; perhaps half a bar of chocolate one day, maybe a spoonful of lemon curd in the evening, and so on.

'If we are not to be here much longer we ought to have a feast,' said Stirling.

'Well, if we're going to be shot that seems sensible. How shall we eat it? Perhaps a four course meal?' replied Pringle. Cooking facilities were somewhat limited; the only utensils were a single porcelain bowl and one spoon.

'No, we'll mix it all up into one big sort of stew.'

Gilbey, who considered himself something of a gourmet, was perturbed but not of a mind to contradict Stirling. Pringle protested that this would not be the best meal in the world. Stirling overrode all objection saying that mixed up the food would contain the best possible combination of nutrients and best value would be gained.

One parcel was opened and mustard, creamed rice, biscuits, chocolate, bully beef, jams, sugar, salt, everything of the most vaguely edible nature went into the awful brew. Stirling appointed himself chef and stooped over the bubbling mess.

'David, this thing's going to boil over you know,' said Pringle, seeing his last good meal turning into a disaster.

'No. It needs to go a little longer.' At that moment the porcelain pot shattered and the gooey mess splattered and ran in animated globules over the cell floor.

'Let's lick it up quick,' said the up-to-now silent Gilbey.

'No,' said Stirling, to the consternation of the others, 'Pass me the other parcel. We'll have another go. It's typical of the bloody Germans to give us a pot that cracks up on us.' Another pot was obtained and the process restarted. Within minutes and ignoring the reminders of his first attempt, now hardening rapidly on the floor, Stirling had nursed the meal to bubbling point again.

'David, remember, REMEMBER, it's going to boil over again,' warned Jack Pringle.

'No, no, that was a faulty cooking pot.' Inevitably the

same thing happened and a second layer of goo rained onto the floor.

'I don't care what you say, I'm going to lick the bloody stuff up. Come on, one third each,' said Gilbey.

'You know, these jam jars are absolutely impossible,' said Stirling as he retired to bed apparently unperturbed.


In Brunswick Stirling had time to think and began to apply his mind to the war effort once more. All of them were convinced that the end of the war in Europe was not far distant and Stirling turned his mind to the Far Eastern war and the part that could be played by the SAS he was convinced he would soon be rejoining. Although maps of Germany were forbidden it was easy, under the guise of study requirements, to get hold of maps of China. His thoughts were interrupted by the news that the Allies had invaded Europe and that an attempt had been made on Hitler's life.

The latter news, which was a declaration that there could be a resistance movement amongst the Germans themselves, started him along a chain of thought which would soon be put to the test. In August 1944 Stirling and Pringle found themselves on their way to the camp which was fast becoming a legend – Colditz.

'It was something of a relief to arrive at Colditz; even though we had been told where we were going there was still the nagging doubt. Were we in fact being taken off to be 'shot while escaping'? We had heard more and more stories of these quiet murders. When we arrived it was almost like a reunion – lots of old friends from Gavi, Märisch Trübau and other places along the route. It was quite serene for a while. The company was good* and the food was very palatable and

---

* In fact Stirling and Pringle shared a room with the legendary Douglas Bader, the legless fighter pilot who carried on his own never-ending private war against the Germans. It is easy to imagine the scenes in a cell which contained three such intelligent, dedicated and humorous individuals.

in a sufficient quantity even for a fully grown boy. To attempt to escape seemed foolhardy at first simply because the Germans had issued a bald statement that anyone attempting to do so would be shot. We knew by now that they meant it.'

Christmas in Colditz was pleasant but far from riotous. Stirling's thoughts were mainly of long-term plans for the SAS in China and of his family in Keir.

'I was rescued from total boredom by stimulating company and the astonishingly good library – I read more books during that period of my life than ever before or since. Despite the dangers of escape there were plans aplenty ranging from schemes to make rope with which to abseil the 300-foot cliff, to an ingenious glider which really was a work of art. There was plenty of "goon-baiting" to pass the time of day, but it was all pretty ineffectual I suppose. The war just seemed to drag on and much of my thinking time revolved around what Paddy Mayne and the boys were up to – had the SAS survived, or had it after all been closed down at the end of the African campaign?

'Things took on a different dimension when the SBO, Colonel Willie Tod, a fellow Scot, called me in for a chat. Just before Christmas Willie had been told that command of Colditz was to pass from the Wehrmacht to the SS. It was a moot point as to whether we prisoners were going to become hostages as a last-ditch tactic by Hitler. There were some pretty important people in the camp, after all; relatives of the Queen, of the Prime Minister, of the American Ambassador to London and a host of others. They were all secured separately from us shortly before Christmas and this lent strength to the hostage possibility.

'The thinking was that Hitler would make his final redoubt in the Berchtesgaden area taking all manner of hostages with him. Willie Tod had surmised that there was a good chance of us being caught between two stools with the Russian and Allied front lines getting closer to us by the day. He wanted to know what the chances were of repeating the operation we had mounted in Märisch Trübau and getting a local liaison under way with the Germans. I was a bit cautious. We were in the Third Reich's most closely guarded hostelry for a start, but more than that Colditz was filled with occupants of long standing. Many of them had come to terms with the place and it would be nowhere as easy as it had been in Märisch Trübau to motivate them to partake in a single cause especially when the benefits were tenuous to say the least. It was a stimulating thought all the same and I naturally discussed it first with Jack Pringle.

'Between us we pulled the problem apart. There was one quite unique factor at our disposal. Because Colditz held so many long-termers many people had built up relationships with the guards and traded regularly. It was small time stuff; chocolate and other Red Cross goodies were swapped for the odd bottle of schnapps or a bit of gossip or even a useful tool. I knew there was an emergency store of Red Cross parcels set by against a rainy day. These were accumulated by extracting a percentage of parcels from each delivery and it had been going on for so long that no one even missed them now.

'The only thing we had going for us was that trading system. We had to maximise on that and put it under the control of specialists. I asked for, and got, complete control of the emergency stock of Red Cross stores and the SBO's backing to instruct everyone to cease individual trading immediately. Dissenters were persuaded that they could actually benefit from a share of the result of centrally controlled bartering.'

Again, Stirling is modestly dismissive of his powers of persuasion. If anything this was an even greater coup than Märisch Trübau. Stirling and Pringle set about assembling their team. They knew all the inmates well by then and had no difficulty in gaining the support of de Vomécourt, a Frenchman; Chaloupka, a Czech, and a third man, known as 'Dick Jones', whose exploits were known to Stirling from his days in Africa. A man of mystery he claimed to be British but certainly was not as he hardly spoke English. He had therefore been under suspicion throughout his time in Colditz. He passed the scrutiny and tests devised by Stirling and Pringle and was taken on, albeit with some initial caution.

'We [Stirling, Pringle and de Vomécourt] devised all questions and the development of intelligence based on the debriefs of Jones and Chaloupka who were designated the sole traders in the camp. I was surprised that the sudden switch to a central system never alerted the Germans – perhaps it was because we traded with guards who were not prepared to let their officers know about their illegal bartering. Most of them were senior citizens with a few very young lads mixed in. It didn't take long to get all the tactical information required; all key installations and principal personalities in the area were soon identified and plotted on the maps along with notes on their habits and political affiliations.

'We had the most amazing piece of luck which we were able to develop. It sounds most improbable but Chaloupka actually had a girl friend who worked in the local dentist's surgery. They'd met in Prague, I believe, and the cunning blighter had managed to see her from time to time by the simple expedient of smashing his teeth as an excuse to get to the dentist. Well, he obviously couldn't be expected to keep on smashing his teeth no matter how big the attraction and personal reward. Jack was detailed to think up a method of regular contact.'

This was eventually achieved through the courier services of a young guard who was persuaded by Jones, and proved most fruitful as the girl turned out to be the daughter of the local Nazi Party leader! That faithful and intelligent young lady answered all Pringle's questions and the dossiers grew impressively. The young courier also turned out to be heaven-sent; his father was a leading local moderate who was taken into his son's confidence with excellent results. The system was slowly built upon and through the courier's father there was soon a reporting network which passed on all information received via the Camp Commandant's telephone.

Far from being content to receive timely intelligence well in advance of the Allied Army, Stirling began to try to manipulate events. It was discovered that the chain of instructions to Colditz Castle was by way of the Gauleiter of Saxony. Pringle drafted a letter to that worthy threatening him with death if any harm were to come to the prisoners of Colditz. The letter, which purported to have been written by anti-Nazi Communists, was an attempt to forestall the Gauleiter passing on orders to execute the potential hostages, or any other prisoner.

The influence of the network was extended even further when an early warning system was established whereby a local man would signal the castle of German Army movements in the Colditz area.

'This was what Willie Tod had wanted,' said Stirling, 'advance notice so that he had time to put his contingency plans into effect. What he wanted to know at any given time was "Nothing of note to report"; "Troops leaving"; "You will be moved out" and, of course, "Get the hell out of it". All this was arranged by coded movements of men at a point of the road which was permanently visible to us by day.

'It bloody well worked. One day in April 1945 Willie Tod was ordered to report to the Camp Commandant and told that we were all to be moved. Willie, of course, had known this for some hours, from our signals, so he had thought out the situation thoroughly. He simply refused to have his officers moved from the castle confines. There was nothing the Commandant could do short of slaughtering us all. Willie then demanded that the Commandant surrender the castle to him and this was done! We sat on the walls to watch the final battle as the Americans advanced to the River Mulde. I managed to get down, with our little intelligence cell, to meet the Yanks and we handed over all the information we had collected which must at least have saved them some time. Somehow it seemed an anti-climax. Soon we were on the move and I think it was 16th April when we got back to

England. I was impatient to see my family and get back to
the SAS.'

Only an ex-prisoner can give true testimony to Stirling's
achievements over this period; Jack Pringle had this to say: 'No
one, unless he has been a prisoner-of-war, can fully understand
the difficulty of carrying three thousand men with you on
what was actually a lethal concept. Prisoners are individuals;
they have lost everything except themselves. Somehow David
Stirling did it. He was an absolutely overwhelming influence
on the officers in Märisch Trübau and Colditz.'


# Author's notes:

1.   There is no doubt that if a mass escape had succeeded from
Märisch Trübau and 150 officers had been let loose into Czechoslovakia it would have brought upwards of 5000 SS troops into the area
at great speed. The majority of officers would have been captured
and a large number inevitably 'shot while trying to escape'.

2.   A letter sent to Mrs Stirling (possibly from Randolph Churchill)
in May 1943 describes the briefing Stirling gave to the prisoners-of-
war (which took place in Gavi, not the early transit camp). '. . .
I saw A. in London . . . and though he only left PG 5 on 8
March after eighteen months there, he looks surprisingly fit and
well. . . . Food is short and everybody loses weight – but there is
enough on which to keep alive and Red Cross parcels are coming
through regularly. He himself had hoarded some tinned food which
he passed on to David.
    . . . David, on his arrival, was asked to give a lecture on the
fighting in Africa. The prisoners had had no real news of the 8th
Army's advance since we'd got into Tobruk in November, so there
was a lot of ground to cover. David prepared his notes in his room
(he has a cell to himself) and then went and had a bath. The guards
took this opportunity of going into his room and reading his notes
which they strongly disapproved of on the grounds that they showed
'disrespect to Italy'. They threatened to confiscate them but David
said that he didn't give a damn – he was going to give the lecture
anyway and it would be a better one if he had the notes which he

would willingly turn over to them afterwards, together with his bath towel on which he'd drawn a map of the campaign. This created a further scene as they told him he had damaged Italian property, but finally they allowed him to use both notes and map. Not only the 160 prisoners attended the lecture but the entire prison guard as well, some 480 men. A. said it was a magnificent lecture and David enjoyed himself at the Italians' expense. He referred to Italy throughout as the soft underbelly of Europe and warned them that the bombing they'd already gone through was only a sample of what was to come and that we had 8,000 bombs that would make a big dent in Italy. He told the guards things about the campaign and how the Italian soldiers were treated by the Germans which they'd never dreamt of but which they accepted as truth, and by the end of his talk they were saying to each other, 'It is obvious we have lost this war already.'

David is regarded with the gravest suspicion by the prison staff and they daren't leave him alone for a minute. A. says David is so closely watched that no attempt to escape would be possible . . .'

# 14

## TO OTHER PASTURES

Stirling arrived back in Britain to learn that his beloved SAS were scattered to the four winds. Now under the overall command of Brigadier 'Mad' Mike Calvert, there were small groups in France and Germany on mopping-up operations but the task of disarming the 310,000 Germans in Norway had been given to 1st and 2nd SAS Regiments. Regrouping was going to take some time. The stories of the SAS operations since he had left them in the Western Desert were heart-warming.

The War Office gave Stirling two documents showing the esteem in which the SAS was held by senior commanders:

To Brigadier McLeod*

I wish to send my congratulations to all ranks of the Special Air Service Brigade on the contribution which they have made to the success of the Allied Expeditionary Force.

The ruthlessness with which the enemy have attacked Special

---

* Brigadier Roderick McLeod was appointed Brigade Commander in January 1944 on the formation of HQ, SAS Troops, which was under overall command of Lieutenant-General F.A.M. Browning. At that time brigade strength was approximately 2,500 and it operated under a specially constituted staff branch of HQ Airborne Forces for planning and tasking.

Air Service troops has been an indication of the injury you were able to cause to the German armed forces both by your own efforts and by the information which you gave of German disposition and movements.

Many Special Air Service troops are still behind enemy lines; others are being reformed for new tasks. To all of them I say, 'Well done, and good luck!'

Yours sincerely,
Dwight D. Eisenhower

The other document was the text of a radio broadcast made by Lieutenant-General 'Boy' Browning to troops behind the lines on 8 September 1944.

. . . I saw the Commander-in-Chief [Montgomery] yesterday and told him I would be speaking to you today. He proposes to send you a personal message, and in the meantime I am going to tell you what views are held about your efforts.

It is considered that the operations you have carried out have had more effect in hastening the disintegration of the German 7th and 5th Armies than any other single effort in the army. Considering the numbers involved, you have done a job of work which has had a most telling effect on the enemy and which, I fully believe, no other troops in the world could have done.

I know the strain has been great because operating as you do entails the most constant vigilance and cunning which no other troops are called upon to display . . . To say that you have done your job well is to put it mildly. You have done magnificently . . . I want you to know how we and the rest of the army feel about you . . . I hope I have made that abundantly clear to you all.

Good fortune and happy hunting.

These messages had been issued in 1944. Between then and May 1945 when Stirling read them (and others) bitter fighting had continued for all five SAS regiments (by then the French had grown to two regiments and the Belgians to one regiment with almost the strength of two).

'It was a great sadness to me that brother Bill had been forced to resign command of 2nd SAS. He was, of course, absolutely correct in taking that step. The post-D Day plan had been to drop the SAS not behind enemy lines but between his front-line infantry and his armour. It would have been bloody suicidal. That was not the point, however; it would have been quite ineffective and marvellous opportunities would have been totally missed. Bill stood firm against this misuse of three years' learning and experience and his decision had far-reaching effects because after he resigned hard questions had to be asked; the planning staff took another look at SAS deployment and came to their senses – without Bill's action this would not have happened.'

As things turned out, the SAS were committed to perhaps more tactical operations than they should have been, but towards the end of the war events and battle lines were moving at speed and this was inevitable. McLeod constantly opposed HQ to minimise such operations and without his aggression and intelligent, forceful arguments in the rear, the SAS's true strategic rôle would have been in jeopardy.

It is probable that during operations in France, Holland and Belgium, three seeds were implanted which have been nurtured by the post-war SAS. Firstly there was a very close liaison with Phantom, the field signals liaison element of GHQ, which proved that it was possible to combine a first-class standard of soldiering with a professional ability to communicate from inhospitable sites. Secondly, there was a dependence (on primary targets at least) on close liaison with, and trust in, a variety of intelligence agencies. Lastly, techniques for gaining the confidence of highly individualistic indigenous, irregular fighting forces were formulated.

Major Brian Franks was selected to take over after Bill Stirling's resignation. A highly respected soldier he was held in the highest esteem by all under his command – he was to become a major force in the post-war evolvement of the regiments.

That his concept of operations had proved as successful in Europe as he had always believed it would was gratifying to Stirling but, although the war in Europe was going to be over shortly, there was still the Far East to consider. He had been thinking deeply about this theatre since his period at Colditz and he was determined that the SAS would see action there.

In the Japanese, the Allied Forces were encountering a fanatical enemy such as they had not met elsewhere. Rangoon was back in Allied hands but the campaign in Burma raged on bitterly. The Americans were taking the islands in the Ryukyu group but it was a slow, expensive process though the fall of Okinawa was inevitable. Brunei Bay was under siege by the Australian 1st Corps and the US 7th Fleet and the American 11th and 14th Corps had at least strategic control of the Philippines. In this way the maritime resupply lines of the Japanese 'sea-empire' were being slowly strangulated. In Malaya, the Philippines, Borneo, New Britain, Bougainville and many of the Pacific Islands, remnants (albeit large) of the Japanese Army were without supplies. Their resistance, however, was spirited (or maniacal) and shifting them would take time unless a surrender was forced.

The main island group of Hokkaido, Honshu, Shikoku and Kyushu was still managing to get supplies in from mainland China and it was in Stirling's mind that a major force of SAS operating along the great Manchurian railway, cutting the line and harassing the Japanese on that front could create havoc. The same operations could be mounted against the trunk roads from the north feeding the Japanese Army in Malaya.

In this way it might be possible to complete the strangulation process. There was, as usual, more to Stirling's idea than was at first apparent; always suspicious of Russian long-term plans, his thinking was at least part-political. Stalin at the Yalta Conference in May 1945 had stated that his troops would be ready to move against the Japanese in Manchuria in August of that year. Would an active, fighting Allied presence foreclose on the Russian demands of the gifts of the Kurile Islands,

Sakhalin and the greater part of Manchuria? In addition, there would be further proof that the SAS was sufficiently adaptable to move into a different theatre and terrain at very short notice.

'There was nothing else we could do in Europe or Scandinavia except jobs for which there were far better equipped troops. I pushed the idea most forcefully in the War Office and had, I think, three meetings with Winston. He seemed quite receptive and I even allowed him to talk me into operating with a multi-national force under American command. That didn't worry me too much – once we were committed I had no doubt as to who would be calling the shots. Winston gave me the authority to begin planning the concept of operations and the logistic demands but there seemed to be little urgency about it as far as he was concerned. What I didn't know, of course, was that the atom bomb was going to be dropped on 6th and 9th August on Hiroshima and Nagasaki.'

Stirling believed that the bomb was not necessary – a view shared by many leading combatants of the day. Japan had lost 90 per cent of her shipping capability. Her ground forces were spread to the four winds with no hope of ever re-grouping in defence; air and naval forces were crippled and her people were beginning to starve. The Japanese were already eager for peace; only the Allied demand for unconditional surrender presented a sticking point. Capitulation was inevitable and it can be argued that this point would have been reached without further intensive military action. Tokyo, Osaka, Nagoya and Kobe had already been bombed horrendously by the American 21st and 22nd Bomber Commands which had displaced Japanese civilians from factories producing war materials and had proved to them that their armed forces were impotent to defend them. Whether Stirling's ideas on the Chinese operations would have had any effect is highly debatable – timing would have been critical; in any event Joseph Stalin and the Soviet Union achieved most of what they wanted despite Churchill's misgivings.

On 8 October 1945, Stirling's dream appeared to come to

an end. HQ SAS, 1st and 2nd SAS Regiments were paraded for the last time under Brigadier Mike Calvert. The War Office in its infinite wisdom had decided that any future conflict would be on an infinitely lesser scale and controlled to a degree by those forces which held the atom bomb. Smaller limited intensity campaigns would not require the use of forces such as the Special Air Service. Time, and the foresight and determination of a small number of dedicated ex-SAS officers, was to prove them wrong, but for the time being the war, for Stirling and his L Detachment, was over. Interestingly, the French and Belgian SAS Regiments, which were formally handed back to their national commands on 1 October and 21 September respectively, retained their formation and identity in the peacetime orbats of those countries.

Where do such men go after four action-packed years of thrills and danger, victory and tragedy, humour and tears? A life of high peaks and low troughs is immediately replaced by the humdrum. After reunions with wives, families and sweethearts comes the need to carn a living – but how can the excitement be replaced? For many, of course, the life of adventure was never recaptured – it was exchanged for a quieter but eventually no less fulfilling existence. So, where did they go? To jobs ranging from professional poacher to Member of Parliament, from policeman to defence adviser to a Middle East ruler; from docker to defence college lecturer. Each man took with him fond memories and an ability to face life squarely, but the early stages for all of them were fraught with the physical and psychological problems of trying to cope with what had become an alien form of existence.

Wives and families had developed their own methods of coping with separation and hardship. They had evolved their routines and the returning husband, loved though he may be, was almost an intrusion into an established pattern. Both wives and husbands had changed, sometimes physically as well as mentally. Both parties had their own stories to tell about the war and both had their own, often different perceptions of what peace would bring to the family. First and foremost was the necessity to buckle down to 'normality' and become the provider again. Somehow most of the returners eventually achieved peace of mind. Today the survivors still meet annually in the mess surroundings of one of the post-war regiments.

Blair 'Paddy' Mayne (now with four DSOs to his credit) initially tried the life of expedition member on a South Atlantic survey. He found the job boring and settled uneasily back into work with the legal profession in his native Ulster. This great SAS soldier died tragically in a car accident on 15th December 1955. With deep feeling, Stirling recalled his last meeting with Paddy:

'Just a short time before his death, Sandy Scratchley and myself succeeded in persuading Paddy to spend a weekend at Sandy's house in Sussex. Sandy, who was very well known to Paddy, was a steeplechase jockey before the war and afterwards became a bloodstock advisor to the Duke of Norfolk and also to my brother Bill, with whom he served in 2nd SAS after my capture. The weekend started well; Paddy was at his most mellow and we had lots to talk about; but on the Saturday I saw Sandy suddenly looking very apprehensive. Evidently his employer, Norfolk, had invited himself and his wife to dinner with us that night and Sandy felt unable to refuse.

'Now Paddy had two fiercely held prejudices – against the aristocracy and against Roman Catholics – and of course he knew that Bernard Norfolk was the premier Duke of the United Kingdom and the chief of the Catholic laity though the two had never met. Sandy and I decided to bluff it out with Paddy. Sandy made the introductions almost inaudibly and Paddy sat down opposite the Duke and had a most animated conversation with him throughout dinner.

'The Norfolks left soon after dinner and Paddy asked who was that splendid chap with the bucolic complexion with whom he had talked at such great length.

'"Oh," says Sandy, "he is just a neighbour, you are unlikely to meet him again."

'"But what is his name?" persisted Paddy. There was nothing for it – Sandy had to own up!

'Paddy's reaction was immediate and classic; that wartime steely, ruthless look invaded his eyes. "Stand up, Scratchley, stand up at once at attention – and stay at attention while you fall backwards, and I may or may not catch you."

'Sandy was really frightened, but at the second attempt Paddy was satisfied, catching Sandy's head half an inch off the floor! And then we all laughed (Paddy the loudest) while we had some more whisky served by Sandy with a rather shaky hand.'

Pat Riley DCM, Stirling's staunch right-hand man during the early days, on whose foresight and professionalism in Kabrit and beyond so much had depended, rejoined the police force only to be overcome by boredom which took him back into the army. After leaving the army as a major, Pat involved himself in the security industry before retiring in harmony with his wife, Kay, in East Sussex.

Ernie Bond, a professional soldier before the war, opted to join the Metropolitan Police. A satisfying and successful career led Ernie into command of the first bomb squad in the fight against post-war terrorism (during which period the Spaghetti House and Balcombe Street sieges put him once again in contact with the SAS). He retired as a deputy commissioner of police and an OBE and now lives contentedly with his wife, Mabel, in Kent.

Bob Bennett MM, BEM stayed to be a significant factor in the reforming of the SAS in Malaya as part of Z Reserve and was a regimental sergeant major on leaving the service. Staying in his native London, Bob worked alongside the legal profession and was eventually given the Freedom of the City before settling down to retirement with his wife, Nell.

'Gentleman' Jim Almonds MM retired from the army as a major after his service culminated in him becoming Military Adviser to Haile Selassie. Ever the craftsman, Jim built his own boat and, basing his navigation techniques on his desert days, sailed it from Africa and up the river to the village in Lincolnshire where his family have lived for three generations. Happily retired, Jim and his wife, May, spend their days in the village which is close to Jim's own small, private wild-life sanctuary.

Reg Seekings DCM, MM who 'shadowed' Stirling so capably on those early operations now lives quietly in Suffolk. Reg opted for challenge and the open spaces and he and his wife, Monica, took up farming in Rhodesia only returning to England in the aftermath of UDI.

Johnny Cooper MBE, DCM, youngest of the originals, joined the Green Howards when the SAS disbanded but in a few years he was back commanding a squadron of the post-war SAS in Malaya. He remained a military man until retirement as a lieutenant-colonel, spending much of his post-SAS service in the Middle East. Johnny retired to Portugal.

Jimmy Brough MM, 'the man with a dodge for all occasions' as Stirling put it, rejoined the police force but found it hard to cope with the normality of his beat. Most of all he missed the comradeship and excitement of special soldiering. He eventually adjusted to peacetime life and settled in Cheshire with his wife, Dorothy.

Sir Stephen Hastings MC joined the Foreign Office soon after the war ended and served in Finland, France and the Middle East before taking up politics and becoming Member of Parliament for Mid-Bedfordshire. Now, with his wife, Elisabeth, he enjoys overseeing the family estates in Cambridgeshire and devotes much time to the preservation of the countryside and British field sports.

Like his comrades, the restless Stirling had to think long and hard about his future: 'I did not miss the war anywhere near as much as one would have thought, though of course I was very unsettled. I suppose in part this was due to the weaning process of being a prisoner. There was no point in reconsidering the

Everest project, though it did cross my mind. I could not easily see a way of getting sponsorship in post-war Britain and I had discussed the needs in some detail with Alistair Cram. I don't think the necessary drive for climbing was there either at that time. I suppose the war had got something out of my system though I'm not sure what it was.'

Even with all the other things occupying his mind in Colditz, Stirling had thought ahead to his situation after the war. As a younger son he had no great expectations, though the family interests with the Keir and Cawder Estates were significant. Disinclined to be dependent on anyone, Stirling had mentally explored a number of avenues including continued military service.

The peacetime army, he concluded after reliving memories of Pirbright, was no place for him. He could see that three to four years away there would be problems in the Far East but the interim period, the aftermath of war, would be quite without stimulus. His father had been a soldier and a businessman and his brother Bill looked set fair to continue; why not himself? There remained only the small decision: what to do and where to do it. It was simply a matter of opportunity and creativity.

He had used the prison library well, and given a lot of thought to Africa which had captured his interest in 1941 when his troop ship had docked for a few days in the south. There was a place worth getting to know. Most of the things a man could want were on offer: open spaces, hordes of the wildlife which interested him so much and, in the 'settlers', a comradeship brought about by a common love of the country. He had not forgotten long talks on quiet desert nights with Rhodesians like Mike Sadler – it had been impossible for Sadler to hide his love of the country. He had family contacts in Rhodesia and Kenya and could certainly gain introductions to a wide range of people. More than that the continent was undoubtedly going to experience turmoil; the signs were already apparent. Was there scope for making a living out there? His needs were by no means great.

Stirling decided that the only way to get answers to his questions was to visit the country. In early 1946 he moved to Salisbury, Rhodesia.

# BOOK THREE

———

# GANG FORWARD

---

# 15

# THE INDISPENSABLE
# STUFF

So little done – so much to do.
            Last words of Cecil John Rhodes.

Africa is the second largest continent on the planet covering roughly one fifth of our global land area. The 11,600,000 square miles (approximately) is peopled by only about 505,000,000 inhabitants; people separated firstly by approximately 900 distinct languages and further by the unrealistic borders drawn by colonialists. Host to vast deserts, huge, thundering waterways, tropical rainforests, snow-capped mountains and verdant plains it is an exciting land. Scientific evidence suggests that man first emerged here as a distinct species. When Stirling arrived again on African soil the majority of the continent was still under colonial rule or protection from one Western nation or another.

Scholars of Africa must forgive the simplistic representation which follows. World War II had touched only a small part of Africa; military operations were confined to Italian East Africa and to the northernmost countries. Nonetheless, Africans had participated in the effort and mechanics of protracted battle.

The continent contributed safe havens, very large numbers of troops and vast quantities of the raw materials of war. The Africans were fully aware of their contribution and there was a noticeable effect. There was a quiet but persistent move to the townships and a growing demand for these to be extended, and there was a growing realisation of the rewards of economic development. None of this had gone unnoticed by the British Colonial Office which had begun to make minor moves towards extending the degree of African involvement in local administration.

The populace of the United Kingdom had little awareness of Africa. It was still the 'Dark Continent': remote, albeit romantic, it held little interest for the average family. India was still the focal point of the Empire and though events there had heightened public interest in colonial matters, even in the Colonial Office Africa was only a ripple on the backwater of politics which colonial affairs had become as Britain tussled with the huge debts and physical damage which were the inevitable aftermath of major conflict. Only the dedicated few raised the question of the proper and controlled development of the colonies.

'Nationalism' was not yet an established movement but protest groups were beginning to spring up as the accessibility of education and recognition of the potential for building 'nations with an identity' and individual economic growth structures gave birth to a new awareness in the Africans. These protests at first took the form of peaceful attempts to air local rather than national grievances and the movements were based on tradition rather than on precepts of mature nationalism. At this point all such movements lacked leaders who had benefited from Western education. There was, however, in Britain a number of Africans working or studying who were ripe for exploitation and guidance by professional Comintern agents.

Although Stalin had ceased giving aid to African nationalist movements before the advent of World War II in his desire to forge better relationships with Britain, his support theretofore had inspired a number of dedicated men who refused to drop the ideals of destroying colonialist influence in Africa. Cells which had been active in some form since the early 1920s still existed. Jomo Kenyatta, a principle player in Kenyan politics, was first attracted to Communism whilst visiting London in 1929 to argue the case for land reform at the Colonial Office. This led him to a two-year course in revolutionary tactics in Moscow. Similarly Doctor Hastings Banda, frustrated by the restrictions his colour placed on him as a medical practitioner in his native Nyasaland as well as in Britain, was an easy target for Communism.

World War II had interrupted the Colonial Office response to the British government's edict that the colonies should become self-financing. Two pre-war studies of the African situation still called for action; the Young Commission of 1929 and Lord Hailey's African Survey of 1938 had each suggested the federation of some or all of the British dependencies in East Africa. In the main such a federation was aimed at the capitalisation of the vast agricultural and mineral resources of the country and to a degree this was bringing an unexpected prosperity to Africa. The overlay politically was quite out of synchromesh with economic advancement. Vociferous at the time was Arthur Creech Jones (later to become Colonial Secretary); he was well-known and respected as a colonial reformist but even he believed that it would take generations before the colonies became self-governing.

In 1945 the plans for the British West African territories were well advanced; the Nigerian Constitution had been re-drafted and Nigerians admitted into local councils, but this was considered a case apart from Central and East Africa for two main reasons. In the latter territories there was a much greater preponderance of whites who had settled the country and who had a vested interest in (white) self-government; indeed Southern Rhodesia had been internally self-governing since 1923. In West Africa there was already a large contingent of educated, professional Africans, they having had easier access to Western education than their counterparts in the Centre and East. Some have said that this advancement owed much to the West African commitment to the British war effort. The Royal West African Frontier Force, for example, was the largest colonial army ever assembled and, fighting as equals and in close proximity to Britons, many of its members gained new insights into such matters as voting rights and the voice of Everyman in the workings of government.

This greater access to education on the West Coast made the Central and East African seem less intelligent and progressive, reinforcing the view that Britain should remain in the rôle of surrogate father. The Colonial Office would continue to look after 'native interests' in combating disease, providing basic education, improving amenities and fighting poverty through the provision of work and simple trade training. The practice of making it relatively easy for British subjects to purchase land for farming flourished immediately after the war, particularly in Kenya, as demobilised soldiers took advantage of subsidised schemes. Thus Britain took scant notice of African land grievances such as had been presented by Jomo Kenyatta in 1929, and the scene was set for grandiose ambitions as thousands of Britons fled the post-war hardship in their own country. This was the Africa to which Stirling moved.

'I was offered the job of managing director to a London-based financial development company and asked to spearhead a somewhat superficial study of the vast natural resources both of mineral deposits and agricultural potential of the continent.

'I moved to Rhodesia in March 1946, I think, very excited and armed with a great many introductions. Evelyn Waugh was particularly helpful as was 'Itchy Cock', let's just call him Foster, it's a common enough name. There was a great influx of people after the war, and even though it had been settled for so long East Africa was for all the world as the Yukon must have been during the gold rush.

'My main intention was to carry out a thorough reconnaissance of conditions and business potential. What first caught my attention was the increased move towards urbanisation (what a horrible word). Lots of blackamoors and brownamoors had moved into urban areas during the past few years as the need for labour grew in industries supplying the war effort. The influx of workers was reinforced by large numbers of ex-servicemen who had tasted life in cities in India and Europe. This resulted in temporary townships or shanty towns on the fringes of major cities like Salisbury and Nairobi. Britain was pouring absolute sporrans full of money into East Africa, to be used to improve the lot of the African. The common denominator as far as I could see would be the need for building materials suppliers and contractors.

'I got a good feel for conditions and predictions for the future from old friends like Mike Sadler and other Rhodesians I had met during the war (many from the LRDG). You know, most of the advice I was given would have led me into farming. I was not a stranger to farming – we had quite large concerns at Keir – but it would have been far too static for me and the results are slow. I was interested, however, in how agricultural methods, especially irrigation techniques, could be applied in parts of Africa. I remember reading a study in Colditz, I think by a German, about how the Qattara Depression could once again be filled with water by creating a drop of only about four feet in ground levels and using the Nile as the supply. Imagine the possibilities.

'I spent some months both in Southern Rhodesia, based on Salisbury, and in Kenya where I had many old friends in Nairobi. The whole period was hugely enjoyable. Sabbaticals were originally taken every seventh year but I'm afraid I took mine about every seventh day! I did a lot of travelling and quite a bit of boozing – it was possible then to find some good backgammon which helped the sporran considerably.

'My conclusions were that it would be quite possible to set up a development operation on a number of fronts. I knew that brother Bill would be interested in some aspects of the venture as he was very keen on the construction of a railway line to bridge Tanganyika and Kenya. I felt that the best base initially at least would be Salisbury. Southern Rhodesia seemed to be growing faster, and being semi-independent there was also a permanence which meant that the planning process for new townships and industrial complexes was approached more positively and looked more certain. Africa certainly seemed to me the place to earn the brasso and stock up on the indispensable stuff.

'I got my first real insight into apartheid in the Rhodesias. Not the apartheid of the South African, Johannes Strydom, but certainly enthusiastic colour prejudice. I met Sir Godfrey Huggins (Prime Minister of Southern Rhodesia), an ardent supporter of Cecil Rhodes's vision of a white Africa stretching as far as Egypt, and Roy Welensky (leader of the whites in the Legislative Council of Northern Rhodesia), also committed to the maintenance of a colour bar. He was an interesting man, quite fully grown and very friendly. He had come up the hard way through labouring jobs and the trade union, which had left him convinced that it would be generations before the Africans could take a true part in their own affairs.

'In Kenya I had a short meeting with Philip Mitchell (Governor). He was courteous and committed to economic development measures in line with Colonial Office policy. He was not then popular with the white community – he was viewed as being too liberal and far too keen on getting whiteamoors, brownamoors and blackamoors together. I visited Nyasaland briefly but found that the white population there was mostly administrative apart from the host of missionaries who clustered like fleas on Africa's hide. I do not wish to sound off against missionaries – far from it, I learned a lot from them about the problems facing the Africans. I met some very, very dedicated priests and nuns in Africa who really did work for the common good, but some missionaries had a great propensity for interference and a lack of understanding of tribal customs which had nothing to do with religion. To those who would dispense with harmless, yet to the African, meaningful tradition or custom, I thumb my nose.'

Stirling's analysis showed him a number of avenues ripe for investigation. The scale of building either taking place or planned was interesting and nowhere had he come across a single company specialising in the total provision of building materials. Quarried stone, cements and timber would be in great demand and he decided that this would be his base business. There were other areas of interest, but in these he did not feel quite so confident.

'With the help of geologists and mining consultants we made an intelligent guess of the mineral resources for our selected test area – a two-hundred-mile radius from the Victoria Falls on the Zambesi River. We postulated that, given a proper structure and presuming American levels of skill and pay, a car, with most of the essential ingredients available within the test area, could be produced at two thirds of what it would cost to make in America. This rather fanciful conclusion clearly had to be taken with a pinch of salt. But beyond doubt until there was an understanding between the different races of Africa there was no hope of prosperity. And the Russians by then were aware of the continent's potential.

'The company I was working for showed no real enthusiasm for our findings, preferring a drip-feed system of financial investment which would have rendered any commercial project vulnerable to takeover.'

Stirling decided to go it alone, and resigned his position. As a prime holding company, and to handle the building materials side, he set up the Gemsbok Corporation in Salisbury.

He also established subsidiary companies to investigate and then trade in each of the areas of mining consultancy (he was particularly interested in coal mining), road construction and road transport. He thought it probable that these enterprises could be started with minimum investment and grow rapidly. Agriculture was not dismissed.

'I had read a most remarkable paper by Colin Clark, a

well-known economist, Australian, I think, who had done a study on agriculture in the format of an assessment of African economy. The study, based on about five countries, was a very detailed piece of work. He took a unit of land – I believe he called it the standard farm acre – and applied four variables. Three were known; natural water availability, sunlight within a twenty-four hour period based on latitude, and altitude. The unknown variable which he had to calculate was soil structure in terms of fertility ratios. This analysis enabled Clark to give predictions in terms of a productivity index.

'He concluded that the world should look to Africa and South America to ensure its food supplies. Of course this required much more research into methods of combating soil erosion and precise water conservation methods. I based a lot of the conclusions of my initial study for the other company on Clark's work; for some reason this important contribution appeared to have been ignored. It was outside the scope of anything I had in my own sights at the time but it kept springing to mind over the years.

'Later in the year I went home to discuss my findings with Bill. I had set up the structures for business, and had decided that I wanted nothing more than to live in Africa. In forming Gemsbok and its subsidiaries, and in setting about making them work, I learned a lesson which never stood me in good stead because I kept forgetting it! I am actually not a very good businessman. You wouldn't be surprised to know how many people agree with that statement.'

Stirling was only partly correct. With regard to spotting opportunities, assessing political, social and business trends and developing strategies he was quite superb. His weakness was in refusing to give up personal hands-on control. Gemsbok exemplified his ability to analyse needs and determine a market sector ripe for the taking. Turning such an idea into a profitable concern requires sometimes boring attention to detail and the slow, plodding mechanics of follow-through.

Stirling was in his element in persuading investors that his projects were based on good research and accurate analysis; they were. But the further steps of business planning, with its cost calculations, cash forecasts, cashflow predictions and profit and loss accounts, were anathema to him.

'Accountants have always made me furious. Utterly cautious and utterly pedantic they have a total lack of imagination. Did you ever see an accountant at the racecourse? Of course not, a horse would have to have at least five legs and a turbo charger under its tail before he would place a bet, and then it would be each way. I suppose they are necessary but in my mind they would always be in the front rank of predators, separated only from the Inland Revenue in the rear by a centre rank of failed alter egos calling themselves book-keepers.

'I realise that I should have taken on a manager who was experienced in the business, if necessary winkled someone away from a firm like Wimpey, or at least found a fellow who knew the building suppliers' trade. One of the problems, apart from wanting to control things myself, was that the sort of chap who was willing to spend his time on painful detail tended to be rather dull and unimaginative. I suppose in many ways I treated business in the same manner as SAS operations. There were opportunities by the dozen; decide on the objective, plan the route in secrecy and achieve surprise whenever possible when the decision was made to move.'

Looking at all the enterprises in which Stirling became involved in 1946-7 it is certain that he cast his net too wide. He definitely should have taken on managers for his projects, and no doubt many a good idea foundered for lack of detailed attention and follow-up, but other aspects of Stirling's character also contributed to the seeming lack of progress.

There were far too many opportunities, and he was noting and assessing these almost daily. An opening would be spotted and a plan put together very quickly which he would follow part of the way down the route. If another opening appeared, effort on the first idea would be reduced in proportion to the amount of interest awakened in the new theme. He never dropped ideas

completely, just put them into a separate mental compartment
to be rekindled whenever events or people reminded him. In
this way he lost impetus on many projects which could have
been solid commercial successes. It would not be fair to say
that he wavered or foundered because he did not; he did,
however, keep shuffling his priorities. He very rarely held
to his principle of planning in secrecy. As a man who loved
argument and debate he found it impossible to keep his ideas
to himself and others surely benefited from his acumen on
occasion.

He was also trying, and failing, to come to terms with the
opportunities and imposed limitations in the lives of black
Africans. 'Apartheid was alien to me but it existed in all the
countries I visited to lesser or greater degrees. The word wasn't
used in the Rhodesias, Tanganyika or Kenya, but the principle
was present. Whether the colour bar was based on feelings
of white supremacy *per se*, or whether it was there for more
"paternal" reasons, I was opposed to it and felt very deeply that
it was not right. I trod my way very carefully because I wanted
to settle in Rhodesia and was conscious that I was a newcomer.
I could very easily have put myself in a position where business
avenues would have closed for me.

'I slipped up often in the early days by my instinctive references to Africans; it was obvious that I meant the blackamoors
and, by inference, was saying they were the true Africans. You
have to remember that some of the immigrant Europeans and
Asians had then been in Africa for two or three generations.
They rightly considered themselves Africans, with a birthright
on the continent.'

There were then two mainstream points of view in Africa.
The policy of the Union of South Africa – that the white race
is unarguably superior and has an inalienable right to rule –
was accepted by most European settlers in other countries,
tempered by a feeling that the black African, after generations
of Western education, would take some part in government. In
the other view, held by some black Africans, Africa was for the

Africans and that did not include the white contingent, fourth generation or not.

'I could not accept either of these standpoints no matter how fiercely they were argued. The white supremacy concept totally ignored human dignity. There is no absolute right to power – the power of government has to be earned by those who earnestly and unflinchingly work toward the common good. The same argument could be made with respect to total dominance by the black African – and Africa still had to make enormous strides in technology, administration and education for which she needed outside help. In between was the brown African. Many Asians were also into the third and fourth generations to be domiciled in Africa and they dominated the 'trades'. Distrusted in the main by the blackamoors, they tended to throw in their lot with the whiteamoors who at least tolerated them and didn't object to them improving their status.

'There had to be an alternative to these two beliefs. I could not accept that there was no formula by which multi-racial harmony could be achieved, to the betterment of all. I was also beginning to meet others who appeared to feel the same way. I knew it would be no easy task to tackle – even in England it was proving difficult to cope with the thousands of immigrants from the West Indies. These people had answered our call for help by enlisting in the services during the war; immediately afterwards, with all the bomb-damage still about us, they were resented by the British public. I didn't know whether I wanted to get involved; I felt the situation was grossly wrong but had no initial desire to take action. That came a little later when I realised that others held the same opinions but felt impotent.'

Stirling's preliminary travels to examine business ideas had convinced him that there was a potential for great economic strength in British Central and East Africa if it could be cohesively harnessed. The raw materials for most industries were there, there was space and labour aplenty and the countries were sufficiently attractive to make the recruitment of skilled men easy. Over the next two and half years Stirling worked enthusiastically on business ventures. He earned sufficient to live on and managed to make frequent visits to Scotland. William Stirling was spending almost as much time in Africa as David and many of the ventures were of a joint nature with the Keir and Cawder UK-based main company. More important in the grander scheme of things is the number of contacts Stirling made during this period. Not only did he meet people with whom he established good rapport, he impressed them with his wit, and with his perception of and growing love for Africa.

The more he argued the case for a multi-racial society, the more the difficulties presented by such a system challenged him. 'If one *really* thought about the creation of such a self-supporting society, the problems were immense. The geography was in itself a problem. African boundaries were [and are] purely artificial – they take no account of tribal precincts and, as almost random lines on a map, they cannot be held to contain anything in which a man can take pride. Pride must be a central emotion in creating something worthwhile – something which has to be tangible. There cannot exist a line on a map which halves a river or a mountain which a man can observe and say, 'There on the one side is my country – one step further and I stand on land which means nothing to me.'

'And the hope had to be for the whole of Africa, not for a single territory or federation of territories. If there was a way forward for the idea then the horizon must be limitless; small territorial successes would lead to complacency and a diminution of ambition. The start point would probably be small; I was not so naive as to believe that the whole continent could be taken by storm with radical new ideas, but the aim must be without boundaries. In fact the idea of a multi-racial society was not radical, at least it was certainly not new. Many people in Africa regarded it as the ideal but, like myself, could not see a way forward.

'What if the British Territories were taken as the initial focus for such a society – not limited by their individual boundaries, rather their tribal and economic borders; but contained within a whole continent. It was a huge slice of land with great economic potential; it had masses of fast flowing water and long hours of sunshine to provide power; there was the love of the country in black, brown and whiteamoors. There were also many problems of social and medical welfare, commerce and communications, problems which might be tackled by an integrated nation working together. The joint crossing of such hurdles would be a necessary part of the creation of national pride.'

It seems that Stirling's concept of African life started as a dream – one which recurred so often that it had to be taken seriously. Once he began to analyse it and appreciate something of the enormity of the venture it became an irresistible challenge. Perhaps the challenge was the initial attraction, but total belief followed quickly. The more his proposals were rejected by entrenched traditionalists of all colours, the more he thought about the mechanics. Mechanical solutions which were so dependent on 'ifs', 'buts' and often matters of racial prejudice made him impatiently angry.

Stirling's religious education had taught him that colour, race and creed were unimportant in the eyes of God. He disagreed. They were important: they gave to each man a sense of identity and history. But it was right that they should be of no consequence in determining equality of voice, well-being or aspiration. Men were created equal and there was no reason, given equal rights and opportunities, that they should not work, rest, progress and live as equals. He became determined to sow the seeds for change in Africa. The scale of the matter did not deter him.

Stirling has been wrongly accused of megalomaniac delusions of grandeur in thinking that he could change the status quo in Africa. To Stirling the embryonic ideas were simply right, as a matter of logic and belief. He recognised immediately that he would need assistance if he was to have any impact. He also needed a positive plan, but what – or, perhaps more to the point, who – would be the start point? Much to the detriment of his business interests, Stirling became immersed in thought. There was a noticeable change in him. He pressed his views more vigorously; potential business associates found themselves engaged in enthusiastic debate on the future of Rhodesia. Stirling had embarked on the first part of his plan – the search for like-minded people who could furnish positive assistance.

'Through argument, and some very cruel teasing, I began to see a framework for action. I cannot in honesty say that the ideas were mine – I doubt if any one of us could lay claim to any single, startling idea; by listening to the voices of experience and often questioning them we arrived at the first plan. As I mentioned, the concept had to have limitless horizons but a tangible and manageable root. We decided to base the operation initially in Salisbury and Nairobi and that our concept would in rough terms apply to those lands which lay within the tropic of Capricorn. The land between the Limpopo and the Sahara was of immediate interest.

The Capricorn lands seemed of sufficient size to give us moment, and they imposed no limitations to spreading throughout Africa – or the world. From the start we decided that the Capricorn Africa Society would dissociate itself from any political programme, even though we believed that administrative and economic unity would be necessary before full unity of race could be achieved. Later we realised that this was a fundamental mistake and a severe limitation.

'What were we trying to achieve? At the time, I have to say, it was woolly. We could all imagine the wider framework of the sort of society we wanted but there were many blurred edges and it took some years to fine-tune the principles of Capricorn. The focus was our recognition that a policy for Africa must come from within Africa and it must be acceptable to, and fully supported by, all races on the continent.

'The model had to be the United States of America. Through their Constitution, accepted by all races in the land, their politicians pay tribute to the basic tenets of America's ideology. They work together for the common good – they are a whole people. That is what we wanted to achieve – an association of territories (not a political federation) within Capricorn Africa, founded upon a common citizenship which would be open, subject to some qualification, to members of all races. We could only achieve this by producing a groundswell of multi-racial public opinion within Africa and by procuring positive sympathy and public and political support within the West.'

Although the following extracts from the Constitution of the Capricorn Africa Society (which was formulated some two years after the events described above) are chronologically premature, they serve to demonstrate the massive task:

## Foreword

Capricorn Africa comprises those lands of eastern and Central Africa which lie between the Abyssinian border and the Limpopo River. The Capricorn Africa Society was founded in 1949 by a group of people who believed that a policy for Africa must come from within Africa. The founders of the Society came from many of Africa's territories and races.

## Preamble

The founders of the Capricorn Africa Society affirm in this preamble the beliefs which guided them in the founding of the Society.

The founders hold that all men, despite their varying talents, are born equal in dignity before God, and have a common duty to one another; and that the differences between man, whether of creed or colour, are honourable differences.

The founders believe in a common destiny for the inhabitants of Capricorn Africa, which will lead to an association of territories wherein men of all races may live side by side in harmony, sufficiency and freedom.

The founders believe that to strive towards such a goal will provide a sense of shared purpose and dedication transcending racial differences; and that its attainment will bring untold benefits to Africa and its people and to mankind.

Bound by these convictions the Founders of the Society submit that:

1. Africa south of the Sahara is comparable in natural resources with other continents of the world. The extent of its mineral, agricultural and industrial potentialities is only now being estimated by research and development.

2. The peoples of Europe have two responsibilities in Africa and these are complementary to one another. They have an obligation to mankind to develop that continent jointly with the Africans and other inhabitants, so that it shall contribute from its great resources to the wealth of the world. They have an equal obligation to give to the African both incentive and opportunity to achieve higher standards of life, and so make possible a living partnership between the races.

3. The African people as yet lack the technical skill, the industrial maturity and indeed the numbers to secure by themselves the timely development of the continent. The twofold responsibility of all the Europeans cannot be discharged by reserving all Africa's sparsely populated areas for gradual development at a pace determined by the Africans' birth rate. It can be discharged, and Africa's development quickened, by an increasing combination of Western immigration, capital and technology with the latent capacity of the African and other races.

4. Capricorn Africa is divided into many separate territories with separate administrations. The divisions are for the most part arbitrary and are seldom based on considerations of geography, economics or race. They deny the urge, increasingly felt among all races, to become part of a greater communion, racially and economically. In a larger economic unit, problems which are obstinate of solution within individual territories can be more readily resolved.

5. Sustained social and economic progress for any race demands sound administration and political stability, which at the outset will call for European leadership and guidance in federal and

territorial government. This leadership can be claimed only by right of administrative ability and experience, not of colour. It will not endure, nor deserve to endure, unless it encourages the participation of other races.

6. The future stability of Capricorn Africa depends essentially upon a policy of human relations which is flexible enough to meet the special requirements of each territory; and broad and liberal enough to face with confidence the scrutiny of enlightened opinion throughout the world.

7. The policy must promote the spiritual, economic, cultural and political progress of the African and other races. All those of all races who have attained the necessary social and educational standard must be accorded the responsibility of franchise and the full rights of citizenship. At the same time, those Africans who are unable or unwilling to accommodate themselves to the new economy and way of life must be protected and helped to develop at a pace consistent with their abilities.

The Constitution of the Capricorn Africa Society which follows has been designed by the founders as a vehicle for all those who wish actively to support the principles laid down in this preamble.

## Objects

The objectives of the Society shall be:

(1) To encourage the development, jointly by all the races, of Capricorn Africa which is comprised of those lands south of the Sahara and of the Abyssinian border and north of the Limpopo River.

(2) To maintain and advance true civilisation and cultural standards while helping all members of all races in Capricorn Africa to attain these standards.

(3) To define and establish a policy of human relations based on a common code of loyalty to Capricorn Africa, and which will bestow the full rights and privileges of citizenship on all those who have achieved the qualifications necessary to enable them to sustain the responsibilities implicit in this status.

(4) To make known the principles and ideals set out in the Preamble of this Constitution and strive towards their fulfilment.

In this way the Capricorn Africa Society was started; in all manner of ways it was to be in Stirling's mind for the rest of his life.

# 16

# NOT BORN OF FEAR

In early August 1951, Stirling caught a severe cold while he was in Salisbury. Having noted the cure-all effects of modern antibiotics, he took a healthy dose of penicillin to cure his running nose, and penicillin poisoning took effect on a flight back to England. He made it to Morar Lodge without shoes and with hands and feet swelling rapidly.

'This was particularly annoying as at that time of the year hands and feet were urgently needed for grouse shooting and fishing. Bill was at Morar and ribbed me mercilessly for my ineptitude – no doubt he was quite pleased not to have competition on the grouse moor. I was bedded down for a short time and I did some real thinking about Capricorn which by then would have been about two years old. But I couldn't completely ignore my businesses; I'd been taking a look at the Umtali area. A great chum, Viktor Chitty, was interested in setting up a hardboard factory, which required black wattle and coniferous timber waste. I knew some people with the Rhodesian Wattle Company and also some in the forestry and timber business so I went to see them.

'I had formed a company called Central African Commerce Limited, with Bill Brown as chairman; Bill was general manager of the South African General Investment and Trust Company. I also had Peter Allsebrook, a director in Keir and Cawder and other of our interests; he was then living in London but had just spent two years in South Africa and Rhodesia so he knew the scene fairly well. We had, too, Olaf Bakke who owned the Bakke Timber Company and had been negotiating for black wattle waste for some time, for different purposes. A huge amount of such waste was simply being burned or thrown away and there had been precious little research into its uses. Olaf had the idea that it could somehow be used in the production of rayon and was talking most enthusiastically to a company in Italy.

'The idea behind Central African Commerce was to try to take advantage of all the new ideas and proposals then being put forward in Africa. The Rhodesias especially were attracting a lot of investment interests from the UK, Europe and USA and it appeared that a company which could effect fruitful introductions and perhaps carry out limited research for those investors could make a little brasso.

'I needed the brasso too. We had a steady flow of piecemeal business but no single company was really going strong and my sporran was in a constant state of emptiness. I was then spending more and more time on Capricorn which, of course, did not create an income; I was able to lay off some expenses against it, but not until later. I did manage to get a lot of investment interest in the City but as usual most people wanted to know every detail and analyse every risk down to the last ha'penny – very few real risk takers about at the time.

'I was relying on supplies from the Soffe Syndicate to make the hardboard company viable. I knew the syndicate members quite well; Lord Salisbury, the Duke of Devonshire and Schroeders Bank. Management was in the hands of Andrew Soffe and they were planting about two to three thousand acres per year. Andrew had been in Southern Rhodesia for some forty years and was a hugely successful businessman. The syndicate had a market for their offcuts but I had pointed out to them that the market would soon become flooded as the results of their planting increased supplies. I got the promise of a good deal in the planning stages by offering him wattle timber at par

price. Central African Commerce was still negotiating for the
concession for wattle but I didn't have to tell him that.

'I seem to remember that we were also trying to get investment to set up a cattle breeding farm using Afrikander bulls –
we were involved in so many schemes, most of which took a
lot of travelling and hard work and didn't amount to much at
the end of the day, that I'm afraid life was often something of
a jumble. Immensely enjoyable though!

'Brother Bill was running Stirling-Astaldi and Keir and
Cawder as well as Derbyshire Granite and the interests were
very wide. They spread across road building, ore concessions,
quarrying and everything which was remotely connected.
Despite spending most of our time in the same countries
we didn't see an awful lot of each other in the early fifties
but we corresponded pretty regularly. Keir and Cawder then
had an office in Upper Grosvenor Street and I tended to make
that my London headquarters whenever I was in town.

'I must have been a complete frustration at times to my
business partners as I was really getting the bit between my
teeth with the Capricorn Africa Society. Some of my business
partners, of course, were staunch supporters of Capricorn
anyway – Andrew Soffe was a real star and needed no urging
to inform influential people about the movement.

'The Africa I was involved with was in disarray. Kenyatta
was making his presence felt in Kenya with the Mau Mau
and the Kikuyu and it looked certain to me that a state
of emergency would have to be declared soon. The British
government public relations was terrible. The whiteamoor
planters in Malaya were hailed as heroes but the settlers in
Africa were portrayed as landstealers insofar as the general
public was concerned. Earlier in 1951, Kwame Nkrumah
had become Chief Minister of the Gold Coast by way of
riots and violence and there was always the fear that this
could set a precedent for action elsewhere. In the Rhodesias
and Nyasaland the white leaders continued to argue for a
federation of the three countries, much against the wishes of

the Africans, who saw this as another stage of solidifying white supremacy.

'By that time I had got some really good people working for Capricorn, people of good standing in Africa whose views carried weight. We were already working towards a major convention but we had a long way to go. Michael Wood had become a great friend – he moved out to Kenya in 1946 and he and his wife, Susan, were pure gold. Susan was born in the Congo and a third-generation African. She had obviously settled in Kenya and she knew and loved the country as only a real African can. She and Jeanine Scott (who later married Rear-Admiral Josef Bartosik, and between us we shamelessly hustled him into helping – but more of that later) did the work of twenty people. They both have a tremendous sense of fun too, which was indispensable.

'Roy Welensky, who favoured the colour bar in the beginning, slowly came round to our point of view and became a great side-liner. Laurens van der Post, who knew the country and the people better than all of us put together, was an inspiration, but he came later. He was a great expert on African agricultural methods and tribal traditions and history. His voice was listened to with respect throughout Africa and his deep knowledge put mine to shame. If these people were the gold dust then Dr John Oldham had to be the diamond. His voice also carried weight internationally, and he was absolutely invaluable to CAS. Arthur Stokes was marvellous – he tried hard to keep me in order both on the business fronts and with Capricorn, in which he was a firm believer.

'We were still, in 1951, groping a little blindly in terms of properly defining our aims. We knew beyond doubt that the principles were fundamentally correct and we were clear in our objectives, but we were still not happy with the clauses of what had become the Capricorn Declarations.

'We had for some time been discussing a London base. By late 1951 we had representative offices at Salisbury (Southern Rhodesia), Luanshya (Northern Rhodesia), one in Tanganyika at Dar-Es Salaam – perhaps we had two; we eventually had another in Tanganyika, at Ol Orion. Michael Wood was to become the chairman of the Kenya office. To call them offices is a bit cheeky; we scrounged a chair, table and address from those who didn't mind too much. To pass the word out of Africa we had been dependent on my trips abroad or the good offices of people like Soffe and Bakke who happily informed their contacts on their business travels. We were missing opportunities because we did not have a fixed point of reference in the UK or America, though in the USA we had acquired a sympathetic group of friends.

'We needed an office and staff who would make influential political and commercial contacts and at the same time be capable of understanding Capricorn and answering questions from interested parties and the press. If we managed to achieve a Convention, there would be a lot of publicity, which we wanted. We wanted people who could open doors in high places for us and advise us of how best to gain the interest of bodies and individuals we had set our sights on. In short, we required an executive London Committee and that was what we called it even though it didn't then exist.

'Money was very tight and I was conscious that we were making heavy demands on Keir and Cawder both financially and on Bill's time. Later that year we set up office in London or rather we set up a room in the Keir and Cawder office in Upper Grosvenor Street. I was nowhere near approaching people for the committee, but I was convinced of the need for this London base. I was travelling there more and more, usually as a staging post between America and Africa, and wanted a focal point for CAS. There was also a commercial need; in London in early July, I approached an old friend, Dudley Clarke, for assistance.

11 July 1952

My dear Dudley,

I am writing to confirm the approach that I made to you,

when we met the other night, for your services on a part-time
basis to set up an African Intelligence Room at 9 Upper
Grosvenor Street. It is obviously impossible at this stage to
go into any great detail of what the job would entail but in
broad outline I would summarise it as follows:

1. Supervising the layout and setting-up of an Intelligence and
Map Room equipped with all the necessary maps, library of
reference books and a film projector and film library, etc.,
covering the six territories of East and Central Africa in detail,
the surrounding territories and the continent as a whole in
less detail.

2. The setting-up of a Commercial and Company Information
Service covering the same area.

3. The establishing of a comprehensive card index of all
information available on Africa.

The emphasis . . . would be on those factors which . . .
determine or influence land values.

*Setting up of the Intelligence Room*

A room will be put at your disposal in 9 Upper Grosvenor Street
for this purpose. Main features of this room will be:

(a) All the maps necessary to provide basic information of
physical features of the continent, its geology, rainfall, soil
structure, etc.

(b) A sand table map of the continent on a large scale which
could provide the main basis for information collected.

(c) Film projector and a film library.

(d) A library of reference books.

(e) Commercial intelligence library.

It will obviously be necessary for you to employ expert
consultants on the question of layout. Before I return to Africa
on 24th July we should discuss in particular detail the sand table
project.

*Company Information System*

All services such as the Exchange Telegraph and Moody's

Services, etc., should be taken relating to the African continent and all other information available should be collected on all companies operating in East and Central Africa.

*General Intelligence Index*

Obviously it would be very costly to purchase all publications on the subject of Africa, but it should be practicable to build up a card index system indicating the whereabouts of every such publication with information as to its availability.

We would make available to you a capable female secretary who, in the early stages, would, I suggest, be sufficient to look after your immediate needs.

We suggest £600 a year as a starting salary on the understanding that this figure would be reviewed in about six months time, when you would know more exactly what scale of work is entailed in carrying out this assignment.

Yours sincerely,
David Stirling

Brigadier Dudley Clarke CB

This letter highlights the degree of understatement Stirling could employ at initial meetings with people he wished to recruit. There is little doubt that Brigadier Clarke did not expect the immense work load implied in the letter; nonetheless he accepted the challenge and worked tirelessly on a project which was to draw him more and more into its intricate network.

Although Stirling was merciless in extracting huge efforts from his associates no complaints are evident. Excerpts from his 1952 working logs show that he drove himself equally hard:

*Tue, Aug 26*: Salisbury. Meetings with Colin Kirkpatrick (African Finance Corporation – Investing House). John Baines (MD of Associated British Investments [Rhodesia] Ltd & MD of Brush Electric and ABOE Group of Rhodesia. Wattle & other franchises). Harold Poole (Norton Factory – all 6 territories).

*Wed, Aug 27*: Salisbury. Meetings with Tony Graftey Smith (Financial Adviser to Rhodesian Govt. Friend of Hugh Kindersley of Lazards Bank). Andrew Soffe (Founder Joint National Council & Area Development and Publicity Board, Southern Rhodesia. Timber & afforestation expert – friend). Dr Chikari (Consulting Geologist. Partner Sir Digby Burnett – Mining Engineer). Rex Reynolds (late political correspondent *Sunday Times*. UCAA, editor *British African Review*).

*Sun, Aug 31*: Dep Salisbury 0630 hrs. Arr Livingstone 0815. Drive to Kazangula arr 1700.

*Mon, Sep 1*: Meet Wilson (Manager Kazangula Area project). Return to Livingstone.

*Tue, Sep 2*: Leave Livingstone for Lusaka. Meet Harry Grenfell (manager BSA Company's Northern Rhodesian interests).

*Thu, Sep 4*: Leave Lusaka 0940 for Tabora. 1630 – flight to Southern Highlands (Sao Hill). Stay at Lady Chesham's house. Dinner with Bishop Beltrinno and Father Sciolta re Salisbury Declarations.

*Fri, Sep 5*: Southern Highlands Club. Driven to Wattle Scheme in Njombe. Meet Mr Senior & Dr Hitchin.

*Sat, Sep 6*: Inspect coal mines. Leave pm for Suddaby Coal Field. Stay Night.

*Tue, Sep 9*: By air to Entebbe; pick up Harris & Cawley. To Mbarara; collected by Spiro Poulos taken to Kabale Hotel.

*Wed, Sep 10*: Visit Wolframs Mines. Meet Fan Joudis (mine owner). Evening meeting with E. Christansen (Uganda Electricity Board).

*Thu, Sep 11*: Dep Kabale 0830. Arr Mbarara 1145. Dep 1155 for Kasase. Arr 1230. Meet Professor Kennedy (Kilembe Copper Mine). Fly Nairobi via Entebbe. Dine with Mervyn Hill & Michael Blundell.

*Fri, Sep 12*: Meet Kendall Ward (discuss retainer). Alistair Gibb (chairman Alexander Gibb & Partners. Southern Tanganyika Communications Report).

Between 26 August and mid-October Stirling's diaries never indicate more than one day without some form of commitment, whether on behalf of CAS or on business. Many people named in these extracts became supporters of the Capricorn Africa Society as the net widened.

'Late in October 1952 we heard rumblings of discontent from Bulawayo; one of the African leaders [Ngebetsha] was accusing other Africans of being traitors to their fellow men by supporting CAS. He claimed to have "spies" in our midst who reported to him on the "sinister motives behind the scenes". There were accusations of secret meetings and of us paying large sums to get the support of Africans in spreading pro-federation propaganda. We rectified this by getting an article into *African Weekly* stating the openness of CAS and its aims. It did help motivate us, however, to get a move on with publishing the Capricorn Declarations which were still being discussed. As the Salisbury Declarations these had been signed in April 1952, the first two signatories being Godfrey Huggins and Roy Welensky.

'I was also having a little trouble with the Capricorn Africa Development Corporation. People were confusing it with CAS and putting two and two together to come up with five. In some areas it was thought that CADC was a vehicle to introduce foreign capital into Rhodesia in order to further the political aims of CAS. In fact I was spending very little time on commercial matters during that period.'

As is borne out in this letter:

31 October 1952

The Hon. Wilfred Havelock
Memorial Hall
Delamere Avenue
Nairobi

My dear Wilfred,

... In respect of the Declarations the die is now cast, and

all that can be done is to delay the actual publication date by a week or two. I think that somewhere around 25th November should allow for some quietening down of the press jamboree on Mau Mau . . .

. . . I had over an hour's talk with the Queen Mother last night, a lot of it about Africa, and told her of our plans. Immediately after the Coronation she is coming out to Southern Rhodesia to open the Bulawayo Rhodes Centenary Show. She is immensely interested in Africa and is intensely looking forward to . . . this visit.

. . . My time has been so taken up with the . . . Society that I have unfortunately had to completely neglect the commercial side of my life. However both Wenner-Gren and Lillas are in New York this week having discussions with World Bank Officials and others on our development plans in Africa. After November I hope to be in a position to pull my weight on the commercial side but I have to make it plain to both my partners that my first allegiance, even if it means withdrawing from the partnership, must lie with the Society, at least until publication of the Declarations. So far I must say they have been marvellously tolerant. The Africa Room is gradually taking shape under the extremely able guidance of Dudley Clarke . . .

Yours sincerely,
David Stirling


The Capricorn Declarations (as opposed to the Salisbury Declarations) were in fact published on 8 December 1952, and seventy-eight newspapers, covering Africa, the UK, the USA, India, Hong Kong, the West Indies, Belgium, France, Canada and Malta, carried comment. Almost all reported in favourable terms, and expressed real hope for success. At the time of publication Stirling was in London, and he wrote a personal article for the *Birmingham Mail* in which he expressed CAS's views so clearly and positively that it is worth reproducing it in full.

## A New Dominion in Embryo

You will ask what the purpose is of the Capricorn Declarations. To appreciate the answer . . . you must look at Africa on the map. Note specially the territories of Northern Rhodesia, Southern Rhodesia and Nyasaland. Nearby are Kenya – so much in the news today – Tanganyika and Uganda. Upon the destiny of these six territories may depend Britain's standard of living and her continued greatness in world affairs.

Altogether the territories cover over 1,000,000 square miles, an area almost half the size of the United States. Except for oil and soft timber, their natural resources are rich in proportion to this huge area. All of the minerals needed to free the British Commonwealth from dollar dependency are there in plenty.

Properly irrigated and farmed with modern methods and fertilisers, the agricultural possibilities are sufficient to sustain the full needs of an expanding industrial economy. The rivers which tumble down from a central plateau of 3,000 feet above sea level have an enormous potential electrical energy.

### Emigration prospects

The present population of these six British-controlled territories is about 25,000,000 but, planned and developed, they could absorb at least 5,000,000 white people in the next 20 years without depriving the African of one acre of land. Within the next century they could support a black and white population of 90,000,000.

These territories and their development are the subject of the Capricorn Declarations.

The case for the current official proposals for the Federation of Northern and Southern Rhodesia together with Nyasaland has already been widely debated. The sponsors of the Capricorn Declarations support these proposals and see the achieving of Central African Federation as an indispensable stepping-stone towards the larger federation which, in addition to the Central African territories, would embrace Kenya, Tanganyika and Uganda.

Thus a great new dominion would be established whose economic and social significance could in the next century equal that of the United States today.

The importance, however, of the Capricorn Declarations

does not lie only in the economic aspects of the proposals, but also in the solemn recognition implicit in them that the future of East and Central Africa can only be built on the partnership of all races, creeds and colours – and not on the principles of racial domination as expressed in Malan's policy of apartheid.

Obviously for many years to come the responsibilities of leadership must rest primarily upon the European, but as the other races develop so they must be able to participate in this responsibility. The sponsors of the Declarations believe that the quality of this leadership would be strengthened, rather than weakened, and the standards of our Western civilisation heightened by the progressive participation of the other races in the responsibilities of government.

## Agreed principles

The Declarations represent a solution to African problems in terms of Africa. They embody principles agreed upon as the result of exhaustive investigation and discussion by White, Black and Asiatic leaders throughout the territories and men and women of varying political beliefs in Britain.

We believe the Declarations to be important, firstly, because they represent an opportunity to lift the discussion of Africa's problems out of the ordinary political context; secondly, because they provide what may be a last chance of preventing relationship between the races deteriorating into a vicious struggle between the extravagant ambitions of the African on the one hand and naked White domination on the other; thirdly, because they provide a challenge to men of goodwill of all races and creeds to combine to build a new Dominion in Africa which could decisively influence the position of the West in the balance of world power.

The sponsors of the Declarations are satisfied that the White Paper on Central African Federation makes adequate provision for the safeguarding of African interests, but they wish to go further than this and therefore emphasise the need to encourage the African in his climb up the ladder to full rights and dignities of citizenship. They lay down that members of all races should be entitled to these rights on passing the necessary tests.

The Declarations also suggest that new European immigrants to the Federal States should not be entered on the franchise registers until they have passed similar tests and given an oath of loyalty to the principles of the Declarations which would be embodied in the Federal Constitution.

### One goal for Africa

The apparently overwhelming problems of race relations in Africa would soon fall away if all the races of these territories accepted one goal for Africa and were prepared to work towards its attainment. The Declarations are an effort to define this goal and set a common purpose for all races.

You may ask why the principles submitted in the Declarations were not advanced previously by such men as Sir Godfrey Huggins, Prime Minister of Southern Rhodesia, and Roy Welensky, Leader of the European Elected Members in Northern Rhodesia. In fact, the principles contained in the Declarations have long been supported by these two great leaders and also by other responsible European settlers in East and Central Africa.

But it must be remembered that these principles are only valid and can only be effectively applied within the framework of the six territories, and until recently it was not within the realm of practical politics to talk about the big federation.

### If they fail –

It is the conviction of those who sponsored the Declarations that the orderly development of the African continent will turn on the outcome of the present negotiations for Central African Federation. If these negotiations fail, then the outlook in Africa is indeed bleak.

If they are successful, then there is every hope that we will have entered into a new phase leading to steady improvement of racial relations and to great advances in the standard of living and well-being of all the inhabitants of British East and Central Africa and to an ever-rising contribution by the African continent to the wealth of the world.*

The publication of the Capricorn Declarations brought a

---

* Reproduced by kind permission of the *Birmingham Post & Mail*.

flood of interest and assistance, both with finance and the acquisition of further supporters as Stirling's letter to Arthur Stokes shows:

December 30, 1952

Arthur Stokes Esq
Salisbury

My dear Arthur,

*Capricorn Africa Society and the Declarations* . . . I am at last getting round to establishing a small London Committee of the Society, perhaps under the local chairmanship of Sir John Slessor. Slessor is at present Chief of Air Staff and only retires on 1st January. There are a great many very big jobs in the offing for him and he is reputed to have been offered the ambassadorship in America. However, he has determined to take a job which deals primarily with Africa. We can have the pick on our London Committee because the Declarations have generated a really remarkable degree of enthusiasm for Africa among just the sort of people who could be of great use to us. Could you let me know if there are any particular names anybody in the Salisbury Branch would like me to approach while I am in London.

Prince Yuri Galitzine, who was chairman until last week of the London Committee of the United Central Africa Association, is very anxious to be asked to join our London Committee. He is convinced that our Declarations have done far more good to the cause of Central African Federation than harm.

I am having a couple of thousand copies printed of all the main comments in the British and African press. Therefore please send at the very earliest moment the leaders in the *Bulawayo Chronicle* and *Northern News*. I shall write a short introduction and a short conclusion to make the resulting pamphlet a suitable basis for our appeal for funds in the City and elsewhere. I shall aim to raise £20,000 for the . . . Society, making clear that we will need a considerable proportion of it as a contribution towards the campaign fund for Central African Federation.

Some of the press cuttings from Europe are beginning to come in. A particularly good and full account of the

Declarations appeared in *Le Soir* of Brussels. I meant to send you the enclosed Kemsley Press cover of the Declarations last week. This came out in all their main papers and covers an enormous aggregate of circulation. I was not very pleased with it because of the personal references; however, according to McCormick, the foreign editor of Kemsley Group, these made it easier to give the Declarations prominence. He has promised that in any follow-up story he will not again refer to that Phantom Major.

I have had some really heartening letters; for instance, I enclose one from Sir Alfred Vincent . . . a very hard-bitten old boy and an extremely successful business man. He was at one time Leader of the Elected Members and has great status as an elder statesman in Kenya. Taking all this into account I feel that his letter is very encouraging for the Society . . .

I will be leaving for America shortly to take the first steps to set up our Africa Room in New York. There I shall have full meetings with my partners before returning to Africa via Lisbon sometime in early February. I naturally want to get back to Salisbury as soon as possible but the Society I am sure will appreciate that I have so badly neglected my business affairs that I must try to make some amends in this respect . . .

Yours ever,
David

'What was particularly pleasing at this stage was the degree of vigorous, active support we were getting from the Africans and Asians. This is surprising as some of them (the Africans) were taking the risk almost of martyrdom. The effect of the publication of the Declarations was dramatic – in one short step most of the world knew about CAS. Freddy de Guingand, who was writing a book about his jumbo-chasing days in Africa (but not about how he spent his ivory money in the casinos of the south of France), had half promised to set out the Declarations as an appendix to the work.

'I should say much more about Laurens van der Post, who by this time was firmly with us. It was reading his book *Venture to the Interior* which first drew my attention to him. The book had been born out of his intense emotions after losing a friend

by drowning in Malawi. But his descriptions of Africa and his
sharply drawn truths about the continent and its peoples were
the hooks which caught me. I vowed that I would meet him.

'I think it must have been late 1952 or early 1953 when we
eventually did meet in London. We were both just back from
different parts of Africa and I told him of Capricorn and my
years working for the Society and that I thought his help was
crucial to us.

'He asked me to paint a picture of Capricorn. When I got
as far as our tremendous press coverage, about thirty column
feet of mainly front-page news and editorials, he interrupted.
Though he admired the concept outlined in the Declarations
he was critical of the Society's evident support of the inferior
and sterile official proposals. Moreover he pointed out that the
Capricorn Contract previsioned the foundation for the Six Territory federation and, of course, for the smaller Central African
federation – but the foundation should have been laid first.

'It was, of course, a most valid observation and I had to
explain to Laurens that tactical timing had obliged us to set
out just the Society's 'Territorial Imperative'. But having been
pre-empted by the official plan which was now preoccupying
the politicians, and recognising the objections to its terms of
most African leaders, including those already members of
the Society, we had decided to concentrate our energies and
resources on the Contract.

'Laurens welcomed our decision and said he was ready to
campaign for us. From then onwards his enthusiasm and
knowledge of the African people propped up our morale.
If many contributed to the Capricorn Africa Contract, it was
Laurens who analysed it and steered us along the right path
and with the magic of his pen was most responsible for drafting
the document which was to be our flagship. He constantly
prompted our thinking and supported our sense of purpose.

'The real powerhouses for drawing up the Contract were the
Citizenship Committees; we eventually had more than twenty,
in permanent offices of some description. These gave venues

for people making enquiries, allowed the staff to spot local
opportunities for extending influence and gave us speaking
platforms for our periodic tours. On these speaking tours
Laurens was superb, he and I together made two tours
through the six territories, often addressing hostile meetings.
I particularly remember one, crowded with a largely hostile
white audience; I can recall the essence of his address but not,
alas, the elegance of his words.

'He asked: "Who are the cowards and who the heroes
amongst us tonight? The majority of you appear to be opposed
to the Capricorn concept. We do not believe that the white
man can secure his destiny in Rhodesia and in Africa, nor that
this country, well endowed in natural resources, can achieve its
economic potential until the black man has a majority of the
votes and the same access to land purchase as the white man.
Our proposals for the right to vote, based on the multi-vote
system, would establish perhaps the most intelligent electorate
in the world; but it would certainly yield more votes to the
Africans than to the Europeans . . ." It was a courageous
speech, so typical of Laurens.

'I really wanted to get the Aga Khan on side. I knew his
daughter, Princess Joan Aly-Khan, very well and I managed
to get her to dinner with myself and Laurens in London early
in 1953. The intention was to create an opportunity for Laurens
to present the case for Capricorn Africa to the Aga Khan.
Laurens is probably the greatest expert on farming practices
in Africa; he had led field expeditions looking into ranching
and plantation projects all over the continent. But his greatest
virtue is his wisdom and perception in all matters concerning
race relations in Africa. I have seen him verbally knocking hell
out of a Bloomsbury socialist and a reactionary Kenya settler
at the same time.

'A lot of the CAS business was done over the dinner table
in London. A relaxed atmosphere with good food and some
carefully applied boozo was a great way of ensuring that controversial argument didn't result in people stalking off in high

dudgeon – and if they were obliged to stay for the whole argument there was a more than sporting chance that they would be
convinced. I would usually try to weight the balance of guests
in my favour of course; my family were a great help and quite
often I was able to get my mother and Irene along in support.'

Stirling had mentioned martyrdom. On 28 January 1953 an
African office orderly, Robert Phelan, was sentenced to jail
for five years by a court at Lusaka for threatening murder.
The evidence, extracted from a letter he wrote to two fellow
Africans, was: 'You people, Capricornists, you are the people
selling your brothers to Yengwe at Ndola. At first you wanted
to kill Nkumbula. You even received revolvers from your
master, the general superintendent of Capricornists. We are
now awaiting that our elders may give us freedom. You will
lose your lives in the Lusaka area . . .' (Apparently Yengwe
is the name for a mythical lion which eats only human flesh.
Nkumbula was then President of the Northern Rhodesian
African Council which was staunchly opposed to federation.)

'Generally speaking, in parliament, we were getting more
and more support from both sides of the House but the Colonial
Office turned quite bloodyminded about the Declarations; they
mistakenly saw them as something which would interfere with
their selling the process of Federation. Quite ridiculous. We
started to organise a proper finance committee. I got Clive
Salter to head this up in Kenya and Andrew Soffe in Central
Africa. In the City I was working on Keswick of the Hudson
Bay Company, Lord Perth of Schroeders, Tom Davies of
Courtaulds Export and others of their stature to help with
fund raising.

'It was quite tricky setting up these committees as it was
easy to ruffle feathers unintentionally. People, once they had
decided to support us, were willing to take on enormous
workloads and often felt slighted if they were not given first
refusal of any new extension to the Society. We didn't then
have a proper financial structure in Salisbury; Arthur [Stokes]
was working on that.'

19 January 1953

My dear Arthur,

*Finance Committee*. Thank you for your letter of 14 January concerning the Finance Committee. Rather than asking Frank Davidson in preference to Albert Davies I would prefer, if the Society agrees, to ask neither at the moment. I don't want to hurt Albert's feelings and in any case I don't think a representative is required in N. Rhodesia at this stage, particularly taking into account the very strong support we have there from the Chester Beatty Group. (Hochschild, President of American Metals, which controls Selection Trust, is giving a small dinner for me in New York in order to help us raise funds) . . .

A person who is really keen to help . . . and who has suitable status in the City is Ian Malcomson, a partner with Abel Smith & Cotton in various tobacco projects in Southern Rhodesia. In spite of the fact that Cotton has tried to damp his enthusiasm for the Society he has held fast in support of us. I reiterate that we should keep our Finance Committee very small and absolutely top-notch.

*Statement by Stanley Evans.** I enclose a copy of a speech by Stanley Evans which is a very gallant performance considering the mood of the Labour Party as a whole at the moment. I think it would be a great encouragement to him if somebody from the Society in Salisbury (I suggest John Baines who already knows him) writes him a letter of congratulations.

*My American trip*. I am going to see quite a few nobs while I am in America. I am starting off with Bernard Baruch, who is regarded as something of an elder statesman by both the Republicans and Democrats. I will ask him to give me introductions to those in the Administration who might be interested in Africa. As I have been introduced to him on purely a personal basis I shall not overdo the Capricorn angle on my first talk. I think it would be wise for me to go rather gingerly until I know more about the American attitude in the matter . . .

Yours ever,
David

* Labour MP for Wednesbury.

Stirling's visit to America was a great success and laid the foundations for a support centre for many years to come. Between 30 January and 11 February he met twenty-five influential American businessmen all of whom pledged support. He located a facility for the New York Africa Room (free of charge, of course), got the editors of *Time*, *Life* and *Fortune* on side and set up the basic element of a fund-raising mechanism to be activated later. He did some personal business in Nassau, then returned to Washington where he concentrated on the State Departments and those concerned with overseas development and investment and Africa in particular. He stayed in the USA, flitting between New York and Washington, until 16 March with never a gap of more than a few hours in his work logs.

Back in London he was just as busy with meetings and briefings until departing for Dar-es-Salaam via Nairobi on 24 March. In London he had checked with Laurens van der Post on the timing for the proposed Capricorn Convention and they had decided on October provided that funding was available. He also urged Randolph Churchill to keep Bernard Baruch (with whom he had established a great rapport) on his toes when the latter stayed with Winston later in the year. Stirling was beginning to show signs of physical exhaustion – his fierce migraines had begun again – but he gave himself no quarter.

'I got something of a break with the Coronation. I was privileged to be a Gold Stick Officer, and the ceremony is so complex that there were lots of rehearsals; these were physically very tiring but they took my mind off things. It was the most marvellous occasion, one of the highlights of my life. I've never been one for too much pomp and ceremony even in the services but the beauty and solemnity of a Coronation and, I suppose, the sheer happiness of it all, will test the tear ducts of the most miserable man.'

Shortly afterwards, Stirling received a letter from Major W.E.P. Miller, who officiated alongside him, and who wrote: '. . . what enormous enjoyment the whole of the Coronation period was for me – the more so because it seemed that our respective senses of humour blended in well together, and that is a vital necessity in a job such as we had . . . My normal existence down here does not lend itself to many laughs so it was all the more desirable that such a break-away from a cabbage routine should entail working with someone who could appreciate the lighter side of things – and you, my dear David, certainly filled that role in full measure! What fun it was and what a great experience . . . I have just received "The policy for Africa" but my enormous pile of letters must come first. Then I will endeavour to direct my third-form brain on to this colossal project. I feel we should keep in touch . . . we should always welcome you down here to have another laugh . . . Remember me to Randolph if you see him again and I hope he is none the worse for the rough treatment we gave him.'

'I did take the opportunity to get Randolph more firmly on side and try to prod him into more positive action. He was then editing his father's speeches but he was also on the board of a New York television company run, I think, by his brother-in-law and he was syndicating newspaper articles. Most of his friends and associates were well-placed for our means. He was very willing but he kept forgetting to act. We had a tremendous following across the complete racial spectrum and spanning all business areas and all flavours of politician. I was conscious that our administrative capabilities were not up to scratch and needed fine tuning. Finances were very tight indeed.'

On 15 July 1953 Stirling wrote to Peter Allsebrook:

1. It is my conviction that we have now arrived at the point where administration facilities must catch up with our commitments in the field.

2. My plans remain as they were and are outlined below:

*First stage.* In early August we start our appeal for the first £12,000. The appeal will be launched by our African Interim Committee. The first £12,000 will be used to pay:

a) the money which will by then be owing to Newman Neame for the documentation now being printed (i.e. the World Press and the Capricorn Declarations, which will be used as the basis of appeal for that first £12,000).

b) the launching of our Association in all six territories in East and Central Africa and a heavy advertising programme.

c) the first few months' travelling expenses and salary of my full-time executive officer (this will probably be Sandy Galloway).

d) the publishing of the book of essays which will cost about £3,000.

e) my personal travelling and other expenses during this phase.

f) note that none of the first £12,000 will be employed in repaying Keir & Cawder.
   I hope to raise this £12,000 partly in Johannesburg and partly in London.

*Second stage.* The raising of funds in this stage will start after the publication of the book of essays, that is about the third week of October and after the setting up of a comprehensive London Appeal Committee. Our target in this appeal will be £100,000. The purpose of this fund will be:

1) to pay off all debts owed by the Capricorn Africa Society to Bill, Keir & Cawder and others.

2) to continue the standing charges already entered into in the first phase and to pay for the additional administrative staff which by then will have become necessary.

3) to pay off all the setting up charges of the Convention.

*Third stage.* A further appeal launched during December in America under the Chairmanship I hope of Baruch . . . The purpose of this third appeal will be to make up our funds to the £100,000 mark if we fail in achieving our target during the London appeal; and to provide further general funds for the Capricorn Africa Society (funds will be needed for the building of our permanent Convention Centre at Mbeya and possible other projects).

3. In the meantime I hope you will realise that literally tens of thousands of people of all races in Africa are pinning their hopes on the Capricorn Africa Society.

4. If you had been recently in Africa you would understand the grave threat of the Pan African Nationalist Congress at present being organised by Nkrumah, Nehru and others. The promoters are trying their utmost to catch Kidaha, Tschekdi and others of our Africans to join them. If we slowed down the preparations for our Convention, they would probably succeed in catching them. It is literally our Convention against theirs. More and more people realise here that our Convention is the last bid in Africa to get Asian and African leaders to join with the European settlers . . .

'We had first planned to hold the Convention at Mbeya in late 1953 but fund-raising did not go as easily as we had hoped and we were also under some pressure to delay it from the Colonial Office mainly because of the White Paper on Central African Federation and the India-Africa Council's Cairo Conference. We eventually set a date for early 1954.'

Between October 1953 and February 1954 Stirling threw himself vigorously into the tasks of fund-raising and setting up administrative centres in the six territories. These efforts took their toll on his health and twice he was ordered to bed for a complete rest. The pressures were very grave. In many African countries there was great dissension; Egypt, Tunisia, Morocco, Uganda, Kenya, Nyasaland, Nigeria, the Gold Coast and South Africa were all intermittent scenes of unrest and the Cairo Conference threatened to gather all the continent's black racialist elements together under one banner.

In early 1954 on the immediate 'home front' the security forces in Kenya were only just beginning to break up the Mau Mau rebels, even though Kenyatta, Kubai and Kaggia had been jailed the year before. CAS took a full page of newspaper space on 28 February to publish articles by prominent members of the Society; they included the Earl of Portsmouth (President of the Kenya Electors' Union), Colonel C.M. Newman CBE, VD,

ED (Alderman of the City of Bulawayo), Dr V.S. Patel (leading member of Kenya's Hindu community), Sir Eboo Pirbhai
(leading member of HH the Aga Khan's Ismaili community
in East Africa), A.C. Soffe (a founder of the Joint Council
of Southern Rhodesia), Aron Jacha (President of Southern
Rhodesia African Farmers' Union), G.T. Thorneycroft (leader
of the coloured community in Southern Rhodesia), T.W. Tyrell
(President of the Tanganyika European Council) and Chief
Kidaha Makwaia (member of the Royal Commission then
sitting in East Africa and member of the Tanganyika Legislative
Assembly).

Within the layout of these articles Stirling inserted a notice:


## Not Born of Fear

The Society originally planned to hold its Convention as long
ago as March 1951, but, at the request of the Colonial Office
and other territorial authorities, consented then and on two
subsequent occasions to postpone it.

This point is emphasised to show that our preparations for the
Convention predate the Mau Mau insurrection, the parity issue
in Tanganyika, the White Paper on Central African Federation,
and the recently disclosed plan of the India-Africa Council to
hold the Cairo Convention.

The impulse behind our Convention is not born of fear.


Despite the problems, the Kenya Branch of CAS was flour-
ishing under the chairmanship of Michael Wood. 'Michael was
in an ideal position for CAS purposes; he was a superb surgeon
and a pilot to boot. He started the first "Flying Doctor" service
in Kenya and was consequently on the move much of the
time. His wife, Sue, was chairman of a number of women's
organisations – no way better of getting to the husband than
through a totally converted better half. Michael had a great
sense of humour and I flew with him quite often. I remember
once when he was being a touch pomposo about his flying skills,
I asked him what he would do if the engine failed. He made

some comment about it being no trouble to a man of his skill – a bumpy landing, that was all – so I switched the engine off.

'He yelled, "You bloody fool, David, there's no way to restart the damn thing", then the plane went into all sorts of strange manoeuvres much to my discomfort. Michael was looking very serious and wrestling savagely with the controls and terra firma was getting decidedly close with precious few clearings in the scrub. I was getting seriously worried but trying very hard to keep it from showing. The crafty beggar knew I was scared and waited until the absolute last moment before he started the engine, at the touch of a button it seemed. That was one joke which really backfired on me.

'Sometime in 1954 Michael and I were returning from a dinner party close to Nairobi. We were in tuxedos, and decided to walk back and enjoy the night air. We were set upon by two blackamoors intent on murder – of that there was no mistake. We turned the tables and they were despatched to their maker in rather short order. To say the least this was a disturbing incident and I vividly remember calling in on a priest I knew and asking for confession. I told him of the two "murders" without fully describing the incident. I went back to the house we were staying in and I can remember asking my sister, Irene, to clean the "strawberry jam" stains off my shirt.

'I had breakfast with the priest the next day and told him the full story; that the pair of unfortunates had certainly been out to kill and that they were undoubtedly part of the Mau Mau remnants who were still causing trouble. He made no real comment on the matter which I suppose is not surprising – those were after all troubled times and spasmodic killings were still taking place as the Mau Mau movement went into its death throes.

The Interim London Committee, working closely with the London Consultative Council led by Dr Oldham, recruited amazing support. Dudley Clarke's Africa Room was copied in New York, a most important funding centre. Stirling played very heavily on old contacts, making them feel guilty for not dropping everything to support CAS. The committee meeting of 15 July comprised the following members: Colonel D. Stirling; V. Bartlett; Colonel F.T. Davies; J. Gerber; the Earl of Ranfurly; Sir John Slessor; H. Tevis; P.W. Allsebrook; Brigadier Dudley Clarke; Prince Y. Galitzine; I.D. Malcolmson; D. Rhydderch; Colonel W.J. Stirling; Major Kendall Ward; (Colonel Laurens Van der Post, Absent on business).

Stirling's technique of recruiting did not change much:

23 October 1953

Dear David,

. . . In reading through the minutes of the meeting held last Thursday . . . I notice . . . that it was accepted that I should be chairman of the Finance Appeal Sub-Committee. I was not actually aware of this and whilst, as you know, I am prepared to give what help I can, my spare time is very limited . . . I thought, therefore, that I should make it clear that I must rely on you to initiate any meetings, etc. that may be required . . .

I think it only fair to you that I should put these views in writing as you may consider it advisable to have somebody who is in the position to give much more time . . .

Yours ever,
Ian Malcolmson

27th October 1953

Dear Ian,

Thank you for your letter of 23rd October and the points you make are fully appreciated by me. We are very grateful to you for being prepared to act as chairman of the Finance Committee and will, of course, see that the call on your time will be reduced to the minimum . . .

Yours ever,
David

By late 1954 CAS was in some financial trouble. The team

was making great efforts and many individuals had dipped into their private purses. Stirling was then taking no salary from any of his business concerns and relying purely on a small allowance from his family. Travel was expensive, and vital to reach the Americans and Europeans. A meeting of the London Committee on 22 December 1954 assessed the debts in Africa alone as reaching around £3200 by early the next year. They accepted that this figure was calculated only on what information Stirling passed to them. His cash forecasts rarely took account of existing debts.

The London Committee decided that the only course would be to put the financial arrangements in Africa also under their control. The unanimous decision resulted in the following cable to Stirling:

> One. As result of talks between Jack Slessor and London Committee following conversation with Prain certain decisions unanimously taken with which I am in full agreement as consider absolutely essential to further progress. Two. Overdraft position is NOT as you stated in your letter to Hoey of 12 December it seems certain that neither short-term money nor essential long-term finance will be forthcoming unless certain conditions fulfilled. These will be explained by Gerber to Michael Wood and Johnson when he visits Nairobi 16 January. Please meet him there. Three. Meantime if you cannot do without money from London it can only come out of the £2000 I have promised so hope you will avoid any demands on London especially as I have also had to pay £800 for Capricorn London debts. You must realise that future of Capricorn is at stake and must depend first on putting it on sound financial basis. You will realise that my contribution was based on your raising the balance of £8000 and from my point of view position very serious unless you can agree to committee's proposals via McIndoe. Bill Stirling.

The financial affairs of CAS were indeed put under the control of the London Committee but no committee would ever have been capable of controlling Stirling. He was a man in a desperate hurry, and such men do not always stop to count the cost. He left a trail of bills to be collected by CAS for travel and the like; but he first emptied his own 'sporran' and ran up personal overdrafts and credit lines until they were exhausted.

In 1955, Longmans, Green and Co Ltd published simultaneously in London, Cape Town, Melbourne, New York, Toronto, Madras and Dacca, the book *New Hope in Africa* by Dr John Oldham. In this book, specially commissioned by CAS, Oldham expressed in very clear terms the history, meaning and aspirations of the Society. The author was an important member of CAS and an acknowledged expert on African affairs. He emphasised the vital work done by many members of CAS, white and African alike, in the attraction of finance and the education of a wide readership.

Target dates for the Mbeya Convention came and went. Without funds to subsidise travel and accommodation, to build the centre (no matter how simply), to hire transport and purchase provisions, there could be no Convention. It was to be a further year and a half before a Convention was held at which the Capricorn Contract was formally endorsed and signed by 140 representatives of the Society's branches. From then on CAS was to campaign to have the document adopted as the basis for a common citizenship in Capricorn Africa.

The pistol reputed to have killed Adolf Hitler is handed over to the SAS Association by some of the 'Originals'. Left to right: Pat Riley, Chris Hackney, Dare Newell, Ernie Bond. (*c.* 1976). (*Courtesy of Ernie Bond*)

Stirling and Brummie Stokes discuss the next assault on Everest (1984). Lord Hunt looks on. (*Permission of Michael Joseph Ltd*)

Stirling unveils the plaque to open Stirling Lines on 30 June 1984. (*Family collection*)

'The Dirty Dozen' (well, almost). Standing left to right: Jimmy Brough, Jim Almonds, Dave Kershaw, David Stirling, Pat Riley, Ernie Bond. Seated left to right: Bob Bennett, Jock Byrne, 'Whacker' Evans, 'Tubby' Trenfield. Front: Johnny Cooper. (*Author's collection*)

David Stirling and Georges Bergé at
Sennecy-le-Grand (1989). (*Terry
Fincher, Photographers International*)

Standing for the Dedication at Sennecy-le-Grand (1989). Left to right: Mike Calvert,
Fraser McLuskey, John Slim, Georges Bergé, David Stirling. (*Terry Fincher,
Photographers International*)

To Col. David Stirling – With appreciation, best
wishes & regards.
Ronald Reagan

With Ronald Reagan (1987). (*Family collection*)

Stirling explains desert warfare to the Omanis; on the right is Johnny Watts. (*Family collection*)

Stirling relaxes in Cheyne Court (1989). (*Family collection*)

At a lunch celebrating Stirling's knighthood. Left to right: Mrs J. Phipps, Richard Lea, Nell Bennett, David Stirling, Janet Hoe, David Sutherland. (*Author's collection*)

The Commando knife **presented** to Stirling by the Amicale des Anciens Parachutistes, after his knighthood in 1990. (*Author's collection*)

Stirling flanked by George Caitucoli (right) and Philippe Reinhart (left) after the presentation of the Commando knife, with M. Benoit and Rodier and the author.

Some of Stirling's doodles.
(*Family collection*)

Morar Lodge. (*Author's collection*)

St Cumin's Church, Morar, where Stirling's funeral was held. (*Author's collection*)

The view from Stirling's final resting place on the shores of Loch Morar. (*Author's collection*)

---

# 17

# THE WIND OF CHANGE

By the end of 1956 the Capricorn Africa Society was as streamlined and as functional as it could be. The organisation then had offices in Nairobi, Salisbury, Luanshya, Kiliman-jaro, Dar-es-Salaam, Ontario and London, and the following officers:

President: Colonel David Stirling DSO, OBE
Vice-Presidents: T.J. Hlazo; The Hon. A.B. Patel MLC. Sir Frank Wilson CMG, DSO
Chairman of Consultative Committee: Dr J.H. Oldham CBE
Treasurer: The Earl of March ACA
*London Branch*
Chairman of Committee: Marshal of the Royal Air Force Sir John Slessor GCB, DSO, MC
Chairman of Working Party: H. Crookenden
Executive Officer: J.T.S. Lewis
Assistant Executive Officer: Mrs J. Scott

The CAS concept was now under challenge from African nationalism. Nkrumah's success in the Gold Coast was held up as the state of the possible. The proposal for qualified franchise was being questioned vigorously despite there being no proven working models of multi-racial countries with a universal franchise. There was no let up in enthusiasm by the now widespread teams of CAS though the effort was slightly realigned. The Capricorn Declarations became the basis for 'common citizenship' and resulted in the evolution of the College of Rhodesian Citizenship Association which was eventually to produce a college proper, and this pattern was followed in Nairobi.

The colleges were aimed at the English-speaking middle strata of African society – clerics, engineers and the like, and the residential courses were designed to demonstrate how society works. The common citizenship theory and the concept of nationhood were central, but the scope was wide: the constitution; law procedure and enforcement; functions of local government; national governments and political organisations; social sciences; national history and literature; world history; national economy and geography and contemporary affairs. The concept sprang from CAS, which designed and built on the Kenyan facility.

The fact that CAS was losing impact did not stop Stirling and his teams, but Harold Macmillan's African tour in early 1960 put the writing on the wall for the future of the Society in its original conception. Aware of the likely attitude of Prime Minister Macmillan, Stirling managed to get a meeting with him prior to the tour.

'I saw him with Alec Douglas-Home and Ian McLeod and we tried very hard indeed to change his views and get him to recognise Capricorn for what it was. Alec was right behind us and spoke very eloquently, based on personal experience of the Colonies. We must have had some two or three hours of his time but it got us nowhere. The speech he made in London was only slightly changed when he gave it in Africa.'

On 3 February 1960 Harold Macmillan made his famous speech to both Houses of Parliament in Cape Town, South Africa. To the Capricorn Africa Society, the damage was done when Macmillan expounded his feelings on the rise of African nationalism:

Fifteen years ago this movement spread through Asia. Many countries there of different races and civilisations pressed their claim to an independent national life. Today the same thing is happening in Africa, and the most striking of all the impressions I have formed since I left London a month ago is of the strength of this African national consciousness. In different places it takes different forms, but it is happening everywhere. The wind of change is blowing through this continent, and whether we like it or not this growth of national consciousness is a political fact. We must accept it as fact and our national policies must take account of it . . .

The letter to members sent later that year from the office of the Kenya President (Michael Wood) showed that despite disappointments, Capricorn was to live on in more than just spirit.

Dear Member,

The year 1960 was generally expected to be an important year for the Capricorn territories in Africa – it certainly lived up to its expectations.

Central Africa had its first emergency amid rising pressure for the break-up of the Federation. The Monckton Report was published. In East Africa, Tanganyika went peacefully into responsible government, while Kenya suffered an economic decline and increased tension as the first common roll elections approached. Uganda's divisions increased in ferocity and bitterness. Everywhere there has been a strengthening and growing of African racialism. Superimposed on the internal tensions and changes of East and Central Africa has been the chaotic course of the Congo transmitting its tragedy and bitterness to all parts of Africa. Added to this, 1960 saw the Sharpeville incident, and the subsequent difficulties in South Africa, and closed with a revolution in Ethiopia.

During such a year of conflict it has been a difficult task for Capricorn to keep its balanced middle-of-the-road course. Divisions have been reflected even in the fabric of the Society itself. Nonetheless we have learnt by them, and from our difficulties has come a reassessment of our position . . .

In mapping our new course there are several difficulties

under which Capricorn operates which should be taken into consideration:

(a) the difficulty of raising money for the propagation of an idea.

(b) the lack of a political front which would give the Capricorn idea an impact on the thinking of a country.

(c) the lack of a project (following the independence of the citizenship colleges) through which members could express Capricorn.

(d) the change of emphasis in racialism in Africa from European to African origins, the growth of intimidation, and the difficulty in Capricorn leadership (mainly white) opposing African racialism without appearing to be racialist itself. Hence a tendency to silence.

We now intend to tailor-make our plan to the needs of Africa and the difficulties encountered.

First of all I believe we should train our branches and organise them to operate almost without funds. In order to achieve this I suggest that we organise ourselves as a network held together by a new and lively communication.

The communication between us as individuals and branches will be carried on through a newsletter which . . . will require the active participation of members and branches. It will be published through . . . the London office and distributed to all members in the UK and Africa. It will thus depend to a great extent on the definite production of news by members and branches . . . We shall also hope to use the newsletter as a forum of opinion and a means of discussion . . .

The London office will be doing a great service . . . by providing this link which could grow into a real strength for the movement in Africa. Branches in Africa should therefore make a contribution . . . by paying for their copies either individually or in bulk. The newsletter is . . . the most important single thing which we propose to initiate forthwith.

We need also to provide a mechanism for handling numerous new projects . . . I suggest . . . the appointment of one person by the local executive to handle a particular project . . .

There are already two projects on the horizon – an educational survey in East and Central Africa . . . and the

Commonwealth project, in which the Capricorn network could play a vital part. In each case the branch chairman will ask a member . . . to handle the project . . . Branches themselves will have a chairman and small executive . . . but the bulk of the work will now be done not so much by committees as individual members. Funds will thus not be absorbed in running expenses; and the keeping up of our lines of communication, i.e. the compilation and circulation of the newsletter, will receive priority.

. . . Projects under way already, such as the mobile educational unit in Melsetter, Zebra Club, Nairobi and Zebra House, London will continue to receive every support we can offer.

There is one piece of news which will hearten you. Peter Marrian who stood so courageously on a Capricorn ticket in 1956 has been elected by an overwhelming vote in the common roll elections in Kenya. My wife, Susan, standing as a National member for the Kenya Legislative Council, has received the unanimous support of KANU and KADU, the two leading African parties. These are victories shared by all Capricorn members and it shows that, despite disappointments, the battle carried on by you all has not been entirely in vain. Indeed, as they join the legislature here they will find many members already . . . share the Capricorn idea. Perhaps . . . the Capricorn idea is no longer just the property of Capricorn, but is . . . held by a large and undefined company of people in Africa. This is the measure of our success, and it may be that . . . the full acceptance of the Capricorn idea will come through them as well as ourselves.

Storm clouds are already gathering in the opening stages of 1961. The process of transition in . . . every territory of Capricorn Africa could still end in failure and chaos, or success and national growth largely on a Capricorn pattern. No one who is aware of the scene in Africa is any longer under the delusion that the cold war can be kept out of Africa. It is here, and it is here to stay. The communists are stepping up their efforts to win the continent. Chaos has always suited their book (a perfect example of this is the Congo), and we must expect every method of subversion and destruction to be used in the coming struggle. Capricorn and those who feel with us must prepare to fight the battle by demonstrating that we have a better idea.

The situation everywhere remains drastically in the balance.

From now on every individual member of Capricorn counts in
the effort we must make in every sphere of life to develop
communities in East and Central Africa in which all inhabitants
shall be happy and proud to lose their racial and tribal identities
in a common citizenship and patriotism.

By late 1962 Michael Wood had taken over as Capricorn
Africa's President; Stirling had been forced to resign to make
some headway with personal business; he had little money
and considerable debts, since he had always spent whatever
he had in the cause of CAS. He was very tired and his health
had suffered. Those close to him saw little diminution in his
efforts on Capricorn's behalf despite his resignation – he was
still the person to whom everyone turned for inspiration and
a renewal of faith. The Society newsletter of September 1962
gives a recap of the Society's achievements to that date:

It is 14 years since the Capricorn Africa Society was started, by
a group of people in Africa led by David Stirling. They were
African, European, South African and Indian by descent but
all with homes and futures in British East and Central Africa.
Their objectives for each territory were:

1.   A community, knit together by a common patriotism, in
which there should be no racial discrimination, and in which
the individual's standing and his share in the government of
the country should be determined by his personal qualities and
not by the colour of his skin.

2.   The vigorous development of the country's resources for
the benefit of all its people.

3.   The maintenance and advancement of moral, cultural and
material standards and the extension of education to the limit
that the country can afford.
    In 1954 the Society published their *Handbook*. In 1955 J.H.
Oldham devoted his book *New Hope in Africa* to the ideas of
the Society. In 1956 came the celebrated Convention at Salima
on Lake Nyasa where delegates . . . endorsed the Society's
'Contract', subsequently published . . .
    In those and subsequent years, the Society had a considerable

effect on the social and political outlook of forward-looking people in Africa. Their ideas have been increasingly reflected in the utterances and actions of political and other leaders.

On a more material plane the Society's important achievements have been . . . the establishment of adult citizenship colleges at Nairobi and Salisbury; two hostels in London for students from Africa of all colours (Zebra House, and Impala House which comprises flats for married students with their families); the work done among women by the mobile unit run by the Melsetter branch; the Zebra Club in Nairobi, a meeting place for people of all races.

Against these successes must be set a decline, during the last two or three years, in African participation in the work of the Society. This has been due to the worsening of the political weather, resulting in a feeling among educated Africans that if they wanted to make an effective contribution to the political development of their country they could not afford to be associated with an organisation in the leadership of which there was an important 'white element'. This falling-off of African support has led inevitably to a decline in European and Indian membership and the present state of the Society may be summarised as follows:

In the Federation activity is confined to Southern Rhodesia, and virtually to the Salisbury and Melsetter Branches. In Kenya the Zebra Club is supported by a few members. The presidency may be described as in suspense, Michael Wood having recently resigned, through pressure of his work as a surgeon, and no successor being plainly visible. The Society continues to have a number of correspondents and supporters in Africa and overseas, but for the spectator of the African scene the political drama inevitably fills the stage.

The UK branch is now the most numerous and active. The London office provides as always a meeting place for people ... interested in the political, social and economic development of Africa. Most of the work of launching the hostels . . . was done in Cheval Place. So are the recruiting and admin for the Capricorn Africa Trustees' scheme for sending teachers of English to the Congo. The Trust and London office are now assisting one of the members with a home for children in Suffolk . . .

. . . Members . . . may see the successful, philanthropic activities sponsored by the Trust and organised from Cheval

Place as a counterpoise to the decline in the activity of the
Society's membership in Africa. It is hoped that they will
continue their support and interest and will let the Executive
Office have any suggestion that occurs to them for extending
the good work.

Some would say Capricorn was years too early – some years
too late – and that is why it failed. This will remain conjecture
unless a future historian answers the conundrum. Was Stirling
too early? Was he too late? Did Capricorn in fact fail? Was it
the impossible dream of the romantic few? Stirling simply came
across a problem which he could not ignore. He could not have
begun ten years earlier. He could perhaps have waited longer,
but it was not in his nature to wait when he could clearly see a
solution, and in 1949 there was little to indicate that patience
was required – indeed quite the opposite.

Richard Hughes, a well-known architect, was living in Kenya
during the early stages of Capricorn and worked closely with
Stirling as a Capricorn member and on later ventures. He
played a key part in the long preparations for the Salima
Convention. He is a very logical man, and unstinting in his
praise of Stirling's enthusiasm, dedication and innovativeness.
He shrewdly observed:

'It is not particularly innovative to say, "Here is a problem
and here, perhaps, is a solution." What was innovative was
to recognise that there was a problem at all. I believe that
racialism in Africa at that time was largely based on ignorance;
if the whites were beastly to the black Africans, and I don't
mean in the sense of beatings or anything like that but more
in the sense of being offhand with them, this was to a degree
based on the fact that they knew next to nothing of how they
lived and the deprivations they may have been suffering.

'In the large towns and cities the whites never went near
where the black Africans lived. They didn't have to; their daily
journeys were probably from the house to the office then to the
club for drinks or tennis and back to the house. The blacks were
housed often miles from the white areas and there was neither

business nor social need to travel through their quarters. The only people then who knew anything about how the Africans lived would have been the priests. Their churches had to be in the areas where they did their proselytizing.

'You see, to the whites in Africa there was no problem. When Anne and I married in Nairobi cathedral in 1951 I don't suppose either of us doubted that our own children would be married in Africa – and our grandchildren for all we knew. You don't think about the sort of problems David considered if they are not under your feet.'

Stirling had no experience of Africa when he arrived there in 1946 and the circles in which he first moved were based on prior social and military contacts and would have fitted Hughes's description neatly. Religion meant a lot to him and it is possible that he became aware of African living conditions through contact with the church, and that this pricked at his conscience. It is more probable though that his awareness was slowly awakened over his initial year of investigatory business travels and occasional meetings with people who were beginning to realise that the future could hold problems.

Stirling had first become interested in the continent for purely business reasons. His reading in Colditz had given him the urge to look at this vast country which seemed to offer all that he could want. It would be quite in character for him to deduce that the business potential, already great,could be much greater still if all the country's resources, which included the people, could be harnessed. Man only works with willingness if he is fairly treated and given opportunity for betterment, a voice in his own future and peace of mind.

Just as he ambitiously viewed not merely a small part of the open flank during the war in North Africa, but the whole of it on the grand scale, Stirling could not be expected to create a small niche in a small country if he could see his way to carving a large niche on a continent. This is not to denigrate his Capricorn effort; once his interest had been captured he threw himself into the campaign wholeheartedly and very much to his own financial detriment.

Richard Hughes commented, 'I often wondered where he did get his cash. It couldn't have been coming from Capricorn because we were often so hard up we couldn't afford duplicating paper. He spent absolutely all his time on CAS and he travelled very widely – the cost of that and communications must have been very heavy.'

In fact the whole Stirling family were immensely supportive. Keir and Cawder subsidised much of his travel costs and his mother made him an allowance, and his own small earnings from business ideas left him with almost sufficient to his needs. In Britain, Mrs Stirling readily spread the concept of Capricorn and recruited many a good disciple, and his sister Irene worked immensely hard both in Britain and in Africa where she spent as much time as she could. Keir and Cawder never recalled their debts.

Though Stirling did not view CAS as a failure, he firmly believed it could have been more of a success had he worked harder in some areas. Lord Richmond (formerly the Earl of March and the CAS treasurer), Jeanine Bartosik and Richard Hughes are steadfast in his defence. Nobody, they say, could have worked harder than David Stirling. One of his greatest strengths was his ability, within minutes, to revive flagging spirits and rejuvenate motivation. His charm and sense of fun were legendary and when it became known that DS was coming to town there was great competition to be first to invite him to dinner.

In Jeanine Bartosik's words, 'David was an inspiration; he seemed tireless and never lost faith in Capricorn. He could talk you into doing anything without you actually realising what he was up to. He worked so incredibly hard himself but was always so very good-humoured. There was so little room in Cheval Place that he would often have to sit on the top of the stairs with the telephone which was not easy at his height. He said that nobody could tell from the telephone from what impressive offices one may be speaking so it didn't matter. Life was great fun when David was around London.'

Where did Stirling think he was lacking? 'I believe I could have done more with the Colonial Office in London, stirred the pot with a little more determination; but we did have local Colonial Office support and I thought that might be sufficient. I was wrong. They thought that to have a front-line recruit with Capricorn would somehow contaminate their own pure approach. It was balls, of course, but the attitude seemed to be, "who the hell is Stirling that he thinks he can shift borders". But I really had stretched the Europeans in Africa to the limit and I tried to nail down the Colonial Office coffin lid by threatening a huge international publicity campaign. All it did was frighten them, and cause them to intervene and persuade the nervous to pull out of Capricorn on the promise that they were going to go for a much closer liaison themselves anyway.

'I held to the deadline and we achieved enormous attention when the Declarations were published. It helped a lot but it was only momentary against the eventual time scale. I think I could have done more in South Africa. I argued the case but they wouldn't shift. I remember on one occasion in the Republic, it must have been the late forties or early fifties, there was a visit by the King and Queen, and Ernest Oppenheimer and I were invited to dine at a function they attended and the Capricorn Africa Society was freely discussed. In retrospect I believe I should have made the case stronger at the London end where they were more vulnerable and perhaps gone on to the attack at some time.

'One of man's greatest assets is the capacity for true friendship and in that we succeeded on the grand scale. I have had dealings with many of Africa's modern leaders and I haven't met one who would argue enthusiastically against what we were striving for. "Mzee" Kenyatta was very staunch in his support you know. Kenneth Kaunda, in his younger and stronger days, paid a lot of attention to Capricorn. I remember taking him to

White's when he was a young man. It was very amusing, KK's hair always stood on end very impressively and he was not the sort of chap expected in the club. There were a few gasps and snorts from the pomposo as I introduced him – it was a great tease. I was seriously trying to get to him but he was thoroughly nationalist even then though his arguments didn't hold water, then or later. I very much liked old "Scram from Africa" Mboya. He was on side really – he was a trustee with me on the Kenya Students' Scholarship Fund for many years.

'It was easy to understand those fellows' frustrations – things just didn't move fast enough. I don't think any more effort could have been put in that direction though. We had several great women and men serving the cause at one time or another – many still serve. Michael and Susan [Wood], Leopold Takawera, Jeanine and Laurens, and many, many others. They were all an inspiration but Laurens in particular had that quality of the spirit. After I had been grappling for nearly four years with Africa's supreme problem – how to draw up a contract between all the races, all the tribes, all the religions inhabiting the six territories – Laurens helped put it all into a context with which we could all identify emotionally.

'John Oldham, who was such an eminent theologist, was unstinting in his support. When he was preparing to write *New Hope in Africa* he interviewed over a period of about a year, and always with a member of the Society present, the leaders of all the main religions on a reconciliation in Africa. We all owe him a great debt for his lucid book.

'It would have been late 1957 when Simon took over the post of Governor-General of the Federation of Rhodesia and Nyasaland. It was a difficult for him in the beginning, but he is a very robust chap and he was a great help to us. Governor-General was not a political task in the true sense as administration was still based on the edict of Westminister; this helped, as no political overtones could be put on dinners or luncheons he hosted. It was very nice to have someone 'en famille' with whom one could discuss problems and progress.*

'Once the African members started to leave Capricorn we were losing effect. It was very sad. But many dear and lasting friends were made in Capricorn and they are treasured years. The same long-range thinking was behind the Gemsbok Corporation – a possible revitalisation of the Qattara Depression scheme – the futility of short-term loan monies and "drip-feed" financing; it would have been so much better if it could have been backed up with a long-range vision of Africa in strategic investment terms.'

To write off the Capricorn Africa Society would be folly. It lives on in much more than spirit. What did it achieve? It opened up the African scene in stark reality to an international audience and created an atmosphere in which things which had never been openly discussed were brought to the political table. How much can be seen of the Capricorn work in current activities in South Africa? Strong relationships were forged, and those friends and allies across all races still talk; and whilst people can still debate without fear the prospects of violence must lessen. Such personal alliances have smoothed the path to independence in more than one case.

In Kenya and Zimbabwe the colleges still function though the prospectuses have changed. In tandem with this educational project, though it came some years later, is the television network set up largely on David Stirling's initiative. Although separate from CAS, it was Capricorn's philosophy which caused Stirling to analyse the benefits of television as effective mass communication through educational programmes, and to a point the Capricorn network eased the path for him.

The Kenya Students' Scholarship Fund still makes grants to

---

* Simon Ramsay married Stirling's sister Margaret in 1940, and assumed the title of 16th Earl of Dalhousie in 1950. He held office in the Federation for six years. The 16th Earl is in fact the third in his family line to be appointed Governor-General; the 3rd Earl was appointed to Canada in 1819 and the 10th Earl was appointed to India in 1847; both held their offices for nine years.

students who may otherwise have to forfeit the chance of a western education. The Zebra Trust, begun in the early 1960s, is still receiving devoted attention from Jeanine Bartosik and Peter Comyns (who nurtured it from the beginning) and has gone from strength to strength. It now has four hostels in London and one in Bristol, all on an international basis rather than solely Africa. Richard Hughes still acts as a trustee of the Zebra Trust which with his wife, Ann, he helped to set up and which provides low-cost accommodation for post-graduate Commonwealth students.

The Zebra Houses are more than just a place to live in a strange country. Registered as a charity, the trust is self-funding and makes no profit. The atmosphere encourages frank discussion and multi-racial harmony through mutual understanding, in the manner of the original Capricorn philosophy. The behaviour of the host country to these students is the impression which they will take back to their own countries and will affect their attitudes when they become politicians or members of the professions. The legacy of the Capricorn Africa Society, therefore, after a little more than four decades, lives on. Perhaps, as Michael Wood said, the Capricorn idea ceased to be the property of Capricorn and came to be accepted by a large part of the nations of Africa.

# 18

# BALLY SHOE AND
# BALLY-HOO

The 1960s were the busiest years of Stirling's life. Until 1962 he was still greatly occupied with CAS (though he had handed over the presidency and was based in London and the Middle East for much of the time), but not to the exclusion of other world events and business opportunities. His performance would have astounded the most competent juggler as he kept more and more balls in the air.

In early 1961 Stirling became depressed at what he saw as a lack of impact on the African scene. He could not convince the major investment houses to take his own long-range strategic vision of Africa as the 'continent in reserve', to be developed slowly, not rushed by greedy Western capitalism looking for fast profit. That Western governments and financial manipulators could not see beyond the day-to-day politics of a nation in a state of innocence, passing through acceptable turmoil as it settled to its future, frustrated him. Capricorn had brought him international attention, but his efforts had branded him, in many quarters, as a political agitator. Not that Stirling objected to the term agitator – he was often to introduce himself as such – but he strongly objected to the misunderstanding of motive behind the description. Of course, had CAS succeeded, Stirling would have been in a strong position to take commercial advantage with his Gemsbok and Capricorn Development Corporations, but that was never his motive.

Stirling's preoccupation with Africa led him into his next major venture. Politics, in his view, was largely a matter of three elements; intelligence or information, communication, and timely distribution to correctly predetermined targets. Whatever the success of CAS, and in my view that was much greater than Stirling gives it credit for, it was, apart from the enthusiasm and dedication of its members, due to reasoned argument and the dissemination of information and ideas. This was not swiftly accomplished; communications were poor in Africa at that time, but the local committees served as collection and distribution centres. Despite outstanding effort, they were still only able to attract to the local-dwelling and educated African. The heart of the populace remained in ignorance much of the time. How could CAS reach into the heartland of the minor townships and change the pulse rate?

Stirling's fertile mind was captivated by the power of television to achieve swift communication direct to the 'masses'. If townships, even on an area basis, could be provided with a television which carried firstly an educative series of programmes and then easy-to-understand discussion on real-time events, surely this would be worthwhile. He had been examining the potential of this medium since the later part of 1959 and had learned four things. Such an enterprise required significant cash investment; it was a complex business; many established television companies were beginning to take an interest in the third world, and lastly, he was technically ignorant. This last did not deter Stirling. He did not fear competition and the technicalities could surely be learned or the expertise hired. If there was anything of merit to his embryonic idea then investment capital should not be difficult to obtain.

Stirling's approach was, typically, on the grand scale. His experience in Africa had shown him the potential for television and his blossoming interest in education provided the spur; but why limit it to Africa? He decided to make Central and East

Africa his first thrust, but at the same time to look wider, with a view to encompassing the Middle East and India, where he saw a need similar to the Africans'. In these countries too, major political events were taking place in administrative and business capitals, but the rural populace often remained in ignorance of the events and of the Western influences on those events.

In particular he had been observing the unfolding drama in the Middle East: 'I believe the British government acted very stupidly with regard to Nasser. As early as 1954 I think Eden had decided that he [Nasser] had to be removed from power. I never could subscribe to the belief that he was responsible for all the anti-Western feeling throughout the Middle East. The truth was that he was getting more and more active in his support of the anti-colonialists in Central and East Africa at a sensitive time. It was unforgivable not to support the Aswan Dam project financially – look what a colossal nonsense resulted from that.'

Stirling was referring, of course, to the decision taken by the USA and Britain not to meet the conditions of a World Bank loan to Egypt which stipulated that they should jointly fund the hard currency costs. They argued that the economy of Egypt was too unstable to take such a financial risk. This led to Nasser's far-reaching decision to nationalise the Suez Canal Company and place management in the hands of an Egyptian Canal Authority. Seeing no other option Eden agreed to the use of force and joined the French and Israelis in a joint invasion of Egypt which began on 31 October 1956 with a bombing operation, followed on 5 November with the capture of Port Said and a canal which had already been blocked with ships sunk by the Egyptians.

'It was a most peculiar style of thinking which caused Eden to decide that world opinion would be with the alliance and the invasion of Egypt. The Commonwealth was already beginning to break up, there was great antagonism from the USA and Russia was openly stating that she would step into the breach and finance the Aswan Dam. Of course the bloody Egyptians could manage the Canal perfectly well; that was obvious to anyone who had spent time in the country. And it was also perfectly obvious that Nasser's popularity would increase rather than fade as Eden seemed to think. Not only did Nasser score a very significant moral victory despite what can loosely be called a military defeat, but Britain and France lost millions in seized assets and indirect income from the thousands of expatriates who were thrown out of Egypt.

'I was sure then and I am sure now that sensible negotiation would have saved the day (and an awful lot of brasso) and put the West in a prime position to extend southwards into Africa – I even offered, through Alec Douglas-Home, to take a part in negotiations myself. By forcing Nasser to take action over the Canal, Britain was largely responsible for his escalation in power afterwards. Without the support of the young Arabs whose imagination had been thoroughly massaged by his stand against the West there is a good chance that he would not have formed his Republican Constitution and been reaffirmed as President. King Hussein swung towards Nasser, Lebanon sat on the fence and King Saud agreed to assist Jordan financially whilst confirming a military alliance with Syria and Egypt. The only remaining friend we had in the Middle East immediately after the Suez Crisis was Iraq and that wasn't going to last long. Nasser was never the man to unify the Middle East; he was a temporary focal point and he allowed himself to be carried away on a tide of public feeling which bore no relationship to the realities of rule; he could not possibly continue to be an international voice of any significance. Because the West was unable properly to analyse him and the situation he was able to sustain himself on their cock-ups; the Middle East splits which closely followed his death show how shallow any apparent unification had been. If anyone with half an eye for strategy and half an insight into the workings of Nasser's mind had stopped to look at the map they would have seen that the blighter could well have been casting his eyes on the oilfields of Saudi Arabia even at that stage.'

Stirling was not always so scathing about Gamel Abdul Nasser. He admired the man's vision and faith in the Aswan Dam project which was set to be the foundation of a new economy in Egypt. This harnessing of the River Nile was predicted to improve agriculture by thirty-five percent, and the vast water storage facility would dramatically reduce both drought and the dangers of flooding along the Nile banks. Stirling probably felt some affinity with the man whose vision was so close to his own with regard to the flooding of the Qattara Depression.

If Stirling's attention to and appreciation of Middle Eastern and African politics seems to indicate that his interest in television was spurred by a desire to influence political events, then this is incorrect. Of course he perceived that television could be a major propaganda medium in the third world but his primary motivation was to foster and feed a community sense in the 'outback'. Only from a solid community spirit could he see springing a communal desire for learning. Paradoxically, only from learning would emerge the community spirit.

'The critical factor was not in actually running the stations but in influencing what was put over the air. To attract people into a learning process one first had to attract them to the screen, and that meant entertainment; at that time all eyes were turned to the USA as a mass producer of popular programmes. On the educational side, and especially for children, I wanted a strong British involvement as I reckoned that this was where the more applicable programmes were going to be made. The BBC had been quick to spot the educational powers of TV and were already embarking on school series – but these were made for an English-speaking audience and needed dubbing; in any case they were lacking in sheer entertainment.

'It was important to me that I didn't start anything which would be easily corrupted by politicians. Obviously government would have to have its say but that should be as limited as possible, so the enterprise would need to be financially self-supporting. I felt it should be possible to set up stations

under the aegis of government and then sell advertising time
and the programmes of other big television companies.'

In reflecting on the educational use of television in the early
sixties one must consider the predominant criticisms which
faced Stirling during his early research. The argument about
the hypnotic effect of audio-visual teaching methods was a
case in point. The reasoning was that the student became so
involved in screen action that he actually became part of it,
leaving reality behind. Stirling would have answered that an
audio-visual medium was able to convey a much wider range
of experiences. The key was that it be treated as just another
medium, only with a more exciting capacity to stimulate the
senses used in learning and not dependent upon full literacy.

It was also suggested that because television could only allow
the teacher one-way communication, that teacher could not
cater for individual student requirements. This weakness is
surely a minor one when one remembers that one superior
teacher using simple instructional techniques could reach
audiences of thousands where before one teacher could only
reach the few who were able to attend the rural schoolroom.

Stirling was firmly of the view that this medium was unique
in that it could vastly extend both the influence of the best
teachers and the students' horizons of experience. Science
students in under-equipped schools could witness experiments,
first-class working models and demonstrations of techniques.
Arts students could experience the classics delivered by fine
actors and readers, have moments from history brought alive,
and relive news broadcasts and political debate. Television,
rather than inhibiting the intellect, Stirling proclaimed, should
be seen as a direct line to it. It offered direct experience and
participation without demanding literacy.

One of Stirling's early and immensely valuable acquisitions
was Colin Campbell who was to become a close friend and
remain involved with Stirling and television for many years. He
was on the point of retirement from the army in Africa when
Stirling made his approach. He recalls the moment well.

'Have you ever thought of getting into television, Colin?' asked Stirling.

'I've never thought about it. I don't know the first thing about it.'

'Neither do I really but it seems to be a good thing to be in. Why not join me and give it a go?'

As Campbell said later: 'I had just left the army after having had a great deal of fun and I wasn't looking forward to a boring life in business. David knew I needed a job and any reservations I may have entertained about business being boring were quickly dispelled. Life and business with David were never boring. By that time he had started Television International Enterprises Ltd (TIE) but he had no real budget.

'My only experience of television had been in the Sudan. In the infancy of TV in that country I had visited Omdurman and on the roof of the military barracks just across the river I'd been watching the local television company putting together a show with a local band. Those chaps were recently from the Thompson TV School (the BBC also had one) and they were going out live. I decided to take a look around the town.

'I walked through a park and was quite surprised to see a television set hanging from a tree in a small bandstand area. In front of it were four people fast asleep on a bench while the music played on and on. I walked a bit farther and suddenly I heard 'baroom, baroom, baroom, boom, boom' – the signature music for Hopalong Cassidy. I rushed back to the TV set. A black and white film was showing and instead of four dozing chaps there were now at least twenty wide-awake people all goggle-eyed and transfixed to the screen. Their own music bored them; they could see and hear it live in the streets anytime, but here was something different. This was free cinema! Such was the drawing power of American television.'

'Colin is a marvellous chap; he has energy and a sense of humour. I suppose it really was a case of the blind leading the blind but we made a lot of quite quick progress. The great rival was always Rediffusion but we managed to stay a jump ahead most of the time. That was largely a matter of studying where they were likely to go next and having a lot of mutual friends who should have kept better security. It was great fun though. We struck up an alliance with Scottish Television which proved most useful while we were learning how to put together technical proposals – we cheated dreadfully. If we spotted a technical-sounding name for a piece of equipment or a filming technique we put it into the proposals to make it sound as though we knew what we were talking about; I often had to hide behind the coat-tails of "my technician back in England" – of course he didn't exist.'

During the frantic early stages of TIE the company's income was derived from a series of small but faithful investors and the skilful application of sales franchises of mainly American produced programmes. The bigger companies were able, when they knew what Stirling was about, to undercut him drastically as they could afford to sell their products at prices which barely covered the cost of printing. He got around this firstly by demonstrating that he was there to stay and that his motives were more beneficial than his competitors'; secondly by laying false trails about his future targets, and thirdly by putting tremendous energy into making his assessments and proposals accurate.

'Those were the halycon [sic: one of Stirling's many deliberate and continual mispronunciations] days; we were always busy, always excited and, I suppose, always broke but life really was funny. We needed a London office and Jeanine [Scott] came to the rescue with her tiny house in Cheval Place. It was most amusing; we had one small room which Colin and I took turns to use. The other had to sit at the top of the stairs. Consequently we never, but never, allowed visitors. If anyone turned up at the door he or she was politely informed that whoever they had come to see was out for the day.'

Colin Campbell remembers those days with fondness. 'There were so many laughable moments when David was around. I don't know if you ever heard him speak French? It was by no means perfect. I remember one occasion when we had both just returned from different parts of Africa; apparently David had sat by a chap from the Belgian Congo on his flight back and started a conversation in French, their only common language. The fellow was head of the Congolese Boy Scout movement, so David offered to introduce him to Chips Maclean, then head of the British Scouts. For some reason he also asked him if he would like a kilt and said that he would fix that with Chips too.

'It was David's turn to sit at the top of the stairs when the Belgian rang and David was obviously taken by surprise as he replied something like: "Oui mon vieux, j'ai fait arranger un kilt pour vous avec mon grand ami, Chips . . ."

'It was hilarious to hear him struggling along obviously wondering where the hell he was going to get a kilt from at short notice and I burst out laughing. I took the mickey at every opportunity, but it wasn't so long before he got his revenge. I took a telephone call from my ex-boss who was the Governor of Kenya. David only heard my end of the conversation which went something like, "Oh. Thank you, sir . . . Very good of you, sir . . . Thank you very much, sir . . . So good of you to call, sir . . ."

'When I looked up after the call David was crying with laughter: "Haw, haw. Colin. Good of you to call, sir. Thank you very much, sir. Have a nice day, sir. Three bags full, sir. You were almost as good as me with the Frenchman." I was never allowed to forget it.

'We were talking about David misusing words. Many years later I went to see him in hospital after he had a major operation for an aortic aneurysm.* I had undergone major surgery some time before and David was determined to prove that his operation had been much more serious than mine. When I

* Campbell's recollection refers to April 1982. In February of that year Stirling was examined by the Queen's physician, Sir John Batten, who suspected an aortic aneurysm. This was confirmed and he was operated on in the King Edward VII Hospital for Officers in April 1982.

got to his bedside he pulled his dressing gown aside and said, "Take a look at that Colin, non-swanks, I had seventy eight stitches – much more than you."

"'Come off it, David", I said, "you're counting the holes not the stitches, you can't double up like that."

"'Hmph. Well, all right, there were only thirty-nine stitches, but you didn't have a cafeteria in your cock but I jolly well did.'"*

In the years during which TIE was very active Stirling was once again working practically non-stop. What he considered a rest period would have been an assault course to many other men, as it consisted of late nights of merriment in clubs during which he rarely lost an opportunity to expound on his theories and enterprises. This was not, as he would have put it, 'swanking', but he enjoyed persuasion and conversion and loved argument. He found it physically difficult to rest during the day; his brain refused to be dormant unless he was totally exhausted. The result was profound tiredness, physical and mental. This manifested itself in a number of ways and Stirling often mistook the effects of stress for physical illness. His manner of treating such 'illnesses' was to fast – something he could never explain satisfactorily; it could almost be compared with a religious act of purging. Quite naturally a tired body which is not getting sustenance will rebel and refuse to function but there may have been more to it than that. It is almost possible to place these 'attacks' at points in Stirling's life when he was at the centre of attention, something his natural shyness made him detest unless he was with close friends. It is possible that some sort of psychological defence mechanism took over when he was very tired, as though he could, by being unwell, escape from a situation in which he was ill-at-ease.

Stirling enjoyed nothing more than a good party amongst friends once he was there, but if he thought he was going to be the centre of attention getting him there was very difficult. He

* Stirling, of course, was abusing the word 'catheter'.

was capable of inventing the weakest excuses and persuading one that they were valid. His reluctance could be so strong on occasions that he would let people down and then be overcome by remorse.

The following story is similar to several about Stirling when his work had pushed him to the limits of endurance and he was faced with the need to meet strangers on business.

It was told by an American who was working for CBS (London) and knew Stirling well. Stirling had involved NBC in his efforts to obtain television franchises in Nigeria and two American NBC executives had been sent to Lagos to meet him. Stirling was staying with Antony Head, then High Commissioner of the Federation of Nigeria. He had suffered one or two sharp reminders from his body that he was not being fair to it in the form of fainting attacks. He had also picked up on the fact that Antony's wife, Dorothea, was worried about him which he thought was great fun. So he took to coming down for dinner, bending over the drinks tray and falling into a dead faint which may or may not have been real. At dinner Stirling would simply push his food around his plate.

The meeting with the Americans was scheduled to take place in a newly opened hotel in Lagos – a huge place with no pillars so the lobby area was vast and open. The NBC executives had simply been told that they were to meet a tall Scotsman. As they entered the lobby a tall, tanned man walked over to them, introduced himself as David Stirling and shook their hands. They were then amazed to see him spin like Nureyev, go into an ever-quickening pirouette until he crashed into the lobby wall and slump unconscious on to the carpet. This was the real thing, not an attempt at off-beat humour, and Stirling was ordered to bed for a few days' rest. As the Americans put it later, their introduction to the entrepreneur who was going to open up Nigeria to them was quite unforgettable; but then most first meetings with Stirling were that.

TIE moved from strength to strength and Stirling's days were full for the next four years. In a short time offices became affordable and he took premises in Sloane Street. Number 21 was entered through a door between two shop window displays of Bally Shoes and then upstairs to the offices which, after the 'camp-style' arrangement in Cheval Place, were luxurious. As one of his visitors put it so aptly, 'Bally Shoe downstairs and Bally Hoo upstairs.'

Life was not without fun. Lord Jellicoe remembered the occasion when Stirling told him that they were summoned to France in order that, '. . . our French gongs be updated or something'. Desperately short of time due to Stirling's casual treatment of the summons, they made it to Paris with no real idea of where they were going. By dint of questioning taxi drivers and the like they eventually found themselves at a military barracks where a medals parade did indeed appear to be taking place.

'David said, "Come on", and we dashed up behind the files on parade, tacked ourselves on to the end of the last rank and stood to attention. The General got closer, pinning medals on to chests on the way. He seemed somewhat surprised when he reached us and found that the tray which had held the awards was empty. He could only look at us and give a Gallic shrug: 'Messieurs, pour vous, je n'ai de rien.'

'We were of course at the wrong parade at the wrong time and in the wrong barracks. It was all sorted out eventually but it was typical of David's organisation.'

At the peak of TIE activities while Stirling was involved the company raised twelve independent stations and supplied them with a number of programmes. There were financial side benefits from the provision of equipment and the building of specialised premises to house the stations. Stirling was also the first to spot and experiment with the possibilities of solar-powered television, having noted the flexibility of this power source as a result of space technology spin-off. He tried the system in Jamaica, but it failed through lack of human attention to the servicing requirement of keeping the rainforest hill sites clear of vegetation.

The high spot of Stirling's personal endeavours on behalf of TIE has to be his success in Hong Kong. His proposal was masterly and took some two years to put together.

'I was very proud of it. Non-swanks, it was a very good piece of work. We had researched every particle of the proposal and ensured that we had every conceivable support at every conceivable level even if we didn't need it. We took no chances.' Stirling's face began to crinkle into his infectious grin as he relaxed into his armchair preparatory to a good belly laugh. 'Do you know the only thing that was missing? The bloody advertising rights. I was so wrapped up in getting the technicalities and the politics absolutely prim and proper that I forgot the one thing which would have made us an enormous fortune. The advertising potential!'

Few people could have laughed at themselves as Stirling could over that incident.

Though he makes light of it, Stirling's hard work had created an impressive track record for TIE, which became a major force in its field. Had he sustained his direct effort there is no telling what status the company would have reached, but other places and other events were again to persuade him to shake off his tiredness with his usual tactic. A change of direction.

# 19

# JEHUDI, FEDHATI AND ONE THOUSAND GIFFELS

From the beginning of the sixties to the end of his life Stirling's activities overlapped so much that it is not possible to present a cohesive chronology. Whilst he was travelling primarily on behalf of TIE he might also have been conducting negotiations on several quite different fronts. During those two decades he was forming alliances and companies approximately every two years. Some came to naught, some had significant success and some fell halfway between. He delved into the diverse worlds of the mercenary, the international arms trade, security at the highest levels (heads of state), trade union reform, the British educational system and commodities trading. He was also involved with furtherance of the cause of the SAS, the protection of the British countryside and the nation's right to enjoy it, the preservation of African wildlife and many other matters, whilst maintaining his instinct concerning what he described as 'political agitation'.

In all these endeavours there is a series of common threads characterising Stirling's view of the world he lived in. Every project was conceived on the grand scale in that it could, given local success, be transposed on to the international scene. All fell within what Stirling conjectured should be the interests of the British government (politicians did not always share his perception). In many of his ventures he was to involve old and new friends from the SAS. None of his schemes were directly motivated by personal gain – quite the reverse; he was capable of throwing considerable amounts of his own money into the pot if he believed he was right.

The projects have other features in common, but ones which Stirling would be loath to point out. He was an immensely loyal man, loyal to those he served and to those who served him. He was deeply disappointed on the many occasions when he was let down by those he had trusted. Those who knew him well will recognise the hurt he suffered. It was a peculiar trait of Stirling's that he would always give a second chance and only when, as so often happened, he was let down yet again would he close the doors against the individual. He never sought retribution, however – he would juggle with his conscience and find a way to blame himself. This often led to temporary bouts of depression. Such was his sense of honour that in his mind, he as leader or employer had been the guilty one in not exercising the leadership qualities rightly expected of him. In keeping faith with Stirling it would be wrong of me to highlight those incidents in this book.

I think it is worth at this point referring to a conversation we had in mid-1989. It gives an insight into Stirling which has to be borne in mind when examining his enterprises and achievements. We were in his flat in Cheyne Court, surrounded by his chaotic floor-filing system – dozens of papers, files, newspaper clippings, etc liberally sprinkled with cigar ash, awaiting the attention of his new 'aide-de-camp', Donald Craven. We had dined on my Chinese 'carry-out' washed down with quantities of Sancerre and we had considerably lowered the Plimsoll line on a litre bottle of Famous Grouse; it must have been about 2 a.m. when Stirling remarked, 'You know, Spike, it's time you turned off that fiendish little machine and we relaxed a bit. After a hot meal and a bit of boozo I'm fed up of trying to dredge my memory.' I was treated to 'the look'.

The 'fiendish little machine' was my tape recorder and lest I stand accused of cruelly keeping Stirling awake, let me say that it was he who was the nightbird, rarely making for his bed before about 4 a.m.; he preferred to listen to the World News broadcasts of the BBC on the principle that it was better to get the news first-hand and to interpret it before the journalists mutilated the facts to fit their own theories.

At such hours he was alert and communicative. I can remember 'the look'. He was sitting back in his comfortable, disreputable old armchair, swathed in his favourite dressing gown, with one foot on the glass coffee table; the displaced pyjamas showed the slowly healing scars on his leg from yet another fall. I had seen him some weeks earlier when he had been treating the wound by smearing it with some sort of cream and holding the edges together with sellotape. He had a mannerism with his cigar, which was always in a stubby holder, holding it just below jaw level with thumb and forefinger gripping the end of the holder and the rest of his fingers slightly curled in the manner of a fencer's grip on his épée. The cigar smoke would partly obscure his lower face and all that one was aware of was his piercing, strangely hypnotic eyes. 'The look' was usually the prelude to a leading question or a sharp observation but if it was accompanied by a silence then it meant that Stirling expected the recipient to do the talking. I had been given 'the look' too often to be diverted, however, and we locked eyes and listened to the ticking of the clock and the quiet gurgle of the upstairs plumbing as the inhabitant above coped with his nocturnal emergency.

'I must ask Don [Craven] to get me a long stick so that I can thump the ceiling. It's disgusting the noise that chap makes stumping across the floor at all hours. I've had enough, I'm going to bed.' Saying which, he recharged our glasses, waving away my weak protestations.

'David, we've covered a lot of ground and I think I now

know what the reasoning was behind most things, but we haven't talked much about your childhood and youth. Do you believe that upbringing and the surroundings of a child actually form the man?' There was a long pause as he reflected.

'In principle I believe that to be partly the case but I also believe that the genes will out. Certainly when I was looking closely at our educational system I foresaw a distinct effort being made on children between the ages of three and six. It should be a matter of getting the cognitive process of the child's mind active so that he goes to the real pursuit of knowledge knowing his alphabet and being numerate. That was the great attraction of the Sesame Street franchise for TIE; there was a series of programmes which offered just the sort of stimulus required – it was hugely successful. Thereafter it becomes a matter of reforming teacher training and looking closely at the curriculum. The over-riding principle has to be honesty. You will have to talk to my sisters about my childhood at Keir. It was mostly happy but I have difficulty remembering.

'School was something of a misery for me. I was a failure at most academic subjects except perhaps history – no, not so much a failure but uninterested. I could have been better at sports but it was all marred by a tremendous anxiety neurosis – I'll come back to that. I was Master of Beagles for a while and during that period I just ran and ran and ran; it was a mindless physical exercise I could get quite lost in. At Cambridge I was totally vague though I did have periods of great enjoyment – usually non-academic. I was quite convinced that I was a great artist and even though I was bad at drawing I was deeply involved with picture composition. Even after André L'Hôte gave me the bad news that I was not going to make it as an artist I remained a constant doodler.'

'What about marriage, David? Was it a case of never having met the right person? I know that many women have found you attractive and I understand that some at least were in love with you.'

'There's a question,' an infectious chuckle. 'Fear, Spike,

sheer fear. Seriously, I don't think I have ever lived the sort of life which I could ask a woman to share. If I had, I can't imagine that it would have lasted and I consider that the marriage vows are very serious. If an idea really took me I wanted to be able to follow it up, no matter where I had to go or what time I needed to spend on it. Of course I have been close to it – what fully grown man has not been in love several times? I am tremendously fond of children – they are the future of this country and we owe them a good start along the learning path. As a youth sex caused me no end of problems and I was in a total mess over it. This is one of my points about honesty and understanding in education. Puberty brings its problems, but they are problems halved if you understand what is going on with your body and mind. I didn't know what was happening to me apart from the schoolboy dissertations to which we are all subjected.

'My religion placed impossible standards on me without any understanding or sympathy. Every sexual thought and action was a sin – why was it a sin and why was it never explained properly? It is a part of growing up and simply cannot be bottled up as I tried to do. The bottling up of emotions, mainly guilt, left me in a real mess which I don't think I got out of until I made the decision to climb Everest. It's a fact that Puritanism, as taught by most religions, has more of the divils than God in it. My first real sexual encounter was as a schoolboy, and with a woman I might say, and within minutes I went through intense feelings of pride and, I suppose, wonderment, followed by an even more intense guilt, hence all the running. Maybe I was hoping to escape it through exhaustion. I can't really remember. Certainly in Africa during the war (which brings another set of pressures) I never hesitated to check out the headquarter equipment; since then, "I've taken my fun where I've found it" – Kipling wasn't it?'

'You said that religion placed impossible standards on you and I can appreciate that in the sexual sense you've just discussed. There's a strong religious thread in the CAS Declaration. You've also told me that, particularly during the war, you have known fear. Like many of us ex-soldiers, you've killed, and joked at the expense of religion though I can't recall blasphemy ever being part of your speech or jokes. Apart from the war you've been close to death several times through illness or injury. How big a rôle has religion played in your life?'

'You are right about blasphemy. Any person with a modicum of education should be capable of expressing himself without resorting to blasphemy or foul language. I do swear, as you well know, but it's weakness all the same. I often use the three dirtiest words in the Arabic language when I want to swear, Jehudi, fedhati and a hundred giffels – the number of giffels depends on how bad the catastrophe is – very useful if there are ladies about. I have to say that I've never tried to find the words in a dictionary and I've probably got them wrong.

'Yes, religion does play its part in my life. Quite a big part, though I haven't often felt the need to talk about it. I was brought up as a Roman Catholic and have often shared the company of priests but I think religion is something you fine tune yourself as you mature. There are many manifestations of le bon Dieu and they are all valid as is atheism and even animalism (in the context that human beings are not necessarily superior to other animals) but to me it is not possible to walk this earth and not believe in a Divine Creator. There simply has to be an influence by which all standards can be measured and this is where the personal fine-tuning comes in. If God is acceptable as a focal point for good then perhaps the presence of the Devil as an alternate force for evil has to be accepted.

'If the heart is capable of compassion, tolerance and friendship then the Devil is displayed in envy, greed and violence and their application against the choice of the individual. Yes, my beliefs are important to me, but I often think of the heart and spirit being the counterbalance between God and the Devil. The heart with its infinite capacity for compassion and tolerance and the spirit which must be given free rein to have a go. I have never made up my mind which is the better teaching precept, "Man versus God and the Devil" or "God versus Man and the Devil" – I suggest these in terms of coming to a personal understanding and not the form of mental warfare which it is so easy to be drawn into. I've not obeyed the formal requirements of my religion; I have gone to confession when I've felt the need, often near Christmas time, but I've certainly called on le bon Dieu many times.'

'David, many of your ventures have seemingly had a world platform as the final aim – Capricorn Africa, your thoughts on education, even some of your more military ventures such as Watchguard. Many people have asked and will continue to ask whether you were on an ego trip – how would you defend that?'

'I would not defend it. I have never particularly cared what people thought. Those who understood what I was about would not pose the question. Having said that, I have taken newspapers to the cleaners from time to time when I thought they were in danger of destroying something they were incapable of understanding. Yes, you're right in a sense, many of the things I have tried to do could be transposed to grander scales but, non-swanks, usually to the developing world. In the West we are in a very privileged position; we have been recording our six thousand years of experience, history and human organisation; we can therefore study the past to understand and learn from it.

'Such a privilege confers great responsibility, to our own youth and to the developing world. Apart from the morality of the situation which demands that we assist those nations through bad patches, the sheer economics are inescapable. To arrive at peace and harmony we must nurture other nations in an atmosphere of trust, untainted by envy and greed; only in this way can we hope to share amicably in resources, technology and education to the betterment of the whole. Now, that seems to be a reasonable toast, why don't you splash a little more into these glasses.'

'Cheers, David, here's to the betterment of the world. I wonder how many people would agree with you. You've never hesitated to go to the top of the tree when you were fighting a case. You have an enormous range of contacts and friends. How do you manage to stay in touch to the degree that they continue to support your enterprises despite the fact that you must have embarrassed at least some of them at times?'

'I've been very lucky with my friends and my family. You must remember just how wide was the range of friends and visitors my father and mother had at Keir. Between the Stirlings, the Frasers and the Lovats virtually all the professions, vocations and styles of life were represented. At Ampleforth and Cambridge many lasting friendships were formed, and then there was the war which breeds strange bedfellows. I have always used ex-SAS fellows whenever I could; I did know something about them after all and almost without exception we worked well together. We mustn't forget the London clubs. White's was especially good fun, and a watering hole for many of my chums. I've always leaned heavily on friends for help and in opening doors but I've also tried to help anyone who has ever come to me. I suppose the Capricorn network was especially helpful in later years in Africa because of the huge number of black Africans I got to know and respect, and of course there was a great deal of travel to the USA in those days. Contacts established there were built on when I was devoted to TIE. And every friend had his own circle and I did not often find a door barred; there was usually someone who could create access and access is what business opportunity is all about.'

An interview with Peter Stirling sheds light on David's approach to business. Peter did not see much of his brother in the years immediately following the war and he was settled in Persia before they made any mutual attempt at business.

'There was a curious dichotomy in David's character at that

time. Although he was very much an idealist, not a practical politician at all, he was very conscious of not having any money – younger brothers do lack money, including myself then – and it mattered enormously to him to find a way of making cash so that he was not dependent on our family and so that he could promote his political objectives. It took him almost thirty years to achieve that because TIE didn't make much until he got the Hong Kong franchise – even then it took time and the financing of some property deals, I think; but TIE did give him sufficient to follow up some of his ideas.

'Whatever he did make he was very generous with, as witness a very laughable episode in Teheran. My partner and I had found that the Persian government wanted to buy a fleet of eight shrimping boats costing about a quarter of a million each. David came in to see us en route to Spain and said that he could sort things out there. In Spain he contracted a firm which he told us would make admirable agents (I think he was also involved with them on some other deal), and proposed that we should get a Spanish company to built the shrimpers.

'We duly did this, and it emerged later that the agents weren't reliable after all and also that David had already given one or two percent to all sorts of people including his secretary! This shocked my partner, who was a real professional. They loved David but didn't think very much of his business acumen. The "shrampers" (David and I always called them "shrampers") were delivered on time and seemed to be OK but the agents ran off with all the commission – we never got a penny out of it and neither did David's secretary I think.

'My poor partner bore the brunt of it; he became infested by an admiral who had been bribed to get the contract in the first place. For weeks afterwards whenever I walked into my partner's room I would see this rather mournful admiral sitting there. I don't know how my partner wriggled out of it in the end but the poor chap had been expecting to see about fifty thousand pounds and didn't make a sausage!

'That was my only business deal with David. He had this

great personality and could sell anything, but he had to be controlled and we didn't get control of him on this deal until it was too late. He was always capable of seizing the initiative and starting things off – some really quite important things too – but he was a bit short on finishing them sometimes.'

Peter Stirling pointed out that when his brother first went to Africa with Freddy de Guingand his intentions were simply to set up in business. As we have seen it was only a short while before Stirling divorced himself from what he called Rhodes-type materialistic ambition and set about forming Capricorn.

The success of TIE gave Stirling reasonable financial independence for the first time, and left him with a taste for the entrepreneurial deal, but he remained without the killer instinct necessary to capitalise on opportunity. His sense of fair play usually meant that he left himself with the lesser share-out and his 'agents' rubbing their hands in glee.

The 1960s heralded the age of the coup and Stirling studied the situation with interest. At the same time the SAS were beginning to receive some unwelcome (to them) press attention due to their successes in the Malayan campaign and the startlingly efficient Jebel Akhdar operation in Oman. Mix these ingredients, add a dash of Stirling vision and ingenuity, and the pudding will soon begin to ferment.

---

# 20

# ONE HAND ON THE TILLER . . .

Apart from the brief war with Saudi Arabia in 1934, Yemen had been free from any conflict more severe than inter-tribal skirmishing since the Treaty of Mundros in 1918 had released the country from Turkish shackles into independence under hereditary rule. The war with Saudi Arabia had sown the seeds of peace with that neighbour in the form of the Muslim Friendship and Arab Fraternity Treaty. In 1945 Yemen became the seventh member of the League of Arab States along with Egypt, Transjordan, Lebanon, Iraq, Saudi Arabia and Syria, and looked set for peaceful co-existence with her neighbours. Backward, but fiercely independent under the rule of the Imam Mohammed al-Badr, there seemed little to attract an aggressor to this wild, remote, mountainous land with its pathetically sparse lines of communication. 'Nasserism' was to change all that in September 1962.

Inspired by promises of Soviet aid in establishing Yemen as a People's Republic, left-wing army officers (under the command of the Chief of Army Staff, Colonel Abdullah al-Sallal) who led the coup d'état on 26 September were confident of instant support from Aden and the Federation of South Arabia. Anti-British feelings were running very high – federation was not popular and the fact that the British Army had established

its Middle East Command Headquarters in Aden Colony in 1960 helped fuel the fires of revolution. During the hamfisted coup attempt which left him with an open flank the Imam managed to escape from Sana'a with Royalist supporters into the inhospitable mountains to the north where he joined up with the remainder of the Zeidi tribe. Alive and still kicking he was nonetheless unable to rule his country. Immediately the revolutionaries took Sana'a and declared the Yemen a republic, Nasser began to land troops, aircraft and armour on to Yemeni soil.

The Royalists did not sit idly by; they resisted the Egyptians enthusiastically, but it was a one-sided struggle. In the Royalist favour was the impregnability of the mountains and the ease with which roads and passes could be dominated, but they were untrained troops and badly equipped with only vintage weaponry. Fervour and enthusiasm are admirable and necessary attributes in war, but they count for little if those emotions cannot be harnessed efficiently.

The situation in the Yemen was of great interest to the British government. Nasser's support of the revolutionaries would seem to have bolstered them in their avowed intentions to carry the fight to the south and threaten Aden Colony and the Federation. It was already on the cards that the British would withdraw from Aden at the point of its independence in 1968 but the dilemma facing the government was whether the necessary stability would be achieved by then. Britain was to ignore this factor in the final analysis under what would by then be a Labour government. By the end of 1962 Britain was under tremendous pressure from Egypt and the USA to recognise the new government of Yemen.

Stirling, now financially secure for the immediate future, was present at White's (probably in April 1963) when four Scots and one English member of that bastion of Conservatism met to discuss the implications of events in the Yemen. They had much in common. Julian Amery, Eton-educated Minister of Aviation, had operated during the war in Egypt, Palestine and the Adriatic under direction of the Special Operations Executive, and he had parachuted into Albania in 1944 with another member of the party.

Lieutenant-Colonel Neil 'Billy' McLean DSO, Member of Parliament for Inverness, had met Julian Amery at Eton. Apart from their adventures in Albania and elsewhere he had been a member of Amery's proposed SOE mission to Chungking in the later stages of the war. Also a part of the Chinese project was Colonel David Smiley DSO, MC who appears later in the Yemen episode.

Stirling had been known to Amery and McLean since the war days in Cairo when Shepheard's Hotel had been the feasting venue for those adventurers, and his ideas for SAS action in China based at Chungking had been drafted in parallel with Amery's. With Stirling, and still closely involved in SAS affairs, was Colonel Brian Franks, the driving force behind the re-formation of the post-war regiment and at that time Colonel Commandant.

The senior participant at the meeting was Alec Douglas-Home, then Secretary of State for Foreign Affairs. They met to listen to McLean who, acting in the capacity he described as 'a sort of unofficial shadow minister for Foreign Affairs', had just completed an unsponsored tour of the Yemen. Cognisant of the pressures on Douglas-Home to recommend that Britain follow the USA and the USSR in recognising the revolutionary government his advice, as remembered by Stirling, was uncompromising:

'It is quite ridiculous for us to recognise a new republic in Yemen as a rightful government. It is just not so – I have met the Imam, who categorically states that it is not so. He is in the mountains and the tribes are rallying round him, of this there is no question. Egypt has not got the Yemen. She may have control of a few main roads and the capital but otherwise the troops don't dare to venture out. We would be stupid and quite immoral to recognise a new government because it is not in control.'

Douglas-Home is reputed to have replied, 'Fine. We'll wait and see what happens.'

'With a bit of help, the tribes now fighting under the Imam could easily hold off the Egyptians,' McLean added.

'It was quite obvious at that point,' Stirling related, 'that between them Alec, Julian and Billy had already decided that it would be a good idea if something could be done unofficially. It appeared that Alec had already been advised that it would take the SIS about six months to get agents into the Yemen and get something established, and even then there were doubts as to whether the necessary talent would be available. Billy had already said that this would be far too slow. It was pretty well clear why Brian and myself were there.'

Having mentioned the SIS, it is interesting to note that the CIA report on the situation to the US government predicted that the Egyptians would land in the order of 12,000 troops and that there would be a stable government within seven to ten days. As will be seen that statement as a military appreciation left much to be desired!

'We were then asked directly who in the SAS might be available to help out the Royalists. Brian, of course, knew far more about modern SAS matters and personnel than I did. I had spent so little time in England in the fifties that I was well out of touch. I was President of the SAS Association but I was rarely called on to do anything. I knew Dare Newell well and from time to time we got together for a hot meal and a chat but as to who was available it had to be Brian. He asked the obvious question – would it be possible for HMG to agree to an official deployment of the SAS – but we both knew it would be a no-hoper.

'We had to look to the Territorial Army. In the first instance it should be an officer, and a retired one. We could think of nobody with war experience who would be available except Johnny Cooper and he was committed to the Sultan of Oman; even if he were interested, it would take time for him to get free and it didn't look in the beginning as though the job would have long-term prospects. We decided to approach Jim Johnson; he had recently retired from command of 21 SAS (TA) and he was broking with Lloyds. He was not a battle-experienced officer but he knew the SAS, should be able to organise and administer the operation and would be well placed to recruit having been on the SAS circuit for some years.'

Lieutenant-Colonel Jim Johnson takes up the story: 'Brian Franks asked me to meet him, and got straight down to brass tacks. Without outlining the background he asked how I would like to take on the job of burning all the Egyptian MiG aircraft on airstrips in the Yemen. I had left 21 SAS in January that year and, replied somewhat flippantly that as I had nothing on for the next week I'd be happy to oblige. He then filled me in on the background and I got a measure of the task.

'A short time later I was invited to Julian Amery's flat and introduced to Ahmed Shami, then Foreign Secretary of the Yemen. Billy McLean and David Stirling were also there. Shami asked whether I could help. In a moment of terrible innocence I replied that I probably could do something. Shami's idea was for a small party of men to go into the Yemen with loads of explosives and duff up the aircraft. He explained that the Royalist tribesmen, armed with primitive weapons and having none of the benefits of military training, were becoming increasingly demoralised with being strafed by the MiGs and not knowing how to deal with them. After Shami had left we got down to realities.'

Stirling's part in the project at this stage was as host and cover: 'We knew that security was everything; if the press were to find out about the operation a number of people would be embarrassed and we would probably get no further than making impotent noises. TIE was well-established in 21 Sloane Street, Johnson had to have a focal point, and I offered him the use of the basement – rather a grand term, it was actually more of a cellar.'

On his first visit Johnson felt he had reason to be concerned about security. 'You entered the cellar through a door between two shoe shops – and it transpired that David never locked the door, day or night. I suppose anybody going in would have been thumped by him. Anyway it got us off the ground so to speak and David supplied me with a secretary, Fiona Fraser [daughter of Lord Lovat] who he said was discreet and very loyal. She was marvellous and she stayed with me for twenty-odd years. Occasionally she would lose her temper and go off to work for Mick Jagger or some such but she always came back.

'David, under the auspices of TIE, produced an operating cover for us by starting Rally Films Ltd. I got on with the paper organisation of the operation and started to look for recruits but it was obvious that we should take a look at the situation on the ground. As it turned out there was no time for this if we were to live up to Ahmed Shami's expectations. It was exceedingly diffi-cult to find ex-SAS soldiers who spoke Arabic but we eventually found three. I then sent a telegram to Johnny Cooper in Oman saying that his mother was very ill and summoning him to England. Johnny's mother had been dead for some years and Johnny was to rendezvous with us in Aden.'[*]

Stirling knew that the French, although not necessarily sympathetic to the plight of the Imam al-Badr, were opposed to anything the Americans were up to and therefore could be relied upon to assist. He was also aware that there were French ex-SAS who would respond to a call for action. Stirling made contact with various officials in France including the Deuxième Bureau and at a meeting in Paris with senior French partici-pation, he, McLean, Johnson, Cooper and Roger Falques hammered out the detail of the first in-depth reconnaissance in early June 1963.

_____

* This is the Cooper of L Detachment days. He had joined the SAS when it formed again in Malaya and had been a squadron commander in the assault on the Jebel Akhdar in 1958. Since then he had retired from the British Army and taken on a contract with the Sultan of Oman. Before the telegram subterfuge he had met with David Stirling, Phillip Horniblow (ex-21 SAS Regiment) and Tony Boyle, ADC to the Governor-General of Aden, in Bahrain and had been given some small insight into the task he was to be asked to undertake.

Aware of the political problems overall in the Middle East, Stirling had anticipated difficulties in getting Johnson's team through Aden without attracting attention. Whilst Johnson got on with the initial organising and recruiting, Stirling flew to Aden to meet the Governor-General to make 'suitable arrangements'. The eventual plan was for Cooper's team of four Britons and two Frenchmen to arrive in the Colony, be quickly nursemaided through customs and immigration, and motored as fast as possible north to Beihan on the Yemeni border. In Beihan the local ruler, Sharif Hussein, had agreed to operate a system of safe houses from which operations into the Yemen could be launched. This worked well and the team eventually eased their way into the Yemen dressed to resemble as closely as possible the local Yemenis.

The task was arduous but fascinating; the team ducked air attacks from the Egyptians, picked their way through minefields, witnessed Egyptian attacks on Royalist strongholds and took part in a little 'unofficial but highly explosive' action against the aggressors. Wherever possible short training sessions were conducted in such military essentials as fire control, use of ground and ambush techniques. The trip lasted well over the month allotted, but Cooper's debrief presented a much clearer picture to Stirling and Johnson.

'The team had met a local prince whose feelings were running so high that the planned operation had to be modified. Basically he said that it was all very well for us to go about our business on the airstrips but the last thing he wanted was lots of burning airplanes stirring up a hornets' nest at that stage. What he wanted was professional weapon, medical and communications training followed by a supply of effective weapons, mortars, etc., and then he wanted properly to organise a resistance movement which he couldn't do himself. He pointed out that far from being able to fire machine guns, his men had never even seen them at close quarters.'

This was a much more realistic proposition for Johnson's team; although a few dedicated men acting in the mainly aggressive rôle initially envisaged could have affected the morale of the Egyptian forces it was much more efficient to use them (plus others) to train and advise the Imam's tribesmen to operate over a wider front.

It is probable that the local prince was Abdullah bin Hassan, then commanding the Royalist Army; he had already been influenced by David Smiley. Smiley, wartime comrade-in-arms of Amery and McLean, had been asked by the latter to meet Prince Feisal in Saudi Arabia. Feisal asked him to make a tour of the Royalist areas in the Yemen and find out what the Saudis could do to help and Smiley spent three months on the task which seems to have predated the arrival of Stirling and Franks on the scene, though curiously they appear not to have been told of this at the time.

Smiley's military appreciation of the situation in Yemen called for a training and supply operation and the use of European mercenaries. In the first instance he envisaged that training was required in the use of mines, mountain/desert tactics, machine guns and mortars which of course would also have to be supplied. These recommendations were put to Prince Feisal and the Saudi Arabian Minister of Defence, Prince Sultan; both had agreed to the plan and stated that Saudi Arabia would bear the costs of the project. Before contacting Stirling, McLean, Amery and Smiley had discussed the mechanics. Their only real stumbling block was where to get mercenaries. There were known to be a few remaining in the Congo, and some French and German odds and sods hanging around the usual haunts in Marseilles and the like, but these were not the sort of men required for such important work. The group decided that it must be either serving or ex-SAS soldiers and at that point Franks and Stirling were brought into the equation. In filling the Yemen requirement, Stirling renewed his acquaintance with Lieutenant-Colonel John Woodhouse, then commanding 22 SAS Regiment, and this revived contact was to divert Stirling's attention from full-time commitment to TIE to explore other avenues of business. I shall return to this later.

Stirling had long held Woodhouse in high esteem considering him the founder of the modern-day SAS through his rigid application of selection and soldiering standards, his recognition and extension of the original precepts of the regiment and his far-sightedness in exploring progressive rôles for the future. In looking for serving members of the SAS to further the Yemen requirement (which would have been extremely difficult), Stirling became aware that a variety of fit, experienced veterans of the regiment, though now retired from active service, still had much to offer. Such men were steered towards Johnson.

Cooper's reconnaissance had centred upon the capital, Sana'a, and its surrounds. He had determined that there was no hope of victory for the Egyptian Army so long as the Royalists could be encouraged to go on fighting. In the longer term, if the Royalists had communications through which to co-ordinate effort, military training and good supply lines then the Egyptians would be very vulnerable to well-directed guerrilla operations. It seemed certain that only a Royalist government could hope to control the tribes in the mountainous region surrounding Sana'a known as the Khowlan. The effect on their morale could be devastating. The sheikhs and tribesmen would have to be paid, but the recommendations fitted perfectly with the proposal already agreed by Prince Feisal and funding was apparently no problem.

The operation was given the green light and Cooper returned to the Khowlan where he made contact with the two Deuxième Bureau agents. These two were shortly to leave him and his became a lonely task for many months before reinforcements reached his area. Slowly the teams were built up and an efficient radio network established with a reporting base in Saudi Arabia. An airdrop routine was put into motion and training got under way. The British teams were to train the Royalists in tactics and the use of the weapons and munitions which became available; they were to render what medical assistance they could (this was important in a country which had theretofore spurned medicine, preferring trust in Allah); they were to collect and transmit every scrap of intelligence possible in respect of Egyptian dispositions, tactics and future intentions; lastly, but perhaps most importantly, they were to be the motivating power behind the Royalist effort. In the main the French teams were concentrated on providing effective mortar crews (though it is certain that they held also to their own intelligence brief). They operated in harmony under control of the Johnson structure.

The CIA prognosis that the Royalist cause would fizzle out within ten days was slightly inaccurate; it was to be five and a half years before Stirling's involvement would cease. The Yemen operation was not without political, personality and resource problems and progress was far from smooth. With some notable exceptions such as Johnny Cooper and Bernard Mills, it is questionable as to whether the calibre of man recruited was sufficiently high. The two highly important aspects of their rôle were the acquisition of intelligence and motivation of the Royalists – both achievable given the firm base of supply, training, medical assistance and the fact that the teams were the conduits for the 'fighting funds'.

At the recruiting base in London there was little proper political briefing – many of the men had only the vaguest idea of the background to the struggle or the wider aims. There was little trust of intelligence agencies and little idea of how to set about sifting truth from rumour. The 'directing staff' in London merely briefed the recruits on their destined locations and set up the administration of salaries, etc. Little wonder that a 'them and us' situation developed at the lonely, often exposed 'sharp end'. It was perhaps asking too much at that stage of SAS development to expect soldiers who had operated at junior and senior NCO levels to take on the task of motivating wild tribesmen when they were often incapable of talking with authority about the general political situation in the Middle East. By no means all of the recruits were ex-SAS; these were in short supply, as better-calibre people preferred to soldier on in their regiment. Some recruits were attracted purely by the very good salary; their ambition was to live to spend it and not take undue personal risk.

Command and control were not efficient. On the ground David Smiley was eventually tasked to command the operation whilst Johnson maintained the administrative effort in London with frequent visits to the Middle East. MacLean was still very much involved as the initiator of the project and the adviser to the government and security services in the UK. Aims and liaison duties became confused especially as the ceasefire declared in August 1965 made it necessary to justify continuing to finance the project. With the command thus fragmented, the teams in the field tended to be left to their own devices; even the motivators need motivating and during that period it seems that only Cooper and Mills succeeded in getting positive aggressive action in their individual areas. This criticism of the few rather than the whole is necessary because these matters weighed heavily on Stirling's mind as his thoughts turned to other areas of business; but praise is also due.

The force which Nasser ordered to the Yemen in September 1962 was estimated at 12,000. Sana'a was quickly taken and the majority of East Yemen which lay adjacent to South Arabia was quickly under Egyptian control. When the Royalists started fighting back Egyptian numbers swelled quickly to 30,000 in order that lines of communication and airfields could be adequately protected. When the small British effort got under way the effect was dramatic as co-ordinated operations began. Egyptian strength in 1965 was estimated at a minimum of 52,000 and even then they were unable to make any headway into the Royalists' mountain strongholds. Despite the atrocious reprisals enacted by the Egyptians who bombed and strafed Royalist villages with great enthusiasm and used chemical weapons in abundance, the Royalists not only held firm but continued to mine, ambush and snipe. The Yemeni Republican Army, which had placed such great faith in the invincibility of Nasserism and the might of the Egyptian Army, crumbled and refused to leave fortified bases. Immediately prior to the ceasefire the Egyptian Army was in real trouble, as Johnson recalled:

'At that point we had an entire brigade with all its armour and support, completely cut off in a deep valley. We could have finished off the whole brigade – they couldn't have got out. The Saudis wouldn't allow this and the Egyptians were able to walk out as surrenderees but with all their weapons. It is a fact that four and a half years after we were committed, 68,000 Egyptians were still tied up in the Yemen and still trying to extract themselves from the mountains. They were in no fit state to interfere with the British Army's withdrawal from Aden nor to threaten the Saudis to the north.'

In 1965 Stirling would not have completely agreed with this view. In the early sixties he had struck up a business relationship with Geoffrey Edwards who was working hard to clinch a deal to sell a multi-million-pound package of aircraft and weaponry to Saudi Arabia. His contacts in the Saudi royal family and other organs of government were as impressive as Stirling's; the two found that their aims were compatible and each supported the other's cause at every opportunity. Stirling had always seen Nasser's thrust into the Yemen as a springboard to South and Saudi Arabia and eventual seizure of their oil wealth. When Britain pulled out of the Middle East as it inevitably would do, Saudi Arabia would be left defenceless against the approximately 68,000 Egyptian troops in the Yemen if the Royalist effort had ceased. He saw the Edwards package as being critical to stability. To those who would cast cynical aspersions on his involvement with Edwards I would say look to the amount of money Britain has made through arms deals with Saudi Arabia since the Edwards breakthrough!

By tracing Stirling's involvement in the Middle East it is possible to gauge the thought processes which led him to diversify his personal efforts. His initial interest in the Yemen was largely superficial; he had been called upon to give advice and assistance to a worthy cause and he had satisfied this request with the introduction of Cooper and Johnson. More demands were to be made on him however, and his interest intensified. His meetings with Woodhouse led to his considering rôles for the modern SAS – he was still travelling extensively throughout Africa, the Far East and the Middle East and he had an awareness of political problems and national realities denied to most serving military officers of that period. These were the years of the coup d'état and an idea was germinating in Stirling's mind which was to mature with his continued involvement in the Yemen.

Over a three-year period he contributed more than is commonly accepted. In the early stages of the operation the weapons and ammunition supplied to the Yemeni Royalists were released from stocks held by the Saudi Arabians who obtained them from the USA in the form of aid. The Americans soon noticed that the quantities of stores being written off as training expenditure did not tally with the lack of training then conducted by the Saudi Arabian army and threatened to cut off supply unless credible accounting procedures were instituted. Stirling resolved the problem by arranging for a country with an 'intelligence' interest in the Yemen situation to effect the necessary supplies in return for information.

Through the auspices of TIE he gained a contract in South Arabia to place a radio station in Aden which had duties beyond its local broadcasts and research into the future provision of television services. Thus was an efficient reporting capability offered to the Yemen teams and it gave credible employment to Tony Boyle who by then had retired from active service on medical grounds and required operating cover for his function in organising air resupply. Time and again Stirling was to use his (and Edwards's) contacts in the Saudi Arabian government to ease tricky situations created by unskilled liaison. He was the normal conduit for information being passed back to Amery and MacLean (though by that time government was in the hands of the Labour Party). He was well equipped to pass on opinions often denied to the others through his close contacts with Israeli, Persian and French intelligence agencies.

At the time in question the mercenary structure for the Yemen effort totalled around some forty-eight ex-servicemen of which most were British ex-SAS. One measure of their effect can be deduced from the Egyptian claim that there were at least four hundred British advisers at work in the Yemen. Overall command was still invested in Smiley (who liaised directly with the Saudi Arabians) though he was due shortly to retire from the project; Johnson remained in overall control from London and Mike Gooley, based in the Yemen interior, exercised ground control. Saudi Arabian policies were obscure and ever-changing, creating unease within the Yemeni Royalists as they began to suspect that King Feisal might not continue his financial support.

Against this backdrop Stirling began to plan a commercial venture which was to have far-reaching effects. The immediate question has to be, why? TIE was progressing extremely well; had he concentrated on that business, Stirling could doubtless have acquired a solid financial base for his later years. Why should he turn aside at such a critical time?

There was certainly a frustration factor; he held to his views on Nasser's ultimate ambitions and saw the planned British withdrawal from Aden almost as a betrayal of South Arabia and Saudi Arabia especially when this was linked to what he regarded as an apathetic approach to the achievements of a few small teams in the Yemen. He was horrified of the prospect of withdrawal before Saudi could mount an effective deterrent through the acquisition and training of an airforce. He also thought there could have been greater success in the Yemen and that it might have been better to pay a little less heed to the Saudi government at some crucial tactical points.

He had enjoyed being instrumental in gaining employment for ex-SAS soldiers, and he had been stimulated by discussions with Woodhouse about possible rôles for the regiment in a world of changing threats. He was disappointed by what he

saw as the Labour government's lack of a progressive foreign policy and their intention of drawing out of a number of countries
before Britain had fully discharged its debts to them. Throughout the Middle East and Africa he observed the subversive activities of the USSR and remarked that nothing was being done
to combat the growing and sinister Communist influence.

The Yemen operation had given him an idea of what could
be achieved by advisers and technicians from the pool of
retired Special Forces manpower – both the strengths and
the weaknesses of such workers were highlighted. He knew
roughly the costs of using a 'mercenary' force and he felt
there was scope for setting up a private force whose main
function would be to have a controllable political effect,
but which must produce an operating profit; politics was
the driving force but it had to be financially viable; it
could not be resourced from within TIE, as the one organisation would create distrust against the other, particularly
in intelligence circles. Stirling conceived the idea of forming
a commercial company to operate in areas of paramount
interest to the highest national figures – the heads of state.

Terrorism was barely in its infancy in the middle sixties –
the coup d'état was the tactic then in vogue for crippling or
destabilising second and third world countries. The USSR
was fast becoming masterly at the technique, particularly in
the Middle East and Africa. Definite patterns of events and
activities could be analysed as precursors to probable coup
attempts. Stirling had observed some of these, though he
had not conducted detailed studies, and was fascinated by
the potential for 'prophylactic action'.

Years later he was to recall: 'In many ways it was a hangover
from Capricorn and the potential for the reserve continent in
terms of trading with the West. Only achievable if heads of
state were benignly disposed toward the West. What better
way of getting very close to a head of state than by proving
that you had the means to prolong his active life? In training
those close to a president one had to engender deep trust.

Once that was established it should be possible to put advisors into place who were more than military experts. Of course the whole thing had to be thought out but if it was possible to detect the advent of a coup d'état, it had to be possible to thwart it. One would need to become significantly involved in the setting up of intelligence agencies, and it would not be possible to set them up and train them without gaining access to a lot of information which could be useful to our own boys.

'The SAS were beginning to develop training skills in special forces tactics, including those of personal bodyguards. For years they had been involved in all aspects of guerrilla and counter-guerrilla warfare, and the nature of military life meant that many of those involved in this were the senior citizens of the regiment who were coming up to retirement. Some at least would be interested in continuing in the military sphere. I was already close to a number of presidents and bosses in countries which were far from secure. Apart from some old friends from Capricorn days, the setting up of television franchises always attracted the organs of government interested in 'educating' the population. Usually these characters fell off the branches of some intelligence tree.

'There had to be a start point and the situation in the Yemen seemed likely to be useful from two standpoints. There was an operation already in progress and though it was not of the type I envisaged it would allow me to get people trained to operate under civilian conditions without the vast resources and support of the army. It could equally well get the better personalities known within the Middle East where I reckoned there could be substantial business. Secondly, it would give me the chance to select future team leaders from the chaps recruited for the Yemen. It was also feasible to mount a probe into Africa at the same time. I felt quite confident about the project. At first the finance for travel could be done through TIE as the company had existing business or at least leads in some of the countries which would be targets; time would not be a problem as the concept had to be tidied up and it would take a while to sell – time enough to recruit and train our chaps.

'There was another aspect about which I think I had already talked to John Woodhouse and Dare Newell. The countries we should be selling the service to would fall into two categories: those which HMG could and would be able to assist overtly and those it would like but could not be seen to assist because of political niceties. Perhaps more pertinently, there were countries who were too embarrassed ask HMG for aid. For those in the first category, we ought to be able to engineer a situation whereby the "customer" could ask for, and get, official help from the regiment.

'John Woodhouse had been exploring the potential of such jobs for the SAS but even as commanding officer he did not have a budget to travel and sell the regiment's services. I also knew that he had the best brain and was by far the most respected of senior SAS officers who could help me formulate an effective service and get the thing moving in the right direction. I couldn't, of course, approach him until he retired.'

In January 1965, Colonel John Woodhouse retired from active service and became involved with Her Majesty's Government as a part-time adviser on counter-coup measures in parts of the Commonwealth. Such was the nature of this work that he was able to take on other duties as he wished; therefore there was a natural gelling of national and commercial interests in getting together with Stirling. At first the partnership worked well. Stirling was quite aware that Woodhouse's first allegiance was to HMG and the good reputation of the SAS, and certain ground rules were laid down for the company which was to be formed under the name of Watchguard International (formalised in the Channel Islands in 1967).

One initial result of talks was an amendment to Stirling's early thoughts. The company would provide a service aimed at preventing the violent overthrow of a government but it would not thereafter seek to exert political influence; indeed as a wholly independent commercial company it would be incapable of doing so. The company would not accept as a client any government which consisted of a racial minority; no client which was or looked set to be hostile to HMG would be considered. The company would offer only instructional training and advice and the actual provision of bodyguards or mercenaries would not form part of the service. No serving members of the SAS would be approached and any such person volunteering his services would be referred back to his commander. Although Watchguard International took the decision to report all contracts to the Foreign Office before starting work they would not feel constrained to refuse the task if Foreign Office objections were unreasonable.

The spearhead of Watchguard's operation was to be the Middle East and whilst Stirling busied himself in developing the concept in Iran, Woodhouse and a small team moved into the Khowlan. Their task, when they departed in late July 1965, was to organise guerrilla action around Sana'a with the primary aim of forcing the Egyptians to abandon the airfields in that area. Before they could become effective the ceasefire was declared on 24 August and they reverted to giving medical assistance and maintaining communications. This gave Woodhouse a fine opportunity to make an overall assessment of the work thus far and the potential for the future in the event of hostilities being resumed.

Woodhouse found that the manner and concentration of the Egyptian deployment left them highly vulnerable to night attack by small patrols. Transport aircraft was consolidated at the civil airfield just south of Sana'a with the fighters parked at a newly constructed airfield a few kilometres to the north. The headquarters, broadcasting station and military vehicle sites were all close to Sana'a but separated in such a manner that penetration between and into them would have been easy. The low quality and lack of experience of the Egyptian forces would have assisted the guerrillas enormously but Woodhouse was of the opinion that any raids would have to be British led.

He found that the Royalist forces, under Gassem Monassir, were well led and loyal. Given that reinforcements in the form of French medium mortars and crews was planned, attacks on the Egyptian bases would have created great morale problems. All road communications between Sana'a and Hodeida and to Jihannah and Raida were extremely vulnerable to mining, machine-gun attack and close ambush. In short there was great potential for classic guerrilla tactics, which would be made even easier through the supply of more up-to-date equipment such as time-delay devices, tracer ammunition and the like.

With famine conditions threatening (farming had virtually ceased during hostilities), many Royalist fighters were returning to their homes, but Woodhouse was certain that there would be a swift response to a further call for action should the need arise. The Royalist leaders were becoming suspicious of the motives of the Saudi royal family; they could not readily appreciate why they had been held back from action at various times. It was probable, however, that they would continue to fall in with Saudi wishes provided that their own royal family was secure and that the financial subsidies continued. In his subsequent report Woodhouse made an interesting political point which was to be followed up at governmental level:

*Medical Assistance* . . . the political advantages to Great Britain in providing medical assistance are considerable and can be achieved at little or no financial cost to HMG. The population of this area have been introduced to modern medicine for the first time in their history by the semi-skilled medical assistants among the ex-SAS soldiers who have been in the Yemen. This treatment though inadequate in scale has brought about a revolutionary change in the attitude of the people to injury and disease. Until 1963 the vast majority accepted sickness as God's will, something beyond human capability to correct. Now their attitude is that, God willing, if there are 'doctors' most ills can be cured. The taste for medical services, once acquired, grows strongly. If we, through the auspices of the Red Cross, can provide something, however small, to assuage their very real and desperate need for medical attention we shall provide a service for the people which they will appreciate all the more because it will be for all practical purposes the first positive help they have had from 'Government'.

Politically it is important that the service should at least appear to be directed and actively sponsored by the Royalist 'administration'. In practice this means that Emir Abdullah should give the medical teams his moral support, which he certainly would do with alacrity.

Woodhouse's report, seen both by Stirling and HMG, contained much that was useful to an organisation setting out to cover the wide geographic scope that Stirling intended. The following extracts will show the eventual reasoning behind recruitment policies and methods of operation:

*Organisation* The head of operations concerned himself with liaison and recruiting but took no part in the direction and control of operations in Yemen after allocating men to particular areas. No training or political directives were given the mercenaries. An assistant, concerned primarily with air supply and administrative details, had no training or experience of guerrilla operations; a fact which inevitably was the cause of friction between those in the field and the headquarters in London.

*Achievements* In the field the mercenaries did as they pleased. A considerable amount of weapon training was undertaken, and both Cooper and Mills organised successful attacks. Others did little apart from providing medical assistance and radio communications and taking air supply drops.

The primary and probably decisive rôle of the mercenaries was to encourage the Royalists to continue the war until eventually the military effort became too much for the Egyptian forces to sustain.

In late 1964 expansion of the mercenary organisation and the imminent arrival of heavy mortars would certainly have led to heavy Egyptian losses in men and aircraft. Even then it would have been the morale and not material effect which would have proved decisive. The poor quality of Egyptian forces should not be forgotten in any lessons to be learned from this operation.

*Security* Because no training was given to the mercenaries security was always very bad. It was in any case impossible to disguise the nationality of the mercenaries. The British government was accordingly given the credit/blame for their intervention.

*Conclusions* The mercenary organisation in Yemen played a decisive part in defeating the Egyptian occupation because it raised and sustained Royalist morale.

It could have inflicted much more damage on the enemy factions had it been energetically and efficiently directed in the field. Alternatively, if better trained men had been available its effectiveness would have been considerably greater.

Lack of equipment, particularly suitable radios, was a further disadvantage of the 'amateur status' of the organisation, but this weighed more in the minds of the members than it did in its adverse effect on operations.

National resistance movements can be greatly strengthened at a very small cost in men and equipment by teams experienced in special operations.

Certain lessons from this first foray into mercenary soldiering were to form part of the philosophy of Watchguard in all its undertakings:

1. Individuals had to be carefully briefed on all aspects of the job in hand including the precise aims, scope of activity, expectations, political niceties and operational and personal security.

2. Recruits had to be of the highest order both in terms of experience and strength of character.

3. The director of operations had to be just that, a director who directed, was a leader frequently seen at the sharp end and showed that he was as expert as the men on the ground and fully understood their problems.

Stirling was concerned about the reticence of the Saudi Arabians to take advantage of the ceasefire to consolidate Royalist positions by topping up war supplies, and maintaining

their morale by continued training. The situation remained
almost stalemate with the teams meeting their regular radio
calls and training as and when they were able. With no
direction, and a seeming lack of Saudi interest, it was beginning
to appear as though the teams might be withdrawn from the
Yemen before the termination of the agreed contract and
this, he thought, could stimulate the Egyptians into moving in
and through South Arabia towards their oil objectives. Saudi
Arabia had still not procured the air-defence material which
he considered so necessary to security and he conjectured that
aggressive activities in the Yemen must begin again. He began
to intervene personally, achieving a meeting with Emir Sultan
(Saudi Arabian Minister of Defence) on 4 and 5 March 1966.
It is possible to determine Stirling's thought process from the
following extracts from an aide-memoire he made after the
meeting:

*First Meeting (4th)*
1. There was evidence of Egyptian intentions to attempt the
occupation of the Chizzan and other landing strips on the
border as a possible preliminary to the extension of the war
into Saudi. Some believed that Nasser regarded such action
as a means of galvanising the UN to insist that he withdraw,
thus providing a kind of face-saving formula under which he
could conceivably retreat to a small enclave within the Yemen
while awaiting the phased running down of the British Forces
in Aden. Emir Sultan refuses absolutely this possibility. He
prefers to look upon Nasser as a dictator under duress, capable
and likely to hit out in a last gamble at Saudi Arabia in the
hope of winning an enormous prize.

2. In view of this situation it becomes imperative that the
control arrangements of our mercenaries in the Yemen, and the
directive to which these operatives work, should be adjusted to
conform to the changed circumstances. Prince Sultan welcomed
DS's proposal that . . . the command headquarters of the
Yemen mercenaries should be transferred to Jeddah, and
be at his direct disposal. On implementation of these new
arrangements, the cost of the mercenary force would be met
from Emir Sultan's special Yemen fund.

3. In addition to maintaining existing functions in the Yemen a SAS training cadre should be established capable of recruiting, training, and equipping a SAS-type Special Force able to undertake a full range of the operations characteristic of the SAS rôle. Training and equipment of this Special Force must enable it to approach target areas by air (helicopter, etc.); overland (jeeps, etc.); and by sea (MTBs, etc.). Ideally the training of the Special Force should be taken on . . . officially by the SAS.

4. The Special Force could not achieve a state of operational readiness in less than 9 months to 1 year. Accordingly, to help Emir Sultan in the present crisis circumstances I suggested that the present terms of reference of the mercenaries . . . should be revised and extended; that a further 7 to 10 mercenaries be recruited . . . and that the existing radio facilities increase proportionately, together with the establishing of an appropriate transport unit. During this period certain operations, such as destroying aircraft on the ground at Sa'dah airport, should be undertaken . . .

5. We agreed the need to put a new emphasis on restricting the mobility of the Egyptian forces by disrupting the full length of their communications system from Hodeida to Sa'dah and northwards from Sa'dah. If, however, the Egyptians did succeed in establishing for themselves a forward air force on such as one of the Chizzan landing strips, the mercenaries should be in a position to tackle the aircraft and installations there.

*Second Meeting (5th)* At a very brief second meeting Emir Sultan requested, and I concurred, that I should put in writing and sign a brief but formal undertaking that I would bring out soonest those primarily responsible for the operations in the Yemen to Jeddah. He needed this formal note to reassure King Feisal (who was leaving the following morning for Khartoum) that effective action was being taken. It was agreed that these further meetings should be held from a date not later than March 16th, and that documentation on our verbal proposal be tabled at that time. Finally, I must emphasise that Emir Sultan was most insistent that nobody, apart from those present at the meeting and those with whom I had to discuss the proposals in order to act on them, should know anything about our meeting.

The year progressed with continual meetings which seemed to bring no positive forward movement. The Yemen operation quietly ticked over with Mike Gooley running the Expedient Force as it had become known. Stirling decided to push things a little. His concerns are shown in a letter to King Feisal written in November 1966:

Sir,

May it please Your Majesty that I write to beg an audience to discuss the present situation in the Yemen.

I would suggest to Your Majesty that while the essential supplies continue to flow into the Yemen from Ṣaudi Arabia and while Colonel Johnson's men remain at the disposal of the Royalists, Nasser's army will remain largely immobilised because its only supply route from Hodeida to Sana'a will continue to be under constant threat of disruption. As long as this situation is maintained, Nasser will be inhibited from risking any significant scaled overland thrust to the north. He will have to content himself with the possibly erroneous assumption in these circumstances of his capability of annexing the South Arabian Federation and Aden when the British leave in 1968.

However, should the European technicians be withdrawn from the Yemen, reliable radio communications within the Yemen will be largely eliminated and the morale of the Royalist leaders and of the leaders of the South Arabian Federation will be much lowered, because this withdrawal would inevitably signify to them the disengagement of Your Majesty from the presently concerted defence against Nasser.

In these circumstances I beg to submit to Your Majesty that consideration be given to these following proposals:

1. That Colonel Johnson's men be contracted to remain in the Yemen for a further period of at least six months from the expiry date (December 31st) of the existing contract and allowed to undertake more offensive operations than they are at the moment.

2. That encouragement be given to the preparation of detailed plans by the South Arabian Federal Army to send a fully trained and equipped force of about 100 men into the Yemen.

3. That maximum possible pressure be exerted to delay final withdrawal of the British presence from South Arabia until the end of 1968, by which time Your Majesty's defence procurement programme should be well advanced.

The timing of a renewal of aggressiveness by the Royalists in the Yemen would remain at Your Majesty's discretion; but all the necessary preparations should, I submit, be made forthwith to ensure a proper state of readiness. (It would seem that the time to renew the initiative in the Yemen must now be imminent – because the 'Magic Carpet' token airforce* will be very soon ready to counter Egyptian air raids across the border.)

Furthermore, if the Royalists and the South Arabian Federali are not effectively supported by Saudi Arabia, and consequently their opposition collapses, Nasser will be able to pose as the great liberator and democratiser of the Yemen and South Arabia and his next step will surely be to 'liberate' the whole Arabian continent.

It is therefore with all these points in mind that I request an audience and in the event of Your Majesty agreeing to discuss these proposals I would like to suggest how they could be effectively and rapidly implemented.

Stirling still believed that the attack point in any venture should be at the top of the tree. If he engineered a personal audience with King Feisal he was confident that his powers of persuasion would win the day. In the letter he was already sowing the seeds of a proposal to supervise the recruiting, training and direction of a specially trained force of Federalis should this prove to be impossible for HMG to consider as a task for the SAS; but, as a first step, it was of paramount importance that Johnson's contract be renewed.

In the meantime he had, through his own British political connections, been trying to further the cause of Geoffrey Edwards in getting the all-important airforce established in Saudi Arabia. Edwards had himself attended the meetings of 4 and 5 March, a measure of the esteem in which he

---

* This refers to the air defence procurement deal being masterminded by Edwards.

was held by the Saudis at the time. During this waiting phase
Stirling, as well as exerting pressure on the ministers of the
Federali, introduced a new element with the establishment
of Quail PR International. He had spotted that should his
proposals succeed there would be scope aplenty for setting
up a broadcasting system as part of an active propaganda
operation which could be turned into the basis of a national
broadcasting service on the advent of peace.

A significant meeting took place at the Crescent Hotel in
Aden on 10 December 1966. It is necessary to reproduce
the rather long minutes of this meeting if the far-reaching
possibilities of the conclusions are to be appreciated.

*Meeting with Sheikhs Mohammed Farid (First Minister and
Minister of External Affairs) and Girgirah (Minister of Information)*

A. *Introduction*
I had planned to hold this meeting after I had been to Riyadh
and before going on to Teheran, but the timetable didn't work
out; in the event it was probably better that I saw the Federali
before going to Riyadh.

Before setting up the meeting I checked the present state of
the game with Ashworth. He was helpful but depressed – and
insisted there was no chance whatsoever of persuading HMG
to delay the departure schedule from Aden. His personal
advice to Mohammed Farid and Girgirah (with whom he had
dined the evening before) was to the effect that the Federali
should be prepared to settle for an ambiguous statement
by HMG hopefully causing Nasser to pause before taking
any irrevocable step towards occupying Aden. Ashworth has
obviously great respect for the Federali and admires the way
their government has stuck together, in spite of tremendous
pressures from Cairo and FLOSY. In a word, Ashworth
was feeling thoroughly frustrated – clearly the current HMG
directive was highly distasteful to him, but one to which he
had to conform.

Before inviting Girgirah to the meeting in my room at the
Crescent Hotel, I checked his security status with Mohammed
Farid, who vouched for him with absolute confidence.

B. *Results of Federali Meeting with King Feisal in Riyadh on December 3rd*

Originally, as conceived by Ahmed Shami, Sharif Hussein and Mohammed Farid, the purpose of the meeting had been for the Royalists and the Federali to make a joint presentation to King Feisal. This plan had to be abandoned because Prince Mohammed bin Hussein (in effect the Royalist commander-in-chief), had lost patience with King Feisal's go-slow tactics in the Yemen, and had . . . most inadvisably gone on his own initiative to seek help from the Shah of Persia and from King Hussein; after having predictably failed in his purpose he holed out – more or less incommunicado – in Beirut. (I was in Teheran at the same time as Prince Mohammed bin Hussein, and had been closely questioned by the Shah's Chief of Internal Security on what I supposed was the Prince's motive in visiting Teheran.)

On the failure of the joint approach the Federali team of ministers, through the good offices of Sheikh Hafiz Wahba, were finally received by King Feisal on December 3rd, after having kicked their heels in Jeddah and Riyadh for over two weeks. The main positive result of the meeting was a grant of £612 million for the development of communications in the South Arabia Federation. On the Yemen situation they got no response, and only the vaguest of assurances on the long-term question of a post-British withdrawal military post. (The Federali were, however, exceedingly pleased with the financial grant as it greatly enhanced their political status in the Federation.)

C. *DS's efforts to help reactivate Royalists in Yemen and to delay British withdrawal from Aden*

I showed Mohammed Farid and Girgirah my letter to King Feisal and Emir Sultan – the former had approved a draft of the letter when we had met two weeks before in Riyadh – and both confirmed the unequivocal support of the Federali behind the letter. I then gave them an account of our efforts to implement the letter's main objectives . . .

(a) While last in London (in early December) I had contacted Alec Douglas-Home and written him a letter accompanied by a draft of the letter to King Feisal. I suggested he discuss the position with Geoffrey Edwards shortly due back in London.

This meeting took place, which enabled Douglas-Home to lead the debate in the House of Commons on the Middle East policy with up-to-date and effective ammunition. (Both had already read a full account of the speech – and Girgirah, as Minister of Information, stated that it was a good example of Quail's enterprising technique in PR!)

(b) During my last visit to Teheran I had discussed the situation very fully with the Shah's Chief of Internal Security (General Nesiri), and our conversations had been taped (*and* taken down in shorthand!), to enable him to provide H.I.M. with an authoritative transcript. On my return to London I gave Ardeshir Zahedi a draft of the Feisal letter (in the form of a memorandum) so that he could advise H.I.M. of the position by letter. (Jim Johnson subsequently gave the Ambassador a full sitrep on the Yemen situation.) I explained that I was returning to Teheran on the night of 13th December to see General Nesiri. The Shah is most anxious to see Royalist activity in the Yemen stepped up again and there is no doubt that he will use all his influence with King Feisal to achieve this end.

(c) While in Nairobi I had a meeting with President Jomo Kenyatta, and several meetings with two of the President's inner cabinet. One of the latter, Bruce McKenzie, was returning to London to accompany me to a meeting with the Minister of Defence (Denis Healey, with whom McKenzie has long been a close friend). President Kenyatta's interest and anxiety about the British withdrawal from Aden was easily explained by the fact that Kenya was under increasing pressure from Nasser and the Communists on the Somali frontier, in the same way that pressure was being applied on the Federali from the Yemen. (Both Mohammed Farid and Girgirah were particularly impressed by this point.)

(d) I explained that the purpose of the meeting with the UK Minister of Defence on Friday, December 16th was (1) to add Kenya's voice to the others concerning the imperative importance of delaying the British withdrawal from Aden to the latest possible moment in 1968; (2) to urge the Minister to give every possible help to the Federali Army during the interim period; (3) to suggest that the squadron of Hunters based in Aden should overfly the Yemen and Saudi Arabia en route to or from Bahrain having gained authority to do so from Saudi and the Royalists); and (4) to provide support as necessary to ensure the final signing up of the Saudi Defence deal.

D. *Watchguard International Ltd and Quail PR International Ltd*

I gave Mohammed Farid and Girgirah all information needed on Watchguard International, and particularly stressed that there was no official relationship whatsoever between the company and any government.

It was agreed that the main functions of the Federali task force would be:

1. to harass the south flank of the triangle held by Nasser's army.

2. to carry out various sabotage operations on the Egyptians' communication system between Hodeida and Taiz, and from Taiz to Sana'a.

3. to apply pressure on the tribes in this area to defect from loyalty to the republican regime.

4. to interrupt the flow of Egyptian-trained insurgents infiltrating Aden from Taiz.

The three main methods whereby Watchguard International could assist the Federali to achieve these objectives were:

(a) to advise on recruiting procedures and special training requirements

(b) to help define in detail the precise functions of the Federali task force and to advise on its equipment

(c) to help establish an effective radio communication system maintaining contact with the task force headquarters, say, in Beihan, and with Johnson's force headquarters in Jeddah.

It was also agreed that training should start at the earliest practical date for the Special Intelligence Sections to enable the Federali to take over responsibility for internal security from the UK, and also to be capable of assessing information flowing from the task force in the Yemen. In the likely event of HMG blocking the transfer of responsibility for internal security, the Federali must have the capability of acting on their own initiative. It was also essential to extract from HMG's security system all relevant information on Nasser and FLOSY's subversive activities, and dossiers on the agents involved.

### E. *The Effective Spokesmanship for the Federali Cause*
Effective spokesmanship to the outside world was immediately essential and this could be carried out by Quail International working direct to the Minister of Information (i.e. Girgirah). This work had already been carried out to some extent by DS, but it was essential to have arrangements properly formalised and supported by an adequate budget.

### F. *Provision of Finance for D. and E. above*
It was agreed that the most effective method of financing the objectives outlined in D. above was direct from Emir Sultan's special budget, on the same lines as are already operative for the financing of Johnson's force. Accordingly, I promised to present such a proposal to Emir Sultan.

In the event of there being no response to the Federali appeal as presented by me in Riyadh, it was agreed that I should approach the Shah of Iran on their behalf – after having told the Saudis of our intention. Assistance from this source would be fairly easy to administer, although obviously more complicated than getting the finance from Saudi.

I also suggested that the Federali should establish a special fund, and explained how it could be set up. However, I had to emphasise that assistance from this source would take too long, and would not in any case be enough to cover the Federalis' present needs.

We discussed the scale of the financing requirement, and agreed that something of the order of £100,000 a year through 1968, and an initial outlay of, say, £40,000 for equipment should be sufficient for the Arabian task force consisting, say, of 30 officers and men and 3 Watchguard liaison operatives.

I assured Mohammed Farid and Girgirah that Watchguard International and Quail International would prepare draft budgets for submission to them at the earliest possible date.

### G. *Tentative Time Schedule*
I suggested the following tentative time schedule:

Jan 1st: DS returns with draft preliminary plans and budgets for consideration by the Federali, covering the task force, the establishing of internal security intelligence service and of an overseas public relations apparatus.

Jan 18th: DS accompanied by JW, Director of Operations and an intelligence expert, arrive in Aden with second draft of plans, schedules and budgets.

Feb/Mar/Apr: Provided the Federali plans are completed and approved, and the source of finance assured at the meeting in Riyadh, recruiting both for the task force and the intelligence sections could begin in mid-February, and training started by mid-April. In the meantime a training cadre would be under instruction by JW in the UK and in parallel with this the designated intelligence expert would be studying and preparing a training curriculum.

Apr: Instructors should be ready to leave for Aden.

May/Jun: The initial task force of about 30 officers and men, could be operational by late May, provided that the recruits had already received basic military training in the Federali Force. The intelligence set up, however, might take considerably longer to become operational.

## H. *Task Force Security*
I questioned Mohammed Farid and Girgirah on security, and they were both anxious to maintain secrecy, and stated that the proposals would not, at this stage, be disclosed to anyone even in the Federali except Sharif Hussein. This seemed to make sense.

It must be noted that in order not to embarrass HMG it may be necessary for one of Watchguard International's overseas branches to handle this contract.

## I. *The Federali and George Brown*
Mohammed Farid and Girgirah were particularly incensed with George Brown, partly because of his much publicised discussions with Nasser's envoy in Moscow, and partly due to the Foreign Minister's betrayal of an absolute commitment he made with Mohammed Farid not to announce any specific date for independence until further discussions had been held on the subject and the text prepared for a joint announcement. In spite of this undertaking Turnbull (HC), on his return from London, gave the date as likely to be towards the end of 1967. The implication of this statement is that the withdrawal will have been completed prior to that date.

## K. *Conclusion*
Our discussion convinced us of the great significance that even

a token task force could have in South Yemen. It would have the effect of committing the Federali as a whole, including Aden, to the Nasser front, and might well result in tribes in the South of the Yemen at present wobbly in their support of the Republic to defect on a large scale. This in turn would cut down on Nasser's present capacity to use Taiz as a training and launching base for his agents provocateurs for Aden.

It is my conviction that if King Feisal and the Shah were confident of the Federali taking the initiative in respect of internal security within Aden, and of their capacity to mount an effective task force in the Yemen, both would be prepared to discuss a joint defence pact with the South Arabian Federation, to become operative on the withdrawal of the British presence. Moreover, it would in my view be well worthwhile attempting to negotiate an even more widely based defence treaty – one which would include Kenya and Ethiopia.

Aden, December 10th, 1966
David Stirling

Stirling's follow-up notes to the meetings display the speed with which he took advantage of chance meetings (Morgan Mann) and his flexibility in handling a situation of which he was not aware (Johnson's diplomatic gaffe).

*Meetings in Riyadh, December 12th*
I arrived in Jeddah on 11th December in time to meet Geoffrey Edwards at the airport (he was leaving for London on the aircraft in which I had flown from Aden), and he told me that he had delivered to Shaikh Hafiz Wahba* my letter to King Feisal, and had requested him to make arrangements for me to see HM the following day.

1. *UK Ambassador*
I travelled next morning (12th) to Riyadh, chancing to be on the same aircraft as Morgan Mann (UK Ambassador in Saudi) and was thus able to show him the letter to King Feisal and my

---

* Ex-Saudi Ambassador in London, and then political adviser to King Feisal.

correspondence with Alec Douglas-Home, and to give him a rough draft of the minutes of my meeting with the Federali. The Ambassador was going . . . to see the King that same morning and I prevailed upon him to discuss my letter with HM, with particular reference to the three proposals. Mann emphasised that he would have to raise the subject 'unofficially'. We made arrangements to lunch together with Shaikh Hafiz so that we could discuss King Feisal's reactions to the letter with him, and I could then better plan tactics. (Shaikh Hafiz is a 100% ally of ours.)

## 2. *Shaikh Hafiz Wahba*

On arrival in Riyadh I immediately contacted Shaikh Hafiz, who then went off to see the King; he telephoned later to say that HM had already read the letter and discussed it with his brother, Emir Sultan, whom he had instructed to see me at 4.30 that afternoon.

At lunch Morgan Mann said that at the end of his audience . . . he raised the subject of my letter to HM, who had immediately referred back to what he called 'Colonel Johnson's rude ultimatum'. HM had evidently been very incensed by JJ's paper – otherwise he or his brother would have explained the background and reasons for his present go-slow tactics in the Yemen. HM was evidently still exasperated, but responded to Morgan Mann's explanation that JJ was a highly effective soldier/businessman who was frustrated by the unexplained insistence on inactivity in the Yemen, and had been honest enough to say so, in admittedly untactful terms. (I must state here, however, that HM was so emphatic in his complaint that Morgan Mann has felt reluctantly compelled to note HM's reaction in his official FO despatches – a fact I undertook to pass on to JJ.)

Regarding the letter, Morgan Mann confirmed that HM had passed it to Emir Sultan with instructions to discuss it with me later that afternoon and suggesting that Shaikh Hafiz act as interpreter.

## 3. *Emir Sultan – Minister of Defence*

The meeting with Emir Sultan was satisfactory. Shaikh Hafiz was a superbly good interpreter, because he understood and sympathised with all the points raised. The outcome of our discussions was briefly as follows:

a. The budget for the Johnson Force was to be renewed until the end of February.

b. At an early date after Ramadan he wished to have discussions with JJ regarding an agreement on a longer-term contract.

c. He welcomed and agreed in principle with all my proposals in support of the Federali and requested that I submit an implementation budget in mid-January (we discussed these proposals as outlined in the minutes of meeting with Mohammed Farid and Girgirah at considerable length).

d. He asked that I should be accompanied at this January meeting by one of Sharif Hussein's sons rather than by Mohammed Farid or Girgirah because the latter were too well known in Jeddah and Riyadh and would inevitably excite comment, which would get back to Nasser.

e. He stressed that points (a), (b), and (c) above had to remain subject to the overall decision to reactivate pressure on Nasser in the Yemen, which was unlikely to be made until after Ramadan.

Both Shaikh Hafiz and myself, when comparing notes after the meeting, were convinced that King Feisal's insistence in avoiding all Nasser-provoking activity in the Yemen was due to a conglomeration of reasons, many of which were no longer valid. The most important single factor still relevant was the Saudis' continued vulnerability to air attack until the Magic Carpet deterrent was fully effective, probably in mid-February. It was understandable that King Feisal should wish to make it appear that this further period of inactivity was a deliberate policy in the interests of peace, rather than one imposed on him by circumstances.

During the meeting Emir Sultan recalled somewhat plaintively that when we had last met (on the occasion when Geoffrey Edwards and myself had suggested, with JJ's full support, that the finance for the Johnson force should be paid direct rather than through Ahmed Shami) he had made it clear he expected JJ to conform to the Saudi directive, on the principle of 'the piper paying for the tune'.

In the circumstances I thought it tactful to apologise on Jim's behalf for the aggressive tone of his ultimatum (of which, incidentally, I have never seen the text), but went on to reinforce the Ambassador's observations that JJ was understandably miffed by both Emir Sultan's 'do nothing' directive and by his procrastination regarding a decision on JJ's insistent pleas for a reasonably long-term budget to enable him to plan ahead.

Riyadh, December 12th, 1966

Whilst Stirling was patiently continuing to advance his proposals in Saudi Arabia and the Yemen, tailoring them to meet the ever-changing circumstances, the Watchguard director of operations was making steady inroads into the African marketplace. In London the basis of a supplementary company was being created to work out of Queen Street. Kulinda Security Ltd was to be registered in the UK, and in order to widen the scope of the overall operation it was to examine the potential for capitalising on the domestic security market which seemed set to broaden with the advent of high-technology-based commercial espionage in competitive industries. On board the flagship Watchguard, however, all was not well despite the fact that the concept was viable and could be undeniably useful to HMG.

# 21

# SNAKES AND LADDERS

By the end of February 1967 tacit approval had been given to Stirling's budgetary estimates for the creation of a South Arabian task force. No detailed formal proposal had yet been put forward. Working closely with Bernard Mills (ex-SAS and involved from the early stages in the Yemen project), he had succeeded in setting up an unofficial 'committee' of those close to King Feisal: Emir Sultan (brother); Kamal Adham (brother-in-law); Doctor Rashud Faroun ('special adviser') and Geoffrey Edwards (a founding, and part-funding, member of Watchguard International). Stirling was also keeping his contacts alive in Teheran and informing them of each move – presumably in case back-up finances were required from the Shah.

His early request that the existing Yemen force of mercenaries with their radio network should come directly under his control was met with a rebuff; this was viewed as the personal province of Prince Zaid Sudairy and very quickly Mike Gooley (not of Watchguard) was confirmed in his status as 'Commander of the Advisory Group attached to the Royalist Yemen Army' by the order of the Minister of Defence (Prince Sultan Ibn Aziz Al Saud). Undaunted, Stirling offered all possible support to Gooley and agreed to complement his manpower from Watchguard resources in order that Expedient could expand its rôle. It can be surmised that the loyalty which Prince Zaid had expressed towards Gooley was tempered by another factor. Watchguard was making overtures across the Middle East (including the setting up of a corps d'élite in Saudi Arabia) and Africa; the openness of Stirling's approach in Iran was particularly unwise. He had also made 'discreet' enquiries into the potential offered by Jordan and he still travelled regularly to Israel. Gossip spreads with amazing speed in the Middle East; small wonder that potential clients began to wonder whether their secrets would be safe with Watchguard.

Encouraged by the verbal agreement to the task force initiative, Stirling put forward his formal proposal on 14 July 1967. His introduction includes his suggested interim strategy.

The momentum of the Royalist Yemeni advance following on the partial Egyptian withdrawal has now slackened. While the Royalists have succeeded in negotiating the early delivery of substantial fresh supplies of arms and equipment from Saudi, the Egyptians would seem to be stiffening their resolve on orders from Cairo – orders no doubt prompted from Moscow; to date the only evidence of this stiffening is increased air activity, including one gas attack.

As of now (July 14th) it would seem intelligent to assume that a further increase of Egyptian air activity may well be capable of frustrating any significant further Royalist encroachment of republican-controlled territory – more especially because a Hodeida-based aircraft can become operationally viable before the Royalist resupply can take effect. In these circumstances one must feel anxiety concerning the Royalist intention to remain concentrated in assembly areas now well known to the Egyptians and therefore vulnerable to bombing. We respectfully suggest that it would be a sounder plan if the Royalists resumed multiple but small-scale harassing guerrilla operations based on the new areas recently won, rather than persist in planning formal and frontal attacks on a tactical scale against major objectives.

There are in compensation certain highly favourable factors which, if imaginatively exploited, could enable the Royalists to resume the initiative with little risk of heavy casualties but with war-winning potential.

Let me summarise these factors and then suggest an interim overall strategy:

1. The Egyptians withdrew, during the Israeli War, the bulk of their tanks, armoured cars and mobile guns. Unlike aircraft, these cannot be quickly replaced.

2. The responsibility held by the Hashid for the Sa'adah/Sana'a Road, for the garrisoning of Sa'adah itself and the responsibility, as I understand it, for maintaining the security of the immediate Western approaches of the Sana'a Road to Hodeida must make all those vulnerable to Royalist political and military action.

3. The arrival (enfin!) of the ammunition for the light and therefore 'manhandleable' eight-mile-range mortars under competent French leaders and their positioning at an early date within range of Sana'a on the 'Woodhouse Spur' is of inestimable importance.

4. The clearing of the coastal plain of Egyptians to a point including and beyond the small port of Midi, opens up opportunities of supply of seaborne materials to maintain a further advance down the plains towards Hodeida.

5. The main Sana'a/Hodeida Road is now highly vulnerable.

6. The morale of the Egyptian soldier, already low before the Israeli War, has probably now taken a further dip.

*Suggested Interim Yemen Strategy*
In the light of the facts as outlined above I would suggest the mounting of three major initiatives:

1. The immediate setting up of a sabotage strike force to harass and deny the use of the Sana'a/Hodeida Road to the enemy.

2. In parallel with this, every effort should be made to harass the Egyptians within Sana'a – in particular by the positioning of the French mortars within striking range.

3. The developing of raids on the approaches to Hodeida down the coastal plain and the gradual formation of a substantial force supplied with some degree of armoured capability, supplied through the landing facilities at Midi.

4. Systematic pressure on Egyptian morale.

The organisation Stirling envisaged was for a headquarters based at Jeddah controlling a supply depot at Chizzan and servicing a forward operational HQ which would have at its disposal five sabotage patrols tasked, in an ideal world, to carry out one road-blocking operation every fourth night. Gooley's Expedient Force would provide communications. Stirling would have needed to recruit a minimum of thirty British ex-servicemen. It is interesting to note one of the paragraphs under 'Outline of Organisation and Operational Procedures':

*The Force Commander*, David Stirling, will be responsible direct to the Prince in command of the area. The Force Commander's interpreter may be, it is hoped, Ahmed Al Hazimi. It is not possible yet to say where the Force Commander will be based, but it will be somewhere south of Abst – possibly close either to Haras or Khokopan. It is at present planned that David Smiley will be appointed as adviser to the Prince in command.

Stirling was then fifty-one years old!
The operational timetable left little room for tea breaks:

*July 14th*: Stirling in London and calls emergency meeting of all executive Directors of Watchguard.

*July 15th*: Consultation with Sayed Ahmed Shami. Bernard Mills arrives London.

*July 18th*: Mills accompanied by officer QM arrives Jeddah to check Saudi sources of arms, transport and general equipment.

*July 25th*: Stirling returns Jeddah with first patrol personnel; flies to Chizzan 29th July, meets interpreter and starts reconnaissance for forward command base.

*July 27th*: First supply jeeps start initial lift of supplies from Chizzan to forward base.

*August 3rd*: 2nd patrol arrives at forward base with liaison officer; both teams make reconnaissance of Hodeida/Sana'a Road.

*August 5th*: Stirling takes up command at forward base and operations start.

*August 12th*: 3rd patrol arrives Chizzan. Recruitment and initial training course of Yemeni in order to set up sabotage school for Yemeni. By August 18th the support administrative staff will have been posted to their various assignments in Jeddah, Chizzan and to the forward base HQ.

*August 19th*: Training Officer in Chizzan despatches 3rd patrol team with trained Yemenis; 4th and 5th patrol team arrive Chizzan.

*August 26th*: 4th and 5th patrol teams despatched to forward base accompanied by training officer who will set up training school for local Royalist Yemenis on simple forms of sabotage, including mining of roads. All major demolition projects will be the responsibility of British-led patrols.

*Supplementary Comments*
The road-blocking operation is not likely to be required for a period of more than 6–8 months at the most. Subsequently, however, the five sabotage patrols could be consolidated into a task force with an operational rôle consistent with the then prevailing military situation.

If the Watchguard contract is terminated at the end of six months, the British personnel should be compensated by a three-month terminal pay with a further, and I suggest substantial, bonus added in the event of Watchguard's operation being outstandingly successful.

In submitting the terms of pay for the Watchguard Company and its personnel, I have kept in mind that the operational rôle is a fighting one, demanding the highest level of leadership, courage, skill and initiative. The success of the undertaking would provide incalculable benefits to both the Yemen and to South Arabia as well as to Saudi Arabia itself.

*The Coastal Operation*
Watchguard proposals under this heading are so secret as necessarily to be restricted at this stage to verbal discussion.

*Psychological and Intelligence Operations*
Our proposals on these important activities must be restricted
to verbal discussion.

*Conclusion*
In effect Watchguard in this paper has submitted the proposition
that active fighting mercenary activities in the Yemen, with the
exception of the French Field Force, be centred on Watchguard
International while the radio network remain the independent
responsibility of Mike Gooley's organisation with which we
shall work in the closest concert. We will continue to assist
Gooley in all ways open to us including recruiting and
training, etc. when so required. In our view Gooley is doing
an excellent job and enjoys the complete confidence of Prince
Zaid Sudairy.

If our plans outlined in this paper are adopted and the
necessary financial provision becomes immediately available
together with the necessary equipment and stores, we can
categorically state that we can meet the Road Operation
timetable commitments.

The Watchguard Proposal pursued with vigour and competence provides the Royalist cause with a strategic blue-
print which would enable them to hasten the winning of
the war.


Stirling had sent the proposal for the Yemen task force
directly to Prince Sultan, Minister of Defence; he had not
learned the lesson of his earlier rebuff. On hearing that he
had made a blunder he wrote immediately to try to repair the
damage:

SECRET                                                    Jeddah

23rd July 1967

Your Royal Highness,

I recently had the honour to submit to you a short paper
entitled *Proposals for a CORPS D'ELITE prepared for the
KINGDOM OF SAUDI ARABIA*. I do hope Your Royal
Highness will find it possible to discuss these proposals at
an early date. I have with me on this visit Colonel John

Woodhouse, my Director of Operations, who should, I suggest, take part in our discussions.

Last week I also had delivered to you a paper headed *A Proposal from Watchguard International for the Formation and Deployment of a Task Force in the YEMEN*. This paper was concerned with the destruction on a massive scale (using relatively sophisticated sabotage techniques) of the Sana'a–Hodeida road with the supplementary but vital further objective of destroying gas bomb bearing aircraft on the ground.

After sending you this second paper I was informed that I should have delivered it first to Mr Gooley in his capacity as your appointed Commander of the British mercenaries in the Yemen. Accordingly Colonel Woodhouse and myself have now talked with Prince Zaid Sudairy and Mr Gooley and we have put at their disposal any help that they might wish from us – particularly in respect of the recruitment of suitable individuals to enable Mr Gooley to expand his Force to undertake its additional highly exacting rôles.

I would like to assure Your Royal Highness that Prince Zaid and Mr Gooley can always continue to count on any assistance it is within our capacity to provide.

I beg to remain, etc.

In this instance Watchguard did not succeed in pushing through the proposal although there was to be some commercial return. Sustaining a 'marketing' drive is expensive often out of all proportion to the seemingly healthy rewards. Watchguard had been active in these endeavours for about two years and the Middle East apportionment of effort had eaten heavily into operating funds as the agenda for the board meeting in London in July 1967 of the Kulinda Security directors shows.

1   *Minutes of previous meeting*

2. *Review of financial situation*
A rough survey to be tabled by the Chairman and to be commented on by the Company Accountant and the other Directors.

Offices – decision on alternative to Queen Street premises . . .

3. *Saudi Arabia and South Arabia*
a) Report by Director of Operations and Chairman on 'Y' proposals and the outcome of negotiations.

b) Duties expected to be carried out by the Company in consideration of the £1,500-a-month retainer to be paid by the Saudi government.

c) Chairman's 'Y' visit; its purposes.

d) South Arabia contract – present position involving the continued maintenance of radio station. Prospects of the re-establishment of the contract on original scale.

e) The Corps d'Elite; Chairman's proposal to redesign the . . . project to conform with likely result of Gaunt report on the Saudi Navy, and to make possible collaboration with the Magic Carpet set-up.

4. *Africa*
a) Report from Director of Operations on his proposed negotiating schedule: i) Kenya; ii) Zambia; iii) Tanzania; iv) Malawi; together with an appraisal of the costs involved up to the stage when African activities become viable.

b) Discussion and decision on the best and simplest way of presenting contractual terms for African based contracts.

5. *Renewal of pressure* on [companies and individuals to assist with finance].

6. *UK Operations* A review of Archie Stirling's report; discussion and decision on first steps and the financial implications of any such action. [This report considered the markets possibly open to a security company to establish a firm financial base for Kulinda.]


The notes from which Stirling spoke on item 2, the financial review, show the outcome to date of the negotiations and the extent to which Watchguard had invested in the project.

The decision to cancel Watchguard's contract in South Arabia (apart from maintaining the radio station until the end of this year) – a contract which was to have grossed £126,000 over 12 months – together with the decision to increase the size of the Gooley Force in the Yemen rather than to employ Watchguard for the more aggressive functions, the failure to obtain a decision for Watchguard to establish a Corps d'Elite in Saudi Arabia, and the possibility of securing two contracts in Africa, calls for the drawing up of a situation report on Watchguard's commitments in the UK, Saudi Arabia and Africa.

Below I do a 'blind' assessment of the extent of residual funds at Watchguard's disposal after the winding up of Watchguard's South Arabian contract at the end of the year; presuming a negative decision on the establishing of a Corps d'Elite; and including expenditure on the Company's current negotiations in Africa, and finally an estimate of the cost of setting up an active UK business.

*Outgoings*

i) Total amount expended by Kulinda and Watchguard as at July 31st 1967 (This is a rough estimate and will need detailed accounting by JS for an accurate figure):                    £24,000

ii) Cost of financing the adverse salary differential of Watchguard personnel accepting service with the Gooley Force*:
Name 1: £100.00 per month
Name 2: £ 50.00 per month
Name 3: £ 75.00 per month
Name 4: £ 75.00 per month
Total for 5 months:                              £1500

iii) Staff officer for the Gooley Force, who will be paid entirely by Watchguard at £375 per month. Total for 5 months:  £1875

iv) London and Jersey overheads at £2300 per month. Total for 5 months:

---

* Watchguard personnel serving with the Gooley Force had their pay boosted from company resources. The reasoning was that they would remain primarily on call to Watchguard in the event of one of the proposals being accepted; they were also gaining valuable experience of working in the Middle East with irregular soldiers. The differential ensured that the men would return for such duties.

£11500

v) Return air fares London/Jeddah for Stirling and Woodhouse and continuing negotiations to set up a Corps d'Elite. Total for 5 months:                                                £1200

vi) Negotiating and setting-up expenditure of projects in Africa:                                              £2200

vii) Cost of maintaining South Arabian radio station for 5 months:                                               £5400

viii) Therefore total expenditure as at 31st December 1967 can be estimated to be                              £47675


Although none of Watchguard's full proposals to Saudi and South Arabia was to reach fruition, Stirling did not stop trying until the uneasy peace was finally negotiated. Some of his ideas were modified and accepted into the charter of the enhanced Gooley Force (Expedient). These training operations, increased activities and the risk to the mercenaries can be gleaned from one of the Force's weekly intelligence summaries:

*Yemen Intsum No. 36 (22–29 August 1967)*
1. *General & Political* The week has been eventful. The whole Yemen situation falls at this time in the shadow of Middle East politics and the Arab Summit Conference. There are many indications that the Egyptian position in the Yemen is unstable and that they can only negotiate from a position of weakness. Whether the pro-Royalist factions allow the Israeli question to be used by the Egyptians to Egyptian advantage in the Yemen remains to be seen. Certainly any 'solution' to be worthy of the name should have at least tolerance from the opposing Yemeni factions. It is very difficult to see what solution is going to meet this, the more especially as they do not appear to have been consulted, and certainly the Royalists can be expected to demand a hard bargain to justify their five-year struggle.

Three Expedient members were killed in a savage incident on the afternoon of 24th August near Amarah while on a routine liaison trip. They were buried in the French camp near Najran. The incident is the subject of a separate report.

One member of a Red Cross party was shot in the arm in an incident with the Dahm between Boa and Matama on night of 27/28. They were on their way to Harram. Sarda was announced to be under Royalist control by the Prime Minister, Al Hassan, early on 26th August. The historic area fell to the Royalists despite a concentrated Egyptian air effort in support of the Republicans. It is fair to say that this is the best single Royalist advance for some years. It is also significant that the Egyptians did not resort to gas despite their frantic air effort.

2. *Royalists* Sarda and the area are now under Royalist control. The Prime Minister has moved forward to As Sinnarah, his old home, overlooking the town.

All the fighting Royalist princes are in aggressive positions and a new spirit is apparent.

The ranger teams from Qassim Monasser, Mohammed Shardah and Ali Obeida have now reported to the Ranger School for training. The first course, which was drawn from picked men of the Amarah Garrison, has been completed. The syllabus, especially designed for the situation, included the invention of one new expedient weapon and variations on known techniques. The response of the trainees was reported as excellent.

A raiding force from Ali Obeida attacked the area of the radio station on the outskirts of Sana'a at 262200C. They reported a number of Egyptians killed.

A strong force was sent from the Amarah Garrison commanded by Brigadier Siraj personally to the area of the ambush of the Expedient group. They are reported to have destroyed half the village buildings as a reprisal and have brought back nine hostages against the production of the three killers.

3. *Enemy* Following information from Secretary Conde, just returned from trip round Sana'a-Taiz-Hodeida:
– Russian strength Sana'a: 50 uniformed – estimates 500 Hodeida – some uniformed.
– Sana'a–Hodeida road insecure from sniping.
– Much feeling against Egyptians/Republicans generally.
– Terrorist activity Taiz and Aden nationalist factions squabbling.
– Egyptian presence diminishing especially around Sana'a.

Following from interrogation of Egyptian deserters at Qara (23 Aug):

- Names: Rifat Ali Ashati; Mohammed Abduljelil Razag:
- Drivers in Regt. Q4. Deserted from Sana'a Garrison 25 days before. Egyptian morale very low. Not told of Sinai defeat until 6 weeks afterwards. Estimate Sana'a Garrison and environs down to 7–10000 and 8000 were moved to Egypt via Hodeida during Sinai emergency. Egyptian tour of duty in Yemen is 3 years without home leave.
- Egyptian orbat Sana'a: 5th Div. composed: Infantry Q4, Q14, Q15 Bns. Q311 Arty. Q4 commanded by Maj Shogi Kemal Michael. Previous commander Maj Hafud Heta – transferred to 15th Div (armd) at time of Sinai, majority of which went to Egypt. Commander 5th Div is Brig-Gen Mansur Fetha.

4. *Expedient*:
- FIREBALL is to time scale.
- 5 teams deployed Yemen plus Ranger School.
- Expedient strength 30: 24 Arabia, 6 UK leave.
- French strength 29: 23 Arabia, 6 Europe leave.

Stirling took small satisfaction from knowing that some of his ideas were being used; he had expected more. He concentrated on tailoring his proposals to make the Saudi Arabian Corps d'Elite more attractive. This was not to be, but the studies, the formulation and reformulation of proposals, the budgeting and negotiating tactics all stood the company in good stead in its African endeavours, most of which were in the hands of John Woodhouse and Malcolm McGillivray (recently retired from the SAS). Kenya benefited from official assistance from HMG and in the process Bruce MacKenzie (Minister of Agriculture and powerful within the Kenyatta Cabinet) had become a staunch protagonist of Watchguard, and was of great assistance in obtaining access to Kenneth Kaunda and others elsewhere.

It is perhaps fortunate that Stirling did not become force commander of the South Arabian task force as the results can easily be envisaged. His inspired leadership and personal audacity would most probably have created havoc in the killing fields of Yemen, which would almost certainly have caused an absolute furore in Saudi Arabia and in Whitehall. Perhaps the Saudis were shrewder judges of character than is generally credited; it is difficult to see how Stirling could have stuck to the non-aggressive tactics being employed by King Feisal at the time.

Stirling maintained his interest in Watchguard business in the Middle East until the late sixties, but he was also captivated by the idea of offering a service to the CIA. He deduced that there were far more American interests in South, Central and Latin America than there were British, and there were also distinct possibilities in South-East Asia. In this context he was not looking specifically to the prime rôle of Watchguard but to what he saw as the increasing annoyance to the West of the drugs barons. At that time there was an awareness but little more – very few had paused to consider the future of this lucrative and destructive trade, and the powers held by the 'barons' to manipulate governments. Surely this situation was tailor-made for the covert operator. It is probable that the CIA was still smarting from its abortive entanglements with Fidel Castro; nothing was to come of Stirling's suggestions at the time but he did cement some useful liaisons for future use.

We should note Stirling's utter willingness to turn potential contracts over to the British Ministry of Defence (and thus the SAS) even though he may have committed considerable funds against the projects. Although the Foreign Office benefited from intelligence reports passed on by Stirling or other members of Watchguard there was a growing unease about the organisation. His overtures to the CIA had not gone unobserved – the security services of the world are as prone to gossip as any other business.

Security had been bad throughout Watchguard's Middle Eastern phase; the area is a hotbed of gossip, and secrets are meant to be shared with 'trusted' friends in that part of the world. Stirling had openly declared that his Yemen task force was to be a fighting unit, designed for missions which required 'the highest level of leadership, courage, skill and initiative' from Watchguard personnel who were known to be ex-SAS. This was a departure from the original philosophy of the company. Little imagination is needed to envisage how this might appear to rulers engaged in diplomatic negotiations and civil servants in London. The press was not particularly kind during the sixties and often printed articles which proved little other than that their arithmetic was faulty.

Security problems reached a peak when a sensitive proposal made to King Hussein of Jordan fell into the hands of the Israelis. This had repercussions in Whitehall, but the greater loser was Stirling (who had lost the document); many of his Israeli contacts dried up instantly. Stirling had steadfastly maintained a discreet liaison with the Israelis over the years for a number of reasons. Theirs was a good intelligence network throughout the Middle East and there was scope for reciprocation of information; Watchguard would be in competition with Israeli 'technical teams', particularly in Africa and South America with its large and powerful Jewish business communities (if headway was made there), and he was also interested in keeping abreast of technical advances made in Israel. The company firmly resisted all the Israelis' pleas for assistance in planting agents in Arab countries where they were trying to attract contracts.

The leak of the proposal signalled the beginning of the end of the working partnership with Woodhouse. A number of Watchguard employees at that stage were ex-SAS officers, recently retired from a regiment which was becoming more politically aware as their peacetime rôle developed, and some were ill at ease with Stirling's method of taking political advice.

Though he despised political labels he was certainly at that time well to the right of the Conservative centre with regard to foreign affairs. He did tend to discuss most of his ventures with people like Alec Douglas-Home, Julian Amery and Billy McLean but whether he took their proffered advice or not was very much down to his analysis. Provided he himself was convinced that his actions were in the interests of HMG, he would follow that instinct. He did draw a fine distinction between 'interest' and 'embarrassment' – HMG could stand a little embarrassment in his opinion; it could not, however, afford either to pass by opportunities to lay the groundwork for benefits which may not be apparent for years, or fail to pay the debts sometimes resultant from colonialist policies. He was usually perfectly correct in both diagnosis and prognosis, but his curative methods tended to be unpalatable to those who preferred the slow, negotiated treatments.

Had Stirling been of a mind to take the advice of his co-directors, Watchguard was impeccably set to become a real commercial force in the security world and there would have been little room for the organisations which 'sprang from the rump' of the initial concept and some of his proposals. Politically the time was right in three respects. Firstly, there *were* tasks which HMG could not overtly touch but which it would have liked to see carried out by a trusted organisation of the Watchguard type. Secondly, not only was it the age of the coup, it was possible to foresee the degree and manner of growth of international terrorism. Lastly, it was the age of discontentment in the British Army with little soldiering activity. There was not quite such discontentment in the SAS, but the regiment had a large number of bachelors not averse to shifting horses to put variety into their lives – Watchguard would not have wanted for recruits.

Life is full of ifs and buts; if Stirling had placed Watchguard at the disposal of HMG and played the tune to order there is little doubt that with official direction and his team's ability to convince and sell the future would have been rosy; the SIS certainly had no 'on call' service of this nature. Watchguard did do reasonably well in Africa, but its reputation was damaged before it was fully matured and this denied it many lucrative markets in the sixties. Acknowledgement has to be given to Stirling's personal philosophy that profits were secondary to patriotism and that patriotism is largely in the eyes of the patriot rather than elected government; nonetheless he failed to see that had Watchguard been accepted as an unofficial arm of the

Foreign Office or the SIS he could, as founder and motivator, have been in a superb position to put his arguments forward at senior levels of government and would have gathered around him a superb team of operators.

A measure of the loyalty which Stirling could still inspire is demonstrated in the way in which senior members of the company severed their employment. Convinced that Stirling was on the wrong track by not working more closely with the Foreign Office, they were tempted to vote him off the board. With more executive power in their hands Watchguard could then have been steered towards the commercial success already indicated. The Director of Operations, John Woodhouse, was in any event committed to HMG as Stirling well knew; he found himself in the impossible position of trying to serve two divergent causes when the masters of both could have been aboard the same ship. In the last analysis they amicably resigned, feeling that the other route would have been a 'stab in the back' to Stirling.

It was only a few more years before Stirling removed himself from the scene of commercial/military business; meanwhile there was one more brief operation. Known to the world as the 'Hilton Assignment', it has been the subject of many media articles and at least one book and does not require a further blow-by-blow account here. It is interesting, however, to note parts of the project from Stirling's standpoint.

By way of setting the record straight; there were in the late sixties rumours that Watchguard had actively recruited and trained saboteurs to infiltrate Rhodesia with a view to cutting off road and rail supplies to that beleaguered country. Although discussions to this effect took place (Watchguard was urged to seek mercenaries willing to mount such operations from Zambia under payment from Kenya), no action was taken and the results of all such meetings were passed to the appropriate authorities.

The Watchguard contract in Zambia was an open secret – there was no reason why it should not have been. Stirling

was well known to Kenneth Kaunda to whom the religious
undertones of the Capricorn Africa Society had some appeal. A
number of ex-SAS men worked for Watchguard, selecting and
training a paramilitary unit to operate both as a counter-coup
force and as a field force in defence of the Zambian borders.
The contract, initiated in 1967, ran for some two years and
was followed by a similar operation in Sierra Leone. Stirling
had been under surveillance by the Rhodesian authorities since
late 1956 due mainly to his Capricorn activities and frequent
trips to South Africa. Stirling knew this and, having nothing of
significance to hide, chose to ignore it. Once an official file is
opened, however, rumours and suspicions become rife and the
truth of the Zambian involvement was tarnished by innuendo.

It was later to be a matter of deep regret to Stirling that
one of the ex-SAS, ex-Watchguard employees was commonly
believed to have assassinated Herbert Chitepo on 18th March
1975. 'Chuck' Hinds, fellow Scotsman, had certainly remained
in Africa after resigning from Watchguard on the completion
of the Sierra Leone contract but his activities thereafter were
a closed book to Stirling.

During the small hours of the morning on 1st September 1969,
a young lieutenant in the Libyan army took advantage of his
King's absence from his country to promote himself to colonel
and declare himself Head of State. Muammer Qadaffi had
deposed King Idris and entered the arena of world politics. One
of his early decisions was to close the strategically important
American and British air bases of Wheelus and El Adem. To
compound the 'insult' Britain lost out on a huge air defence
sales and training package. Should one wonder that when
Stirling was approached in August 1970 to assist in a move to
make life unpleasant for Qadaffi he assumed that there would
be at least tacit approval from both sides of the Atlantic?

In late November 1988 I was spending some time in Scotland
with Stirling taping interviews and generally discussing his

adventures. We had stayed for a few very relaxing days at Brechin Castle impeccably hosted by Stirling's brother-in-law, the Earl of Dalhousie. The tenor of life had been unhurried; I would walk in the mornings through the crisp early snow and we would talk in the afternoons and evenings alongside a log fire. The time came to motor across Scotland to Loch Morar where we were to spend a few days at Morar Lodge at the kind invitation of Irene Stirling before I headed south.

With Stirling made comfortable in my car we set off and climbed at a modest pace into the Highlands. Stirling was dozing and I was enjoying the quiet roads and the majestic beauty of the snow-crowned peaks and ridges as we meandered east. Stirling gave a sudden snort and sat upright.

'Rather a comfy car for two grown boys, Spike. What is it?'

'An Audi,' I replied.

'Hmph. Foreign. Is it "owdi" or "ordi"? How big is the engine?'

'Two litres.'

'What's that in pints? Does it mean you can go faster? There's some quite interesting road ahead of us.' This with a pointed look at the speedometer which was indicating about fifty-five mph.

'I expect it does, David, but I'm enjoying the peace. We're well on schedule and I've got a valuable cargo. I daren't write off our founder.'

'Well, Spike, le bon Dieu is not going to extract me from a car, you have my word on that, He's had enough opportunities in the past. Anyway we won't be on schedule soon because there's a little hostelry just around the corner where we're going to pause for a dram.'

There was indeed a quaint old inn around the corner. There was no parking area and I pulled off on to the right-hand verge so that Stirling wouldn't have to contort himself getting out of the car close to a hedge. He swung open the door and, without looking either way, stalked across the road being narrowly missed by cars from both directions which he totally ignored.

By the time I got inside he had a brace of large whiskies and had found an armchair by the fire.

'Here you are. It's very kind of you to drive me – most people don't like it. You're allowed only four of those, by the way.'

'To be truthful, David, I've found it extremely relaxing so far. Brechin was marvellous. I don't seem to find enough time for walking these days.'

'Simon's an excellent host. I can remember a rather jolly occasion when I had Ian Crooke and a lot of his boys from 23 SAS for a reception or something. There were a few French there as well. Between them they'd got through an impressive amount of boozo and Ian decided it was time for them to depart. What he hadn't realised was that they'd had time to do a thorough reconnaissance and as fast as he shunted them down one set of stairs, they were disappearing round the corner, going up the servants' stairs and joining the party again. It took hours to get them out. A really good party.' He raised his glass in toast.

'Here's to good parties. Tell me about the car smashes, David, though I think I've heard about most of them.'

'Did you know that I've written off about five cars and never lost my no-claims bonus?' A quiet chuckle. 'Had a Rhodesian driving licence for years, long after it became Zimbabwe.' I never managed to work out how a Rhodesian licence could affect a no-claims bonus, and I'd heard that more than five cars had suffered at his hands. Perhaps strokes of luck like this one recounted by Colin Campbell affect the tally.

'David had a Mini Cooper – I don't know how he managed to get into the thing but it was like watching Houdini when he got out. He was driving it quite ferociously on one occasion in 1967 or thereabouts when he was stopped by the police. He hadn't been drinking, but his licence had been issued in Rhodesia in 1953 and had expired in 1958. Rhodesia wasn't even a country then! Anyway the licence was sent off to Guildford, and the story goes that it was processed by a sergeant who had been a troop commander in the

SAS and fortunately he just threw the documents into the wastepaper bin.'

Stirling continued. 'I think one of the most impressive happened not far from Morar, I'll show you on the way. That was a foreign car too, a BMW I think. Damn thing went right off the road, down the hillside and virtually lost its roof on the way. That put me off seat belts for life. That would have been in 1970. I spent quite a long time at Keir getting over that one. My sister was also driving and I thought she was ahead of me and I was trying to catch up with her. She was in fact behind me which is fortunate because it was Irene who found me.'*

'1970. David, that would have been when you were first approached on the Hilton Assignment wouldn't it?' More chuckles.

'Yes, but I wasn't anywhere near as closely involved as people imagine. True it was an interesting proposition and I think we should have had some support. That's the problem with politicians, they have minds which work in three- and four-year electoral cycles. They can't look at things without the clutter of electoral policies – they rarely, at least when they're in office, think twenty and thirty years ahead. There comes a time when politics demands the application of intelligent action; getting rid of Qadaffi at that time would have been a good move. Once Nasser went he was sure to take the world stage – any fool could see that. The Americans were more sanguine than we were because they saw him as anti-Communist in the extreme; they were right in essence but wrong in respect of the

---

* Stirling neglected to relate how serious this particular car accident had been. He was in fact found by the police and not his sister (as he remembered). Apart from severe concussion and a variety of broken bones, one of his lungs was punctured and he was later to lose half of the organ. He was in the Stirling Infirmary for over a month before being allowed home for convalescence. This early discharge was largely due to his own obstinacy. It was during this period of convalescence that Irene remembered a succession of strange visitors who well fitted her perceptions of what a mercenary soldier would look like. Invariably the visits took their toll on Stirling leaving him quite exhausted.

threat he presented to the West. He is a troublemaker and will always have an open chequebook for other troublemakers. But the point is that he seized his position through coup tactics. We simply cannot have this – government has to be democratically elected. The plot was not to assassinate the man – rather to create a situation where he would be on the receiving end of his own tactics; the established ruler would be reinstated and the people free to remove him democratically if they desired.' Stirling became slightly morose and there was a silence. I had, presumably, speeded up sufficiently, though I am sure on a number of occasions he was on the point of asking if he could drive himself!

'The whole affair was something of a débâcle from the start. I was approached mainly because Watchguard had become quite well-known even though it wasn't then very busy. There was never any question of the company being used to recruit or control the operation regardless of the rights and wrongs but I was certainly not adverse [this use of 'adverse' is a Stirlingism], in the beginning at least, to looking at the plans and lending resources under the counter as it were. It seemed certain that both the USA and Britain would speedily acknowledge Qadaffi's government despite being considerably miffed by it all. It was not an undertaking in which to become involved with a high profile – perhaps at all, if HMG was totally adverse to it. After I moved down to London from Scotland I went to the top to find out what was what with SIS and the Foreign Office.'*

The plan, at the time of which Stirling speaks, was to mount a seaborne operation to liberate the 140 or so political prisoners in Tripoli. After their release they were to be left with arms while the mercenaries departed. It is a moot point whether the prisoners would have opted to fight or just flee! The prison was

---

* Stirling must have met with Anthony Royle, Parliamentary Under-Secretary of State, who had served with 23 SAS Regiment and would have understood the high chance of success of the planned operation. Stirling intimates, in going 'to the top' of the SIS, that he would have spoken to Maurice Oldfield, whom he knew well.

known as the 'Tripoli Hilton' – hence the press dubbing of the 'Hilton Assignment'.

Stirling's investigations with his Foreign Office and other contacts left him in no doubt that a British operation would be highly undesirable. This he accepted.

'I certainly got the impression that there would be great satisfaction if the operation was successful even though the use of British (hence Watchguard) personnel was out of the question. Such an operation would have been remarkably easy; mostly a matter of administration and logistics. I gave a hand in introductions to the French circle, but took a back seat from then on, though I was kept in the picture. The whole thing took much longer to put together than it ought to have done.'

Though Stirling had mentally washed his hands of the affair, he was constantly contacted for advice and names which he freely gave. He certainly hosted a number of the Libyan 'plotters' at Keir on one occasion 'a really ferocious bunch' as the hostess recalled); he did not see this as being contrary to anyone's interests. His own security was as lax as ever; he was quite happy to chat about the operation in his own peculiar form of veiled speech to trusted friends in White's Club. Perhaps, knowing where some of their loyalties lay, he was passing on progress reports. The result was that however much Stirling felt he was standing-off from the business he was, in the eyes of all interested agencies, involved in the planning.

It is interesting to note that though some of the most powerful intelligence agencies in the world were focused on the Hilton Assignment, they did at one point miss the boat. Jim Johnson remembers an incident:

'I was approached by MI6 who knew that David was launching the operation in Libya. They knew it was going to be done by French mercenaries and they knew the name of the boat (*Conquistador*?). They were horrified at the lack of security and the general talk going the rounds. I was asked if I could help. I checked the Lloyds Register but couldn't find where the boat currently was. I happened to mention it to my wife who knew exactly where it was – lying in harbour in Malta. We had been out there visiting friends and she had noticed it because there were clothes-lines all over the deck cluttered with khaki underpants and such; she had said to herself, 'That's a mercenary boat.'

'About a week later I was asked to go to France urgently. I was met by Roger Falques who told me he wanted to give me a warning that everybody knew about the Libyan job; that it was going to be a complete fiasco and that the French did not want to be associated with it through David's recruits. I was asked to tell him "to lay off". The next day, before I left Paris, I was approached by the resident Mossad man who told me they had intercepted so much information about the operation that David should realise that "everybody knew about it". Apparently every mercenary had talked in every bar between Marseilles and Italy. I told David, but he seemed to brush it aside.'

Stirling's interpretation was a little different. He believed that the intelligence services had been sharing information from the beginning – and why not – he himself had made no secret of the affair and his knowledge of it. He thought the agencies were quite prepared to see the operation succeed, until the assassination of Nasser. This focused world attention on Qadaffi, as Nasser's successor in the furtherance of Nasserism; a political fusion of Egypt, Libya and the Sudan was looking likely. Tripoli was now in the public eye. The *Conquistador* was by then in Trieste and ready to move. Shortly before she was due to weigh anchor (March 1971) she was taken, with full crew and passengers, into custody in Trieste. Stirling, with some chagrin, believed that the British deliberately "blew the operation" to the Italians and requested containing action from them.

The failure of the Hilton Assignment was one of the reasons why Stirling abandoned the mercenary business and retreated from active involvement with Watchguard. The company had made some money – little enough for him to reconcile with his conscience. A profit was necessary in order to maintain a corps of staff and to on-sell the services, but he was becoming quietly disgusted with the financial return being demanded by operatives; in particular the Hilton payments had, to his mind, been out of proportion to the risks implied in the original plan.

Stirling took nothing out of the operational purse except to pay for renting London premises in the early planning stages. Stirling's views on the financial morality of mercenaries are perhaps naïve; he was reasonably financially secure, but many of the 'soldiers' on the assignment were not, and they had wives and families to support. Probably Stirling was more annoyed by the huge profits often gleaned by those who put together such operations at little personal risk.

In 1972 Stirling ceased all activity with Watchguard though the philosophy behind the nature of the work quite soon interested other people, and Stirling would eventually return to close that circle of his activities.

---

# 22

# A BETTER BRITAIN?

Stirling played down the after-effects of the car crash; it was almost a year before he regained full mobility. The long convalescence left him prone to bouts of depression caused by what he saw as a personal inadequacy to cope with long, self-imposed responsibility. The wartime migraines returned and he said that the early seventies were nonproductive years for him. This is difficult to credit; his travel pattern changed hardly at all; perhaps he stayed a little longer in the countries he visited but his passports show constant trips to Africa, the Middle East, Hong Kong and Indonesia. In the previous ten-year period the longest spell he had taken in the UK spanned the funeral of Sir Winston Churchill in January 1965 (he attended as a family friend, with great personal sadness). Though he travelled mostly on behalf of TIE and related business, this was also his final fling at establishing a toehold in the Middle East. He chose public relations as his platform.

In an interview in 1989 he recalled, 'As far as I can remember there were then three recognised dimensions to public relations operations. The first was the informative process by which the recipients, carefully targeted for effect, were educated in a style which they found easy to believe. Second was the seductive process which flattered them into thinking that they had reasoned out a case for themselves and third was the manipulative process; they were persuaded to present the argument to others. These precepts were usually confined to one country and directed towards internal politics. There was, however, a fourth dimension which I saw as being an overseas branch of a national PR effort.

'Iran was the main target; we thought it imperative to British interests and the good of the Gulf as a whole that the Shahanshah should stay in power. "We" were Quail International, an amalgam between Frank O'Shanohun Associates (I'd known Frank for quite some time) and TIE. O'Shanohun had a very good press, radio and television lobby based on news and information distribution; TIE had the better intelligence, political, economic and commercial liaisons, all still bolstered by our television programme distributions and our overseas research. Through blistering Quail on to these facilities we were able to offer a first-class and rather different service to the Shahanshah.

'Frank could cover the orthodox facilities and I could put together the unorthodox and covert side. We proposed to make available all our sources of information from Europe, the UK, the USA and the Middle East, combine them with the not insignificant Iranian resources and plan an international PR operation from there. I would be responsible for helping the Shahanshah to convince key British ministers of Iran's importance to British interests and Middle East stability and relieve him of any accusations of "special pleading" which might have caused him aggravation locally. I would meet regularly with British ministers and pass on and interpret the Shahanshah's problems, in a way that would have been impossible for his ministers due to the inhibiting official etiquette.

'Through the auspices of Frank's organisation and TIE we could boast full-time residential representation in Paris, Vienna, Zurich, Frankfurt, Copenhagen, Stockholm, Milan, Beirut and New York while both our headquarters were, of course, set in the world's most sensitive news centre, London. It was a very successful commercial operation for quite some time and I think both countries benefited considerably in terms of advance information and defence trading spin-offs. We certainly got the Shahanshah an ear in Parliament.'

'David, who was, or is, Yuri Galitzine? He featured in many of your business affiliations and you seemed to have respected his advice. He appears on the fringes of Quail also.'

'Ah, he's quite a man. I was introduced to him by Brian Franks not long after the war. Brian met him when Yuri was working with the War Crimes Organisation; he's the son of a Russian prince and had been working very courageously in the front line of intelligence in Europe. I believe he was one of the first of the Allies to enter a Nazi concentration camp in the closing stages of the war in Europe. When Brian and Bill Barkworth put together the special team to track down the bodies of the SAS soldiers executed during the war, Yuri was immensely helpful. Brian set up a London headquarters, and while he and Randolph Churchill made sure that the operation went unhindered – with a lot of direct help from Winston – Yuri kept the base together, looked after communications and made sure that they didn't run out of brasso. That chap who was involved in the SAS TV film project wrote a book about it.* Yuri was a very shrewd businessman and I turned to him a lot during the Capricorn days particularly. A delightful man though I fear I often didn't take the advice he freely gave me.'

The early seventies were probably Stirling's heyday in White's. I asked about his apparent penchant for telling the club about his activities.

'It was a very good sounding board. I don't think I was really as loose as people say, you know. Perhaps; but no matter now. It's a very convivial place and I was gambling quite heavily in those days. Do you know I was accused of cheating at snooker – in the friendliest manner, of course. It wasn't cheating at all. To dip a finger in one's kümmel and pop it on the tip of one's

---

* *The Secret Hunters* by Anthony Kemp.

opponent's cue is simply tactics. The secret was to keep him talking while you did it.

'White's has all sorts of people in during the early evenings and it was interesting to bounce ideas around and confound the press which had usually made facts fit theories rather than simply reporting the truth. There are well informed people there and with a bit of an argument raging it was often possible to glean rather more than they intended. Jolly fine place to start a rumour too! It is also a prime source of stimulation; I often heard people saying how impossible this or that situation was becoming and it was interesting to pick up on them and get a jolly good free-for-all in motion.'

Stirling is remembered with great esteem in White's. The staff remember a very gentle man who never forgot a name, always had a joke on his lips and never failed to inquire after friends and families. His contemporaries remember him as a raconteur par excellence when the mood was upon him; as the eternal practical joker; as a man who could not resist a challenge whether at the snooker table (at which in White's the rules can be decided as the game progresses), backgammon board, chemin-de-fer or in political or purely intellectual argument. A story often related concerns the 'clock incident'. Sir Stephen Hastings, one of Stirling's brother officers in the Western Desert and fellow member of White's was witness to it:

'David was playing snooker with Dickon Lumley and I was watching when I had to leave the snooker room. I heard the crash and when I returned David was lying on the floor with clock springs and little wheels scattered around his head which was bleeding. It seems that the ball had been thrown and David had stepped back and stumbled against a stand from which had fallen a really rather valuable clock. The results were obvious. In the following weeks David was constantly asked to apologise for the misdemeanour which he steadfastly refused to do. It got to the point where it was suggested that he would be asked to resign. I remember saying to him, "What are you going to do about it, David, we can't have the club asking for your resignation – in any case you'd probably refuse, wouldn't you?" Of course he said yes. In the end he did write a very short letter of apology – one sentence, I believe, to which he added a postscript: "Tempus fugit – which roughly translated means, Stirling fucked by clock." Very amusing. The clock was eventually replaced, by Dickon I think.'*

Stirling's description of the early seventies as 'fallow years' does not accord with newspaper articles of the time. Before examining the activities which brought him back to the attention of the media, it is interesting to note some comments made by an acutely observant man who became involved with Stirling for a three-year period during the Capricorn days. They highlight some of his leadership techniques; his reticence or perhaps embarrassment in financial matters; how easily he could become distracted by anything akin to the old SAS work and his major business deficiency.

Charles Richmond, then Earl of March and now Duke of Richmond and Gordon, was introduced to Stirling by Michael Wood in 1956 just after he, Richmond, had qualified as a chartered accountant. He was immediately captivated by the ideals of Capricorn and persuaded to become treasurer of the Society. His memories are quite distinct:

'I made a tour of Africa with David Stirling and my great friend David Hamilton, who was to stay on in Africa as the Executive Officer in Rhodesia. Before you ask about that let me tell you a story which shows the difficulties of controlling the finances of an idealistic organisation. We had a meeting in London, in Jeanine's [Bartosik] flat – David, Jonathan [Lewis], Laurens, Jeanine and one or two others. Laurens was talking

---

* Dickon Lumley, now Earl of Scarborough, is married to Stirling's niece and was a partner in many of his business ventures including Capricorn and Watchguard. He told me that when he was controlling the funds of one company (probably Capricorn), Stirling had asked for a cheque to cover travel expenses; this was refused due to a cash shortage. Stirling's response was to take the money from Lumley in person at a game of chemin-de-fer, afterwards expressing the opinion that this was a much better way of accounting!

about the future of Northern Rhodesia in words that only he could use.

'About every half an hour I said, "That's very exciting stuff, Mr Chairman – but how's it going to be paid for?" Jonathan took me aside afterwards and said, "Charles, There's something you ought to learn. You can't bully poets." Of course he was quite right. That was the problem, Laurens was a poet, and though David was not – he was more of a prophet really – the same applies.

'On the trip to Africa he quickly showed what a great motivator he was but I spotted one of his techniques very quickly. He would visit one location and tell them how well the people he had just visited at another branch were doing, and perhaps imply that there was room for more effort here. Fortunately they didn't communicate much with each other so they never found out.

'We were in the middle of that tour when the Hungarian uprising took place and for a week or more I couldn't get David to concentrate on Africa. We were supposed to be giving the African branches an uplift but he was completely distracted, on the telephone half the time to Anthony Head, then Minister of Defence, plotting a drop into Hungary. He was wild about the idea and wouldn't stop talking about it. One morning as we sat down to our grapefruit at 8.30, he started again, and I said, "Look, David, I'll listen to you for the rest of the day but for God's sake not at breakfast." But he'd had this great idea about Hungary and he wasn't moving from it. I pointed out that if he had to do the job within the next fortnight he had problems. He had to recruit people, he had to get back to London which would take at least three days from where we were. I just couldn't see the logistics working out. His reply? "Purely administrative, purely administrative."

'In other words, if the idea was good then it was really good and the practical difficulties – somebody else could get on with that. Perhaps David was too idealistic; too prophetic to function alone. I think I said to him once, "David, what you need is a superb chief-of-staff who respects you for what you do so well and whom you would respect because you would know what he did so well." I don't want to be unfair to David but that man would have had to be a superman to stay with it for any length of time.

'When we arrived in Salisbury I'd put together all the figures. We'd been to the three main branches in Africa and I had to tell David that the excess of liabilities over assets of Capricorn at that moment was about £15,000; I asked what he was going to do about it. He told me he would arrange to spend the weekend with Stephen Courtauld, who lived near Bulawayo; he was a very rich man and might "do the job".

'We duly went to see Stephen and over dinner the first night he asked what we wanted to talk about. I said, "Well, sir, if we may we'd like to talk about Capricorn and especially the current financial situation." He said that was fine; we would talk the next morning at 10.30. I assumed that David and I would see him, I would put the situation and we'd discuss it. I was electrified when at 10.15 the next morning David said, "Oh, by the way, Charles, I've got to go to Mass. I'll be back in about an hour."

'Luckily, when I told Stephen, he said, "Right, We'll wait till he bloody well comes back." Wait we did and after we'd explained the situation Stephen asked how much we wanted. I said we needed about £10,000 and he and his wife wrote out cheques on their current accounts for £3,000 each, which in 1956 was quite a sum of money!

'Yes, David was a great motivator and leader of men. I've always felt that there was a slightly sad aspect to him; the SAS was a tremendous achievement and he was fêted in high places – 10 Downing Street and all that – in the war. He never really grew out of that – always wanting to go back to rushing in with a pistol so to speak.

'One of the things which emerged for me out of my association with David and Capricorn was an invitation in 1960 to join a little group which was thinking of the Northern Rhodesian

Constitution; a constitutional conference was about to go on and I got together with Chris Chataway and Charles Janson, and the idea of this little newsletter emerged. Charles Janson invited me to play some part in it so he and I and John Vernon and others came together, as partners originally, now directors, and out of it grew *Africa Confidential* which is still going and still pretty highly regarded in Africa. We just set it up to try and produce something reasonably objective about what was going on; so much of the news then was slanted in one direction or another. Not only does the newsletter now have a great reputation amongst some of the most important people in Africa, it actually makes money.

'In 1959 I moved up to the Midlands and was not well placed to continue with Capricorn and I eventually resigned. I don't think David liked me very much towards the end of my involvement as I wouldn't sign cheques unless I knew we had the money in our account. I was never involved in finding funds; the treasurer's job is to control the finances not seek them. He was a delightful man, most interesting, with a very lively mind.'

I asked him about Stirling as a businessman.

'To use my accountant's language, David was rather like the last balance sheet of a very large company. There were terrific assets on the one side and terrific liabilities on the other.'

The Duke of Richmond's life, like so many others', had been touched by his relationship with Stirling and Africa. I challenged Stirling several times on his attitudes to business and partners (in fact this was to have personal relevance in later years) but I never got a satisfactory answer. I eventually concluded that he was never quite certain that he had fully imparted his reasoning to his partners; he therefore maintained a slight mistrust of them and was forever cross-checking to see that they were on the course he had set out. Most men could accept this; but Stirling was prone to forget that the course of action was ever deviating as he continually spun off new ideas or tactics, and that he didn't always impart the new bearings to others. The result was frustration on both sides.

Stirling was beginning also in those years to touch again on SAS matters; he began to attend Association meetings occasionally. He had been President of the SAS Association since its inception and first dinner in 1946 but had rarely become involved.

'I was receiving a lot of column inches in the newspapers throughout the seventies, and whether it was warranted or not it didn't seem a good idea to be in any detectable way involved with the serving regiment. Of course I took great pride in what they were up to; who can forget the successful ascent of Everest by Brummie [Stokes] and Bronco [Lane] in May 1976? I was mainly involved only with the fund-raising aspects, and I had chats with the various directors, who I suspect invited me for the odd hot meal out of politeness. Association meetings could bang on a bit. I remember once when this person was getting a little pomposo and I decided to do something about it. He was waxing most lyrical when he suddenly began to stoop, slid backwards on to his chair and began to disappear under the table. I'd got under the table and had got my hand up between his legs with an extremely firm grip on his headquarter equipment. It certainly stopped him sounding off. There was no real need for me; Brian Franks and Dare Newell were doing such a tremendous job that the President was just a figurehead, but it was enjoyable to know a little of what was going on.'

If there was a high degree of levity and fun in Stirling's life during this period there was also a serious sense of political duty. In 1974 Wilson slid into government on the back of Heath's 'surrender' to the miners and this was a portent of doom to Stirling. He had predicted something like this the year before and he had not been mentally idle. He had been not so quietly sounding out friends and ministers on their views on the current state of the nation.

'There was a blindness to something which was really so very obvious if one stood off and looked at the situation clearly. For the past half a dozen years the country had been subjected to a carefully laid-out strategy which would carry us inexorably towards totalitarianism. Those who accepted this seemed to see it as a sort of sword of Damocles from which there was no escape.'

Stirling's answer to the problem was first to try to explain it, then to devise a carefully calculated plan of action. First he wished to impress upon a select gathering of influential people the need to take action. For this he formed the Greater Britain League. His reasoning is outlined in a paper he wrote in 1974.

The United Kingdom would seem an unlikely candidate to join the ranks of the totalitarian countries. Historically, we have shown great dexterity in dealing with external and internal threats and pressures. In the building and defence of the Empire, our tiny country survived the external pressures with a mixture of opportunism and ingenuity (much helped by the luck of being an island), together with a preparedness in extremity to confront an enemy four-square with patriotic gallantry and determination. On the other hand, we have dealt with the internal sociological pressures for emancipation and for the rights of the individual by a readiness to compromise before these pressures could become so great as to be resolved only in revolution.

After the last World War, we matched the spirit in which the United Nations Organisation was founded by transferring power from Whitehall to our erstwhile colonies and dominions as fast as was practicable. Internally, we pioneered a welfare state and nationalised those industries and public utility services which were judged to have grown beyond the scope of private enterprise. To finance the welfare state and to bring about a radical redistribution of wealth, we endured massively increased direct and indirect taxation.

About five years ago, in spite of these huge external and internal adjustments . . . and in spite of the many inevitable residual problems, it looked as if, within the framework of our mixed economy, we were within distance of attaining an ideal of what the democratic state could be. Why then are we so ignominiously sliding . . . towards some form of totalitarianism? And why are so many of us still blind to an already far advanced conspiracy by the broad Left to topple our democracy – a conspiracy which, in retrospect, will look to have been so entirely obvious?

The explanation for this blindness lies, at least partly, in the over-simplistic notion held by so many – that the political Left was the source of social benefits and reform (i.e. 'the goodies'), while the political Right ('the baddies') safeguarded privilege and put the brakes on social reform. At last, but far too gradually, people are realising that the political situation has somersaulted. It is now the broad Left which harbour 'the baddies' and which is devoted to creating a privileged class of rulers hell-bent on demolishing our individual rights and on creating a totally socialistic and, therefore, totalitarian state; while it is the moderates, with the Labour Party Manifesto Group in the front line, which is rallying in defence of our mixed economy and our democratic rights. Today's significant political watershed runs between the Tribune and the Manifesto groups within the Labour Party, rather than between the Labour Party and the Conservative Party.

The first stage of the campaign within the trade union movement by the left wing (the International Socialists, Communists, Marxists and fellow travellers) was to capture many 'commanding heights' of the trade union movement on the backs of a tiny majority of . . . union members on the factory floor. Their undoubted victory has enabled them, through the block vote system, to dominate the last two Labour Party conferences; and . . . to install some union-nominated MPs to reinforce the Tribune Group in the House of Commons. This group, accompanied by a growing band of 'shirt-tail hangers-on', have secured many of the more important individual appointments and won control of the tactically vital committees at every level of the Labour Party organisation and, short of the cabinet itself, of parliamentary apparatus.

. . . This near takeover of the governing Labour Party by its parliamentary left-wing activists in alliance with the trade union extremists . . . poses the most menacing crisis our country has faced – more dangerous by far than the worst period of the last World War.

The status of parliament, under both Conservative and Labour governments, has not been enhanced in the last few years by their initially robust, but eventually faltering and unavailing efforts to curb the raw power of the trade union militants by legislation and to cope with strikes which plainly went beyond particular unions' legitimate rights to protect their members, and wholly against the national interest; nor has it been enhanced by the government's current 'Social Contract' which has been treated by the extremists with disdainful arrogance.

In summary . . . parliament's authority and its credibility have been ominously eroded by the left-wing Members of Parliament. They have demonstrated arbitrarily their power to force extreme socialist-type decisions, often in defiance of the mandate on which they have been elected. In parallel with this, the left-wing trade union leaders, who have been elected at different levels on a derisory percentage of those entitled to vote, are formulating and acting on strike-threat and inflation-exploiting policies which are calculated to destroy Britain's economy. Thus, in collusion with their fellow-travellers in parliament, they are creating circumstances leading – *they will claim constitutionally* – inexorably to a fully socialist state. Some of their MPs succeed in acting bland and even appearing sweetly reasonable; but their mentors inside and outside the House of Commons are entirely without scruple, quick to intimidate and exceedingly crafty. However divided they may be within the broad left, they combine singlemindedly in their determination to convert our democracy into a socialist state. This crisis, which is both organic and of the spirit, cannot possibly be resolved within parliament alone. The sickness lies at the heart of the country itself and of its people, and that is where the cure will come from.

We should remember too that the House of Commons is the 'Mother of Parliaments', and the dousing of its democratic light will diminish the faith of all those worldwide who believe in the freedom of the individual.

Before going on to set out the aims, objectives and pro-gramme of the Greater Britain League, I must first put all the emphasis I can on the immediate and pressing responsibility at present facing parliament. If, as is likely, the left fail in their campaign to take us out of the EEC, and if they reckon that the people of Britain are starting to shake off their apathy and thus become alerted and hostile to the broad left's intentions, their wilder men could provoke major (although not necessarily

national) strike action forcing an economic 'crunch', in the final
throes of which the left-wing faction of today's government
would declare that only they were in a position to negotiate
with the strike leaders and, thereby, take over the reins of
government from Mr Wilson's cabinet. We must keep in mind
that there is little chance of the country sustaining a long
strike which puts the electricity national grid system and, as
a result, all the main essential services out of action, unless
the goverment . . . has made effective contingency plans to
cope with such a situation. But have they?

The other course of action open to the broad left, and the
one they are more likely to take, is an intensification of their
present highly fruitful tactics. This government (which is already
very nearly theirs) has four years to go. To combat the public's
growing anxiety, the left will no doubt put on their blandest airs,
while they continue with their hatchet work on the country's
fabric. They know that the whole structure of the nation is
presently sliding inexorably down the slope, at the bottom of
which lies their prize and our enslavement. Those who have
studied socialism critically (and no one has done a better job
. . . than Hayek in the *Road to Serfdom* and Solzhenitsyn
in his recent writings) acknowledge the inevitability of the
final slide to totalitarianism once central planning, and what
the left-wing socialists like to call rationalisation have gone
beyond a certain point; and, without doubt, we are now at
that point.

Since it is over thirty years since Stirling first expressed a
concerned awareness of the broad left's progress within the
trades unions and some eighteen years since he became actively
involved and wrote the above paper, it is worth looking at how
the Communist element had been able to manipulate events
within the unions up to that point. It was from such a study of
how power was gained and wielded that Stirling, and later some
close friends, evolved the basis for action. In rather simplistic
terms the situation was:

When the Communist Party of Great Britain began in the
1920s they perceived that it was within the trades unions that the
class war was being fought; this was the 'muscle' of the working
class, the regiments, and a training ground for the future. Party

members, whether Trotskyist, Marxist, Stalinist or whatever, believed that they should not only be union members, but active members providing leadership for their common political ends. In the beginnings the struggle for higher wages was seen as political, or as having political consequences, for this raised the traditional questions of ownership, wealth and priorities in society.

During that stage of Communist Party evolution there was a degree of cross-union discussion in terms of political issues to be challenged and tactics to be used. In the 1920s the Party inherited some powerful people in influential positions within the trades unions and on this framework, in about 1924, they formed the Minority Movement which consisted of the militant minority struggling to become the majority. Each union had its Minority Movement and they met through Conference. Progress was quite rapid but the General Strike, with the resultant moderate backlash against the Communists, caused the Minority Movement to be dissolved. When the Party began its rebuild in 1931 it was down to about 2,000 members. By the late thirties the Spanish Civil War, the easing of the Depression in the UK and the growth of new industries in engineering (particularly around the South of England) had brought about a new rise in Communism and the Party began to pick up strength again. It organised rank-and-file movements and there were attempts to forge lasting cross-union links. The Party was totally transformed by World War II; at the outbreak of hostilities it probably had about 10,000 members – it came out of the War with at least 100,000 and in control of powerful unions like the Fire Brigades, the Electricians and with very powerful positions within such organisations as the TGWU, AEU and the NMU.

The old principle of cross-union links fell apart as the people now running the unions, as opposed to fighting for control, became very hierarchical; they were less inclined to take instructions from other unions and people beneath them. So throughout the forties, fifties and sixties the Communist

Party did not function 'across the board', but through the creation in each union of a Party advisory committee. This slightly backfired because very often the members of those committees had become powers in their own right and could defy the Party and even lay down the law nationally.

It is interesting to look at the structures built by the left in the trades unions; the Party advisory committee would create a 'lower order', the Socialist Workers; all members of a union would meet to decide upon the policies for that Union and which members would run for office, and attempt to lead the much broader left. An early priority would be to produce their own paper; for example the official union journal of the CPSA was called *Red Tape* and the left responded with their own paper, called *Redder Tape*, which argued for more militant policies and listed the candidates being supported.

All unions, from the nineteenth century, have had to battle against apathy. Sometimes they argued that branches should be workplace based, and meetings take place at the work site, to get higher turnouts. On the other hand, for example, an engineers' union might have a branch in Poole consisting of twenty different factories, so that meetings might take place in a pub. The meetings could not be about problems at work, since twenty different factories were represented. Television, family life, the difficulty of transport and so on were also given as reasons for apathy – apathy which the left turned into a weapon.

How can apathy be used? A union of 5,000 members does not in reality have anywhere near that number of active persons. The left isolated precisely where the 'points of power' lay. There are two channels of power in a trade union. The first is in the workplace, where direct power is in the hands of shop stewards, power which greatly increased between the late 1950s and the early 1970s; they became more active, had more autonomy and union decisions were decentralised in their favour. Obviously the left was able to exercise some influence at that level but within the structure of the unions they worked more simply.

Take a union with 300 branches, grouped into 10 regions; each region would have a committee made up from the branches. That is one set of structures. In the second set they would have an Annual Conference consisting of, say, 3 delegates from the 300 branches and an executive committee of, say, 30 members elected regionally. Add together 300 branch secretaries, 300 branch chairmen; in each branch then there may be a committee of 6 (door stewards and the like) (1800); then 10 regional committees of the union each with 15 members (150); take these to Annual Conference at which there will also be 3 elected delegates per branch (900). In addition to that there will be an executive committee of 30 added to the 60 full-time union officials. This comprises the Annual Conference which will decide the general policy of the union.

When all these figures are added (300 + 300 + 1800 + 150 + 30 + 900 + 60), there are 3540 apparent points of power in this union. Obviously it is not necessary to have 3540 people to run the union; probably only 1200 are necessary. If this third of the total are clear about what they are going to say and do not behave stupidly by advocating completely objectionable policies, the results are predictable. But in reality one person can occupy five of those points of power, being branch secretary, member of regional committee, member of Conference, member of the executive committee and also branch chairman. So, the number of posts could fall to say, 2900 and if 1200 of those are held by the left then it effectively owns the union. If the left holds a post with influence to appoint the full-time officials, either by executive interview or the seconding of those put up for election, the case is sewn up. Thus a small number of committed people can exercise amazing influence. The apathetic help them – they do not hinder.

The left's recruiting platform also had an effect on Stirling's thinking later on. Although the Communist Party attracted more than its share of social misfits, drop-outs and so on, it also had its share of people of outstanding ability. In the post-war years and before, the majority of working-class children did not go on to higher education, or even grammar school, because they could not afford it. They went to work unsatisfied; they had to take jobs which were often boring and beneath them intellectually. It was much more interesting to argue with the boss than weld all day – the cleverer ones were ripe for recruiting and a person recruited at eighteen will probably rise to the top of the tree.

The left had other advantages over the moderates; they had classes and training schools at which recruits were taught how to argue, how to speak in public and how to write effectively in pamphlets which they were also shown how to produce. They also had their own newspaper, the *Morning Star* (formerly the *Daily Worker*). Although it had a limited circulation, it provided a platform on which people could be promoted to stand as leaders. The paper was skilfully used to create personalities often far removed from reality. A candidate for a top slot in a union would not be described as dedicated Brezhnev supporter Joe Spot; he would be hard-working, popular, first-class negotiator Joe Spot, who recently won equal pay for thirty women at London Airport; this, rather than the man who spends his annual holiday by the Black Sea. The moderates did not have access to printing presses at little or no cost. Even a small organisation like the Socialist Workers' Party could have enormous printing presses, which were often put to commercial cash-earning work – e.g., *Private Eye* was, and may still be, printed by the SWP. Whether he wished it or not the presses of Rupert Murdoch would be of no use to the moderates to print leaflets – they needed a small jobbing printer.

So it was that in 1974, the moderates within the trades unions, their sense of purpose awakened, found themselves fighting a battle against huge odds and hampered by lack of support and finance.

In that same year the then retired General Walter Walker made headlines with his 'strike-breaking' organisation Unison. General Walker was a highly respected soldier who at one time, as director of Borneo Operations, had the SAS under his command and was later to hold very senior office in NATO. He had a deep mistrust of the Labour government under Harold Wilson and was convinced, like many others, that conditions were right for another General Strike and a collapse of law and order. He had, with George Young (ex-MI6 officer) and Ross McWhirter, a right-wing Conservative, formed a committee to plan a response to the foreseen strike. Unison intended to put pressure on government to act in time to avert a crisis, and set about recruiting thousands ready to take over vital services. Stirling was invited to become involved.

Although Stirling and Walker, who knew each other, did exchange ideas, there was no joint operation. Stirling was reticent. He felt that such a body had to be governed by a tighter, more acceptable set of rules. He contended that to be trusted and effective the group must accept that they would be deployed only on government instructions. Also, Unison appeared to be in contact with senior serving army officers, or so the press insinuated, and Stirling would have no part in this highly controversial aspect. He decided that Unison lay too far to the right wing which could not, in the longer term, be completely trusted.

Stirling was prompted, however, to look closely at the idea of mobilising skilled support in the event of major strike action, but he decided to tackle it in a slightly different manner. He already had his committee of advisers from political, business and intelligence circles as a result of his studies on behalf of the Greater Britain League, and from there it was a short step to the mounting of the operation which became known as GB75.

# 23

# THE PEN IS
# MIGHTIER . . .?

Stirling did not for one moment regard the Great Britain 1975 Organisation (GB75) as what is normally accepted as a strike-breaking force. He was painfully aware through discussion with political contacts that a general strike was indeed feared by government, which was ill-prepared for such an event; there was no evidence of contingency planning. In particular a shutdown of power generating plants would have a devastating effect on the country. While he did not doubt that the army, both Regular and Territorial, would be called in, he knew that they also had made no preparations.

It was not in Stirling's nature to sit idly by and be overwhelmed by a problem, however great. If the path being trod by Unison was too extreme and provocative, there must be a path along the political centre line. What was probably necessary was a means of giving government breathing space, and this ought to be possible given the huge amount of support being offered to Walker. Could this not be tailored to the point of acceptability? His working aim was to find a way of 'plugging the gap' for the first few vital days to avoid the government having to negotiate under extreme duress. They would certainly capitulate in the chaos he foresaw happening, with anarchist-inspired violence on the streets.

In the twenties the Territorial Army, boosted by civilian volunteers, had managed to contain the situation by keeping basic services functioning, even if on a very minor scale. The seventies was worlds away in terms of technology and even the relatively sophisticated army did not have the expertise to do this now. The plan was put together in May 1975 and the working committee considered that the flashpoint, if there was to be one, would probably occur about December of that year.

The operation would call for a series of regional committees, each controlling smaller committees, to work to a central executive committee and administrative bureau based in London. Nationwide recruitment would set out to attract those with the technical skills to train others and, if necessary, man and control public facilities. A small industrial conurbation and one rural county area would be the basis for the feasibility study from which the final organisation and operating procedures would be formulated. The onus had to be on maintaining an adequate level of electrical power.

Stirling was never totally at ease with GB75. 'There were grey areas; if the organisation had to be deployed then legal implications had to be considered. We had fine lawyers to advise us and, so far as we could see, an unpaid and demonstrably patriotic rather than political organisation was quite in order. It was ever our intention that long before the crunch came we would have been accepted by government, and that if needed we would move in by invitation. Secrecy was necessary in the early stages, despite its obvious dangers; if we were fully fledged by the time we held our first press conference there was a very good chance that, if we could demonstrate a serious, committed and efficient organisation, we would be a major deterrent to any planned political strike. Deterrence was always preferable to action.

'We drew a clear distinction between a political strike and a legally mounted strike in proper defence of workers' rights and conditions. Inflation was ravaging the country and in their proper and lawful efforts to keep their members on a par with the cost of living there was every possibility that some trades unions would call for strike action anyway. That was their legal and honourable right – we would allow ourselves to be deployed only against the undeniably political strike.

'It is impossible to maintain real security when you are recruiting. We tried to do the maximum through local, established organisations such as the Rotaries and Round Tables, but it was inevitable with the flood of correspondence that the media would pay attention. Walter's [Walker] outfit was already getting a lot of column inches and we soon followed. There was also the expected inrush of oddities such as the neo-fascists and their multitude of mindless clones; we had no truck with them, but once they were sent packing they could be vociferous in their protests and thought nothing of doing a little mischief with their favourite papers.'

Stirling did manage to obtain a minimum of funding – enough to carry out the short-term feasibility study and convince himself and his team that GB75 could be viable. But the press publicity which ran from April to July 1975 was the harbinger of doom as far as his personal involvement with the organisation was concerned. Media attention unleashed a flood of support. Each letter was responded to either by a polite refusal of the offer of services (and there were many refusals) or by the following:

GREAT BRITAIN 1975

22 South Audley Street, London.

Thank you for your most welcome offer of support for GB75. As you know, our objective is to provide, on a volunteer basis, the minimum manpower necessary to cope with the immediate crisis following a General Strike or near General Strike.

Our volunteer force would await a formal request from the government before intervening in a major political strike situation and would thus not be acting outside the law. I am confident that in the event of a General Strike, the majority of the people of our country would be in favour of the use of our volunteer force to sustain the country's basic essential services and that the weight of this opinion would persuade parliament to authorise our intervention.

The recent unsolicited publicity for our activities has resulted in an enormous and most encouraging response from people of all walks of life, offering all manner of assistance. In order to record these offers accurately and fully, I am sending with this letter a proforma which I hope will be completed and returned as soon as possible. Naturally the information given on the proforma will be kept in the strictest confidence. The proforma is in no way a legal document and its purpose is solely to help us to form a comprehensive record of the potential assistance available.

I hope that you will encourage your friends to volunteer. I would like to see whole families joining us where appropriate, and I would stress that in emergencies such as we envisage there are many tasks for the womenfolk.

Finally, you might like to join a new society I am forming called the Better Britain Society (we originally called it the the Greater Britain League). Its general aim is to establish a code of morality and honesty for our lives in this country. Its immediate objectives are:

(1) To define and subsequently to propagate a statement on what constitutes patriotism today.

(2) To define the constitutional precepts and tenets within the framework of which a modern democracy can survive and prosper.

(3) To plan for a nationally scaled one-year citizenship course with a broad curriculum for the 15- to 16-year-old age groups as an alternative to remaining at school. Those taking the course would be boarded away from their homes except for usual holidays.

People joining the Better Britain Society are invited to make a small voluntary contribution . . . towards its costs . . . It is expected that the Society will be granted charitable status . . .

David Stirling

Among the letters received were these two:

Please count me as a member of GB75.
   61 years young. Ex-RAF. Can still use a handful of sand
and a knife.

Good Luck.


Dear Mr Stirling,

   I am delighted to note the contents of your letter published
in the *Daily Telegraph* today. Our enemies are united (under
Moscow direction whether they know it or not) and it is useless
for the opposing movements to appeal for national unity unless
they are themselves in close collaboration.
   Already we can hear the modern equivalent of, 'L'Empereur
récompensera celui qui s'avançerá!' Wellington remarked:
'That must be Ney going down the line – we shall be attacked
in five minutes.' Ney–Callaghan has been going down the line;
the little Napoleon of Lord North Street is making his final
astute dispositions . . .
   How can these politicians have the nerve to talk about
'superannuated Colonels' and 'blimps' when it is all too clear
that politics is now far too serious a business to be left entirely
to civilians?

Yours sincerely,
Tertius


For every such letter there were thousands of genuine offers
of support. The media attention given both to Unison and
GB75 was provocative at times; indeed Stirling took out a
successful libel action against one article. The overall result,
however, was to place pressures on Stirling which could not
be shrugged off.
   'The main problems were that GB75 was too closely linked
to the Better Britain Society (BBS), my main sphere of activity
at the time. I really did want that to succeed. And, inevitably,
the Phantom Major reared his head again and the obvious

references to the SAS were made. I really couldn't afford for the regiment to be brought into disrepute. Of course there was no involvement but the press were speculating that Walter was in close contact with senior military officers and it was only a matter of time before they made the same accusations about me. Even suing them for false statements could have been potentially embarrassing to the SAS, if only because it put the spotlight on an organisation which neither wanted nor needed a public image I decided to resign from the chair of GB75 and concentrate on the BBS.

'One major benefit sprang from GB75; the letters offering support gave a very positive measure of the dismay in the minds of the private citizen about the future of Britain. I suppose GB75 was ill-advised, and had I left that alone I would have been more effective with the BBS in the early stages. It was impossible to ignore the problem, though, and even with hindsight I would almost certainly have done the same thing.

'There was a further reason for my resignation. In 1973 and 1974 the BBS had only two primary objectives. While I was looking in detail at the trades unions structures. I met a very dedicated man, Frank Nodes, who told me about his ideas for TRUEMID (the Movement for True Industrial Democracy). Frank had taken the bull by the horns and, no doubt influenced by the late and great Sir Leslie Cannon, was making a determined study of how to oust the left from power within the unions. We hit it off from the start. I suppose one of the demerits of closeted thinking is that one is often very late in meeting others with like ideals. To my regret, I met Frank only months before he died. There were so many parallels between what he was trying to achieve and what I envisaged that it was not difficult to turn ideal into practice and find a common base for some of our work. He was a very warm, humane person of immense courage and he brought along a very good friend of long standing, Ron McLaughlin, who carried on Frank's work in the same style and with the same enthusiasm. Between them their knowledge of left-wing personalities, unscrupulous activities and tactics was impeccable and invaluable.

'With the newspapers full of "Colonel Blimp" and the "Phantom Major" – we had many more inches than Walter, you know it would have been stupid to be seen to be too close to TRUEMID; that would have immediately brought about accusations of militantism [Stirling's word]. The only militantism Frank advocated was an emotional one; there should be a refusal to let grass-roots apathy become the weapon of the left. It decided me to set another objective for the BBS and disassemble GB75. Here is the letter I wrote in response to an annoying article; it went, I think, to all the national newspapers.'

5th April 1975

Sir,

In his article of March 19th about GB75, your correspondent, Christopher Walker, accused its spokesman of being secretive. Just before that date, we had decided to dismantle GB75 and we were reticent because we did not wish supporters to hear about this decision first from the newpapers. All members have now been written to and we are able to state the reasons why it was disbanded.

Late last August I met Frank Nodes, and we had almost daily discussions up until Christmas time when he died very suddenly. Mr Nodes, an experienced Labour Party man and trade unionist, collaborated with the great Leslie Cannon in proving in the Courts in 1962 that the election of the Communists during that year to key offices in the ETU had been achieved by ballot rigging; from this incident, and others, he gained a full awareness of the union left-wing militants' intentions and techniques.

Our understanding was based on our shared conviction that the organisation he was creating, called the Movement for True Industrial Democracy (TRUEMID), and the Better Britain Society, for which I was acting as convenor, should work closely together; but he set one condition – while accepting the good faith and patriotic intentions of the GB75 members as volunteers on call to the government in the event of a crisis, he was nevertheless adamant that the Better Britain Society must undertake to sever all connections with that organisation before he could feel able to consummate our understanding by becoming a founder member of the Society. On my assurance that we would meet this condition, he joined the Society as its first vice-chairman.

It became evident earlier this year, however, that there was no way completely to honour our commitment to TRUEMID (because of the substantial cross-membership between the BBS and GB75) short of actually disbanding GB75; and this we have done. The decision became all the easier to take when we realised from Frank Nodes's many friends that an increasing number of trade unionists acknowledge the extreme threat to the country and to themselves posed by the left-wing activists, and are determined to rally the moderates under the TRUEMID banner and fight the militants at every level from the factory floor upwards.

The position now is that the Society has pledged all the support it can muster for TRUEMID as an anti-extremist counterforce within the trade union movement although, of course, only those who are trade unionists can join it as full members. The Society has two other prime objectives. The first is to create from the grass roots of the country a demand for a new constitutional settlement embodying a Bill of Rights with entrenched clauses to safeguard the various freedoms of the individual (rights which are already being challenged by the left-wing cancer within the Labour Parliamentary Party); and, secondly, to generate support for a drastic re-ordering of the curriculum and the present educational facilities for the 15- to 16-year-old age group.

During the last few months, members of the Society have gained the very highest regard for the trade union moderates and, even though there may be difficult times ahead, we are convinced that, during the course of this year, their influence and judgement will begin to prevail over the wild men of the left.

David Stirling

In the reasoning and objectives of the Better Britain Society, the visionary element of Stirling's character comes once more to the fore; he had reasoned that what he saw as the 'long continuing crisis in Britain' was grave and multi-dimensional. It was a malaise which both government and opposition had either failed to recognise or simply lacked the courage to tackle at source. The solution, he argued, required creativity; only through an exciting, creative, positively progressive programme could the fundamental element become inspired – the fundamental element had to be the British people.

Surely, demanded Stirling, the politicians are the servants of the people even though they often forget that; therefore, in resolving a 'crisis of this magnitude' the curative process should directly involve the people. He likened the disease to a cancer; from an already known number of 'hot-spots' the inexorable, malignant web would spread unless the hot-spots were treated effectively. His concept was of a nation rising up in response to a challenge. The BBS challenge was to the people not to Parliament; the restoration of Parliament's authority would be an offshoot of the movement which would have no leanings toward any political party.

The objectives of the BBS as defined by Stirling (after the meeting with Nodes) were:

1. The enactment by Parliament of a constitutional settlement, superseding the settlement of 1689.

2. The enactment of an Educational Bill drastically revising the schooling methods and curriculum of the 15- to 16-year-old age group.

3. To back the Movement for True Industrial Democracy (TRUEMID) in every way open to the Society.

4. *Long Term Aim* Britain, since shedding its overseas possessions, has been without a rôle in the world and is, indeed, so lacking in economic muscle that it is beyond its powers to sustain one of significance. First, we must achieve as a nation the goal of being self-supporting and . . . achieve a standard of domestic prosperity at least equal to the average of Common Market countries. We can then get down, for instance, to leading the

world in devising ways of halting and even helping reverse the present rapid deterioration of the environment; helping resolve the problem facing the developing countries and the world problem of over-population. Historically, as the oldest of the Western democracies, it is fitting that we should again assume leadership status in world affairs.

I was interested to know why Stirling thought that those three objectives could inspire the 'fundamental element'.

'David, we've had a Bill of Rights since 1689, that's three hundred years during which we've had no civil wars. The same Bill has been used to help formulate similar Bills for other Commonwealth nations and ex-colonies and part of it was even used as an amendment to the American Constitution. On top of this we've got the Universal Declaration of Human Rights as drafted for the United Nations; parts of that came from our own Bill. I feel reasonably well protected in law, understand and value my rights of freedom of speech. Why do you see the need for what you refer to as a "constitutional settlement" which implies changes to an already satisfactory state of affairs?'

'You're making mischief, Spike. The Bill of Rights is not just about the rights of the individual and, as you should know, but there's a possibility that you don't, you have to look to three documents to discover all your rights. The Magna Carta of 1215; the Petition of Rights of sixteen something-or-other and the Bill of Rights of 1689; you've then got to examine common law; then treat yourself to a visit to Scotland and you'll find differing laws. You've read the objective without bothering to look at the supporting papers and that's unfair – or are you practising to be a journalist?

'The constitutional settlement we envisaged was aimed at parliamentary reform. Much of what affects the grass roots of our country today stems from that which was written when the class system was fully operative, and in a society where there was nothing really wrong with the class system in many ways. Aristocracy is one of those words whose meaning has become corrupted over the years. It is best used alongside meritocracy, because in the original Greek context it signified a person who had reached a point of respect amongst his fellow men as a result of his own efforts – birthright was not a factor.

'Britain should be a meritocracy and there should be no legal or sociological bars put in the way of the budding aristocrat (in the Greek sense). Part of the settlement would have been electoral reform; I staunchly support James Goldsmith's proposal of alternative voting. That does away with splinter groups and frightens off the extremists; a consensus of opinion is readily available and Members of Parliament elected by their constituents continue to represent them. All the resultant MPs under such a system would be obliged to take an oath of allegiance to the Crown and the Constitution.

'There was to be provision within the settlement for a substantial devolution of legislative, administrative and financial powers to Scottish, Welsh and English Assemblies, but under conditions which would promote and preserve an economic unity of the Kingdom which would be subject to the Supreme Court of the House of Commons. We believed in the necessity of a Supreme Court, in the manner of the USA, as being the highest Appellate Court in the country, charged to protect and interpret the Constitutional Settlement and the Bill of Rights. The law, which is a strange mixture of common and statutory legislation, needs a huge overhaul to bring us in line with our obligations to the EEC and the United Nations Organisation. A great deal within the law needs simplifying also so that those whom it is designed to protect can readily understand it.

'The House of Lords has little credibility with the people of this country, perhaps the more so now that it is televised! It is inconceivable to imagine the House of Commons without the checks provided by the Lords, but consider how many of them are there by hereditary privilege or by being shunted upstairs after either a very good or an embarrassing career. The House of Lords, with properly elected members, could well assume the mantle of the Supreme Court. I am not saying that the

House lacks sagacity; there are some very wise men there – when they choose to be present. The members of the Supreme Court would be obliged to fulfil their responsibilities.'

'Did you, David, in 1974 set yourself a timescale for this massive undertaking?'

'You mustn't credit me with all this. I talked to an enormous number of people about the BBS and I stole all ideas which were in keeping with the Society. No. There wasn't a timescale as such; the approach was to try to get the objectives properly drafted with supporting papers under the advice of the best legal and political brains before going to the public for support. The support would have had to be massive but I believe it would have been attainable. Then the idea was to get a substantial number of Members of Parliament from both main political parties, I think we set our sights on a hundred or so with a few from the other parties – we decided to leave out Creaming Lord Crutch and his Monstrous Raving Things, of course. We were aware of how long this could take. Given a suitably massive groundswell of support, MPs would not have been able to ignore the concept and we then aimed to have those who were firmly committed begin to submit the Constitutional Bill under the Private Member's Bill. I suppose the best time-frame would have been about five years but I would have hoped for something much quicker because the whole thing was dependent upon the people and keeping motivation up would have been quite difficult.'

Privately I thought that if anyone could have done it, it would have been the man who had taken 60 soldiers on their first operational parachute drop behind enemy lines in atrocious weather; maintained an influence over all the inmates of a prisoner-of-war camp; kept the Capricorn Africa Society in good spirits for so long, and who was already being overwhelmed by support from complete strangers for a cause which they knew little about (GB75). We went on to examine objective two.

'David, I've seen a 1976 news clipping. Some three years

later you began to re-examine the possibilities of the Society. The article would put me off, as a parent, from wanting to see your influence anywhere near my children's education. What were you really trying to achieve?'

'There were a few articles and they were all short on the truth.' Stirling rooted around in the seemingly chaotic 'filing system' on the floor of his flat. He found what he was looking for amazingly quickly.

'Here's my response to the *Times Educational Supplement*. I really can't remember but I might have tucked a little into my sporran from them. That was one of the problems of word getting out before one was ready. People got hold of jottings on bits of paper or heard only part of a conversation or, like this fellow, listened to one but either didn't hear what was being said or more likely couldn't understand it.'

It was the article to which I had been referring and Stirling's letter to the editor read:

29 October 1976

Dear Mr Cohen,

Yesterday, I received this clipping from a friend, who saw it in the *Times Educational Supplement*.

Subsequently, I read the rest of your article, which makes it clear that you were determined in the first paragraph to give the impression that I was trying to establish a modern-day Hitler Youth Movement. Obviously, you assumed that people of normal liberal outlook would refuse to read on, because of the utter disgust you will have aroused in them in this preliminary paragraph.

Before taking the matter further, I suppose I should give you a chance to make some amends by arranging for a very prominently placed apology for, and withdrawal of, the first paragraph. So perhaps you will now let me know what you propose to do. In the meantime, I will withhold any formal legal action until next week.

In addition to the offending paragraph, you entirely failed to mention that the whole project will initially be a voluntary one, on a pilot scale, and will only be expanded to a national scheme if popular opinion so demands. I emphasised this point many times in our talk. There were also many other inaccuracies in the article, which I charitably put down to your inexperience.

Yours sincerely,
David Stirling

P.S. I am sending a copy of this letter to Sir Denis Hamilton. I will not write to others who may have been outraged by your article until I have heard from you.

Sir Denis Hamilton DSO

Dear Sir Denis,
    A junior reporter on one of your papers – *The Times Educational Supplement* – has behaved really abominably.
    The attached enclosures will indicate the good reasons for our sense of outrage.
    In the past I have always let you know when I get into trouble with one of your papers – you will remember that I once lifted £7,000 libel money off Roy Thompson as a result of an article in the *Sunday Times* colour supplement and more recently, the row I had with your Mr Evans of the *Sunday Times* about Watchguard and the Yemen.
    Before starting up proceedings against *TES*, I am following the same procedure, and letting you have the relevant papers . . .
    As the Better Britain Society takes its educational project (so falsely described by Cohen) very seriously, it is obviously necessary to take all steps open to us to combat the effects of Cohen's article.

Stirling carried on with his reply to my question. 'What was I trying to achieve? I can say "I" because, non-swanks, it was my idea in the first place. If you are asked a question on the educational system in this country your mind is immediately, in the first instance, drawn back to your own experiences. Now I had the opportunities for a very good well-rounded education but I was in such a mental fug of uncertainties that I didn't take full advantage. That is by no means unusual in people of my age; before the advent of sex education and before priests of all religions began to temper their imprecations of the devil taking the sinner without explaining why, the pressures were great. That is not to say the same pressures aren't there today – they are in some households. If I had had the courage to ask more questions I wouldn't have been quite so wrapped up in guilt.

'I believe that had I been put into a learning mood earlier the benefits would have been enormous, and why should that not be perfectly feasible? The other aspect of life in this country which disturbed me, and still does, is that if you believe in meritocracy you also have to believe in every person's right to extract the maximum from the educational system. In part we go back to the concept of aristocracy as normally accepted; in this country there is still a "them" and "us" area in education. The public schools dominate the private sector of education, and with very few exceptions the students are there through privilege of birth or wealth. The comprehensive school system lost its way and became thoroughly undermined by teachers with strange thoughts about competition and merit. Many schools do not recognise ability, indeed blatantly stifle it. No teacher could ever convince me that it is an advantage to either party to force the able to adopt the slower pace of learning of the less able. That is utter nonsense.

'How can a responsible person pretend that it is correct to steer a child into thinking that it is anti-social to want to beat his classmates! How absurd. When that child goes into business as an adult the first thing which will hit him is that all business is fiercely competitive, as are most of the professions (including teaching), and he who does not compete will find himself quite quickly on the scrapheap, or stagnating into boredom in a job perhaps well below his capacity, then developing the peculiarly British killer disease – apathy.

'Another major weakness of our system is what the educationalist would grandly call "career planning". What poppycock. How can career planning be successful when it is often run by academics who have never been exposed to business life and who base their advice on reports from teachers who have led equally sheltered lives? Exam results do not necessarily show an aptitude to work in any one direction. A few certificates in the sciences don't mean that a person is tailor-made for engineering or pharmaceutical work – he may have the makings of a first-rate diplomat or negotiator who just happened to find the sciences easy. Only the study of that person in a suitable environment by one qualified to do so will determine what real talent is there.'

Stirling obviously believed passionately in educational reform and he had at least one method charted out. He had taken great care with his proposals which, although not in final form, had been presented to people of different political persuasions and academic experience including the head of at least one public school and friends on the staff of Ampleforth.

The system was initially devised to work in harmony with the new Constitution, and was essentially volunteer based. It provided a means for those interested in broadening their formal education to do so in an informal way, under conditions which would develop their characters in areas which might be restricted by normal school and family environs. Apart from my interview notes there is little written detail on the concept. In essence Stirling aimed at establishing four distinct phases of education, 'from weaning to wage packet'.

He recognised the immense learning capacity a child has almost from the moment of birth, and reasoned that by the age of three a child was easily capable of learning the alphabet and numbers, and would find it fun. (Many do this anyway.) The state would provide either nursery schools or television and radio programmes aimed at three- to five-year-olds. He saw no reason why a normal child should not begin formal education capable of simple reading and arithmetic and filled with the desire to learn.

During the first formal phase of learning, between the ages of five to fifteen years, he envisaged no great change to the national curriculum but did see major efforts being put into teacher training, teaching aids and methods and incentives for teachers. Progression through the system should be based on a child's abilities and the structure must be able to deal with all groupings, from the brilliant to the slowest, with nothing to retard either stream. Healthy competitiveness should be encouraged and teachers should share responsibility with parents concerning children's manners and behaviour.

Up to the age of fifteen years parents would be free to pay for education as they wished and grammar schools would continue, removed from any threat of closure, offering conventional scholarship vacancies to those who achieved the necessary standards. From the age of fifteen years, however, the facilities of both public and grammar schools would pass into the hands of the state and places would be offered on a competitive/merit basis for sixth-form education. This further education would be delayed for one year while the fifteen-year-old attended a course in a totally different environment.

Within a rural setting (Stirling suggested that the many vacant stately homes and country houses would make ideal locations), the youth would be exposed to a dramatically changed curriculum. Conditions would be standard: a dormitory system, austere but not spartan; the atmosphere 'classless' with no child able to outdo others through the trappings of wealth or privilege; set in green fields as far as possible and staffed by the most proficient teachers available. The system would not be obligatory for those who opted to begin a working career, but Stirling hoped to make it sufficiently attractive to leave those numbers small.

Educational streams would continue but the curriculum would be broadened to include a full understanding of the Constitution and an in-depth examination of the aims, philosophies and workings of all political parties (to include Communism). Great emphasis would be put upon lucid explanation of basic economics, including the responsibilities of the West to the developing nations. All subjects would make full use of closed-circuit television, so that students could be exposed to the finest teachers and speakers in the world.

Life outside the academic would be geared towards developing community and family responsibilities through self help. The religious base of the schools was to be multi-denominational and pressure-free with lecturers providing explanations of all the great religions. Sporting facilities and facilities to improve physical fitness would be available, again without pressure.

A major feature would be the private tutorial which would extend beyond the academic. Apart from allowing students to ask questions in private the tutor would be able properly to assess each student's qualities and give advice on developing these. This was a key part of the system which would also expose students to lectures and discussions chaired by highly placed and knowledgeable executives from business, academe, the professions, the vocations and the sporting world.

At the end of the year at this 'interim school' Stirling expected students to be well-balanced, have a sense of family, community, national and international duty; be confident and have no fears of class differences; have a full understanding of their country and a good idea of what they wanted to do with their lives. Those who opted for, or required for their chosen careers, further education would have access to the grammar and public schools as mentioned, en route to the universities.

I am over-simplifying, and it should be understood that Stirling was not so pompous as to want to impose an untried system on the nation; his aim was to achieve approximately forty hours of debate time in the House of Commons; this he was sure would lead to a pilot scheme if he could also muster sufficient public support. He failed to attract enough support, but Stirling never lost faith in his ideal, which was based on common sense, downright patriotism and humanitarian philosophy.

What about the enthusiasm Frank Nodes had awakened in him? The support of TRUEMID led to the third objective of the Better Britain Society.

# 24

# LEFT, RIGHT AND CENTRE

The raging inflation which was to peak in 1975 and result in the worst levels of unemployment for some thirty-five years gave the left-wing militants every opportunity to exploit the difficulties of the nation. In 1974 Britain had lost more than twelve million working days through militant-activated strikes. The growing sophistication of industry created a mutual dependency between plants and factories which gave the Trotskyist groups greater power than ever to create widespread chaos. Within the trades unions, violence and intimidation were becoming unbearable; the unruly element seemed to believe they were above the law. In central and local government, functions were under attack from the Marxists who had virtually destroyed the tradition that public servants carry on with their duties whatever their grievances.

In that year strikes and overtime bans had disrupted London; a postal strike deprived the councils of approximately £100,000,000 in uncollected rents and rates. Communist infiltration into ministries started a series of leakages of confidential documents, resulting in an international mistrust of government in security circles as parts of the Civil Service were discredited. A number of government ministers were apparently in sympathy with a wide spread of Communist-oriented organisations. Reg

Prentice, a cabinet minister, was dropped as the candidate for Newham North-East due to an extremist manipulated vote. His crime was to speak out for his constituents. Britain was beginning to pay the price of apathy.

Stirling left many notes on his involvement with the battles within the trades unions; I am grateful to a number of people who helped me appreciate the significance of his work. Not all considered it of great importance – they were bound up in their own struggles; some saw him as the strategist and motivator without whom they would not have been able to carry on the fight; few would wish to be named, for, as Stirling said, 'This is just a skirmish – it will get nastier and it will not just go away.' This, after he had been working for the cause for some dozen years, and at a time when most people would have said that the battle was virtually over.

A short chapter in a book does no justice to the very courageous work carried out over two decades by the dedicated few whose example inspired others in sufficient force to bring about a radical change.

Frank Nodes saw it as a task for both employers and trades unionists; in his view, the left-wing extremists had already taken over the commanding heights of the more powerful unions, and from this power base would ruthlessly attempt to inhibit government and threaten parliamentary authority. The left had access to money; the moderates who did not were losing the battle despite the complete commitment of the dedicated few in terms both of private resources and time.

Nodes stated that management in both industry and commerce had a high stake in the fight, but felt by the rules of the game that they should not enter the arena. This he said was nonsense. They had much more right to be involved with the shaping of the unions than had any Communist Party or other extremist group. Employer and union member were partners in work and had a close identity of interests. Surely, he argued, the moderate had the right to say: 'Our fight is your fight; stand in line beside us.'

It was Nodes's fighting spirit that attracted Stirling in 1974, when TRUEMID was an infant movement, but he sensed that Nodes and others were perhaps fighting in isolation with platoons rather than taking to the broader battlefront with an army. Nodes had no rear echelon support, he did not have sufficient committed lieutenants to cover his flanks nor any defined strategy to meet the wider front. It was important to define the threat, convince the few and then broadcast to the many to elicit their support.

Stirling was quite aware that in many ways he was a liability and that it would be sensible for him to stay away from the TRUEMID offices, once established. He set about determining how best he could help a cause very dear to his heart. He planned a series of small, intimate dinner parties at which he met highly placed union executives; his offers of help had a mixed reception.

Frank Chapple (later Lord Chapple) was to say in an interview many years later: 'I only met David Stirling on one occasion. I had great sympathy with what he was trying to do which was similar to what I was trying to do myself. Any contact with him would have made me less effective at that time. I'd have been seen as a tool of this strange man who formed the SAS. Nobody wanted to be seen as a direct associate as this would have tarred them with being semi-fascist. My arguments always were to stay clear of any obvious or well known right-wing activist. Those were personal feelings but I know that would also be the position of people like Jim Skinner. I knew John Ogier slightly better than I knew David Stirling; I believe Ogier knew Stirling but I certainly didn't get that from Ogier himself – I'm guessing. His [Ogier's] great weakness was that he knew very little about the trades unions.'

Small wonder that men like Frank Chapple were reluctant to form liaisons with Stirling in the aftermath of the publicity of GB75 which hung on him labels of 'fascist', 'Blimp' and 'eccentric' which he certainly did not deserve – a first-class example of how the left set about character assassination.

Chapple was making good headway in his own brave and lonely battle within the ETU; he could do without the extra pressures such an alliance would have produced. Stirling's diaries show that he regarded Chapple highly, as being 'cast from the same mould as Leslie Cannon'. Although many declined to treat with Stirling on the same grounds as Chapple, a host of others did not, but wisely the relationships were kept quiet. If anything this added to Stirling's determination to act.

Early on, Stirling advised the moderates to get a newspaper organised. He largely took upon himself the onus of acquiring funds for this. His reasoning would have resembled Roger Rosewell's; Rosewell had in his youth been an active Trotskyist (since then very positively converted) and, in Frank Chapple's words, 'a real pain in the backside as a youngster'.

'For the moderate camp to have a chance it had to have an organisation that at least matched that of its rival. There were two basic necessities. First, a single candidate at elections so there was a direct choice between one Communist and one moderate, no dilution of the anti-Communist vote by two or three moderate or other candidates. Second, it needed a newspaper. For all left-wing organisations in whatever walk of life the first thing to be organised is a newspaper.

'A newspaper is not only a propaganda vehicle where ideas are written down and you sell it to someone else; the discipline of producing a paper once a month – collecting reports, writing it, printing it, gives a reason for the organisation to continue; it lives around the paper. The paper is not only the way in which it expresses its ideas to the outside world – the paper tells *them* what to do as well. You can't be a member by going to the pub, you can only be a member by selling a paper – it's an activity you can't avoid. People have to give money to support the paper, and thus become involved – get locked in.

'The moderates needed to publicise themselves and their activities. When a union puts up a notice on a board announcing a branch meeting for such-and-such a date, the agenda this and that, it was hardly designed to attract anyone but committed union activists – and they were unlikely to be people that didn't want to be run by the Communists.

'One of the philosophical differences within the Marxist movement is worth mentioning; it revolved around the question of honesty. There is a meeting of 1000 people at which pay conditions are going to be the main topic. Do you say, "I'm a revolutionary Marxist. I believe in the overthrow of parliament, the monarchy, the courts and the rounding up of all judges. Because I believe in all this I also think we should have a pay rise"?

'If I said that, maybe I'd get five votes – a triumph, five more members. Wouldn't it be better simply to say, "Let's have a pay rise"? That way I would have 1000 people behind me. I don't necessarily need them to be Marxists – I just need them to vote for me.

'There were many rows about this dilemma – to what extent do you display total belief and to what extent can you dispense with these "unnecessary" confessions? The moderates had to determine who was who and spell out to people exactly what they stood for. If a speaker or an official was a member of the militant tendency but not saying so then someone had to brand them with the truth.'

Stirling's notes show that he saw the challenge to TRUEMID as being to thwart the left's intention of disrupting central government; there was no secret that this was a Communist aim. He was also aware that many fine people were fighting in isolation, seeing only the immediate attack on their own structures, and perhaps losing sight of the greater threat. If the first step was to bring cohesion to the fight, structure it to a common, wider aim, then the second step had to be to involve Whitehall and force it to acknowledge the actions of the few. Elementary to this was the encouragement of moderates in their first challenge – to put the unions back into the hands of the members. Insofar as he could see there were only four real rôles for him personally. He could assist with fund raising; he was willing and able to get involved with the tactical battle; he had conduits into Whitehall, Scotland Yard and the security services and he was committed to the cause anyway, which meant that he ought to be able to motivate its members. He had to do all this without appearing to be too closely involved.

Stirling made one early mistake in attending the inaugural meeting of TRUEMID on 9 April 1975. Though he stood at the back he was an unmistakable figure and reporters photographed him. Syd Davies (AUEW) had agreed to be chairman and the rest of the board comprised John Adams (GMWU), Ron McLaughlin (AUEW) and John Fraser on the national executive committee of NALGO. Some harsh, if predictable, press reports hinged on Stirling's 'anti-trade union' organisation, GB75. An old quote by Syd Davies was hauled out of the filing cabinet; asked about his association with Stirling and GB75 he had said, 'I think he is a totally acceptable figure. It is the Scanlons and the Scargills who are the danger to this country, not the Stirlings.'

TRUEMID published three well-written pamphlets that year: *Towards an Open and Classless Society* by James Goldsmith (aimed more towards the ideals of the Better Britain Society) and *The Labour Party and Trotskyist Infiltration through the Militant Group* and *The Day of the Ostrich* by Frank Nodes, who completed the work just before his death in December 1974. From these evolved the TRUEMID newsletter *Trueline*. Papers were also started in a number of unions by the moderates. Stirling used the response to the old GB75 and the BBS mailing lists to initiate the request for funding for TRUEMID. He had rightly gauged public opinion in that whomsoever was attracted by the BBS had also to be interested in the new organisation. The BBS was by no means dropped, however; Stirling continued that work with no lessening of enthusiasm.

In reply to a particularly vitriolic attack by the left-wing East

Birmingham Trade Union Research Unit (EBTURU) a leaflet was immediately circulated in that city.

## Fact or Fiction?

If the EBTURU has to produce so-called 'fact sheets', then for goodness' sake let them be factual – that much at least is due to the trade union member to whom they are directed and who, thank goodness, is still basically a very factual animal.

TRUEMID, through recognition and respect for this fine quality, from the very beginning made no effort to hide or disguise any part of its structure, aims or activities. Anyone wanting to know more about us – the more the better – need only send for a copy of our Objectives and Constitution . . . names are named – nothing is hidden.

TRUEMID is for responsible trade unionists who resent seeing the unions used to savage our economy and destroy our way of life.

TRUEMID is accused of trying to influence the trade union movement. Of course we try – and very hard too. We are loyal trade unionists and want to influence the movement for a return to its former high standing, its dignity and wide-held affection. We want to influence it for the good of all and especially for the low-paid and those least able to care for themselves in these days of escalating inflation – the aged, the sick, the single-parent family, the first-time house buyer. This is an immense task, which thankfully can be accomplished by proper use of our resources.

Our most valuable asset is our workforce. We have more skilled workers per square mile than any other country. Given the right worker/company relationship, we can quickly become the world's most prosperous workforce. The developing Third World needs our skills – and will pay for them.

We all acknowledge that the major factor in bringing about the present economic collapse and hideous job loss has been acrid industrial relations stemming from inhibited management playing into the hands of political extremists.

TRUEMID wants you, brother, to replace the extremists. TRUEMID wants you to acclaim that *you* are the union, that *you* are best fitted to shape policies which will establish our economic prosperity and at the same time secure our democracy – a democracy which will expose all spurious organisations with pretensions of doing public good . . . with public money.

TRUEMID's money is hard and honestly earned. When accusing companies of funding us, why doesn't the 'Research Unit' name names?

WHAT OF THE EAST BIRMINGHAM TRADE UNION RESEARCH UNIT'S MONEY??? They clearly employ high skills and, as trade unionists, must pay the going rate for the job . . . a rate higher than that paid in engineering. Their printing machines and office equipment are clearly of the best . . . The rent, heating, light and other commitments must also cost a packet.

Who, then, pays for all this? *You*, brother. *You* could well be paying for all this. 186 St Saviours Road, the home of the EBTURU, is paid for and maintained by you . . . the rate payer. *That the City Council is not happy and intends to stop the money supply, must mean something in the honesty stakes*?

The observant will detect the hand of Stirling. Notes from an interview with Mrs Kate Losinska (one time President of the CPSA) show how highly regarded Stirling's input was.

'He showed how the militant tendency was operating like the military – I believe that's why they adopted the name. They worked like an army. People like myself were only becoming aware bit by bit of what the fight was really about, forming our own quite well-organised groups in small pockets all over the place. Then there were people like Frank Chapple, fighting his fight in the Electricians' Union, having just surfaced from another big court case. In local government there were large areas with problems. The shops and distributive trades sounds minor, but trade is the lifeblood of this country. The problem was evidenced by the rise and hopefully the fall of Arthur Scargill – you could see how he managed to wreck the mining industry for a while. British Steel was beginning on its downhill road. The postmen managed to stop the mail for weeks, and remember when nobody's rubbish was collected for such a long time. There may have been some pretty good general secretaries around but they were helpless if the executive was nominated by the left. People like me became aware through TRUEMID that there were others willing to make a fight of it.

'That was David's understanding – he saw what was really going on in total terms, nationally; we saw just a small section. He must have quietly decided that it was time somebody did something.'

Stirling held his cards much closer to his chest than he had ever done, and never told any person he met exactly who else he was talking to without good reason. He organised small seminars to study alternative union rule books, enabling the less experienced members of TRUEMID to speak with eloquence and authority on a wider range of matters. He was very careful in the way that he offered advice. He was much more at ease if people approached him; he felt that to push advice on to them would lessen their stature in their own eyes; far better that they thought through to the root of the problem, then came to him if they felt he had something to offer. He was always cognisant of what the fight meant to the moderates who had decided to act.

'It is impossible to deny the courage of those people though they would probably brush it aside. Frank Nodes, Frank Chapple, Kate Losinska, Les Cannon, Terry Duffey, Sid Weighell, Syd Davies, Ron McLaughlin, John Ogier, John Adams, John Fraser – there was a host of them, far more than most people would realise – they were all in the forefront of the fight with no armour other than their personalities and convictions. Chapple was given rough physical treatment from time to time; Kate actually had her leg broken when she was deliberately pushed down some steps in Glasgow – all because they had the courage to speak out. John Ogier's death was quite strange, though nobody could make accusations over it.*

---

* John Ogier died in a car accident when, apparently as the result of a burst tyre, his car went off the road in Hickstead. Stirling's notes show a certain amount of suspicion but as Ogier was very much his link man he may have been over-reacting. Ogier was very important to Stirling's operation and the outsider may have calculated that the effect of his demise on TRUEMID would be devastating.

I found it quite humbling to discover, where I had thought only apathy existed, good men and women prepared to go down fighting. If I did anything it was in a very small way.'

Stirling was highly critical of the government's handling of the GCHQ crisis and reckoned that it set TRUEMID back considerably. 'The fight was reaching critical stages in the Civil Service and the mess which resulted from the GCHQ affair was horrendous. The fault goes back to when the site was constructed. In tandem with the Americans Britain organised a listening post, to be one of only two such major facilities in the West. There was to be a great deal of collusion between the two countries which required trust and confidence. The Americans quite rightly staffed their facility from the start with military personnel. Only the British could have set up a Civil Service base in Cheltenham. Thirty years later some bloody fool is caught playing around with little boys and the whole system comes under scrutiny and is threatened with closure due to a decision to ban the trade union.

'The mess that followed put us in the position of having to defend a government that took away the basic human right to strike. I know Geoffrey Howe tried to persuade Margaret Thatcher to do a deal by offering to allow GCHQ to keep its union, with a clause that a particular part of its work would be guaranteed free from strike action; she brushed it aside. There really was a case for sensible negotiation there with a bit of give and take and I think she mishandled it badly. The whole business took some weathering – it weakened our case for at least three years.

'I can't say I was ever particularly fond of Thatcher but I did admire her tremendous fighting spirit which was in line with what this country's heritage is all about. Knowing she was there gave many of the people I worked with a very comfortable feeling and the end should not have been so undignified. I'm glad that moderation won through – I hate the labels we pin on each other like left, right and centre, but if I had to choose it is probable that I would opt for left rather than right. The left does have an element of compassion lacking in the right; the centre is really composed of people without opinion who are happy to do nothing. I'm talking about extremes of course – the only real route to harmony is throu;h moderation on both flanks and let the saner argument win.'

To try to find out how senior political figures viewed Stirling and his activities in the seventies, I interviewed Lord Whitelaw, who through that decade served both as a cabinet minister and in the shadow cabinet. During the time of GB75 and the BBS, he had spoken out for Stirling when some noteworthies were being quite scathing. Roy Mason described him as a Colonel Blimp (for GB75) while Lord Hailsham accused him of 'adopting a novel and not particularly attractive heresy in proposing that a preamble to the Bill of Rights should have constitutional precedence over the operative content of the Bill itself' (Better Britain Society). Stirling, in a reply to Hailsham via *The Times*, questioned why 'Lord Hailsham, with his highly trained legal mind, has so profoundly (and unattractively) misinterpreted the intended meaning of the only paragraph he chose to quote.' I asked Lord Whitelaw about his defence of Stirling.

'Mainly I did it out of friendship for David though I thought it was a jolly good idea and very useful. I never really thought it would come off, it was too imaginative. In fact it was David at his most imaginative.

'I didn't see an awful lot of David after the war but we remained very good friends. We were both members of White's and very often one would hear David telling all who cared to listen, in a very loud voice, all his secrets. Really the last place one wants to tell a secret is White's. I remember his great ploy to protect us all from government (BBS) and the raising of the private army to help government (GB75). We would all hear the grand plans. He was a most enjoyable man, very, very remarkable. He became a little reclusive later on and stopped seeing people and didn't get much to the club. Although he was totally different as a man there was a lot of the Lawrence in him; he had an enormous streak of brilliance – all the Stirlings have it.'

Stirling's claim to have helped the cause only 'in a very small way' is contradicted by those I have interviewed. He consolidated their efforts on a national scale; he clarified their aims and assisted in laying down strategies; he made sure they understood just how long the fight was going to be, and prepared them for that. He was unquestionably effective in getting conduits into Whitehall and these efforts bore fruit; central government was eventually forced to pass new legislation on compulsory ballots and the like, as a result of pressures from within cabinet as well as without.

In any long fight the combatants become weary and dispirited from time to time and that is perhaps where Stirling's greatest contribution lay. He was always available for a chat, always ready with words of encouragement and always the first to congratulate members on their achievements. A cause needs a leader, and Stirling provided that leadership in a peculiarly personal fashion, and he was still taking an active, if diminishing, part in proceedings as late as 1988 – fourteen years after the inception of TRUEMID (which still functions).

Stirling's nature, however, demanded other interests besides TRUEMID. Though his health was not as good as he would have hoped – unsurprisingly considering what his body had been made to withstand over the years – nonetheless he was a regular visitor to the shoots, rivers and lochs in Scotland and he began a venture in 1975 which was largely successful and was to engage part of his attention for the rest of his life. Four years in preparation, the plans for the 'Renewal of a Highland Loch' caused consternation in the local community of Morar; they were long and complex and not immediately recognised for what they were. The preamble promises 'An account of how the people, proprietors and crofters of a Highland community, by acting together to launch a locally significant enterprise, can bring gain to themselves, and, hopefully, a better understanding of one for the other.'

At first the Morar community, perhaps influenced by enthusiastic local newspaper reporting, saw this as an attempt by the 'absentee Laird' to make money. They could not have been much further from the truth. Stirling was genuinely motivated by a great love of the area.

'I've become just a visitor to Morar over the years though I view it nowadays as my home and expect to end my days there. I was able to see it through a visitor's eyes. I could notice subtle and not-so-subtle changes which because of their insidious nature perhaps pass unnoticed by the residents. The peace and tranquillity of Loch Morar was fast disappearing. Of course men have to make a living but there seemed to be great flotillas of cabin cruisers there nowadays and the pollutive effect could only be imagined.

'There is a disease in that part of Scotland, Spike, called West Coast Inertia (WCI); a particularly stubborn form of inertia. We do a lot of thinking and talking in that part of the world and we nod our heads wisely when we talk about poachers and fish registers but we don't do anything about it. WCI is to the West Coast what mañana is to Mexico, and Keir and Lovat Estates were as guilty as anyone else.'

In his introduction to the project Stirling gives his three aims as:

a) To save the fishing on Loch Morar from virtual extinction at the hands of the poachers.

b) To arrest the growing scale of pollution in the river and estuary.

c) To preserve the quietness and the beauty of the loch and to prevent its savaging by haphazard commercial exploitation.
    To achieve these aims will require the backing of the people of Morar, of the Morar lochshore crofters and of the proprietors – but the initiative must come from the latter.

During the last few years many of us have talked of ways
of ousting the salmon and sea trout poachers, but have done
nothing. Now we must commit ourselves to winning back for
Loch Morar its true maximum rod fishing potential. The register
on the river fish ladder records a major drop in the number of
fish moving upriver to the loch – a drop far more massive than
can be explained by the general current downward trend of sea
trout stock on the West Coast of Scotland.

Provided the plan set out in this paper can be put into effect,
we should within six years or so restore the count to at least
four-fifths of its old average.

The plan then goes into great detail covering every conceivable argument and all financial ramifications. Stirling invested
a considerable amount of his own money in the research,
preparation and production of the plan and into the project
itself. It was money he did not anticipate getting back, but
he thought the cause vital to the community interest, as his
conclusion says.

Clearly we cannot afford to delay. If we are convinced that the
project . . . is practicable, then we must act with the immediacy
of the timetable suggested . . . otherwise our position, whether
as a proprietor or crofter, or a Morar resident, will become
increasingly difficult. In the past we have enjoyed, and so
have Morar's summer visitors, the peace and serenity of the
loch; but now all that is under threat. Already, for instance,
there is a conurbation of 35 cabin cruisers, of strident colours,
moored at the very point from where many Morar visitors get
their first glimpse of the loch.

As road access to Morar is improved, and as more coaches
and cars arrive, many even of the most loyal of Morar's regular
visitors will go elsewhere . . . and they will be replaced by a
much larger number of . . . trippers in small caravans or . . .
tents, who will be impervious to the loch's deterioration and
add to it with their litter. This well-known sequence of the
tourist . . . pushing out the traditional visitor with all the
severely negative economic consequences to the community
has occurred elsewhere, but has been successfully combated
by strict zoning regulations. *But until the Morar Project organisation exists, what concerted action can be taken?*

An enthusiastic rather than lethargic response to this paper – provided the Morar Community Council's amendments do not remove its 'teeth' – could switch our present dreary do-nothing attitude to one of active commitment to carry out its recommendations, and thereby establish the best 'public permit' fishing loch in all Scotland, greatly enhance the community's material well-being, and, best of all, preserve the Morar way of life.

Dear though it was to his heart Stirling and I did not spend a great deal of time talking about the Morar Project, simply because it appeared later on our calendar of topics, but he did remark over drinks one evening, 'It's one of the toughest battles I've ever been engaged in and I'm managing it in a pathetic way from my easy chair in London. The person in the forefront is dear Irene. She has worked enormously hard and has put up with a very unfair amount of tedious abuse from those who simply can't or won't understand it. If we get anywhere with it, it is really Irene who must be patted very warmly on the back.'

I believe this to be one occasion where Stirling was right in eschewing praise; I had been in his flat when his sister telephoned with updates on the project and had heard the rapid firing of questions and instructions she received. I understand that the plan is well advanced and that there has been a shift from WCI. If so then this will be a Stirling family triumph.

During this decade Stirling reluctantly closed down his 'private intelligence service' in the Middle East which, unknown to many, had been quietly ticking over almost of its own volition since the early Yemen days. It was a nostalgic period for Stirling as he quietly withdrew his finger from a multitude of pies some, as he put it, 'hotter than others'. His forays overseas were infrequent, and made mainly to visit old friends rather than in pursuit of business. Although he drove almost daily from his flat in Cheyne Court to the 22 South Audley Street office (he swore that the initials 22 SAS were purely coincidental – I don't believe it), he rarely went to White's. Harry's Bar in nearby Mount Street became a favoured watering-hole though he much preferred his large, oak-panelled office as a venue in which to relax over a glass of wine with the many old friends who visited.

Stirling did not become the recluse some people have described him as – he simply chose whose company he was going to enjoy at any one time. Those who appeared at South Audley Street unannounced were usually assured of a very warm welcome and a convivial, unhurried chat – if not, they must look to some landmark in the past for explanation.

May 1980 saw the beginning of another interesting period in Stirling's life.

---

# 25

# ENDGAME

I cannot decide whether the following story is true. The 'facts' have been related to me on numerous occasions by people I would have no reason to mistrust other than that they are all possessed of the same sense of humour as Stirling. I have tried to check through Metropolitan Police records, but files on an incident which does not result in court action are destroyed after six years. I asked Stirling to vouch for the story – his reply was, 'Dear me the things people say.' But it is a good story and I leave you to decide on its veracity.

On the evening of 5 May 1980, Stirling was enjoying one of his increasingly rare visits to White's Club. In convivial company he was, on this occasion quietly, watching the snooker world championships. The screen suddenly went blank and seconds later images appeared of black-suited soldiers poised on the rooftop of 16 Princes Gate, Knightsbridge, London. The SAS was going into action to relieve the Iranian Embassy siege which was then in its sixth day. The groans of disgust at having the snooker championships interrupted were quickly muted as the audience watched in fascination an operation which lasted a mere eleven minutes.

Stirling was in rapturous mood as he strolled across Green Park that evening on his way to South Audley Street, he thought perhaps via another toast in Harry's Bar. He was suddenly confronted by two youths demanding his wallet and a struggle ensued; a passer-by on Piccadilly alerted a police car and two officers rushed to the path in the park which paralleled the road. They found one youth suspended by his collar on the spikes of the railings, and could see the other fleeing into the distance. Stirling declined an invitation to Cannon Row police station to make a statement, saying that he was a little tired and would call round the next day – of course he never did. Improbable? Green Park has its share of 'muggers' and Stirling's stooping figure moving at a leisurely pace would have been an attractive target. Impossible? No, even at sixty-four, Stirling was a powerfully built man who would certainly not have meekly handed over his 'sporran'. Given his euphoric mood and a sudden burst of adrenalin, the result as described would certainly have been feasible.

Stirling had long been an advocate, mostly in private conversation, of the SAS's need to be prepared to tackle offshoots of modern terrorism but he was totally surprised at the efficiency of the Knightsbridge operation. He had known they were studying such techniques but not how far this had been developed. He began to take more interest in the regiments.

'I had made it quite plain that I did not want to get too involved in the past. I even shirked my duties as President of the Association, not because I had no interest but I was very aware of the mould I was cast in by the press throughout most of the seventies – I was determined there would be no way of linking me to the regiments to their detriment. I had turned down so many invitations to get-togethers that the SAS had accepted that I wanted to stay out of things. I met a few of the officers from time to time at the L Detachment reunions, but we tended to keep that a fairly private affair. Perhaps this was a mistake because I always found the post-war soldier to be very interested in the roots of the SAS, and the Originals followed post-war progress with tremendous pride.

'I met Peter de la Billière, not for the first time, shortly after the Iranian Embassy Operation – that may have been when I really caught on to the massive progress in training and techniques. I did begin to accept a few invitations after that – never enough to become a burden, I hope. It was such a pleasure to find that the sort of chap who was joining was really no different in spirit to those who came together in Africa. Very much more politically aware, highly technical – certainly to an old buffer like me – and prepared to argue their corner. Such get-togethers were most enjoyable and very stimulating.'

Stirling obviously did get very much more drawn into the network he so loved and if he had, as he put it, been 'vegetating between Cheyne Court and South Audley Street' things were to change. Stirling had not really slackened off – he was merely organising events differently. The telephone had become his instrument of coercion and it was no easier to resist his powers of persuasion over the 'phone than it was face to face. He continued to take an active if more remote interest across a broad business and political spectrum.

There was undeniably a dark, brooding side to Stirling's nature which he freely admitted, though very few people saw it; it comes through in the 'doodles' in his diaries and the scraps of notes he kept. These were intermittent throughout the fifties, sixties and seventies and could be tied in with the periods in between the tailing off of one activity and the formulation of new ideas. Stirling drew up his 'battle plans' in very military style whatever the project, which may have been a hangover from the great wartime success of the SAS. When the mood of battle was upon him and the challenge had been defined his doodles were light and airy, often brightly coloured. When things were not going so well or if life had little stimulus the sketches took on a more sinister nature; in the early eighties they were bright and light – Stirling was seeking a new campaign.

The Loch Morar Project was taking quite a lot of his time (though much was delegated to Irene), mainly in persuading the local community that the plan was in their best interests. On the SAS front he was battling to minimise publicity to the organisation, using his contacts in broadcasting and Fleet

Street, and energetically fund raising for the Association. He was thinking about the possibilities open to the modern terrorist and what could be done to thwart him; he was missing the mental and physical stimulus of the battlefield.

The long-term effects of his early parachuting accident were exacerbated by being catapulted through the windscreen of his car at about 90 mph in 1976. This left him with a very painful back condition which developed into an intense osteoporosis of the second, third and fourth lumbar vertebrae. Standing and walking for long periods were uncomfortable. None of this deterred him from his annual shooting trips to Scotland though he invariably returned with yet another broken rib. Hardly a year went by after the late seventies when he didn't suffer a rib fracture or other minor injury – 'arising out of boyish horseplay', according to one doctor. If Stirling was in pain he showed it to nobody and a stick was to be used only in the direst emergency. In April 1982 he had the operation to repair the abdominal aortic aneurysm mentioned earlier during the interview with Colin Campbell.

The enforced rest period was not wasted as Stirling had decided his next move, though he was not to put it into effect for another couple of years. It was during his recuperation in 1982 that film interest was once again aroused in the SAS story and he was again approached about the early days being recorded for posterity. The first approach had been in 1960 when it was proposed to draft a script from Virginia Cowles's book *The Phantom Major* for a film of the same name. This failed largely because of the economic recession in the film industry, but Stirling was never particularly co-operative – he was too involved in Capricorn and TIE to give time to what he then saw as a 'thoroughly pomposo business'.

1977 brought a second invitation, in the form of Bobby Childs's script for the making of *Who Dares Wins*; again Stirling was never really convinced of the film's merits, and in any event financial support was hard to get at a time when there was thought to be little market for World War II stories.

The venture of 1982, with a script by Frederick Forsyth, was more to his taste especially since he had been appalled by a recent release of *Who Dares Wins*; modelled around the Iranian Embassy siege it showed a marked lack of understanding of the workings of the modern-day SAS and a peculiarly biased misrepresentation of the type of man who serves the regiment. Though Stirling had misgivings even about this film, which was to have been called *The Birth of a Regiment*, he did give his time to draw together the surviving members of the Originals to relate their memories. Once again it was not to be and in many ways it was a great pity, for who but the founder of the regiment could have recalled with accuracy the 'battles' that took place in the Middle East HQ.

There was to be yet another drawing together of the Originals in 1987 as Gordon Stevens and Anthony Kemp began to assemble a documentary history of the SAS. This was not to reach the television screens either, though it was the one project which had Stirling's full backing. The idea of a documentary appealed to him far more than anything which brought an element of fiction into what was already a very exciting story.

Stirling was not displeased with his fringe involvement with the film industry; he knew something of contracts from his television business. 'There was a little change from all this to pop into the Association coffers to defray a few L Detachment expenses in the future.'

In 1984 a small SAS team took on a challenge very close to Stirling's heart. 'Bronco' Lane and 'Brummie' Stokes, who had reached the summit of Everest in the army expedition of 1976, had got permission to take a SAS team to the 'top of the world' via China and the North Face. Stirling was delighted to meet the pair who had both lost 'many inches of finger and toe' on their last attempt; he assisted them with introductions during the fund-raising stages and was flattered to be invited to be patron of the expedition. Sadly the expedition failed with the tragic loss of one life in a major avalanche. Later, when

Stokes was to return once more to the High Himalayas, Stirling was to write, in the foreword to Brummie's book, *Soldiers and Sherpas*:

> Since climbing Everest, Brummie has already been back to the mountain only to be caught on one occasion in a devastating avalanche that broke his neck and killed a friend. Many people cannot conceive why he should want to go again. For Brummie it is unfinished business; the North-East Ridge must be climbed, not so much to prove that he can still do it, even without toes – though that does come into it – but more as a tribute to lost companions. Such determination I can understand and applaud.
>
> His fascination with Everest, that too I can understand. When I was young and Everest still unclimbed, I dreamed of being the first to reach its lonely summit; I even formulated a five-year-plan that was to enable me to do so. I trained in the Swiss Alps and the Rocky Mountains but after two years my plans were interrupted by the outbreak of war. By the time the war was ended, my life had taken a different turn and Everest could no longer be a part of it, but I am proud now to be Patron of Brummie Stokes's North-East Ridge Expedition. If only vicariously I can at least identify with his struggle. I wish him and his team well. He deserves reward for his courage and his persistence and, above all, for his moral guts.

Stirling followed the progress of the climb with avid interest, but once again Mother Nature was to take a hand and put the mere mortals back in their places; atrocious weather led to the climb being abandoned. Stokes, to Stirling's delight, was to return yet again, though as a civilian, in 1988 and this time the team succeeded in climbing through the Pinnacles and conquering the North-East Ridge.

For some five or six years the now traditional home of the SAS, Bradbury Lines in Hereford, had been in a state of rebuild and the founder of the Regiment took a very special pleasure in opening the newly named Stirling Lines on 30 June 1984 in front of many hundreds of serving and ex-members of all of the SAS regiments. He particularly wanted his speech to be reproduced because, as he put it, 'I was able publicly to express my gratitude to my co-founders.'

What a magnificent gathering; it moves me to conclude that our regiment has a special magic in generating for itself an intense loyalty in all who have served it. Indeed we are more than just a regiment – we are a family.

In the SAS it is a tradition never to be heard in public boasting about our regiment's past or present performances. Today, because this is strictly a family occasion, I am going to break that rule – in a modest way.

Almost to the day 43 years ago as a second lieutenant and known to be something of a 'cheekie laddie', and of dubious value to the army, I submitted to Field Marshal Auchinleck's Chief of General Staff a paper setting out in my own nearly illegible handwriting the SAS proposition. Within days I was authorised to raise and command a 65-man unit to be called L Detachment, SAS Brigade; and within minutes of getting that favourable nod, the SAS was underway.

Most survivors of the original SAS foundation unit – and I understand we are known in the regiment as the Dirty Dozen – are here today (and in spirit alongside me). Perhaps you can understand our astonishment, and how proud we are, in looking around this mighty throng.

After L Detachment's first disastrous parachute operation on a moonless and stormy night in November 1941, L Detachment was reduced to only 27 men; but it was more than enough to get on with proving the SAS rôle.

In January 1942 during our drive for recruits we were joined by Georges Bergé and his Free French unit. From this group eventually were born the French SAS Regiments. Bergé's men were of superb quality and they were the bravest of the brave.

In those early days we came to owe the Long Range Desert Group a deep debt of gratitude. The LRDG were the supreme professionals of the desert and they were unstinting in their help. Here among us today is David Lloyd Owen, a wartime commanding officer of this magnificent unit. We are proud to regard the Long Range Desert Group as honorary members of our SAS family.

By February 1943, L Detachment had prospered at the enemy's expense and had become the first SAS Regiment. By then we had acquired our full establishment of jeeps and supply vehicles, and we had consolidated our maritime capabilities by incorporating, under George Jellicoe, the Special Boat Squadron. Thus, sub-units of the regiment could arrive at a selected target area by air, by sea or by land.

Shortly after I was nabbed by the enemy and after a hiccough or two the command of the 1st SAS Regiment passed to the great Blair 'Paddy' Mayne.

In the meantime the 2nd SAS Regiment had been formed by my brother, Bill, and commanded by him until he had a bitter quarrel with the High Command who insisted on his regiment being used in a semi-tactical rôle for which it had not been trained. Although he had to resign he won the argument. He was succeeded by Brian Franks who was allowed to revert to the true SAS strategic function – of operating deep behind the enemy lines. At the end of the war Paddy Mayne was still in command of the 1st SAS and Brian Franks of the 2nd SAS and the SAS Brigade from the end of 1944 was under the command of Mike Calvert; while in the Middle East, George Jellicoe had been succeeded by David Sutherland in command of the Special Boat Squadron.

You will all know of the prodigious range of SAS operations carried out in the Western Desert, Italy, France, Norway, Germany and the Eastern Mediterranean. A senior general, Miles Dempsey, who commanded 13 Corps, in writing to the commanding officers of the 1st and 2nd SAS Regiments, summarised his views on the SAS as follows:

'In my military career, and in my life, I have commanded many, many units but I have *never* met a unit in which I had such confidence as I have in yours. And I mean that.' Surely a marvellous accolade coming from such a famous soldier.

After the war the anti-climax – we were disbanded. Had it not been for Brian Franks we would have been consigned to oblivion – just a meagre footnote in the history of the Second World War. With admirable tenacity of purpose he persuaded the military establishment to form 21 SAS as a Territorial unit. By 1951 the 22nd SAS was being formed in Malaysia and the regiment soon thereafter regained its proper status.

With John Woodhouse and his successors in command there began the post-war heyday of the regiment. Campaigns were fought in Malaysia, Borneo, Aden, Oman, Northern Ireland, South Georgia and the Falkland Islands – campaigns often operationally complex and each of them studded with episodes demanding the full range of SAS skills.

During the post-war period the SAS family was further enriched by the forming of the Australian, New Zealand and Rhodesian Squadrons. Each of them has merited splendid chapters in the history of its own country. The Australian and the New Zealand SAS retain the strongest of links with Hereford. The Rhodesian SAS, sadly now disbanded, had its roots in 22 SAS as C Squadron. Their roll of honour stands alongside that of 22 SAS within these Lines.

At this point I want to emphasise that I have always felt uneasy in being known as the founder of the regiment. To ease my conscience I would like it to be recognised that I have five co-founders; Jock Lewes and Paddy Mayne of the original L Detachment; Georges Bergé who started the French SAS; Brian Franks who re-raised the SAS flag after the war and John Woodhouse who created the modern SAS during the Malayan Campaign by restoring to the regiment its original philosophy.

There are so many others who have played vital parts in the SAS story like Mike Calvert, Ian LaPraik, Eddie Blondeel (who raised and commanded the Belgian SAS), Christodoulos Tzigantes and his Greek Sacred Brigade, a squadron of which fought gallantly alongside the SAS in the Middle East, Pat Riley, Bob Bennet, Johnny Watts, Geordie Lillicoe, Peter de la Billière, Fitzroy Maclean, Johnny Cooper, Tankie Smith, Tom Burt, Roy Farran and 'Mr SAS' himself, Dare Newell – but to mention them all would be almost like calling the roll.

I must specially commend you to the wise words of Neville Howard on the standard of the SAS man. I would go further. The very survival of the regiment, in a society wary of élitism, depends on the calibre of each individual man recruited. This was, is and must remain the cornerstone. I know the regiment believes in this and must always do so.

There is a further imperative which the SAS has traditionally imposed upon itself. The regiment must never regard itself as a corps d'élite, because down that road would lie the corruption of all our values. A substantial dash of humility along with an ever-active sense of humour must continue to save us from succumbing to this danger. Only then can we be sure of consolidating the foundations of these splendid new Lines and shielding the spirits and integrity of those setting out from here on their exacting tasks.

The sum total of all that has been accomplished in all those campaigns waged during the regiment's 43 years; the sacrifices of all those who have died, been disabled or wounded, from the time of our first casualty in the Western Desert to the last just two months ago on Mount Everest; the grief and anxieties caused to the wives and families throughout those years; all this must be added together for us properly to grasp the scale of our investment in the regiment as it stands today. We are deeply proud of our regiment and we are confident that in the crucial years ahead, as we advance towards our 50th anniversary, the SAS will further enhance that standing and thereby its ability to serve our Queen and Country.

And, now, on behalf of the entire SAS family – with a chest fit to bust in sheer proudness, I declare open the Stirling Lines.

In the same year Stirling was able to visit America, where he was given the opportunity to view the training and methods of Delta Force which had such a close relationship with his own SAS. That he would enjoy it was a foregone conclusion but he confessed that he thought the Americans were a little slow to understand his humour at times. He met the President, Ronald Reagan ('He never, ever seemed to answer a question – perhaps I should have given him a script first') and a multitude of high-ranking members of the Administration. He picked their brains mercilessly on such topics as their views on limited intensity conflict, national security, the free-flow of Western intelligence and their philosophies and attitudes to events in Southern and Central America. All of this was to help cement in his mind the plans he had afoot for a new venture.

In the following year, 1985, he made his last major overseas journey, to visit the Sultan of Oman's armed forces on the ground. In command was an old ex-SAS friend of great repute, Major-General Johnny Watts. He had a full and exciting tour of some of the SAS battlegrounds of the seventies (the Dhofar campaign); met many old friends from his own Middle East days and, significantly, saw at close quarters the well-run commercial operation which raised and trained the Sultan's Special Force. In many ways the origins of this could be traced back to Watchguard, as Jim Johnson had been closely involved in getting the Oman contract for his company, KMS, no doubt having learned much about the 'commercial army' business during his Yemen period.

In 1986 Stirling put together his last new business venture, inspired by three prime motives. Firstly, he had been watching the political situation in Africa quite closely over the past few years and believed that coup tactics were going to be used in at least one country which he knew well; the Philippines were also highly insecure. Secondly he perceived that the rise in terrorism would inevitably threaten commerce and industry, as evidenced by the relatively new tactic of 'product extortion' and a more sinister perception of the vulnerabilities of the oil industry to acts of international terrorism – a perception he found shared by the captains in that industry. For these two reasons alone, and despite the plethora of 'security' companies in and around London, he believed there was room for one more – provided it had an excellent pedigree both in its operatives and its philosophies. For the third reason we have to look back on Stirling's life.

Soon after he formed the new company I asked him, 'Why, David, when you're financially secure, comfortable, do you want the pure hassle of getting back into the security industry which is already overcrowded? It's much more of a dog-eat-dog world than it was in the Watchguard days; it's an expensive venture and is bound to raise the old Phantom Major headlines again. If you really want to get involved why don't you become a consultant to an existing, well-thought-of company?'

I was given a host of good reasons: how well he and Ian [Crooke] had thought out the business plan; how exciting the future was if one looked to the areas where there were real problems; how good his contacts were especially in Africa and

America; how the company would very soon be tackling a huge project in the oil industry; how I was wasting my time piddling around with a little two-man company and lacked the vision and courage to grasp the real nettles. I replied that I was grasping a fairly healthy nettle by tackling him about this book, and that being stung once I hadn't been afraid to go back. This led into one of our many late-night conversations.

'I've always said that I've been subjected to four pressures in my life. The first was my mother. I loved her dearly and had the most enormous respect for her but she was always asking what I was going to do with my life. I didn't know, of course; the more I thought about it the less I was able to see anything clearly. She was right, I had to make up my mind, but a combination of that and the totally confused, guilt-ridden years of puberty exerted an awful pressure. It seemed unbearable then.

'Having made up my mind that I would paint, the disappointment of my lack of talent left me feeling pretty useless, and surrounded by quite brilliant brothers and sisters. This was a second pressure. Years later I was able to understand that I was in fact quite normal but such a feeling of uselessness is hard to shake off. I was very worried when I was summoned to Scotland because my mother was dying – I was terrified of being there. I stopped for a drink on the way, not far short of the house in fact. A little bit of me may have been hoping I'd be too late – I still don't know. In fact I did arrive before she died and I think she gave me a bit of a telling-off for being tardy.

'The years in prison had an effect on me and unless you've been a prisoner you can't imagine what the sudden loss of freedom means. I had periods when I felt intensely guilty for being safe, even quite comfortable, while outside there was a war raging. At times there was immense satisfaction at having outwitted the Germans or Italians in some small way but overall, despite one's companions in misfortune, I experienced a great loneliness. Planning a break-out or setting one's mind to problems as we did is only a temporary escape. Reality returns and with it guilt, claustrophobia, secret yearnings and the singular uselessness of one's situation. Since the prison days I've never been at ease in a crowd and I've always been at my happiest in wide open spaces. It's not just a physical thing – it's mental as well; paper commitments, contracts, they've all given me the "jitterbuggers" – I don't like to be tied. Bonds of any sort are a pressure I find very difficult to bear.'

'But you're very close to your family,' I interrupted, 'that's very obvious. I know your word means everything to you and I've not heard of you ever turning your back on an old friend. These are bonds, surely?'

'They're quite different bonds. There's no written contract and it's two-way. There are no expectations – each takes the other for what he is; it gives a "oneness". Family and friends are outside what I'm talking about. That's a different sort of unity, beyond the clinical. It can create a pressure itself of course. I realised some years ago that I'd achieved little in my life except huge personal enjoyment – that makes one rather sad, you know, and just adds to the guilt. The best that I could hope to do is to leave behind some sort of financial trust and I've worked towards that a little; I cut out the gambling years ago and I can probably do something quite satisfactory for some of the youngsters. Perhaps that can be improved.'

I took Stirling to mean his nieces, nephews and a number of godchildren. I believe it was a contributory reason for his taking up the gauntlet of business once again – but probably no stronger a reason than his desperately feeling a need for action in the autumn of his life or having one last fling at leaving the mark he felt he had not made.

Stirling called his new company KAS Enterprises – KAS simply because it was phonetically identical to CAS, one of his great undertakings. About half way through the first year of the company's business Stirling agreed to this book being written but tried to extract a pound of flesh in return. He invited me to lunch at an expensive Chinese restaurant in South Audley Street and over the crispy seaweed got down to business. I listened to his argument that as mine was such a small company and couldn't possibly give me out of life what I really wanted, nay deserved, there was only one sensible route to take. I should amalgamate my minuscule operation with KAS, merge our existing contracts and become a director with 'special responsibilities'. I explained that I was very happy with my minuscule operation, and even though its horizons were limited it made quite enough money for my partner and me. I was sorry but I did not feel able to work for him, or anyone else – I too had my problems of 'personal space' and I too wished to be master of my own destiny.

Having brushed aside my refusals by ordering more wine and telling me that I had not fully understood the import of what he was offering, he went on in similar vein. He told me that I would have a free hand but was careful not to define in what. I would be a small shareholder, say about $2^1/_2$ per cent, beneficial equity of course, and there would be scope for further share purchasing as I proved my merit. The salary would have to be negotiated but the business brought in from my company would be reflected in my bonuses and profit sharing at the end of the first year.

Again I made my polite refusals, this time also saying that I thought it would be disastrous for us even to contemplate working together as my methods of doing business, lacking in vision as he had pointed out, were diametrically opposed to his. Where he had a global strategy, mine was local; where his perceived client base was in the top echelons of government, commerce and industry, mine lay in the private sector only; where he wished to pursue the military training contracts, my days of soldiering were over forever; where he wished to run, I was content to stroll. We would argue incessantly, I told him. Knowing something of his penchant for late-night activity, I told him that my quality of life would become much less comfortable. Thank you, sir, but no thanks.

Over our second and third courses, washed down by numerous bottles of Sancerre, the equity offer slowly rose to 15 per cent and I was invited to name my own salary. It wasn't a problem that he hadn't discussed this with Ian Crooke (his managing director), Ian would understand. The brandies and coffee came and came again and yet again and still I refused. He sat back and looked at me through those famous brown eyes and as he stubbed out the Havana cigar, I knew that at last he had accepted my point of view. I was quietly pleased that there was no acrimony and I had thoroughly enjoyed my lunch. I walked across to his office with him and sat down for a final coffee, building myself up for what I was sure would be an unsteady journey to my club; he appeared quite unaffected by the impressive amount of alcohol we had taken aboard. I stood to leave, held out my hand and thanked him for a superb lunch.

'It was my pleasure, Spike. When you come to work for me, and I'll expect you on Monday morning, do you think you could get hold of a decent blue pin-striped suit?'

I had no suitable answer for the moment!

However, it was a battle which Stirling only half won; I was to do some work for him from time to time, and quite interesting it was. The one exercise I never repeated with him was to accept an invitation to drive back to his flat from the office during the London rush hour. My soldiering days gave me moments of high tension but nothing like the drive down King's Road with my regiment's founder. Small wonder that Reg Seekings preferred to drive in the old desert days! Zebra crossings were a matter of playing chicken with the pedestrian; traffic lights were advisory, not obligatory; anyway, as he told me, 'It's an automatic car.' Automatic beyond the wildest dreams of the manufacturer. This may present an unfair picture of Stirling at the wheel. If he gave no quarter neither did he expect it when walking. Not for him the off-route diversion to a pedestrian crossing nor the unacceptable delay in waiting for lights to change. If he wished to cross, he crossed, eyes never deviating from a point on the opposite pavement. Strangely, it worked for him.

In early 1988 Stirling had two reminders of his wartime exploits. The first was a letter:

8 March 1988

Baron Rüdiger von Wechma
Der Botschafer
Der Bundersrepublick Deutschland

Dear Colonel Stirling,

It was very kind indeed to have agreed in principle to accept our invitation to come to my residence for a small luncheon on March 23rd. We do hope that your health will be restored by then to allow you to attend.

The occasion will be in your honour and we expect Lieutenant General Sir Peter de la Coeur de la Billière, a former director SAS and currently GOC South East District, and Major-General Charles Guthrie, the current Assistant Chief of General Staff who commanded a squadron in the SAS from the British side, and a few Germans to attend.

The reason for such a get-together is quickly explained: the undersigned, at present German Ambassador at the Court of St James's, was a young lieutenant during the 1942/43 campaign in the Western Desert. I served with an armoured car reconnaissance battalion (Aufklärungsabteilung 3) in Rommel's 21st Panzer Division. After our arrival at El Alamein, one of our tasks was to chase your SAS units operating behind our lines.

We were, most of the time, not very lucky. You were not only better but certainly quicker to get away. I remember one encounter just north of the Qattara Depression – it must have been around the end of June 1942 – when we discovered one of your three-jeep-units behind a hill. Before we were able to get close enough and aim our guns, your men were able to dash off in a dust cloud. One of the jeeps, however, seemed to have developed engine trouble (it was two flat tyres as it turned out), was abandoned, and its crew got away aboard one of the other two.

All this came back when I read the German translation of the book *The Phantom Major* by Virginia Cowles, which was only published in 1986, 28 years after the original, and was given to me last Christmas. We have therefore also asked the man who wrote the foreword to the German language edition, Col. Edu Neumann, Commanding Officer of Fighter Wing 27, as well as the chap who sent me the book (also an old Western Desert man) and who is now the chief editor of a Hamburg newspaper, to attend the lunch.

During and after the war we talked about you and your men quite a lot. My father-in-law was the Commanding Officer of the Luftwaffe Fighter Force in North Africa and was there when your boys blew up his planes at Fuka and El Daba. David Stirling had been, and among the old Desert Foxes still is, a household name. It would therefore give me great pleasure and be a very special privilege if we could, finally, meet in person and under more peaceful circumstances.

The luncheon will also be attended by our Defence Attaché, Brigadier-General Count Berthold von Stauffenberg. Like yourself, I was also taken prisoner in Tunisia. I 'served' as an American POW until 1946.

Looking forward to a reunion some 40 years after it all happened, I remain with my very best regards . . .

The second reminder was an occasion at which I witnessed an enormous feat of physical stamina by Stirling. He had been invited to France by the Amicale des Anciens Parachutistes, to attend the dedication of a memorial to the SAS of all nations at Sennecy-le-Grand. As the founder he was asked to make a speech. Stirling was far from well and he asked me to accompany him as it would be a marvellous opportunity to meet some of his French and Belgian wartime comrades. I was very happy to do so. He spent some days polishing up his speech which he was determined to give in French, almost driving to distraction poor Evelyn Le Chêne as she constantly redrafted his almost hourly changes. My duties began the night before the journey – I was invited to stay with Stirling to ensure that he got up in time. He teased me mercilessly the next morning by insisting that he had changed his mind and was not going – John Slim would have to give the bloody speech. I forestalled his last excuse of not having a regimental tie by giving him my own (one of three I was to give him over the years).

It was heartwarming to see the sheer delight on all their faces when Stirling, Bergé and Blondeel met up again, and that set the scene for the whole occasion. On the day of the dedication ceremony (Sunday, 4 September), Stirling arose in great pain. I was sworn to secrecy but I knew the agonies his back injury was causing him. During the ceremony an erect rank of VIP visitors, Stirling, Slim, Calvert, Bergé and Blondeel prominent among them, all, with the exception of Stirling, heavily bemedalled ('Couldn't find 'em, old boy') made an impressive sight to anyone with a sense of history. The French are prone to making long speeches and that day was no exception; whilst all this was going on the VIPs stood erect on a hot, humid day. Both Stirling and Calvert refused chairs. Stirling's exhaustion was showing when the time came for him to make his speech and he sensibly gave it in English asking Charles Cary Elwes to translate. There is a poignant reminder of man's frailty in the speech which centred on urging a closer union between the modern day SAS Regiments of Britain and France:

> . . . I propose – no, I order you, Georges Caitucoli, and you, John Slim, that before our 50th anniversary in 1991 we consolidate this new era by organising a group from the French SAS Amicales to visit Hereford as guests of 22 SAS Regiment, where they will be joined by representatives of our British Association; this to be followed, in due course, by a reciprocating visit of our British Association to Bayonne.
>
> When we have fulfilled these commitments, only then can we feel happy that we have done real justice by those we have been honouring in today's ceremonies and be sure that the bonds between us will be made stronger and bind us together into the long future.
>
> One more word about the 50th anniversary. None of you, least of all my old-timers, has permission to fall out – that is, to croak – even if you want to, before that all-important date.
>
> But I am not sure how far I can trust you to obey; therefore I will supplicate the good Lord, on bended knees, not to grab any of us even if He is so inclined, until after we have concluded those anniversary celebrations.

Throughout the long, arduous day, which did not end until many hours after the dedication, Stirling did not give away by so much as a grimace the pain he was feeling. It was an incredible performance and to witness it at close quarters made all the stories believable.

Many of his plans for the new company came to naught; it was an expensive company to maintain in the heart of London and although his team would have performed excellently had he captured the sort of operation he wanted, business was slow. Having a team consisting exclusively of ex-SAS operators was no longer novel and the economic climate prevented one major operation he had pinned his hopes on from materialising quickly enough. The team, as would be expected from their backgrounds, was not orientated towards marketing and when Stirling decided to select a man to give marketing some direction during the necessary long absences of his managing director he chose unwisely and was badly let down.

Nonetheless, the company kept going. Some good successes in the field of counter-poaching operations on several major salmon and trout rivers and shoots led Stirling to create Country Guard, and here he was in his element dealing with people he knew and respected on issues close to his heart. It is a measure of his integrity that he chose not to accept a number of security jobs which though lucrative were against his philosophies for KAS. Though illness prevented his travelling to his office for days on end he never lost the sharpness of mind which kept a constant flow of ideas being passed on to his team.

We spent many happy nights in his flat talking about the various episodes of his life, he, wrapped in his dressing gown, totally relaxed and chuckling over his reminiscences; the problem was getting him to describe his own part in events – he would far rather discuss the merits of others. I knew I was in for a treat whenever he telephoned. 'Spike? Why don't you come round for a hot bite and glass of wine?'

I knew my Stirling. On the way round I would collect a Chinese carry-out and a bottle of Sancerre to be greeted with apparent surprise: 'Oh. How very, very kind. I was going to make us some toast.'

It is incredible how frequently his telephone would ring: Gardenias, Fionas, Sabrinas, Marias – ex-secretaries, old comrades, old friends and, of course, family. He had the most unbelievable number of friends from all walks of life and he enjoyed every moment of every chat.

When Stirling decided to point his company along a single line of business, it is typical that he should again choose the grand scale. It is fitting, insofar as it closes a circle in his life, that he should select Africa as the fulcrum for his operation. Conservation of the endangered species of wild life had always been a matter of importance to him and when a series of events caused him to look in that direction he hardly paused before committing himself.

The concept of working towards the same aims as the World Wildlife Fund came from a member of his staff who, on reading a newspaper article reflecting the terrible losses of protected species of animals in Africa, remarked that surely KAS could offer real assistance. It would be unfair to discuss the fine detail of the tactics and strategies of an operation which, for all I know, continues still; suffice it to say that Stirling envisaged a network of actions which would close down the activities of the African poacher. Recognising that it was essentially a matter of supply and demand, he was planning to operate against both ends of the chain as well as the middle. Since Stirling's death his name has been impugned as having been involved in a disreputable, if not dishonest, operation in Africa. Much of this has been inspired by highly speculative journalism and a number of malcontents; whatever the final outcome may be, I can speak with authority on his ideals and ambitions for Project Lock as it became.

The efforts of the African poacher come to naught if the demand is removed. That demand, in Stirling's opinion, was created in the Middle East and China. In the Middle East, particularly the Yemen, there is always a market for rhino horn to be carved into the intricate handles of 'khunjas' – the ornamental daggers affected by most males. Being of a fibrous nature the horn is easily worked and polished and will gain in beauty as years of handling impart a deep patina.

'It is quite sickening, Spike, when you think that the rhino horn is actually nothing more than a huge fingernail. It would be understandable, though not excusable, if those fellows [the Yemenis] had tackled the rhino with their own hands, like the Masai and the lions. At least they could take pride in the acquisition having put their lives at risk. No. They must be stopped.'

He considered the Oriental market even more revolting; there, the demand was for an aphrodisiac, nor was it just for the rhino's horn. The Chinese would take any part for 'medicinal' purposes; skin, tails, ears and other organs. The Orient was also the major market for ivory, and in Stirling's eyes the elephant was equally at danger.

In conference with his team he decided that the initial approach had to be on African soil in a concerted action against the actual poachers. He recognised that so long as the market existed there would be work for poachers, and his feelings about them were more of sorrow than anger. If the cash return for a rhino horn or elephant tusk allowed an African family to live reasonably well for a month or so, who could blame the native for taking a risk in the one area where an income was assured? Perhaps, though, through education and the skilled training of game wardens, the risk to the poacher could be significantly heightened.

Perhaps the teams on the ground, through careful analysis of intelligence and surveillance of suspects, could learn something of the channels by which the plunder was smuggled out of the African countries. Such proof could be passed on to legitimate policing agencies for action. Stirling was aware of the corruption in very high places in some countries but this he shrugged aside – proof was the first requirement. Although he had meetings with World Wildlife Fund officials, it was made plain to him in the early stages that there would be no official blessing for his efforts. As a charitable foundation, the WWF could not properly sanction active operations of the sort that Stirling proposed.

Once his ground action commenced, Stirling intended to mount a concerted attack on the consumer end of the business. He collected papers by learned scientists proving beyond doubt that claims that sexual abilities were enhanced by the ingestion of powdered rhino horn, no matter how exotic the mix, were totally unfounded. He accepted that no one was going to convince a culture as old as the Chinese that this was so, but he hoped that if the public were bombarded with strategically placed articles and documentary films, demand might at least decrease. This same onslaught on the public was to cover the network of smugglers regardless of their political or social standing.

Accusers have said that the operation got out of hand and that the ground team began to take their own way forward without reference to Stirling. In my opinion this was not so, though it may have seemed so, given the difficulties in communications. Consider the need for security and the extended (and public) lines of communication between him and his team; think about the political sensitivities of working to such ends on foreign soil where a team of such a background is bound to give rise to suspicions; imagine how many influential persons would have been at odds with the aims, and it is logical that a two-way flow of information would have been sketchy to say the least.

When I visited the team in South Africa at Stirling's invitation I found what I expected to find. A dedicated team working professionally, in very difficult conditions, towards a goal in which they all believed. It must also be said that Stirling's health was on the decline and he tired easily during those hours when normal people were wont to communicate. This frustrated him and often made him answer aggressively when questioned on this, his pet project. When a questioner can get no reasonable answer, whether for reasons of security or the simple lack of desire to communicate, the temptation will be to construct answers from 'facts' which have been assumed rather than presented.

The cost of the operation must have been enormous and the personal investment against an entirely unpredictable return (after all, who would pay for the results?) undoubtedly concerned Stirling. He was determined not to deplete completely the trust fund set up to benefit his family. The prolonged absences of his managing director placed strains on the London end of the organisation. The acquisition of business was slow against the expense of running 22 South Audley Street. The recession was starting even then and the office missed the sheer charisma of Stirling's presence and the blunt, uncompromising attitudes of Crooke – so often a winning combination in presentations to captains of industry and foreign dignitaries.

Although he was to close down KAS some months before his death, he remained very much in favour of the African project and was in the process of setting up what might have been called the Stirling Foundation as a trust to work against the poaching community and the unprincipled 'barons' who kept the market alive.

In the Honours List of 1990 Stirling at long last received an accolade commensurate with his great achievements. To honour his 'services to the military' he was to become a Knight Bachelor. He almost didn't! Having received the statutory notification asking whether he would be accepting the honour, he mislaid and forgot it. Irene found the form and invited him to complete it – he claimed he had no idea that it required a reply.

Lord Whitelaw told me how determined the SAS lobby had been: 'It wasn't until Dwin Bramall came to see me that I realised just in what reverence David was held by the SAS. He really was the father to them.'

Though he was at great pains not to show it at times, Stirling clearly took enormous pleasure in the knighthood, and the staggering amount of congratulatory mail testifies to the equally great pleasure of others. It was late, but somehow it was entirely fitting that it should be bestowed in time for the 50th anniversary of the SAS, at a time when the public had become aware of their great contribution to the free world. A letter from the US Delta Force Commander particularly pleased him as it confirmed the solidity of the relationship between the special forces of the two nations. Especially pertinent to his pleasure was the passage:

> We of the Delta Force have built upon your philosophies, organisation, and operational concepts in creating this unit. Your principles and ideas are as sound today as they were in World War II. The common bond among the special forces of the Western world is that we all trace our roots back to you and your innovative design.

Stirling's last public appearance was on 26 October 1990 when he attended the one function he had never missed – the reunion of L Detachment, the Originals. He was then resident in the London Clinic. The reunion was held as usual in the drill hall of 21st SAS and although there were people waiting to assist him up the three flights of stairs, Stirling, typically, insisted on making the ascent alone. There was a great amount of joking about the knighthood which Stirling thoroughly enjoyed and it was a tired but happy man who left at about ten thirty that evening. His descent of the stairs was again unaided and he took time out to chat to many of the 21 SAS soldiers who had just arrived back from annual camp.

Stirling was by no means finished with business and in case his physical weakness has given the impression that

he was ineffectual, I quote from a letter I received late in
December 1990:

Dear Spike,

   You know, I think, that David, on my invitation, became
president of Saladin Security Ltd shortly before he died. I
was in touch with him throughout much of 1990, and always
marvelled at how lively and innovative his mind continued to
be, even though his body was in poor health.
   The story that perhaps illustrates this best is that he
telephoned me on Friday 2nd November from the London
Clinic to say that he was very keen to have a good session
with me before I departed for Africa on Tuesday 6th. We
arranged to meet at midday on Monday in the Clinic. I asked
how he was and he replied that he felt very much better; he
was speaking to his doctors about coming out of hospital at
the end of the following week. He expected to be up and
about and was keen to get heavily involved in a number of
projects that we had been discussing. In particular . . . he
was keen to discuss security requirements in the North Sea,
the need for covert operations to be started against Saddam
Hussein, possibilities of raising finance for Joseph Savimbi to
allow him to undertake training and preparation for long-range
sabotage operations, drugs problems in Colombia, and not
least to ensure that I would touch base with various old
friends of his in Uganda during my visit. Though his voice
was very weak, the imagination and mental agility were as
strong as ever.
   As you well know, he then died just a few hours before
we were due to meet. I think the story well illustrates
what a remarkable man he was right up to the moment he
died . . .

With all best wishes,
David Walker

The end of an era came when Stirling collapsed whilst
exercising along the corridor of the London Clinic. He
died some hours later, but not alone; his sister, Meg, was
at his bedside and he was sufficiently aware for her to

note the flash of recognition in his eyes before he passed away. He had earlier taken communion in his room with Monsignor Miles from St James's Catholic Church. Late that night his coffin was carried by members of his family into a side chapel at St James's. There the Director of SAS covered the coffin with the Union flag and laid out an SAS beret, Stirling's DSO, the Orders of Officer of the Légion d'Honneur and the Orange Nassau, his war campaign medals and the recently bestowed badge of a Knight Bachelor. On 6 November a private requiem mass was held at St James's, Spanish Place; even at such short notice representatives of some of the great names in British history were present, united by marriage to the Stirling family: Dalhousie, Salisbury, Cranborne, Scarborough, Maclean and representatives of the SAS and his old regiment, the Scots Guards.

The funeral took place at St Cumin's – a church built by Stirling's grandfather on the shores of Loch Morar where Catholicism had survived the Reformation and the lands had been in the Stirling family or their kinsmen since the Middle Ages. The hymns were in English and Gaelic as the service was performed by Canon MacInnes assisted by Stirling's old friend from Ampleforth, Father Maxwell Stewart. Angus MacLennan, a local piper, led the bearer party of Archie and Johnnie Stirling of Keir, James and Johnnie Ramsay, Chips Keswick and Jeremy Phipps. 'Lord Lovat's Lament' then 'Flowers of the Forest' accompanied the coffin across the fields with crofters, villagers, estate workers and members of the SAS and Scots Guards taking turns to carry the coffin.

At the graveside, and in the old Morar tradition, the ropes lowering the coffin into the grave were held not just by the bearers but by all others who were there: family, friends, relatives and old comrades all taking part in this last earthly ceremony. And so Colonel Sir David Stirling came to his final resting place in his ancestral lands overlooking Loch Morar to the hills beyond, guided into his grave by the hands of those who knew him and loved him.

It is sad that after his death writers should persist in insinuating that Stirling was involved in shady goings on. They are apparently persuaded that the public will readily believe such things of so controversial a man. Though Stirling was of course devoted to the SAS: he would never have done anything which, while appearing to defend its interests, could in the long run have endangered the organisation or its reputation. The book, *The Feathermen*, deliberately influences the reader to believe that Stirling was the founder of an undercover organisation set up to hunt down the so-called murderers of a number of SAS soldiers.

The writer is guilty of two fundamental misunderstandings of Stirling's character. Firstly, the methods of the fictional 'Feathermen' were quite alien to his nature; he never condoned torture or murder. Secondly, in the unlikely event of his being persuaded, the organisation would have operated efficiently instead of spending fourteen years chasing shadows! Would this and other such insinuations have been published before his death? He would certainly have sued!

On 7 February 1991 a memorial service was held in the Guards Chapel in London. It was a day to remember. The weather was so foul that many people were simply not able to travel in the freezing fog and thick snow. The IRA chose that day to launch their 'mortar' attack on 10 Downing Street which successfully closed off part of the public transport access to the area. One person remarked, 'How typical of David. Now that he's sitting up there with the Almighty he turns the matter of getting to his memorial service into a SAS selection course. Who but him would have laid on snow and bombs?'

There was a huge turnout of course. The address was

delivered by Sir Fitzroy Maclean of Dunconnel and it struck to the heart of what the name Stirling had come to mean:

... Of David Stirling's greatness there can be no doubt. As a leader, a man of action and a man of ideas, he left an enduring mark on the military thinking of his age ... No one could have given more anxious moments than David to those who loved him. But, equally, no one could have made them laugh more or, in the long run, have given them greater cause for pride ... There are people who pride themselves on showing a proper appreciation of the art of the possible. David was a specialist, if ever there was one, in the art of the impossible. Another thing that David did was to make it all great fun. Even at the most difficult moments, you felt how lucky you were to be there ... Even after fifty years of friendship and a number of shared experiences that are not easy to forget, David's character remains a difficult one to assess. There was about him, as about many great men, an element of mystery, an intangible quality, akin perhaps to what Lawrence called 'the irrational tenth, like the kingfisher flashing across the pool' – an irrational tenth that sometimes confused Middle East HQ every bit as much as it confused the enemy ... David was a man of ideals as well as ideas. What is for sure is that when he got hold of an idea – or, for that matter, an ideal – he didn't let go. And this was as true after the War as during it ... But I shall always remember him in the desert, when he was young, a great soldier and a great friend, and take heart from these words: 'Death is only an horizon and an horizon is nothing more than the limit of our sight.'

What was Stirling's greatest achievement? Perhaps those who knew him would each think differently. Was it the creation of the SAS? Was it that he pricked the conscience of so many in Africa during his Capricorn days? Was it the quiet, patient urging behind the scenes of TRUEMID? Those who knew him will make up their own minds for he touched the lives permanently of every one of them. How did he touch them? Was it the inimitable

sense of humour (which decided him to form the Younger
Brothers' Club, meeting annually to feast right royally and
charge the entertainment to the accounts of their elder
brothers)? Was it the flash of sheer inspiration which
led to the formation of a very successful private intelligence organisation (for that was what Quail International
became)? Was it his visionary quality, which drew into
his net anyone who stopped to listen for more than a
few moments? Was it simply his obvious and deep love
of his country? I for one accept that there was a part of
David Stirling which no one was allowed to know; but I
shall not forget the grand exciting manner of the man in
full flow on a topic in which he believed. I am certainly
not of the stuff from which heroes are made, but I am
quite sure that if I had been invited into his aircraft
on that fateful day in November 1941 I would willingly
have gone.

Perhaps Stirling can yet speak for himself. The following
poem (punctuation as recorded) was found amongst his
jottings. It was in his handwriting and is squeezed between
notes on other topics; it has proved impossible to trace and
therefore it is believed to have been written by him. Saanen
is a lake in the part of Switzerland where he did some of his
early climbing training.

### Saanen Loch

Yet cradled within that mountain
Is a deep blue nameless lake.
And silent it lies
Facing the skies
Yet some how most deeply awake.

So perhaps in our inner being
There is also a great blue eye
Which watching all, and knowing all
Says nothing itself to belie?

Nothing? Well only in dreams
For dreams are our real inner freedom
Like the lake they reflect the sky
And they tell us the truth of our being
But with faith, and unable to lie.

Field Marshal Bramall made an observation which perhaps
makes a valid epitaph: 'He was a true knight.'